D0179285

READING OPERA

Reading Opera

EDITED BY ARTHUR GROOS
AND ROGER PARKER

PRINCETON UNIVERSITY PRESS
PRINCETON, NEW JERSEY

ML
2110
R4
1988

LP

Copyright © 1988 by Princeton University Press
Published by Princeton University Press, 41 William Street,
Princeton, New Jersey 08540
In the United Kingdom: Princeton University Press,
Guildford, Surrey

All Rights Reserved

Library of Congress Cataloging-in-Publication Data

Reading opera / edited by Arthur Groos and Roger Parker.
p.   cm.
Includes bibliographical references and index.
ISBN 0–691–09132–3 (cloth)
ISBN 0–691–02709–9 (pbk.)
1. Libretto. 2. Music and literature.
I. Groos, Arthur. II. Parker, Roger, 1951–   .
ML2110.R4 1988
782.1'2—dc19   88–25984

This book has been composed in Linotron Sabon

Clothbound editions of Princeton University Press books are
printed on acid-free paper, and binding materials are
chosen for strength and durability. Paperbacks, although
satisfactory for personal collections, are not usually
suitable for library rebinding

Printed in the United States of America by
Princeton University Press,
Princeton, New Jersey

03/15/91

CONTENTS

v

CONTENTS

vi

ACKNOWLEDGMENTS

Most of the essays printed here were first presented at a conference on opera libretti held at Cornell University in October 1986. Other presentations at the conference will appear elsewhere: Herbert Lindenberger, "Opera as Historical Drama: *La clemenza di Tito, Khovanshchina,* and *Moses und Aron*"; Harold S. Powers, "Metastasio into *melodramma*"; Richard T. Dillon, "The Poetic Process: A Close Reading of Two Passages from *Simon Boccanegra*"; James Boon, "Between New World Mythology and Wagner's Libretti: Cycles of Return Upon Endless Transition"; Frederick Ahl, "The Word Fighting Music: The Creative Warfare of Gilbert and Sullivan."

We should like to thank the various institutions within Cornell that contributed funds to the conference: the College of Arts and Sciences, the Society for the Humanities, the Western Societies Program, the University Lecture Committee, and the Departments of History, Music, German Literature, Romance Studies, and Soviet Studies.

As the book took shape, Carolyn Abbate offered many helpful suggestions. We should also like to thank Gisela Podleski for assistance with editing and word processing, Jane Dieckmann for preparing the index, and the staff at Princeton University Press, especially Eric Van Tassel and the Press's Director, Walter H. Lippincott, who was from the first an enthusiastic and energetic supporter of the project.

A.G.
R.P.

READING OPERA

INTRODUCTION

Habent sua fata libelli.

The fact that this collection of essays is devoted to opera libretti of the later nineteenth century may necessitate a few introductory remarks. Most people familiar with opera have read a libretto, and many of these share the widespread opinion mentioned by *The New Grove*:

> The study of librettos was for a long time neglected by historians of opera and oratorio, and it has generally been taken for granted that the vast majority of them are as literature beneath contempt.[1]

Although the article proceeds to qualify this opinion, the uses of libretti cited—recovery of information not in scores, or study of performance practice—confirm the general cultural prejudice it seeks to mitigate. That prejudice denigrates libretti vis-à-vis literature and music with antithetical judgments such as "the compilation of a librettist" and "a real poem" or "rhapsodical librettist" and "uninteresting music."[2]

This attitude toward libretti as something sub-literary and intrinsically uninteresting is a phenomenon with which scholarship has only begun to come to terms.[3] The elevation of music to a "universal language" in our post-Romantic culture has had a far-reaching impact on the general conception of verbal texts attached to musical forms. Most listeners appreciate *Songs Without Words*; many demonstrably prefer "operas without words." Nobody seems to want "operas without music"—the mere rumor of having to sit through one provokes audience unrest in Tieck's *Der gestiefelte Kater*. We certainly do not deny the primacy of music in the performance of opera and in opera scholarship, and would scarcely be interested in opera were it not for the music. Nonetheless, there are compelling reasons for interest in libretti, not the least of which are the longstanding prejudice against them and the scholarly tradition that has, until recently, reiterated it.

---

[1] *The New Grove Dictionary of Music and Musicians* (London, 1980), X, 822. The article is by Edward Dent and Patrick J. Smith, who present a further section on libretti in the article on opera, XIII, 610–17.

[2] London *Times* entries (8 October 1891) and (3 August 1862) cited in the *Oxford English Dictionary*, s.v. "librettist."

[3] The basic studies are Ulderico Rolandi, *Il libretto per musica attraverso il tempo* (Rome, 1951), and Patrick J. Smith, *The Tenth Muse: A Historical Study of the Opera Libretto* (New York, 1970). The following discussion primarily cites research that has appeared since *The New Grove*.

1

I

Libretto-bashing has a distinguished tradition in the blood sport of opera. The word *libretto* ("little book"), like other variants such as *libricciuolo* or *libriccino*, derives from the small format (usually duodecimo) of late seventeenth-century editions, printed for performances and designed to be read in undarkened auditoria.[4] Early references often employ the diminutive form to imply a value judgment, as in the impresario's directions to his principal female singer in the Intermezzo to Metastasio's *Didone abbandonata* (1724):

> Il libretto non deve esser capito;
> il gusto è ripulito,
> e non si bada a questo:
> si canti bene, e non importi il resto.

(The libretto isn't supposed to be understood. / Taste has been refurbished / and one doesn't care about this: / Let one sing well and the rest needn't matter.)[5]

These instructions satirize a contemporary preference for bravura singing over intelligibility.[6] Indeed, it seems likely that melomania has always been fundamental to the success of opera as a performing art. Nonetheless, the allusion to reversals of taste reminds us of periodic "reforms" and the continuing debate over the primacy of words or music in the conception of opera.[7] This debate also reflects a difference in emphasis on these components between French and Italian opera. Quinault's libretti,

---

[4] See Rolandi, 14–20, for early usage of the term; Wolfgang Schivelbusch, *Lichtblicke: Zur Geschichte der künstlichen Helligkeit im 19. Jahrhundert* (Frankfurt/Main, 1976), 179–201, for developments in lighting.

[5] Fausto Nicolini, ed., *Pietro Metastasio: Opere*, I (Bari, 1912), 65.

[6] A letter of August 1701 from Apostolo Zeno to Lodovico Antonio Muratori places the success of the libretto and the opera in an inverse relationship: "se'l libretto ha qualche lodatore, ha poco concorso" (if the libretto has any admirers, the theater will be poorly attended), *Lettere di Apostolo Zeno* (Venice, 1785), I, 121. The text was reprinted by Muratori in *Della perfetta poesia italiana* (Modena, 1706), II, 55. According to Muratori, contemporary taste emphasizes the music and its vocal realization; one goes to the theater to experience this, not the libretto: "il Gusto de' tempi nostri ha costituito l'essenza tutta di questi Drammi nella Musica, e la perfezion loro nella scelta di valorosi Cantanti. Per udir questa sola si corre ai Teatri, e non già per gustare la fatica del Poeta, i cui versi appena si degnano d'un guardo sul libro" (II, 43).
See also the first chapter, "A poeti" (To poets), in Benedetto Marcello's satirical *Il teatro alla moda* (Venice, 1720), 11, which advises not to correct indistinct pronunciation by singers, since "parlando schietto potrebbe minorarsi l'esito de' *Libretti*" (speaking clearly could reduce the success of libretti).

[7] See Herbert Lindenberger, *Opera: The Extravagant Art* (Ithaca, N.Y., 1984), 108–44.

for example, were certified by the Académie Française, whereas Meta-stasio, whose works were performed as spoken plays in their own right, struggled with uncertainties attending the validation of operatic texts.[8] It will be helpful to examine an early example of such uncertainties before proceeding to the nineteenth century and its attitude toward libretti.

Shortly before Metastasio began his career, Pier Jacopo Martello pub-lished a dialogue on opera that reflects both the early reputation of libretti and the difficulty of dealing with them within a conventional system of neo-aristotelian poetics.[9] The discussion examines—often with consider-able wit—the unique situation of the librettist, observing that he depends on the wishes of all others involved in the production of opera: the com-poser, singers, architect, machinist, painter, and impresario. A prelimi-nary judgment is therefore clear-cut. In tragedy and comedy, poetry oc-cupies the principal place, whereas in opera it should occupy the lowest, functioning in the former—according to a commonplace metaphor—as mistress and in the latter as servant. Yet this rhetorically neat placement of libretti at the bottom of a hierarchy of genres fails to satisfy Martello, who proceeds to locate writers of libretti somewhat higher, between the extremes of poet and verse-monger, without being able to find an appro-priate intermediate term:

> We have need, then, not of Poets but rather of verse-mongers [*ver-seggiatori*]; but no, not of verse-mongers, either, for there must be a plot, and that calls for something more than a verse-monger: not mere verse-mongers, then, nor true Poets—I am at a loss what to call them.[10]

More than a century later, the vocabulary that Martello found lacking emerged in the Romantic revolution that shaped the modern reception of libretti and—indirectly—the beginnings of opera scholarship. The de-scription of a premiere at La Scala by Stendhal (1823), who introduced the word *libretto* and other operatic terms into French,[11] provides a vivid example:

> It is worth remarking that, at the *première* of any opera, the applause for the singers and the applause for the composer are always kept

[8] See Piero Weiss, "Metastasio, Aristotle, and the *Opera Seria*," *The Journal of Musicol-ogy*, 1 (1982), 385–94.

[9] Hannibal S. Noce, ed., *Scritti critici e satirici*, Scrittori d'Italia 225 (Bari, 1963), 270–96; translated by Piero Weiss, "Pier Jacopo Martello on Opera (1715): An Annotated Translation," *The Musical Quarterly*, 66 (1980), 378–403.

[10] Noce, 277; Weiss, 385.

[11] See *Revue de philologie française*, 45 (1933), 26; T. E. Hope, *Lexical Borrowing in the Romance Languages* (Oxford, 1971), II, 446; *Trésor de la langue française*, X, 1183.

perfectly distinct. As you may well have guessed, nobody gives a damn for the librettist [*poète*]; for who indeed, unless it were a French critic [*littérateur français*], would dream of judging an opera by the *words*?[12]

The passage juxtaposes two different types of discourse about opera. The French tradition, here an object of Stendhal's irony, reflects the continuing dominance of neoclassical drama in post-Revolutionary French culture, emphasizing literary values measured by the word;[13] Italian practice continues to reveal a clear preference for singing and music,[14] a preference that—according to Stendhal—involves not merely lack of interest in the text, but complete disdain.

This disdain is now grounded in the far-reaching "paradigm shift" in cultural values that took place during the age of Romanticism, fundamentally changing our conception of artists and the arts.[15] Stendhal's provocative criticism of the typical Italian opera aria of his day again provides a point of departure:

The excruciating doggerel which forms the verbal skeleton of the average Italian aria is hardly ever recognizable as verse of any description, owing to the multiplicity of repeats; the language which greets the listener's patient ear is pure prose. Furthermore, the language of poetry does not lie in its bold and melodramatic exclamations, such as *I hate you like poison!* or *I love you to distraction! etc.*, but in its shades and subtleties, in the skilled ordering or selection of words; and it is these *nuances* which convince the reader of the poet's sincerity, and which ultimately awaken his sympathy and understanding. But there is no room for *nuances* among the haphazard jumble of 50–60 words which go to form the text of the average Italian aria; and so language, *as such*, can never be anything more than a *bare canvas*.[16]

In general terms, his opprobrium differs little from that of eighteenth-century critics,[17] using literary standards to condemn libretti without con-

---

[12] *Life of Rossini*, trans. by Richard N. Coe, rev. ed. (New York, 1970), 147; for the French text see *Vie de Rossini* (Paris, 1854), 113.

[13] In contrast to Germany, reviews of French opera at this time generally begin with the libretto. See Brian Primmer, "Unity and Ensemble: Contrasting Ideals in Romantic Music," *Nineteenth-Century Music*, 6 (1982–83), 97–140, esp. 100–105.

[14] Cf. the comments of Muratori (n. 6 above).

[15] See M. H. Abrams, *The Mirror and The Lamp: Romantic Theory and the Critical Tradition* (1953; rpt. New York, 1958).

[16] *Life of Rossini*, 368.

[17] See Muratori (n. 6 above), II, 42–45.

sidering the limitations in meter and vocabulary imposed on operatic texts by the structure and slower pace of musical forms. In this particular argument, however, libretti have acquired a further liability. An aria consists not of "verse of any description" with a "skilled ordering of words," but of "excruciating doggerel" in a "haphazard jumble." Nor does the text provide the outline for musical color, as a traditional eighteenth-century analogy with painting suggested,[18] but something more preliminary: a background on which the true medium is imposed. Libretti are no longer on the margins of literature, but beneath it.

Libretti continued, of course, to be written to conventional rhetorical standards of meter, rhyme, and stanzaic form in order to accord with traditional expectations of fixed musical forms, and they continued to be criticized—particularly in Italy—according to those standards.[19] But they could now also be judged, and found wanting, by a Romantic aesthetic that Stendhal's writings and criticism did much to disseminate through Europe. Based on the expression of individual experience ("the poet's sincerity") rather than on imitation and variation of universal standards, Romantic theory found its literary ideals realized not in the genre closest to the libretto—verse drama—but in the lyric and the prose novel. Moreover, the differentiation of genius from talent, and "high" literature from "applied" literature, which began in the late eighteenth century,[20] also made it possible to exclude libretti from the new critical debate that redefined the canon of genres and individual works.[21] Paradoxically, the exclusion not only helped identify a more clear-cut hierarchy of literary discourse, but also created pressure for libretti to approach the status of poetry.

Discussions of opera in Germany,[22] the leading exporter of Romanti-

---

[18] For a representative sampling, see Ulrich Weisstein, *The Essence of Opera* (1964; rpt. New York, 1969), 69 (Francesco Algarotti); 126 (Goethe, "the familiar comparison"); 177 (E.T.A. Hoffmann). Andrea Maffei uses a variation in his preface to the libretto of *I masnadieri*, quoted in Franco Abbiati, *Giuseppe Verdi* (Milan, 1959), I, 718f.

[19] See, for example, the criticisms leveled at Piave's libretto for *Macbeth*, in *Verdi's Macbeth: A Sourcebook*, ed. David Rosen and Andrew Porter (New York, 1984), 140f, 370–401.

[20] See Jochen Schulte-Sasse, *Die Kritik an der Trivialliteratur seit der Aufklärung*, Bochumer Arbeiten zur Sprach- und Literaturwissenschaft 6 (Munich, 1971).

[21] For an introduction to the diversity of the debate and the institutionalization of literature in Germany, see Friedrich Sengle, *Biedermeierzeit: Deutsche Literatur im Spannungsfeld zwischen Restauration und Revolution 1815–1848*, 3 vols. (Stuttgart, 1971–80), and Peter Uwe Hohendahl, *Literarische Kultur im Zeitalter des Liberalismus 1830–1870* (Munich, 1985).

[22] See John Warrack, "German Operatic Ambitions at the Beginning of the Nineteenth Century," *Proceedings of the Royal Musicological Association*, 104 (1977–78), 79–88, esp. 85ff.

cism, were directed toward creating a national tradition for the emerging empire, partly by selecting indigenous subjects and partly by differentiating their artistic realization from prevailing French and Italian models. The latter trend is illustrated by a taxonomy of libretto types posited in Wagner's review of Halévy's *La Reine de Chypre* (1841).[23] Drawing on the new standard of individual expression, Wagner requires a "poetic genius" with a "sensitive heart." Still only vaguely articulated, the resulting German art work of the future is by implication far superior to current French practice, which does not require a poet (*Dichter*), but only a libretto-maker (*Operntextmacher*) with sufficient skill—like a cobbler or harness-maker—to ply his trade (*Handwerk*), combing sources such as newspapers, novels, and history for appropriate subjects. A third and even worse model, implicitly based on Italian opera, is the refuge for those without skill who can only "write reviews, smoke cigars, spend evenings in bed," putting together a farrago in which the characters behave "like clouds or flowers."

One indication of the gap separating genius from talent, and "high" literature from "applied" literature, in mid-nineteenth-century aesthetics is the creation of a new term to replace "poet" as a designation of writers for libretti. Wagner's characterization of the predominant French type as a "craftsman" (*Handwerker*) finds a parallel in the Italian "poeta di mestiere."[24] The more specific "librettist" soon enters the vocabulary of Italian and French.[25] A rhyming dictionary of 1839 offers the following definition: "*librettista*—a title of contempt for someone who makes opera libretti, as if unworthy of that of poet."[26] The changing attitude is strikingly illustrated by the reaction of Felice Romani, the foremost writer of libretti in the 1820s and 1830s (for Rossini, Bellini, and Donizetti) and subsequently an essayist on cultural subjects. In 1841, he wrote a response to the charge of having been a *librettista*:

[23] *Sämtliche Schriften und Dichtungen*, 6th ed. (Leipzig, [1911–16]), I, 244f; translated as "A First Night at the Opéra," *Wagner Writes from Paris: Stories, Essays, Articles by the Young Composer*, ed. and trans. Robert L. Jacobs and Geoffrey Skelton (New York, 1973), 163–77, esp. 166f.

[24] Cf. Rolandi (n. 3 above), 114.

[25] Nicolò Tommaseo, *Dizionario della lingua italiana* II.2 (Turin and Naples, 1869), 1844, defines the word without citing sources; Carlo Battisti and Giovanni Alessio, *Dizionario etimologico italiano*, III (Florence, 1952), 2223, refer only to its nineteenth-century provenance. B. Quemada, *Matériaux pour l'histoire du vocabulaire français: Datations et documents lexicographiques* 2.2 (Paris, 1971), 134, lists a series of references in French beginning with Théophile Gautier in 1844; The *Oxford English Dictionary*, s.v. "librettist," records the first usage as 1862 (cf. n. 2 above).

[26] Francesco Antolini, *Rimario italiano di voci piane, sdrucciole e tronche; ossia, Vocabolario ortografico-desinenziale* (Milan, 1839), s.v. "-ista."

Do you know that last night a friend (or perhaps an enemy, since nowadays in the matter of letters nobody can distinguish enemies from friends)—do you know what this person said on hearing the circumstances in which I find myself? He said that I would have done well to devote myself to the trade of *librettist*. By this name [. . .] certain literary critics [*baccalari della poesia*] call authors of music dramas, and with this name they would now call Apostolo Zeno and Pietro Metastasio if they had the fortune to live among us.[27]

The altered situation could hardly be clearer: Zeno and Metastasio considered themselves, and were called, *poets*. Writers of libretti have now been demoted and ghettoized, to the consternation of the conservative Romani, and are identified only with the product of their labor.

The first recorded use of *librettiste* in French, Théophile Gautier's review of a revival of Rossini's *Otello* at the Opéra (1844), adds a further dimension. After lavishing praise on the composer's music in general, Gautier raises a different and more critical issue:

we believe that the choice of *Othello* is an unhappy choice—not that the score does not sparkle with sublime beauties. But the work in general is heard in this Italian style which is completely heedless of the situation, and which is troubled little by whether or not the melody agrees with the sense of the words, provided that the phrase be lively, alert, sparkling. In effect, what do the syllables matter that the poor poet-librettist has grouped in lines or in stanzas! Surely nothing is more immaterial; and yet when this poet is the great William Shakespeare—no more, no less—the case is more serious.[28]

Gautier frames his discussion by one standard of Romanticism, only to find it deficient in the light of another, more important consideration. The first, essentially the assumptions governing Stendhal's deliberately exaggerated comments, grants the music not only primacy but also autonomy, unconcerned by its relationship to the words of "le pauvre poète librettiste," to whom he seems to condescend with a specific designation that segregates him from poets in general. The second standard in Gautier's argument undercuts these assumptions, pointing out the essential identity between the text of that presumed theater hack and his source, "le grand William Shakspeare [sic]." A great work of literature, even in its transposition into a libretto, imposes a serious obligation on the composer.

As this example suggests, the differential between the new concept of

[27] Article from Turin's *Gazzetta ufficiale*, no. 59, in *Critica letteraria*, ed. Emilia Branca (Turin, 1883), I, 441.
[28] *Histoire de l'art dramatique en France*, III (Brussels, 1859), 266.

"high" literature and traditional libretto practice did not invariably lower the status of librettists and their art, but sometimes demanded higher standards of the libretto, and this also exerted a powerful influence in the choice as well as the treatment of opera subjects. The shift from mythological or historical sources to works of literature, a fundamental change that reflects the emergence of the nineteenth century as a "literary" culture, established a potential dialectic between the "superior" and "inferior" types of discourse. A literary text could, as early Italian Romantic opera suggests, provide only the subject matter for a libretto that still "served" conventional musical structures.[29] But it could also—and increasingly did—stimulate as well as legitimize operatic practice that respected and even celebrated the literary source. The spectrum of possibilities opened during the course of the century is exemplified by the *Otellos* of Rossini and Verdi.

The new importance of "high" literature as an alternative to traditional libretti can be seen in a variety of other developments in operatic culture. It is particularly ironic that Italian "libretto language," which has drawn the fire of so many critics, actually represents the attempt of librettists to remain in the literary mainstream by employing the same *linguaggio poetico* as other writers.[30] The emergence of poet-composers such as Wagner, Musorgsky, Berlioz, and Boito, who strove to represent the fusion of the arts in one person, also incorporates the libretto into a basic Romantic ideal of genius. One practice that may reflect the desire to bridge literary and libretto discourse is the employment of poets as well as librettists in the production of opera, as exemplified by Puccini's team of Giuseppe Giacosa and Luigi Illica. Another development, perhaps the clearest reflection of the impact of literature on operatic culture, is the emergence at the end of the century of *Literaturoper*—a play set to music nearly verbatim. These few examples suggest only some of the possibilities that open up in response to the more variegated poetic discourse of the nineteenth century.

II

Musicology, which—like other historical disciplines—is indebted to the influence of German Romanticism on academic institutions, has to some extent recapitulated these developments, coming late to a differentiated appreciation of libretti. Traditionally, it treated opera in a stepmotherly

---

[29] Cf. John Black, *The Italian Romantic Libretto: A Study of Salvadore Cammarano* (Edinburgh, 1984).

[30] See Piero Weiss, " 'Sacred Bronzes': Paralipomena to an Essay by Dallapiccola," *Nineteenth-Century Music*, 9 (1985), 42–49.

fashion, preferring older or purely instrumental music for establishing canonical norms, often abandoning the study of nineteenth-century opera to amateurs. Although opera has recently become a more legitimate subject in academic criticism, this progress has often been achieved at the expense of the text that the music expresses. A critic who proceeds with the goal of demonstrating coherent musical structure may demonstrate only that. It is not difficult to find lengthy analytical discussions offering only passing reference to "the words." Nor is it surprising to encounter assumptions that musical understanding remains the only legitimate goal of opera scholarship.

This bias does not originate entirely with musicologists, but represents a problem for Anglo-American speakers in general, expressing our linguistic insularity as well as the innate prejudice of a culture with a dominant tradition of spoken drama and no indigenous opera. It reflects the instinctive if unspoken assumptions that a libretto "reads" like a drama *manqué* or that it is inevitably deficient unless redeemed by music.[31] Under these circumstances, libretti have understandably been neglected by English-speaking literary scholars. The situation has always been different in Italy, where a vigorous opera tradition persists with little spoken drama—i.e., where libretti represent the cultural mainstream of dramatic texts, and can be discussed as such. The "libretto" entry in the *Dizionario della musica e dei musicisti*, for example, even warns against an exclusively literary treatment of the genre, thus approaching the opposite stance to its counterpart in *Grove*:

> Although history is not lacking in libretti that have aroused interest because of their autonomous poetic merit or that have been considered as literary artifacts, an evaluation of the libretto cannot leave out of consideration its purpose and its need to link the various arts that comprise *melodramma*: poetry itself, the dramatic, visual, and choreographic element of theater.[32]

Not surprisingly, Italian scholarship on opera continues to produce new insights into the typology of operatic drama and the libretto based on familiarity with a respected indigenous tradition.[33]

[31] The defense of Italian opera in Richardson's *Pamela* (IV, 13), which introduces the word *libretto* to English, repeats an indigenous belief that "One Play of our celebrated *Shakespeare* will give infinitely more pleasure to a sensible Mind, than a dozen *English-Italian* Operas" (Oxford, 1929), IV, 91f.

[32] II (Turin, 1983), 690. The article is by Bruno Cagli.

[33] See, for example, Mario Lavagetto, *Quei più modesti romanzi* (Milan, 1979); Daniela Goldin, *La vera fenice: Librettisti e libretti tra Sette e Ottocento* (Turin, 1985); Folco Portinari, *Pari siamo! Io la lingua, egli ha il pugnale. Storia del melodramma ottocentesco at-*

However, the fact that Italians can also share the antipathy of other cultural groups toward libretti reflects a further problem.[34] Until recently, disciplines other than musicology were wary of the genre, historians frequently being constrained by a narrowly defined "history of ideas," literary critics by a post-Romantic bias and a New Critical emphasis on the canon of "great works." The preconception of libretti as hack-work, dependent on pre-existing sources as well as on a host of other factors—ranging from the composer and impresario or publisher to singers, theater and stage directors—can scarcely have stimulated the interest of either discipline. Recent developments have changed all this, as studies by intellectual and economic historians as well as literary scholars interested in cultural history testify.[35]

The most extensive of those developments, however, reflect the expansion of literary scholarship to include the nature and types of literary discourse as well as texts traditionally excluded from consideration as literature. An unsuspected variety of approaches to libretti has emerged. Theoretical attempts to differentiate opera from both drama and music have led to greater awareness of the ways in which libretti seek particular modes of expression.[36] As adaptations of pre-existing literary works, libretti pose questions of intertextuality, transposition of genre, and reception history; as verbal artifacts, they invite the broad spectrum of contemporary reading strategies ranging from the formalistic to the feminist; and as texts for musical realization, they raise issues in the relation between the two media and their respective traditions. According to such perspectives, libretti are not "beneath contempt as literature," but very much within the purview of contemporary humanistic scholarship.

THE following articles reflect this variety of approaches. The editors left the options for contributors open, specifying only that each should deal with some aspect of libretti between the age of Metastasio and the early twentieth century. The majority of those essays collected here focus on subjects from the second half of the nineteenth century. It is obvious in

---

traverso i suoi libretti (Turin, 1981); Guido Paduano, Noi facemmo ambedue un sogno strano: Il disagio amoroso sulla scena dell'opera europea (Palermo, 1982).

[34] See the examples provided in Rolandi (n. 3 above), 96–99, 119–22, 136–38; and Weiss (n. 29 above).

[35] See, for example, John Rosselli, The Opera Industry from Cimarosa to Verdi (Cambridge, 1984); Paul Robinson, Opera and Ideas (New York, 1986); and Caryl Emerson, Boris Godunov: Transpositions of a Russian Theme (Bloomington, Ind., 1986).

[36] See Herbert Lindenberger, "Towards a Theory of Musical Drama," Yearbook of Comparative and General Literature, 29 (1980), 5–9, and Opera: The Extravagant Art (Ithaca, N.Y., 1984); and Ulrich Weisstein, "Librettology: The Fine Art of Coping with a Chinese Twin," Komparatistische Hefte, 5/6 (1982), 23–42.

retrospect that certain topics would claim attention—Wagner, Boito, and the varying types of *Literaturoper*, broadly defined. This may suggest a lingering insecurity on the part of literary scholars in dealing with libretti of the eighteenth and early nineteenth centuries, periods with a predominant emphasis on musical forms and traditions; it certainly suggests the growing ability to extend new methods of literary analysis to unjustly neglected texts and problems.

Inasmuch as the interdisciplinary study of libretti is rapidly changing and expanding, individual scholars tend to concentrate on single works or single writers and composers. For the moment, a wider focus seems possible largely in collaborative efforts, such as those exemplified by recent European publications.[37] The possibilities seem endless, and the present collection, though diverse both in scope and approach, can only scratch the surface. If it stimulates others to join the enterprise of reading opera, it will have served its purpose.

Arthur Groos

[37] The number of collections has multiplied in the last few years: Jens Malte Fischer, ed., *Oper und Operntext* (Heidelberg, 1985), with an excellent bibliography; Albert Gier, ed., *Oper als Text: Romanistische Beiträge zur Libretto-Forschung*, Studia Romanica 63 (Heidelberg, 1986); Philippe Berthier and Kurt Ringger, ed., *Littérature et opéra: Colloque de Cerisy* (Grenoble, 1987); Jürgen Maehder, ed., *I libretti di Puccini e la letteratura del suo tempo*, Atti del II° Convegno Internazionale sull'opera di Puccini a Torre del Lago 1984 (Pisa, in press); papers from the conferences "Perspektiven der Opernforschung," held at Bad Homburg in 1985 and 1987, are planned for publication under the editorship of Albert Gier, Jürg Stenzl, and Jürgen Maehder.

ARTHUR GROOS

Appropriation in Wagner's
Tristan Libretto*

I

Opera libretti traditionally have a more uncertain status than conventional literary texts, in part because their genesis as well as their reception involve them in a different complex of considerations. Literary critics and musicologists frequently isolate two different relationships in discussing nineteenth-century libretti: that between the literary source and the libretto, and that between the libretto and its music. The relative emphasis within and between these relationships has of course changed during the history of opera, but for our purposes it might be formulated in the following terms: the increasing importance of "literary" sources in libretto production lends the source-libretto relationship an important role in the *genesis* of late nineteenth-century operas. Nonetheless, the finished libretto is then subsumed in its *reception* by the libretto-music relationship, a status suggested by the fact that the libretto usually appears in print for the first time in conjunction with the premiere of an opera and—unless the librettist achieves the independent literary status of a Metastasio or a Scribe—is reissued only in conjunction with subsequent revivals of the opera.

The libretti of Wagner's maturity require a more differentiated examination, with respect both to their music and to their sources. Whereas the title pages of first editions through *Lohengrin* (1850) identify the libretto as part of a larger musical work by designating it as an "Oper," the title pages of his subsequent libretti avoid any such limitation.[1] Indeed, their publishing history provides them with an independent status well before

---

* This is a revised and expanded version of a paper, "Goethefried von Straßburg?," presented to a conference on Gottfried's *Tristan* in 1986 at the Germanic Institute, London. The conference papers are planned for publication under the editorship of Roy Wisbey and Adrian Stevens.

[1] According to the *Mitteilung an meine Freunde*, "I do not write *operas* any more. Since I do not wish to invent arbitrary names for my works, I call them *dramas*." *Richard Wagner: Sämtliche Schriften und Dichtungen*, 6th ed. (Leipzig, [1911–16]), III, 343n. Subsequent references to Wagner's writings are to this edition unless otherwise noted.

the first performance of the operas,[2] the most famous example being the *Ring*, a version of whose libretto appeared twenty-three years before the first performance of the entire cycle at Bayreuth. The text of the *Ring* first appears anonymously in a private Zurich edition of fifty copies in 1853, then in Leipzig (1863 and 1873), and finally in Mainz (1874). One could view these editions as an extreme case of traditional pre-performance publication, anticipating and advertising the first Bayreuth *Ring* in 1876. But the appearance of the *Ring* libretto in the 1871 Leipzig edition of Wagner's *Schriften und Dichtungen* and the appearance of the entire cycle as well as individual works in two separate editions before performances, one for the book trade and one for the performance, suggest a dual existence for Wagner's libretti, one independent of and one dependent on their musical realization. Unlike Berlioz, Musorgsky, and Boito (to take the most prominent examples of contemporary composer-librettists outside Germany), whose libretti generally first appear in conjunction with their operas, Wagner demands to be considered not only as a composer but also as a poet—a demand to which contemporary readers responded.[3] The new conception of his double calling is emphasized throughout the *Mitteilung an meine Freunde*:

> My career as poet begins at the point where I abandoned that of making opera libretti [. . .] With the *Flying Dutchman* I took up a new career, becoming myself the poet of a subject that previously existed only in simple, rough outline in popular tradition. (*Sämtliche Schriften*, III, 266 and 316)

This situation obtains also for *Tristan*. The libretto first appears in Leipzig in January 1859 without any indication of its future musical status ("*Tristan und Isolde* von Richard Wagner"),[4] a year before the publication of the score and six years before the edition for the Munich premiere. Other evidence, such as Wagner's letter of 15 April 1859 to Mathilde Wesendonck wondering whether it was wise to publish the *Tris-*

---

[2] The following is based on Horst F. G. Klein, *Erst- und Frühdrucke der Textbücher von Richard Wagner*, Musikbibliographische Arbeiten 4 (Tutzing, 1979).

[3] Cosima claimed (12 December 1870) that Wagner's libretti were unique even without music; less biased readers also responded in similar fashion. Gottfried Keller, for example, recommended the *Ring* cycle in a letter of 16 April 1856 to Hermann Hettner as "powerful poetry, pure German, purified by the classical tragic spirit." *Gottfried Keller: Gesammelte Briefe*, ed. Carl Helbling, I (Bern, 1950), 429f. A thorough study of the reading reception of Wagner's libretti remains to be done.

[4] The title page is reproduced in Klein, 30. The subtitle, "Eine Handlung"—a literal translation of the Greek *drama*—was added later.

tan libretto separately, also suggests the dual status of his libretti.[5] Wagner's general comparison "between a poem that is entirely intended for music and a purely poetic stage play" reveals the limits of a libretto vis-à-vis a play and thus the ultimate unity of the text and its setting, the libretto being "completed and perfected [*vollendet*] through the music." The larger context of the letter, however, Wagner's reading of *Tasso*, also documents the alternative reception of both Goethe's work and *Tristan* as *Lesedramen* independent of their intended performance media.[6] As we shall see, Wagner's comparison of his libretto with a play by Goethe is not accidental.

But Wagner's *Tristan* differs from libretti by other composers not only in a relative independence from musical realization; it also differs in an unusual relationship to the source. The majority of later nineteenth-century libretti derive from works of recent or contemporary literature and usually reflect a relationship with those works, either celebrating the source by keeping it more or less intact, or celebrating its revision or transposition to another medium.[7] In either case, the inherent intertextual relationship with "literature" serves to enhance the more tenuous status of the libretto, legitimizing the opera text by means of its source.

One is tempted to say that Wagner, in contrast to this tendency, legitimizes his sources by means of his operas, reflecting a negative, albeit widespread, contemporary opinion of medieval literature. The paucity of references to Gottfried von Straßburg among the hundreds of allusions to the opera *Tristan* in Wagner's essays, letters, and diaries implies a value judgment that the letter of 29–30 May 1859 to Mathilde Wesendonck states in no uncertain terms. Leafing through San-Marte's *Parzival* translation causes him "to be immediately repelled by the incompetence of the poet. (This already happened to me with Gottfried v. Straßburg in regard to Tristan)."[8] Not surprisingly, Cosima's diaries record discussions of the medieval *Tristan* on only three occasions.[9] The sole entry (14 March 1870) that documents its having been read, stimulated by her reminis-

---

[5] *Richard Wagner an Mathilde Wesendonck: Tagebuchblätter und Briefe*, ed. Wolfgang Golther, 33rd ed. (Berlin, 1908), 124–26. My translations from the Wesendonck correspondence follow this edition.

[6] Goethe's plays, especially *Tasso* and *Iphigenie*, were generally considered to be untheatrical, i.e., reading texts, an opinion that was fostered by Hegel's *Aesthetik* and Gervinus' *Geschichte der deutschen Literatur*. See Karl Robert Mandelkow, *Goethe im Urteil seiner Kritiker*, II: *1832–1870* (Munich, 1977), 157, and III: *1870–1918* (Munich, 1979), 5f, and the entries s.v. "*Tasso*."

[7] For a model study of the latter kind of transposition, see Caryl Emerson, *Boris Godunov: Transpositions of a Russian Theme* (Bloomington, Ind., 1986).

[8] Golther, 146.

[9] 12–14 March 1870; 18 October 1877; 21 June 1879.

cence of a quote, ends with another version of Gottfried-bashing: "In the evening read Tr[istan] und I[solde], which makes me realize ever more clearly how great and unique R.'s conception of it is."[10]

It is important to emphasize, as Germanists have recently done, that this attitude was shared by contemporary opinion, which followed aesthetic criteria developed during the age of Goethe and exerted a strong influence on the reception of earlier literature through literary histories such as that of Gervinus.[11] *Tristan* suffers from the inability of nineteenth-century readers, schooled in standards of taste based on the works of Lessing, Goethe, and Schiller, to conceive of medieval romances as unified and consistent wholes, and bears the additional onus of its French origin and "salacious" content. Although basing an opera on a medieval text considered deficient by contemporary standards runs counter to the trend toward setting more recent and more respected literary texts, it provides Wagner's libretto with the same unusual degree of independence vis-à-vis his source that it has with respect to its musical realization. As we shall see, this independence has far-reaching consequences.

Wagner's few references to his treatment of Gottfried's romance seem at first glance to suggest that he subjects that work to drastic reduction and transposition. The comparison in *Mein Leben* of Karl Ritter's plan for a dramatization of *Tristan* with Wagner's different conception of the material is brief but explicit:

> At the time I had pulled no punches in pointing out to my young friend where the defects of his draft lay. He had confined himself to the adventurous incidents of the romance, while I had been immediately struck by its innate tragedy and was determined to cut away all the inessentials from this central theme. Returning from a walk one day, I jotted down the contents of the three acts in which I envisaged concentrating the material when I came to work it out at some future date.[12]

This broaches the fundamental issue, transposition of genre (and ultimately of medium), which requires the reduction of a multiplicity of epi-

---

[10] Cosima Wagner, *Die Tagebücher*, ed. Martin Gregor-Dellin and Dietrich Mack (Munich, 1976–77), I, 209; trans. Geoffrey Skelton, *Cosima Wagner's Diaries* (New York and London, 1978–80), I, 199. The citations given here follow Skelton, with occasional emendations.

[11] See, for example, Marianne Wynn, "Medieval Literature in Reception: Richard Wagner and Wolfram's *Parzival*," *London German Studies*, 2 (1983), 94–114.

[12] *Mein Leben*, 2nd ed. (Munich, 1915), III, 84; cited from the translation of Andrew Gray, *My Life*, ed. Mary Whittall (Cambridge, 1983), 511. Cf. the similar reference to *Parzival* in the letter to Mathilde Wesendonck of 29–30 May 1859 (Golther, 146–48).

sodes and adventures to three acts, i.e. a shift from defective breadth to effective depth, from romance to drama.

As part of this transposition of genre, Wagner's libretti also undergo a shift of viewpoint from objective to subjective, a shift that is based upon his consistent preference for drama over the novel. *Oper und Drama*, his principal theoretical writing, emphasizes the relative merits of the two genres with a series of antitheses. Whereas the novel proceeds "from without inward [. . .] from complex surroundings intelligible only with difficulty [. . .] and sinks exhausted before a portrait of the individual," drama proceeds "from within outward [. . .] from a simple, universally intelligible surrounding to an ever richer unfolding of individuality."[13] As we shall see, the preference for the subjective over the objective, for character over milieu, is crucial to an understanding of *Tristan*. For the moment, we need only emphasize that this bias underlies Wagner's proclivity to present extended "narrative" matter from the perspective of individual characters. The most spectacular example of this process in *Tristan* transposes the medieval narrative to dramatic form by shifting the description of events prior to the love potion (some 11,000 lines of Gottfried's romance) to Tristan's and Isolde's reminiscences during the course of Act I.

Although it would thus not be incorrect to consider the *Tristan* libretto as a "transposition" that "reduces" narrative to drama, such a designation ultimately proves inadequate. In a normal transposition, a literary source and its libretto adaptation differ primarily in a generic sense; the transposition itself does not necessarily alter our estimate of their relative merits. But Wagner's comments about his source, as we have seen, do not concede it any value beyond that of a preliminary stimulus in the genesis of his own works. References in the letter of 29–30 May 1859 to Mathilde Wesendonck, for example, which assert that medieval narratives are immature ("unreif") or incomplete ("nicht fertig"), deficient products of their distant age, imply their true "fruition" or "completion" only in Wagner's modern transformation. We might therefore consider the *Tristan* libretto not as a simple transposition, but rather—owing to the underlying teleological conception of the source-libretto relationship—as a work that *appropriates* the medieval romance into Wagner's "definitive" modern dramatization.

Given this implied teleology, it should not seem strange that the above-cited comments by Wagner on his condensation of Gottfried's *Tristan* echo a major historical thesis of *Oper und Drama*: that modern drama evolved out of medieval romance by reducing episodic narrative to an

[13] *Sämtliche Schriften*, IV, 47f.

internal unity grounded in the individuality of the poet and his characters. We perceive in this development, Wagner states, the dramatist's striving

> to master the varied subject matter from within outwards, to give his formation a firm center, and to derive this center as the axis of the art work from his own view of life. [. . .] From the vast mass of external appearances, which previously could not be too manifold and variegated to suit the poet, the related component parts are sorted out, the multiplicity of moments condensed to a particular illustration of the participants' characters. (*Sämtliche Schriften*, IV, 8)

On the basis of the correspondences between this general statement and those describing his adaptation of *Tristan*, we might say that Wagner's libretto appropriation also attempts to reproduce the general development he posits for the transformation of medieval romance into modern drama.

This implicit unity of conception between Wagner's main theoretical treatise and his libretti—a unity not always conceded by scholars—raises a musical issue that should be mentioned before discussing the *Tristan* libretto itself. As we have seen, Wagner demands to be considered as a dramatic poet, publishing his libretti for the book trade before as well as independently of their operatic performance, a tactic that isolates the libretto and celebrates its realization of a source. At the same time, however, separate publication also reminds us of the imperfect status of any libretto *per se*, a tactic that—paradoxically—also draws attention to the musical means by which it ultimately transcends conventional literary texts: through its realization as music-drama.[14]

The libretto's involvement in two sets of relationships, first as the dramatic appropriation of a narrative source and then as a text that is appropriated in turn by its musical realization, is implied in an alternately self-congratulatory and obsequious letter by Wagner to Ludwig II during the first performance run of *Tristan*. The fact that Gottfried's romance remained incomplete and also that August Wilhelm Schlegel, Friedrich Rückert, August von Platen, and Karl Immermann—not to mention Robert Schumann—had all attempted to write *Tristan*s during Wagner's lifetime, but left them "unfinished,"[15] posed an enticing cumulative challenge

---

[14] In addition to the letter to Mathilde Wesendonck of 15 April 1859 cited above, see the preface to the first edition of the *Ring*, which Wagner presents as a "poetic work," while simultaneously reminding his audience that it is also only a "draft for that intended actual work of art," i.e. a staged musical performance (*Sämtliche Schriften*, XII, 289).

[15] On Schlegel's rendition, which did not progress beyond the story of Riwalin and Blanchefleur, see his *Sämtliche Werke*, ed. Eduard Böcking (Leipzig, 1846), I, 100–26. Rückert's attempt to continue Schlegel's fragment, published in the journal *Die Jahreszeiten*

to posterity. Although it begins with the triumph of meeting this challenge, the letter proceeds to celebrate much more. Through repetition of words based on the ambiguous verb *vollenden* (to complete *or* to perfect), Wagner first emphasizes his "completion" of Gottfried's romance by its transposition to drama, but gradually moves to the true "completion," indeed, the unique "perfection" of its realization as a music-drama:

> This singular *Tristan* is—completed. You know that whoever else wrote a Tristan left it incomplete, from Gottfried von Straßburg on. It almost seemed as if the ancient curse would extend to my work: for it was completed only if it came to life before us completely and truly, as [performed] drama, and spoke directly to heart and mind. This has been attained. The ancient love poem lives and speaks loudly to the people, who inform me of their emotion in moving testimony. What we—my noble beloved—have accomplished with this completion, you will understand at some future date. I proclaim it boldly: nothing similar of this kind can be compared with our *Tristan*, as it will reverberate and resound today.[16]

Not surprisingly, the letter bears two dates, a conventional one of 13 June 1865 and another referring to the new era, "the second day of *Tristan*."

II

Even if we conceive of Wagner's later libretti in general as appropriations, the strategy itself is not always immediately obvious from a reading of the texts themselves, owing to the drastically reduced congruence with the narrative source that results from its transposition to drama. In *Tristan*, however, Wagner discreetly calls attention to his appropriation at the climactic moments of Acts I and II, the drinking of the potion and the conclusion of the *Liebesnacht*, which recall the equivalent scenes in the medieval source (Act III is based on material found not in Gottfried's fragment but in his sources). Both scenes are central to the structure of each work, presenting, as it were, the beginning and the end of Tristan's

---

(Summer 1839), itself remained a fragment. Platen's attempts, known today only from the poem "Tristan," include both poetic and dramatic fragments—see the *Sämtliche Werke*, ed. M. Koch and E. Peret (Leipzig, 1909), VIII, 269–75, and X, 375–82. On Immermann's fragment, see the *Werke*, ed. Robert Boxberger, vol. 13 (Berlin, n.d.). Schumann's scenario for the opera, written in 1845–46 by Robert Reinick and well known in the Dresden intellectual circles frequented by Wagner, was published in *Die Musik*, 17 (1925), 753–60. For a survey of modern *Tristan*s, see Michael S. Batts, *Gottfried von Straßburg* (New York, 1971), 109–50.

[16] Translated from *König Ludwig II. und Richard Wagner: Briefwechsel*, ed. Winifried Wagner, I (Karlsruhe i. Br., 1936), 106.

and Isolde's physical relationship, and thus lending particular emphasis to any self-conscious intertextual reminiscences. In accordance with the distinctive style of Gottfried's romance,[17] Wagner draws attention to his appropriation through rhetorical patterns, particularly chiasmus, a characteristic feature of both works.

The first instance of this technique occurs immediately after the drinking of the love potion in Act I, scene 5. Gottfried uses oxymoron to suggest the unexpected, external compulsion of the potion, followed by an extended allegorical psychomachia narrating the lovers' struggle against it.[18] Wagner's libretto, in accordance with his emphasis on grounding events in the subjective responses of characters, uses verbal and visual chiasmus to express the release of their mutual longing in a spontaneous exchange of names and embraces, dramatizing the internal process whereby the lovers become aware of their long-repressed attraction to each other:

> ISOLDE: Tristan!
> TRISTAN: Isolde!
> ISOLDE (*an seine Brust sinkend*): Treuloser Holder!
> TRISTAN (*mit Gluth sie umfassend*): Seligste Frau!
> (*Sie verbleiben in stummer Umarmung.*)

(ISOLDE: Tristan! / TRISTAN: Isolde! / ISOLDE [*sinking upon his breast*]: Faithless beloved! / TRISTAN [*ardently embracing her*]: Most blessed lady! / [*They remain in a silent embrace.*])[19]

A second dramatic chiasmus in the ensuing passage emphasizes the growing affinity between Tristan and Isolde:

> TRISTAN: Isolde!
> ISOLDE: Tristan!
> TRISTAN: Süßeste Maid!
> ISOLDE: Trautester Mann!   (VII, 28; Balling, 115f)

[17] The most recent—and most provocative—study of Gottfried and rhetoric, Winfried Christ, *Rhetorik und Roman: Untersuchungen zu Gottfrieds von Straßburg "Tristan und Isold,"* Deutsche Studien 31 (Meisenheim am Glan, 1977), also surveys previous contributions to the subject.

[18] See esp. Peter Ganz, "Minnetrank und Minne. Zu *Tristan*, Z. 11707f," in *Formen mittelalterlicher Literatur: Siegfried Beyschlag zu seinem 65. Geburtstag*, ed. Otmar Werner and Bernd Naumann, Göppinger Arbeiten zur Germanistik 25 (Göppingen, 1970), 63–75; and Wiebke Freytag, *Das Oxymoron bei Wolfram, Gottfried und andern Dichtern des Mittelalters*, Medium Aevum 24 (Munich, 1972), 186–91.

[19] *Sämtliche Schriften*, VII, 26f. In cases where the text is elaborated in the score, I cite according to *Richard Wagners Werke*, ed. Michael Balling (Leipzig, 1917)—in this instance V, 110.

19

(TRISTAN: Isolde! / ISOLDE: Tristan! / TRISTAN: Sweetest maid! /
ISOLDE: Dearest man!)

These lines seem to represent a deliberate reminiscence of the high-point
of Gottfried's prologue. In the nineteenth-century translation of Hermann Kur[t]z, Wagner's most likely source:

Ein Mann ein Weib, ein Weib ein Mann,
Tristan Isold, Isold Tristan.

(A man, a woman; a woman, a man: / Tristan, Isold; Isold, Tristan.)[20]

The reminiscence is not fortuitous: Wagner emphasizes the initial emotional effects of the potion just before these passages with a long reprise
of the prelude to the opera; he now signals the beginning of the hero's
and heroine's consciousness of that compulsion with the most famous
lines from his source's prologue.

Yet Wagner's highly self-conscious musico-dramatic citation of beginnings also relativizes the medieval text by making it only a prologue to
the further development of Tristan's and Isolde's love. The climax of the
scene, which follows an interruption by the chorus announcing the ship's
arrival, again renders their parallel reactions—but far more intensely.
Tristan and Isolde are now, so to speak, completely attuned to each other,
as their vocal unison suggests:

BEIDE: Jach in der Brust
         jauchzende Lust!
         Isolde! Tristan!
         Tristan! Isolde!
         Welten-entronnen
         du mir gewonnen!
         Du mir einzig bewußt,
         höchste Liebes-Lust!

(BOTH: Suddenly in the breast / exulting joy! / Isolde! Tristan! / Tristan! Isolde! / From worlds escaped / you won for me! / Of you alone
I am aware, / highest love-bliss/desire![21])

[20] Hermann Kur[t]z, Tristan und Isolde. Gedicht von Gottfried von Straßburg, 3rd ed.
(Stuttgart, 1877), 3. On the quote, see Peter Wapnewski, Der traurige Gott: Richard Wagner in seinen Helden (Munich, 1982), 75. Given the uncertainty whether Wagner used the
Tristan translation of Kurtz, which was in his Dresden library, or that of Karl Simrock
(Leipzig, 1855), it is interesting to note that Cosima's quote of lines 5067–69 recorded for
12 March 1870 is from the latter.
[21] I have rendered both meanings of Lust (joy and desire) in the translation here and

Rhymed couplets further underscore the congruence or harmony of the lovers' desire, the past participles *entronnen/gewonnen* in particular suggesting the completion of an irreversible process: Tristan and Isolde have escaped from the feudal world and found each other, moving from the public sphere of medieval society to the exclusive realm of their newfound private consciousness. The only unrhymed lines in the passage, with the chiastic exchange of lovers' names, emphasize that they now comprise a separate unity "consonant" only with each other, while the doubling of the exchange in the duet suggests that this new state represents an intensification and culmination of the love intimated earlier by the reminiscence of Gottfried's romance.

But how do we evaluate this relativization of the medieval romance within the larger context of the libretto, i.e., what is the nature of the love for which Gottfried's hero and heroine are only precursors? That there is indeed a conscious appropriation of medieval patterns by modern ones is suggested in general terms not only by the transformation of the linear narrative of the romance into the circular pattern of the hero's and heroine's reminiscences throughout Act I,[22] but also by a similar structural appropriation in Act II, whose basic framework, that of the medieval dawn-song, Wagner updates to include reminiscences of modern conceptions of love and death from Lessing and Schiller through Novalis, Schlegel, and Schopenhauer.[23] Given the appropriative context posited here, these reminiscences should be viewed not as indications of the poverty or derivative nature of Wagner's poetic imagination but, rather, as part of a highly developed strategy.

As if to emphasize the difference between the medieval source and its modern appropriation, the metaphysical explorations at the end of the *Liebesnacht* (Act II, scene 2) proceed by binary opposition: Tristan and Isolde long to negate the frustrations of the feudal day-world, suggested

---

elsewhere; the tension between fulfillment and longing that they express perfectly characterizes the interrupted climaxes in Acts I and II.

[22] While the ship moves relentlessly toward its destination, the lovers undergo a different journey of the mind, moving backward through the past to the present and a consciousness of their repressed affinity. The convergence of objective linear and subjective circular motion is a central structure in Romantic literature. See "The Circuitous Journey," in M. H. Abrams, *Natural Supernaturalism: Tradition and Revolution in Romantic Literature* (New York, 1973), 141–324.

[23] See Thomas Mann, "Leiden und Größe Richard Wagners," in *Wagner und unsere Zeit*, ed. Erika Mann (Frankfurt/Main, 1963), 96f; Dieter Borchmeyer, "Welt im sterbenden Licht—*Tristan* und der Mythos der Nacht," in *Das Theater Richard Wagners: Idee—Dichtung—Wirkung* (Stuttgart, 1982), 261–87; Jürgen Maehder, "Ein Klanggewand für die Nacht—Zur Partitur von *Tristan und Isolde*," *Bayreuth Programmhefte* 1982, II, 27–29.

by the preposition "ohne" (without), and replace them with a future state
that affirms their longing, suggested by the adjectives in alternate lines:

Ohne Wähnen
sanftes Sehnen,
ohne Bangen
süß Verlangen;
ohne Wehen
hehr Vergehen,
ohne Schmachten
hold Umnachten;
ohne Scheiden
ohne Meiden,
traut allein,
ewig heim,
in ungemess'nen Räumen
übersel'ges Träumen.   (VII, 50)

(Without deluding— / gentle longing: / without fearing— / sweet
yearning. / Without woes— / sublime dying. / Without languishing—
/ lovely darkening. / Without avoiding— / without separating, / intimately alone, / forever home, / in unmeasured space / most happy
dreaming.)

The actual transition from a medieval world that both lovers would like
to do "without" to a future realm beyond time and space (a realm hy-
pothesized by Novalis's *Hymnen an die Nacht*[24]) requires a further nar-
rowing and intensification of their already isolated subjectivity. Wagner
leads his hero and heroine from self-conscious deliberations on the conjunction that reminds them of their conjoined fates ("Tristan *and* Isolde")
to a heightened form of chiasmus.[25] In affirming death as a way of destroying the separation of individuation ("But that little word 'and,' / if it
were destroyed" [47]), the lovers again move through an exemplary rhetorical pattern, progressing from conjunction to chiasmus as the vehicle
for realizing a union beyond consciousness.

The expression of that chiastic union—and the shift from medieval to
modern paradigms—at the end of the *Liebesnacht* involves a second,
more extensive reminiscence of Wagner's source, the scene in the garden

[24] "Zeitlos und raumlos ist der Nacht Herrschaft" (Timeless and spaceless is the rule of
night), in *Novalis: Schriften*, 2nd ed., ed. Paul Kluckhohn and Richard Samuel, I (Stuttgart,
1960), 132.
[25] See the discussion of this nexus in Wapnewski, *Der traurige Gott* (n. 20 above), 71–
79.

near the end of Gottfried's fragment, in which Tristan and Isolde, having been discovered by Marke, take leave of each other for the last time, using the conceit of a *Personenwechsel* or exchange of personalities (18355ff) in order to overcome spiritually the physical necessity of separation. In Kurtz's modern German translation of Isolde's words:

> Nun gehet her und küsset mich:
> Tristan und Isolde, Ihr und ich,
> Wir Zwei sind immer Beide
> *Ein* Wesen in Lieb und Leide.
> Der Kuß soll ein Insiegel sein,
> Daß ich Euer sein soll und Ihr mein
> In Stete und Treue bis an den Tod,
> Nur Ein Tristan und Eine Isot.   (209)

(Now come here and kiss me; / Tristan and Isolde, you and I, / we Two shall both be forever / *One* being in love and sorrow. / The kiss shall be a seal / that I shall be yours and you mine, / in constancy and fidelity until death, / only One Tristan and One Isolde.)

As in Act I, Wagner's placement of a reminiscence from Gottfried's romance establishes a self-conscious and highly appropriate structural irony: his operatic lovers unwittingly recapitulate the parting exchange of their medieval counterparts a few moments before their own King Marke will discover them in the garden, precipitating the separation that will find its resolution only in death.

Wagner's adaptation reveals additional differences from the medieval source. The most obvious is that the transposition from narrative to music-drama enables the revelation of the lovers' inseparability to be presented not episodically in successive monologues, but simultaneously in a duet—hence the shift from the romance's description of their *Personenwechsel* by oxymoronic play with unity and duality to the libretto's expression of it through chiasmus. More important, whereas the romance's rhetorical figures suggest a static pattern of anticipation and fulfillment between the drinking of the potion and the parting scene in the garden,[26] the libretto's increasingly elaborate chiasmus suggests a continuing process of intensification between the same episodes in Act I and Act II:

ISOLDE: Du Isolde,
           Tristan ich,
           nicht mehr Isolde!

---

[26] See Freytag, *Das Oxymoron* (n. 18 above), 190–91.

23

TRISTAN: Tristan du,
ich Isolde,
nicht mehr Tristan!   (VII, 50; Balling, 271–73)

(ISOLDE: You Isolde, / Tristan I, / no longer Isolde! / TRISTAN: Tristan you, / I Isolde, / no longer Tristan!)

On the surface, Tristan and Isolde yearn to become "nicht mehr Tristan" and "nicht mehr Isolde" respectively; they seem to long for death, the state that according to Schopenhauer affords the great opportunity to be "nicht mehr Ich" (no longer I).[27] But a Schopenhauerian conception of death merely as the negation of consciousness does not adequately characterize Wagner's lovers, since they also desire to merge personalities with each other. Isolde expresses this wish in the form of a chiasmus, as does Tristan; both exchanges of the speaker's personality, through a reversal of the sequence in Isolde's chiasmus and Tristan's, also combine chiastically to establish a meta-chiastic relationship between the two in which— by denying *self*-consciousness—they become *one*-conscious, "ein-bewußt."

As they strive toward this disembodied relationship, where each will exchange consciousness with the other and be subsumed into a larger unity, first- and second-person pronouns—the characteristic expression of the Romantic consciousness's division of the world into *Ich* and *Nicht Ich*—disappear from their discourse, and Tristan and Isolde invoke a metaphysical journey beyond the division of individuation into the brave new world of night beyond the limits of space and time:

BEIDE: ohne Nennen,
ohne Trennen,
neu Erkennen,
neu Entbrennen;
endlos ewig
ein-bewußt:
heiß erglühter Brust
höchste Liebes-Lust!   (VII, 51)

(BOTH: Without naming, / without parting, / new knowing, / new enflaming: / forever endless / one-conscious: / of ardent glowing breast / the highest love-bliss/desire!)

In the climaxes to Acts I and II, then, Wagner appropriates reminiscences of his medieval source into a larger modern context, shifting atten-

---

[27] *Ueber den Tod und sein Verhältnis zur Unzerstörbarkeit unsers Wesens an sich*, in *Schopenhauers sämtliche Werke*, ed. Max Frischeisen-Köhler, III.4 (Berlin, n.d.), 526.

tion from the static relationship between the medieval lovers to the progressive development of his hero's and heroine's common subjectivity. He makes this progressive development especially clear at the very end of these climaxes as well as at the conclusion of Act III through a remarkably similar series of concluding lines, lines whose finality emphasizes the precise development of this subjective consciousness:

Act I, scene 5	*Act II, scene 2*	*Act III, scene 3*
Du mir einzig bewußt,	ein-bewußt: [. . .]	unbewußt—
höchste Liebes-Lust!	höchste Liebes-Lust!	höchste Lust!

In each case, the word beginning the final rhyme derives from the root *bewußt* and articulates the basic concern with the consciousness of the hero and heroine. The exclamation "du mir einzig bewußt" at the end of Act I, scene 5 characterizes the effect of the love potion, which makes Tristan and Isolde "conscious" of their attraction for each other at the same time that it makes them aware of nothing else. The ecstatic "ein-bewußt," which climaxes their exploration of love and death in Act II, scene 2, evokes the transcendent union of "one-consciousness" that they can realize only by casting off the shackles of individuation that separate them. Finally, the *Liebestod* at the end of Act III calls upon the heroine quite literally to expire "unbewußt" into the surrounding universe, thus becoming "un-conscious." These simple variations, *conscious, one-conscious,* and *unconscious,* epitomize in telegraphic style the trajectory of consciousness and desire that begins with Tristan's and Isolde's awareness of their love and concludes with its realization in death.

III

In revealing *Tristan und Isolde* as a paradigmatic tragedy of modern consciousness (born out of the spirit of medieval narrative), these final couplets raise an intertextual issue beyond the appropriation of Gottfried's romance. We noted above that Wagner's procedure differs from the tendency in other countries to base libretti on recent or contemporary works of literature. The traditional explanation for Wagner's choice of medieval sources, the central role of myth or of the Middle Ages in German Romanticism, and particularly the projection of a German cultural-political unity backward into the past, still avoids the absence in Wagner's operatic plans of works from the age of Goethe and Schiller, an absence made all the more striking by the constant and intensive reading of such works documented by Cosima's diaries. *Tristan und Isolde* does respond, however, to the challenge of that era of German culture through a form of what Harold Bloom has called the "anxiety of influence,"[28] indirectly taking issue with the work of German literature most capable of contesting the unique position Wagner wished to claim for his music-drama: Goethe's *Faust*.[29]

The major reminiscence occurs—not surprisingly—in the final line of our first two climaxes in the rare compound word *Liebeslust*, which receives maximum emphasis as the concluding word of two duets. The word *Liebeslust* first appears, according to Grimm's *Wörterbuch*, in three famous passages of *Faust I* and *II*—the only source cited for this word—and rhymes with the same words as in *Tristan* ("bewußt" and "Brust"). The initial occurrence is the famous description of the Faustian character:

> Du bist dir nur des einen Triebs *bewußt*;
> O lerne nie den andern kennen!
> Zwei Seelen wohnen, ach! in meiner *Brust*,
> Die eine will sich von der andern trennen.
> Die eine hält, in derber *Liebeslust*,
> Sich an die Welt mit klammernden Organen;
> Die andre hebt gewaltsam sich vom Dust
> Zu den Gefilden hoher Ahnen.   (1110–17)

(You only know one driving force, / and may you never seek to know the other! / Two souls, alas! reside within my breast, / and each is eager for a separation: / in throes of coarse desire, one grips / the earth with all its senses; / the other struggles from the dust / to rise to high ancestral spheres.[30])

The second passage centers on Faust's command to Mephisto after meeting Gretchen to procure him a kerchief or a garter to excite his passion, "Liebeslust" (2661f); the third—at the very close of *Faust II*—involves the final resolution both of Faustian striving and of the Gretchen tragedy in the petition of the Doctor Marianus that the Mater Gloriosa accept that which is borne aloft to her in love's sacred rapture, "heiliger Liebeslust" (12001–4). In *Faust*, then, this unique compound word also traces the course of the action and epitomizes it.

Wagner's lexical counterpoint with *Liebeslust* suggests what other evidence confirms: that he also considered *Tristan und Isolde* as a corrective to and improvement on Goethe's *Faust*. Cosima's diary makes it clear

---

[28] *The Anxiety of Influence: A Theory of Poetry* (New York, 1973).

[29] Cf. Dieter Borchmeyer, "Idee eines *Faust*-Theaters," in *Das Theater Wagners* (n. 23 above), 48–56.

[30] This translation and the following paraphrases are from Stuart Atkins, *Johann Wolfgang von Goethe: Faust I & II* (Cambridge, Mass., 1984).

that Wagner followed contemporary opinion, which since the 1830s had elevated *Faust* to the central work of the age,[31] in designating it as *"the book"* (13 April 1882).[32] But Wagner's high estimation of *Faust* did not deter him from asserting—at a crucial juncture in the genesis of *Tristan und Isolde*—that Goethe's ultimate concern with the totality of Faust's striving ruined the even more significant potential of the original love tragedy. The famous letter to Mathilde Wesendonck of 3 April 1858— intercepted by Wagner's wife Minna, kept by her during their ensuing separation, and finally published in the Burrell Collection in 1953—attempts to clarify a heated argument about *Faust* the previous evening. Instead of focusing on the Gretchen episode and redemption through love, Wagner's constant and unremitting theme, Goethe extricated Faust from this love,

> so that the authentic great world, the classical world of art, the practical world of industry, can be *played out* before his decidedly objective scrutiny in the greatest possible comfort. Thus for me Faust really signifies only a wasted opportunity; and this opportunity was nothing less than the only one he had of salvation and redemption. The old sinner feels this himself in the end and tries to make up for it in the final tableau—outside the whole affair, so to speak, after death, when it doesn't bother him any more but can be very pleasant to be taken up in the arms of an angel and even, no doubt, awoken to a new life.[33]

Wagner sees a fundamental antithesis between Faust's progress through the world and the transcendent "depths of love." By "objectifying" Faust's striving in a multiplicity of episodes, Goethe neglected the true realm of salvation, the subjective consciousness, since in Faust's progress

---

[31] On the following, see Karl Robert Mandelkow, *Goethe in Deutschland: Rezeptionsgeschichte eines Klassikers*, I (Munich, 1980), 240ff.

[32] Other references praise the work as "the finest book ever written in the German language" (30 September 1882), "a kind of Gospel" (12 November 1878). In fact, *Faust* should be the modern equivalent of the Luther Bible, "the new Bible . . . everybody should know all its verses by heart" (20 March 1873). Although Wagner's reading of the work would be considered highly selective by modern scholarly standards, there is no doubt that he held a high opinion of the passages cited above. Of the *Osterspaziergang*, Cosima reports "Richard moved to tears, as he says, by every encounter with so noble a spirit! Admiration and amazement over every word" (2 April 1875), and specifically of Faust's definition of his two drives, " 'that,' he says, 'is the Faust who grips us' " (9 April 1882). The Gretchen tragedy, in particular, represents "all the power of sensuality" (12 September 1880).

[33] Cited according to the translation appended to the English translation of *Mein Leben* (see n. 12 above), 779. The original is in John N. Burk, ed., *Richard Wagner: Briefe. Die Sammlung Burrell* (Frankfurt/Main, 1953), 491.

through the world "the subject never gets to take up the object, the world into himself." Inherent in this criticism is the familiar genre difference— or rather genre bias—from *Oper und Drama*. *Faust's* epic breadth prevents the work from attaining the subjective depth and concentration characteristic of modern drama; it reveals affinities with the novel without attaining the true synthesis of genre and medium postulated by Wagner's theory of music-drama.

According to his autobiography,[34] with this letter to Mathilde, Wagner sent the pencil sketch for the opera's prelude to celebrate having sent the orchestration of Act I of *Tristan und Isolde* to the engraver, thus adding to the letter's criticism of *Faust* his own realization of Goethe's "wasted opportunity," namely "the only one of salvation and redemption." As if to emphasize the certainty of his conviction, Wagner's *ad hominem*—or rather, *ad feminam*—peroration on Goethe's *Faust* concludes with an invocation reminiscent of the final scene of *Tristan und Isolde*. Rejecting the blind Faust's attempt to win "the world and peace from outside,"[35] Wagner directs his vision to Mathilde, his own Isolde-surrogate, and—in a passage whose literary-biographical confusion of subject and object intimates their mutual "one-consciousness"—echoes Isolde's own empathetic *Liebestod* in a celebration of the salvation to be found within the depths of her "wonderful, sacred eyes":

> I sink into them! Then there are no more objects and subjects; then everything is one and the same, deep and immeasurable harmony! . . . He is a fool who tries to win the world and this peace from outside! A blind man, if he has not recognized your eyes and not found his soul within them! Only inside, within us, only in the depths is salvation to be found! (492f)

On one level, Wagner's extension of his appropriative technique to include Goethe's *Faust* represents no unique occurrence in mid-nineteenth-century intellectual life. The "*Faust* fever" of the 1830s and 1840s, the formative experience of a generation of students which helped establish Goethe's masterpiece as *the* work of German literature, inspired not only the young Wagner to begin his first *Faust* compositions but countless other writers as well, so that Gervinus felt obliged to observe:

> Upon its appearance, everyone found himself—as Niebuhr affirms— moved in his innermost being and felt inclined to continue it; one tested one's own ability against it, and everyone thought to help the

---

[34] *Mein Leben*, III, 153; in Gray's translation (see n. 12 above), 562.

[35] The rejection of Faust itself echoes Faust's rejection of supernatural transcendance (11442–44).

28

mysterious poet by imputing to him and imposing on him one's own sentiments. But all the endless imitations that Faust underwent were not resolutions of the unresolved riddle; they were not continuations, but rather—as Goethe himself said—repetitions.[36]

Wagner's *Tristan und Isolde* differs, of course, from such adaptations or "repetitions" in its tendency to subsume Goethe's work into a completely different text, and ultimately into the larger context of the composer's life and work.[37] Numerous subsequent events, ranging from the Wagners' celebration of the anniversary of Goethe's death to the stylizing of Cosima's diaries as a counterpart to Carlyle's biography or Eckermann's conversations, suggest a desire also to institutionalize Wagner's position generally as Goethe's successor—a program that becomes clear in the emerging tension between Weimar and Bayreuth as "centers" of German culture in the late nineteenth century.[38]

IV

Although the type of appropriation in *Tristan* discussed here is not unique (the combination of older German literature and the competition with Goethe appear again, for example, in *Die Meistersinger*),[39] it does not appear to comprise the only such pattern in Wagner's later libretti. My concluding remarks will therefore attempt some preliminary suggestions concerning related strategies in *Parsifal*, a work also derived from a masterpiece of medieval German literature but even less indebted to its source. Wagner's subtitle alone, "Bühnenweihfestspiel" (Stage-Dedication-Festival-Play), already suggests the greatly increased importance of extrinsic factors in a work that retrospectively validates the preceding operas by consecrating an already existing theater at Bayreuth. Indeed, it represents a potentially more general program of appropriation, both with respect to other texts and its cultural context.

As is the case with *Tristan*, there is a paucity of references to Wolfram

[36] Georg Gottfried Gervinus, *Geschichte der deutschen Dichtung*, 4th ed. (Leipzig, 1853), V, 105.

[37] See, for example, the entry in Cosima's diary for 24 October 1881: "R. talks about *Faust* and remarks how unique it is [. . .] The children perform a charade outstandingly well, then R. plays *T. und Isolde*, and all, all that is sorrowful dissolves, and the fair bliss of melancholy flows through our veins."

[38] See the comments in Mandelkow (n. 31 above) I, 229f, on attempts to regain Weimar's cultural leadership by making it an "anti-Bayreuth."

[39] See Peter Wapnewski, "Wagners Sachs in Goethes Werkstatt," in *Richard Wagner: Die Szene und ihr Meister*, 2nd ed. (Munich, 1983), 67–74.

von Eschenbach, and these are primarily negative.[40] Wagner's statement that only "a few images" of Wolfram's romance "stuck in my mind" and Cosima's accompanying assertion that the composer's text "has in fact no connection with it" (21 June 1879) seem to represent one of the couple's more justifiable claims. Rather than appropriating and completing a "deficient" medieval source, the valedictory focus of *Parsifal* generates a complex web of allusions to Wagner's earlier works, turning the text back upon his entire *oeuvre*. The genesis of the opera, for example, is closely associated, not with Wolfram's romance, but with the problem of longing and redemption in *Tristan*. Wagner's discussion of his first draft for that work in *Mein Leben* (cited above, n. 12) explains the connection:

> I wove into the last act an episode I later did not use: this was a visit by Parzival, wandering in search of the Grail, to Tristan's sickbed. I identified Tristan, wasting away but unable to die of his wound, with the Amfortas of the Grail romance.

Even more revealing is the fact that after deleting the episode he continued to define the future work in terms of the earlier one, describing the Amfortas of Act I to Mathilde Wesendonck (29–30 May 1859) as "my Tristan of the third Act with an inconceivable intensification." The technical term intensification (*Steigerung*) is revealing: used to characterize a variety of processes and their results, ranging from concentration and refinement to metamorphosis, it also attained a well-known literary extension in Goethe's reference to his Tasso as "an intensified Werther."[41] Inasmuch as intensification can transform shared characteristics into different, even opposite ones, the intensification of longing from Tristan to Amfortas also generates a larger unity underlying the apparent reversal from passion to compassion, sex to chastity, in the two texts. Moreover, Wagner's letter to Mathilde Wesendonck stating the opposition of *Tristan* and—by implication—the as yet unwritten *Parsifal* ("active sympathy," "saint") to *Faust* intimates their common subjectivity in contrast to the "objectivity" of Goethe's play:

> people may well also call it objective that the subject never gets to take up the object, the world, into himself (which can only be done by active *sympathy*), but only displays the object for his own scrutiny, and loses himself in it in contemplation, not in sympathy (for

[40] Documents for the genesis of *Parsifal* are presented by Martin Geck and Egon Voss, *Dokumente zur Entstehung und ersten Aufführung des Bühnenweihfestspiels "Parsifal,"* in Richard Wagner, *Sämtliche Werke* 30 (Mainz, 1970), 11–67; see esp. nos. 4, 5, and 12.

[41] See Elizabeth M. Wilkinson and L. A. Willoughby, " 'Tasso—ein gesteigerter Werther' in the Light of Goethe's Principle of 'Steigerung,' " in their *Goethe: Poet and Thinker* (New York, 1962), 185–213.

that would make him become the world—and the subject's becoming the world is a matter that concerns the saint, and not the poet of *Faust*, who has ended up as a paragon for philistines).[42]

As this nexus suggests, such operators as intensification and appropriation seem to be important forces unifying what on other levels appear to be opposite or contradictory elements of the composer's *oeuvre*. It is not surprising that readers other than specialists in medieval German literature often find *Parsifal*'s intertextual relationships with Wagner's preceding works more significant than the connections with its source.[43]

Wagner's valedictory opera, however, also represents an intensification of claims on contemporary society by extending its sphere of appropriation from a canonical individual text such as *Faust* to a larger cultural context. *Parsifal* establishes this extended claim by means of a highly appropriative pattern of thought that surfaces most succinctly in a letter of 7 September 1865 to Ludwig II: extra-Biblical typology. Responding to Ludwig's question about the significance of Kundry's kiss, Wagner relates the story of the fall (emphasizing—again with an oblique connection to *Tristan*—the role of "consciousness") and its resolution in Christ, and then extends the pattern to his own work:

> Adam and Eve became "knowing." They became "conscious of sin." Because of this consciousness the human race had to do penance in shame and misery until it was redeemed by Christ, who took upon Himself the sin of man. My dear, can I speak about such profound matters other than in metaphor, through comparison? But only the clear-sighted person can inform himself of the inner meaning. Adam–Eve: Christ.—What if we added to them: "Anfortas–Kundry: Parzival"? But with great caution![44]

Great caution indeed! Traditionally, typological patterns are used to link the Old and New Testaments, e.g. Adam's fall with man's restoration through Christ (the "new Adam"); or they are used "extra-Biblically" to establish a connection between Biblical and post-Biblical events or fig-

---

[42] Cited from Gray (see n. 12 above), 779; the original is in Burk (see n. 33 above), 491f.

[43] On *Parsifal* as a "summation" of central concerns of earlier works, see Borchmeyer, *Theater*, 287–301, and Carl Dahlhaus, *Richard Wagners Musikdramen*, 2nd ed. (Zürich, 1985), 143f. One of the earliest records of the reception of *Parsifal* illustrates the relative unimportance of Wolfram for Wagner's libretto. Gustav Adolph Kietz's recollection of Wagner's reading of his prose draft of *Parsifal* emphasizes, "you know the poem by Wolfram von Eschenbach, but you shouldn't think of that; it is something completely different, inexpressible." Geck and Voss (see n. 40 above), no. 31.

[44] *Briefwechsel* (see n. 16 above), I, 174.

ures, e.g. between Christ and the "imitatio Christi" of a saint.[45] Wagner's analogy is more complicated, beginning with the central Adam-Christ typology between Old and New Testament, which then forms (in a manner reminiscent of the intensified Tristan-Isolde chiasmus in Act II of *Tristan*) the first component of a larger meta-typology between Biblical figures and the principal figures of Wagner's opera.

The extension of Biblical typology to *Parsifal* seems unexceptionable at first glance, part of a pattern of appropriation operating on the level of genre rather than through motifs or rhetorical figures, as was the case with *Tristan*. Wagner intensifies Wolfram's superimposition of genre elements from the saint's life onto the basic structure of knightly romance, creating instead a saint's life with knightly elements.[46] His major changes all point in this direction: incorporation of the Eucharist into the ritual at the Grail castle (the only extensive intertextual borrowing); deletion of all major female figures except Cundry, as well as elimination of the pervasive love interest, including the story of the hero's parents and the parallel adventures of Gawan (which comprise nearly half the work); and—most important—the drastic reduction of Parzival's adventures and the shift of the Good Friday episode from the middle to the end. Whereas Wolfram's extensive series of knightly adventures articulates the development of a hero who is "brave but slowly wise," Wagner's transposition reduces the romance episodes to three static situations characteristic of the saint's life (anticipation, temptation, completion), fulfilling the prophecy of a "pure fool, knowing through compassion" (*durch Mitleid wissend, der reine Tor*).

Unlike the traditional saint's life, however, the typology of Wagner's libretto does not suggest a relationship of anticipation and fulfillment between New Testament and post-Apostolic history. Following San-Marte, Wagner conceived of the Grail community as an alternative to organized Christianity, revealing to Cosima on 7 September 1875 that the Grail "evolved entirely outside the church, as a peaceful disengagement from it." But precisely what his particular vision of that alternative signifies has remained a point of contention for more than a century. Whether it capitulates before Christianity, as Nietzsche thought, or incorporates religion into the institution of art, as Ludwig II suggested,[47] might not be

---

[45] See Friedrich Ohly, "Halbbiblische und außerbiblische Typologie," in *Schriften zur mittelalterlichen Bedeutungskunde* (Darmstadt, 1977), 361–400.

[46] The two genres are quite similar. See Max Wehrli, "Roman und Legende im deutschen Hochmittelalter," in *Formen mittelalterlicher Erzählung* (Zurich and Freiburg i. Br., 1969), 155–76.

[47] "Indeed, this art is holy, is the purest, most sublime religion." Letter to Wagner, 5 September 1865, *Briefwechsel* (see n. 16 above), I, 169.

demonstrable from an extended study of the text itself, whose typological and rhetorical patterns often seem more solipsistic ("Erlösung dem Erlöser" [Redemption for the Redeemer]) than imitative or appropriative. Provisional answers about this puzzling work may ultimately have to come from a study that emphasizes the ambiguous structures of the libretto, and then relates them to the reception of *Parsifal* and Bayreuth— and the conflicting perceptions that differing cultural situations impose on us in reading opera.[48]

[48] See, for example, the introductory "Toward a Theory of Literary History" in Robert Weimann, *Structure and Society in Literary History*, expanded ed. (Baltimore and London, 1984), 1–17.

Boito and F.-V. Hugo's "Magnificent Translation": A Study in the Genesis of the *Otello* Libretto

Arrigo Boito's libretto for *Otello* is a complex, multilayered document, the antithesis of a "spontaneous" work of art. It is the product of a slowly and carefully created first draft dating from the Summer and Autumn of 1879, which was followed by seven years of sporadic plot and text revisions, most of them undertaken at Verdi's request.[1] Surely no other completed opera of Verdi's underwent such painstakingly intense "textual thinking." Every word, every rhyme, every metrical choice was meticulously plotted. Even the intricacies of *Falstaff* came to Boito far more easily.

I am concerned here with the earliest stages of the *Otello* text, that period of its initial drafting from July to November 1879—months in which Boito first distilled Shakespeare's *Othello* into a workable libretto. Needless to say, the topic of Verdi, Boito, and Shakespeare is almost fatiguingly perennial. Its treatment has ranged from program-note summaries and college term papers to more elevated statements of how Boito condensed and altered the Shakespearean original: among these last, the writings of Joseph Kerman, Winton Dean, Julian Budden, Stefan Kunze, and several others.[2] Often stressing narrative concerns—an account of the

[1] Boito began drafting the text shortly after the *Otello* project had been broached to Verdi in Milan, c. 30 June 1879. An initial draft of the proposed libretto was given to Verdi in two installments, on c. 1–6 November (probably at least the first two acts) and on 18 November 1879 (the remainder of the opera). For a chronological account of the drafting and revising of the libretto, see James A. Hepokoski, *Giuseppe Verdi: Otello* (Cambridge, 1987), 21–47. See also Alessandro Luzio, ed., "Il libretto di *Otello*," *Carteggi verdiani*, II (Rome, 1935), 95–141; and Julian Budden, *The Operas of Verdi*, III: *From "Don Carlos" to "Falstaff"* (New York, 1981), 295–332.

[2] See, for example, Joseph Kerman, "*Otello*: Traditional Opera and the Image of Shakespeare," *Opera as Drama* (New York, 1956), 129–67; Winton Dean, "Verdi's 'Otello': A Shakespearian Masterpiece," *Shakespeare Survey*, 21 (1968), 87–96; Roy Aycock, "Shakespeare, Boito, and Verdi," *The Musical Quarterly*, 58 (1972), 588–604; Peter Conrad, *Romantic Opera and Literary Form* (Berkeley, 1977), 46–69; Budden, 95–141; Graham Bradshaw, "A Shakespearean Perspective: Verdi and Boito as Translators," in Hepokoski, *Giuseppe Verdi: Falstaff* (Cambridge, 1983), 152–71; Stefan Kunze, "Der Verfall des Helden: Über Verdis 'Otello,'" *Giuseppe Verdi: Otello: Texte, Materialien, Kommentare*, Ro-

deletions and interpolations made to produce an efficient libretto—these discussions have typically compared the ultimate source, Shakespeare, with the final product, Boito's Italian opera text, without probing into the influence of intermediate texts. From many perspectives this is a defensible, and not infrequently a fruitful, enterprise; but we may wish to ask more pointed questions of the libretto. What exactly was Boito's knowledge of Shakespeare? From which cultural and interpretive grounds does his understanding of the play spring? Our understanding springs from a tradition of English-language criticism extending from the commentaries of Thomas Rymer, Samuel Johnson, and Samuel Taylor Coleridge through those of A. C. Bradley, T. S. Eliot, F. R. Leavis, and so on.[3] But whose critical opinions shaped Boito's Continental, nineteenth-century feeling for Shakespeare? More precisely, which factors of critical and cultural mediation helped to transform *Othello* into *Otello*?[4]

Boito, for instance, never hid the fact that he worked principally from translations. In 1887, the year of the *Otello* premiere, the English correspondent Blanche Roosevelt published an account of a discussion that she had recently had with him:

> By the way, I haven't told you of Boïto's personal appearance, nor the literary gods at whose shrine he worships. These latter are three poets, Dante, Victor Hugo, and Shakespeare. . . .
>
> His worship of poetry and his three poets reaches idolatry. Of

roro Opernbücher, ed. Attila Csampai and Dietmar Holland (Reinbek bei Hamburg, 1981), 9–36. Reflecting more modern approaches, Kunze's essay is particularly sensitive to the cultural and aesthetic context in which *Otello* was created, as is Francesco Degrada, "*Otello*: da Boito a Verdi" [1976], *Il palazzo incantato: Studi sulla tradizione del melodramma dal Barocco al Romanticismo* (Fiesole, 1979), II, 155–66. See also William Weaver, "Verdi, Shakespeare, and the Italian Audience," *Otello*, English National Opera Guide no. 7 (London, 1981), 23–26.

[3] Summaries of influential English-language *Othello* criticism may be found in Albert Gerard, " 'Egregiously an Ass': The Dark Side of the Moor: A View of Othello's Mind," *Shakespeare Survey*, 10 (1957), 98–106; Helen Gardner, "*Othello*: A Retrospect, 1900–67," *Shakespeare Survey*, 21 (1968), 1–11; John Wain, ed., *Shakespeare: Othello: A Casebook* (London, 1971), 11–33; Robert Hapgood, '*Othello*,' *Shakespeare, Select Bibliographical Guides*, ed. Stanley Wells (London, 1973). Wain also anthologizes much of this criticism.

[4] On the other hand, recent studies of Verdi's *Macbeth* have addressed some of these issues and mediating elements directly. See especially Francesco Degrada, "Lettura del *Macbeth*" [1975–77], *Il palazzo incantato*, 79–141; Degrada, "Observations on the Genesis of Verdi's *Macbeth*," *Verdi's Macbeth: A Sourcebook*, ed. David Rosen and Andrew Porter (New York, 1984), 156–73; Daniela Goldin, "Il *Macbeth* verdiano: Genesi e linguaggio di un libretto," *Analecta musicologica*, 19 (1979), 336–72, rev. in Goldin, *La vera fenice: Librettisti e libretti tra Sette e Ottocento* (Turin, 1985), 230–82; and William Weaver, "The Shakespeare Verdi Knew," *Verdi's Macbeth: A Sourcebook*, 144–48.

course, he is at his best in the Italian or French authors; he reads Shakespeare very well in English, but told me he had learned *Othello* by heart in "François Hugo's magnificent [French] translation and that of the Italian author Maffei."[5]

Boito's acquaintance with the English text is attested to by the presence in his personal library of three copies of Shakespeare in English. To judge from the present condition of the books, his most frequently consulted copy was a one-volume edition of *The Complete Works of William Shakespeare*, edited by the German scholar Nicolaus Delius and published in 1854 by Baumgärtner in Leipzig.[6] Boito went through several plays in this collection, *Othello* among them, and underscored a few lines of text here and there. At times the underlinings intersect with important lines in the libretto; at times they do not. For instance, toward the end of Act I, on p. 734, he underscored five separate sentences of Iago: "It is merely a lust of the blood and a permission of the will"; "These Moors are changeable in their wills—fill thy purse with money"; "She must change for youth"; "I hate the Moor; my cause is hearted; thine hath no less reason"; and "There are many events in the womb of time, which will be delivered" (*Oth.* I.iii, 326, 336–37, 348–49, 350–51, 353–54).[7] More suggestive, perhaps, is the isolated underlining of Iago's "Ha! I like not that" (p. 742, *Oth.* III.iii, 35; cf. "Ciò m'accora," vocal score 124/1/2),[8] but it cannot be proven that this marking dates from 1879. Other plays in the volume are similarly marked (for example, *The Merchant of Venice*), and the relationship of Boito's *Othello* entries here and the eventual *Otello* libretto remains uncertain.

Probably more important, in Delius's edition of *Othello*, some of whose readings derive from the notorious nineteenth-century forgeries of John Payne Collier, Boito seems to have been concerned primarily with correcting in the margins the words of an annoyingly corrupt text.[9] For

[5] Blanche Roosevelt, *Verdi: Milan, and "Othello"* (London, 1887), 239–40.

[6] Boito's library is now housed in the Biblioteca Palatina in Parma. The Leipzig Shakespeare title reads: *The / Complete Works / of / William Shakespeare. / The Text / Regulated by the Old Copies and by the Recently Discovered Folio of 1632, / Containing Early Manuscript Emendations. / With / Notes, Selected and Original, / A Copious and Almost New Glossary, / The Poet's Life and Portrait.* Concerning Delius, see William Jaggard, *Shakespeare Bibliography* (Stratford-on-Avon, n.d.), 531.

[7] Line numbers within *Othello* refer to The New Cambridge Shakespeare edition of the play, ed. Norman Sanders (Cambridge, 1984).

[8] All references to the opera *Otello* refer to the currently available vocal score published by Ricordi, Milan, pl. no. 52105, ed. Mario Parenti, 1964. Citations refer to page number/ system number/bar number.

[9] The impact of the "recently discovered folio of 1632" mentioned on the title page (see n. 6 above) is elaborated upon in the introduction to the volume, written by "Dr. D." [De-

instance, on p. 736 he changed Desdemona's incorrect last word in the 1854 edition's "How say you, Cassio? is he not a most profane and liberal censurer?" to the proper "counsellor" (*Oth.* II.i, 159–60); on p. 737 he corrected Iago's "If this poor brach of Venice, whom I trash" to the more correct (but still problematic) "If this poor trash of Venice, whom I trace (*Oth.* II.i, 284); on p. 744 he emended the last word in the first line of Iago's "But pardon me; I do not in suspicion / Distinctly speak of her, though I may fear" to the correct "position" (*Oth.* III.iii, 236–37); on p. 745 he changed the second line of Iago's "It were a tedious difficulty, I think, / To bring it to that prospect" to "To bring them to that prospect" (*Oth.* III.iii, 398–99); and so on.[10] His preoccupation with correcting Delius was scholarly, philological—an essential part of his character—but, again, no evidence links these markings directly with the creation of the *Otello* libretto; they might have been made at a different period. His other two English editions, the thirteen-volume compact set of *The Handy-Volume Shakspeare* [sic], probably acquired no earlier than the 1870s,[11] and an apparently later "Chandos Classics" edition of *The*

lius]: "The preparations for the present edition . . . had not yet been completed, when the corrections and emendations of the Shakespearian text, discovered by Payne Collier in a copy of the folio-edition of 1632, became known, and created so great a sensation in the literary world. . . . [The present editor] has received all those [corrections] which undoubtedly are to be called *emendations*" (p. iii). The "sensation" referred to was Collier's newly claimed set of manuscript corrections on the "Perkins Folio," a copy of the second folio then in his possession. Collier had announced these to the world in 1852 in his *Notes and Emendations to the Text of Shakespeare's Plays*, and in 1853 he brought out an edition of the *Plays . . . The Text Regulated by the Old Copies and by the Recently Discovered Folio of 1632 Containing Early Manuscript Emendations* (Jaggard, 56–57, 50; cf. the title page of Delius's 1854 Leipzig edition, n. 6 above). Collier's supposed discoveries, however, were immediately disputed in England and were exposed as forgeries in 1859 and 1860.

Delius's edition—Boito's principal copy of the English-language Shakespeare—is thus textually flawed. It seems likely that Boito was aware of the Collier forgeries; that is, realizing at some point that his English edition of Shakespeare contained corrupt readings, he must have compared its texts with others that he considered more reliable in order to alter the inaccurate words. (He even makes a passing reference to a reading in Collier's 1632 manuscript in the margin of p. 741 of the Delius *Othello*, the beginning of Act III.) The important point is that Boito's concern for textual correction is not unique to *Othello*, and it need not be linked with the libretto-making process.

[10] Not all of Boito's alterations were accurate. For instance, on p. 744 he changed the word "mocks" in Othello's "If she be false, O, then heaven mocks itself" (III.iii, 280) to the incorrect "doth mock."

[11] Containing only two underscored passages (again, "Ha! I like not that," but now continuing through "or if—I know not what" [III.iii, 35–36]; and "But for a satisfaction of my thought; No further harm" [III.iii, 96–97]), Boito's copy of *The Handy-Volume Shakspeare* (c. 3 × 4 ⅝ inches) was published by Bradbury, Agnew & Co. and lacks a printed date. This thirteen-volume set (edited by "Q. D.") was first brought out in 16° in 1866 and 1867 by Bradbury, Evans & Co. and was treated to at least three reprints (in 12°, 16°, and

Works of Shakespeare (London, after 1883)[12] provide little further indication of any close study of the English *Othello*. One's general impression is that Boito struggled through the original version of the play, was happy to have it at hand, but did not rely heavily on it for the libretto.

Nor does the language of the various Italian translations seem to have been particularly important. Curiously, no copies of Shakespeare in Italian have turned up in Boito's personal library. Boito, of course, was aware of the Italian translations, and, as will emerge, he did use some of them for an occasional turn of phrase; but, at least with regard to his own choice of vocabulary for *Otello*, he seems to have been less reliant on them then he would be, for instance, for the *Falstaff* libretto.[13] Although nineteenth-century Italy saw a number of *Othello* translations, Boito would have been most likely to encounter—or to take seriously—only three: the widely circulated and often inaccurate prose version of Carlo Rusconi (1838–39); the poetic version (in *endecasillabi sciolti*, also prominent in passages of Boito's *Otello*) of Giulio Carcano (published 1857–58, initially prepared in 1852 at the request of the Italian actor Ernesto Rossi); and the version mentioned by Boito to Blanche Roosevelt, that of Andrea Maffei (1869, also in *endecasillabi sciolti*).[14] Both Rusconi and Maffei, it should be added, had included Giovanni Gherardini's influential translation (1817) of August Wilhelm Schlegel's commentary (1809–11) on the play. This was surely the most readily available discussion of

---

18°) in the next few years. The first thirteen-volume "Bradbury, Agnew & Co." printing (in 12°) seems to have occurred in 1876. (A thirty-nine-volume edition in 16° followed in c. 1898.) See Jaggard, 539, 540, 544, 546, and 554.

[12] The eighty-volume "Chandos Classics" were issued in various editions by F. Warne and Co., London, from 1868 onward. Boito's one-volume copy of *The Works of Shakespeare* bears the printer's date on the final page, p. 748, "31/5/83." *Othello* appears on pp. 639–61 and is unmarked by Boito. (Some passages of *The Merry Wives of Windsor*, however, are underlined, suggesting that this volume might have been consulted as part of the preparation for *Falstaff*.)

[13] For some of the indebtedness of *Falstaff* to the Italian translations of Shakespeare, see James A. Hepokoski, "The Compositional History of Verdi's *Falstaff*: A Study of the Autograph Score and Early Editions," Diss. Harvard 1979, 13–14, 21–22; and *Giuseppe Verdi: Falstaff*, 30.

[14] The clearest treatment of nineteenth-century Italian *Othello* translations may be found in Anna Busi, *Otello in Italia (1777–1972)* (Bari, 1973). Busi includes discussions of the translations of Rusconi, *Teatro completo di Shakespeare*, originally published in Padua, with numerous subsequent editions published in various cities, the eleventh, for example, in Rome in 1884 (71–78); Carcano, *Teatro scelto di Guglielmo Shakespeare*, published in Milan (78–87); and Maffei, *Otello e La Tempesta di G. Shakespeare, Arminio e Dorotea di Wolfgango Goethe*, published in Florence (91–96). See also Busi's full bibliography of Italian translations, 309–10.

Othello in nineteenth-century Italy, and it profoundly influenced both the *ottocento* acting tradition and Boito's understanding of the play.[15] (Verdi himself seems to have relied primarily on the Rusconi and Maffei translations of *Othello*.)[16]

More immediately important to Boito than either the English text or an Italian translation was the 1860 French version of *Othello* by François-Victor Hugo, the son of Victor Hugo: this is the "magnificent translation" of which Boito spoke to Blanche Roosevelt. Hugo's translation of Shakespeare's complete works was an enormously important literary event for French readers, and his renderings immediately replaced earlier, less careful versions of the individual plays. Paul de Saint-Victor, writing in 1873 at Hugo's death, would summarize the translator's achievement: "François-Victor Hugo has done for France what Schlegel did for Germany: he has naturalized the genius of Shakespeare into our language."[17] And a typical reaction to the translations had been that of Jules Janin, who responded on 24 January 1859 in the *Journal des débats politiques et littéraires* to the appearance of the first volume (*Les Deux Hamlet*): "It is supremely faithful; it reproduces laments and sobs, pain and nuance, melody and groaning, the soul and the body, *the military spirit*, going so far as [to capture] the dark reflection of armor in the pale brightness of the winter moon."[18] Hugo's value lay in the depth and quality of his scholarship (since at least 1853 he had been tracking down not only Shakespeare's own sources, but also contemporary English plays and important English and Continental Shakespeare criticism) and in his devotion to textual fidelity and precise French verbal equivalents. His father, Victor Hugo, described the whole scholarly project as an "oeuvre philologique," an "oeuvre critique et historique."[19] François-Victor Hugo's passion for exactitude, however, did not always find complete approval among French readers. Some were reluctant to acknowledge this meticulousness as a virtue; and even some supportive readers occasionally feared that he had sometimes been, if anything, "excessively close to the

---

[15] Hepokoski, *Giuseppe Verdi: Otello*, 163–89.

[16] See Verdi to Boito, 8 May 1886, in which the composer, in order to clarify an individual point within the *Otello* libretto, mentions the translations of Hugo, Maffei, and Rusconi, in *Carteggio Verdi-Boito*, ed. Mario Medici and Marcello Conati (Parma, 1978), I, 103.

[17] Quoted in Frances Vernor Guille, *François-Victor Hugo et son oeuvre* (Paris, 1950), 197. (Unless otherwise indicated, the translations throughout this study are my own.) The following remarks in the text are based on Guille's discussion of Hugo's Shakespeare project, 171–99.

[18] Quoted in Guille, 197.

[19] Guille, 178.

text . . . too faithful to Shakespeare."[20] Nevertheless, in its authority, thoroughness, scholarship, and "close reading" of the original texts it was something of a non-English-speaking scholar's dream. This was its appeal to Boito.

Hugo's translations passed through three slightly varied nineteenth-century editions. The first two were published by Pagnerre in Paris: the first in fourteen volumes, *Oeuvres complètes de W. Shakespeare*, dating from 1859–64 (the *Sonnets*—originally issued separately in 1857—and the doubtful works, the *Apocryphes*, would appear as later volumes of the set in subsequent years); the second edition appeared in 1865–73. A third, more popular edition, smaller in format, was brought out beginning in 1871 by the Parisian publisher Alphonse Lemerre.[21] Boito owned all three editions, and his copies are still preserved and may be consulted today: the first in the Library of the Museo Teatrale alla Scala, Milan (TE.P.20.2); the second and third in an uncatalogued collection in the Biblioteca Palatina in Parma. Hugo's first edition of Shakespeare (1859–64) remained Boito's principal and most extensively read copy. Containing personal underlinings, markings, and general reactions, it was, as we shall see, the practical working source of the *Otello* libretto. (His copy of the second edition is virtually unmarked—it seems in mint condition, almost unopened. Boito's copy of the third edition does contain a few marginal notes, but far fewer than those found in the first edition. Moreover, most of these later notes seem to have been transferred from his copy of the first edition.)

It is with the La Scala copy of the Hugo translation, then, that we shall be concerned here. The following discussion is divided into two sections. The first of these is an elaboration of the evidence that this copy of the translation is indeed the source from which Boito constructed the *Otello* libretto. This will entail an inventory of the most important of Boito's markings. As will be seen, certain groups of annotations and underlinings occasionally suggest interpretive decisions that Boito made when creating the libretto—lines that he considered important or essential to one or more of the characters. Readers less concerned with a detailed demonstration of this evidence may wish to skip over to Part II, a more general consideration of the ways in which Hugo's translation and scholarly apparatus affected Boito's thinking about *Otello*. It deals with the librettist's conception of his characters in general—a conception forged with a keen awareness of Hugo's views—and with two operatic texts directly

[20] Guille, 182.
[21] Guille, 186, 197.

traceable to Boito's copy of the Hugo translation: Desdemona's "Willow Song" and Iago's "Credo."

I

Hugo's *Othello* translation is to be found in volume V, part II of the first edition (1860).[22] Boito's La Scala copy bears the flourish of his signature, "A. Boito," in red pencil on the half-title page, and the red-pencil, black-pencil, and (especially) blue-pencil annotations within attest to Boito's reactions to the play.[23] The nature of the annotations permits us to date them to the period of the initial *Otello* draft, July–November 1879. Evidence for the operatic relevance of this copy of the first edition is clear even before the opening words of the play. In the list of "Personnages" (Hugo, p. 232) Boito underlined in blue pencil the names of "Othello, le More de Venise," "Cassio, lieutenant honorable," "Iago, un scélerat," "Roderigo, gentilhomme dupe," "Montano, gouverneur de Chypre," the "Gentilshommes de Chypre," "Desdémona," and "Émilia"—the essential characters that appear in the opera. He either left unmarked or provided with a different mark, a blue "check" of omission, the characters that would not be included in *Otello*: Brabantio, "Le Doge de Venise," "Sénateurs," "Matelots," "Le Clown," and "Bianca." For Lodovico and Gratiano he underlined only their description, "nobles vénitiens." Lodovico would be transferred to the opera; Gratiano would not. This last point suggests that the underlining occurred at an early stage of libretto-making, one in which the precise extent of the roles of Lodovico and, possibly, Gratiano had not yet been determined.

Within Act I of the Hugo translation, the contents of which Boito was largely to discard, one finds several scattered lines underscored in blue.

---

[22] Because Hugo preferred to group plays thematically, *Cymbeline* and *Othello* are presented together in this second part of volume V, "Les Jaloux." (Part I of "Les Jaloux" [1859] had contained translations of *Troilus and Cressida*, *Much Ado about Nothing*, and *The Winter's Tale*.)

[23] I would like to thank M.º Giampiero Tintori and his staff at the Museo Teatrale alla Scala, Milan, for the opportunity to examine this copy of Hugo's *Othello*, on which the present study is based.

The existence of this volume with Boito's markings was first noted—briefly—by Piero Nardi, *Vita di Arrigo Boito* (Verona, 1942), 566 and 594, and *Arrigo Boito: Tutti gli scritti* (Verona, 1942), 1541. Subsequent studies of the later Verdi operas have ignored this point, and no account of Boito's markings in the Hugo volume has appeared in print. Nardi mentions that Boito's copies of the Hugo translations of *The Merry Wives of Windsor* and the two parts of *Henry IV* also contain marginal annotations and were the immediate sources of the *Falstaff* libretto. Those plays, however, are less thoroughly marked than is *Otello*; moreover, some "non-Verdian" Shakespearean plays are similarly annotated. Whether the Hugo translations played the same role in the creation of *Falstaff*, then, remains uncertain.

As might be expected, many of these are lines that he decided to retain in the subsequent action of his libretto. (Boito's Act I is based on the play's Act II, with a few notable interpolations from the "deleted" Act I.) These include several summary-lines that refer to Iago's motives and initiate his plotting with Roderigo; [24] a line in which Roderigo gives vent to despair ("Je vais incontinent me noyer" [p. 257], "I will incontinently drown myself" [I.iii, 301], "d'affogarmi" [vocal score, 31/1/3]); Roderigo's racial epithet for the Moor ("l'homme aux grosses lèvres" [p. 235], "the thicklips" [I.i, 67], given by Boito to Iago, "quel selvaggio dalle gonfie labbra" [32/2/2–32/3/1]); and so on. Throughout Act I the blue-pencil underlinings stand out as key phrases that Boito wished to call to his own attention, evidently things that he wanted to keep in mind while preparing the libretto in the Summer of 1879.

The carving-out of potentially operatic text is especially clear with relation to the opera's Act I Love Duet. This piece—Otello's and Desdemona's reminiscence of how they came to be enamored of each other—is a composite of three extracts from Shakespeare's play: Othello's narration of how Desdemona fell in love with him after hearing the stories of his past adventures (I.iii, 127–69); a single line of Desdemona, "I saw Othello's visage in his mind" (I.iii, 248); and various lines from Othello's victorious entrance into Cyprus (II.i, 174–93, "O my fair warrior!" etc.). Within these three extracts only those lines that would be directly transferred to the Love Duet are underscored in blue pencil in Boito's copy of the first edition of Hugo. The blue-penciled Hugo translation, therefore, graphically illustrates Boito's "extraction" process. Here, for instance, is a list of the phrases that Boito underlined in the Love Duet passages of the play; I have re-ordered them to correspond with their representation in the duet:

[OTH.] Si après chaque tempête viennent de pareils calmes, – puissent les vents souffler jusqu'à réveiller la mort! [Hugo, p. 269; Oth. II.i, 177–78]. . . . O ma belle guerrière! [269; II.i, 173]. . . . Pour écouter ces choses, – Desdémona montrait une curiosité sérieuse

---

[24] For example, the first words and sentences that Boito underlined in blue pencil in the Hugo translation are: [IAGO:] "Tudieu!"; "Cassio, un Florentin, – un garçon presque condamné à la vie d'une jolie femme, – qui n'a jamais rangé en bataille un escadron"; "N'importe! à lui la préférence!"; "Et moi, qui, sous les yeux de l'autre, ai fait mes preuves – à Rhodes, à Chypre et dans maints pays – chrétiens et païens, il faut que je reste en panne et que je sois dépassé"; "et moi, je reste l'enseigne (titre que Dieu bénisse!) de Sa Seigneurie more"; [RODERIGO:] "Par le ciel"; [IAGO:] "jugez-vous même – si je suis engagé par de justes raisons – à aimer le More" (pp. 233–34; I.i, 4 [" 'Sblood"], 20–22, 27, 28–30, 33, [Roderigo] 34, [Iago] 38–40; cf. Otello, Act I, "Quell'azzimato capitano," etc., vocal score, 34/1/2–35/2/1 [see n. 8 above]).

[251; I.iii, 144–45]. . . . [il me demandait] l'histoire de ma vie, – année par année, les batailles, les sièges, les hasards – que j'avais traversés. – Je parcourus tout, depuis les jours de mon enfance – jusqu' au moment même où il m'avait prié de raconter. – Alors je parlai de chances désastreuses, – d'aventures émouvantes sur terre et sur mer, – de morts esquivées d'un cheveu sur la brèche menaçante, – de ma capture par l'insolent ennemi, – de ma vente comme esclave, de mon rachat, – et de ce qui suivit [251; I.iii, 128–38]. . . . [J'y consentis, et] souvent je lui dérobai des larmes [251; I.iii, 154–55]. . . . C'est dans le génie d'Othello que j'ai vu son visage [255; I.iii, 248]. . . . elle m'aimait pour les dangers que j'avais traversés, – et je l'aimais pour la sympathie qu'elle y avait prise [252; I.iii, 166–67]. . . . Si le moment était venu de mourir, – ce serait maintenant le bonheur suprême; car j'ai peur, – tant le contentement de mon âme est absolu, – qu'il n'y ait pas un ravissement pareil à celui-ci – dans l'avenir inconnu de ma destinée! [DES.] Fasse le ciel – au contraire que nos amours et nos joies augmentent avec – nos années! [OTH.] Dites amen à cela, adorables puissances! – Je ne puis pas expliquer ce ravissement. – Il m'étouffe, c'est trop de joie. – Tiens! Tiens encore! [269; II.i, 181–90, including "And this, and this," the source of the "Bacio" passage]. . . . [IAGO, à part] Oh! vous êtes en harmonie à présent! – Mais je broierai les clefs qui règlent ce concert, – foi d'honnête homme! [269; II.i, 191–93].

Figure 1 is a transcription of two relevant pages of Boito's Hugo (from *Oth*. I.iii). At the bottom of p. 269 Boito has underlined Iago's eavesdropping, "Oh! vous êtes en harmonie à present" and so forth. These lines were included in the first version of the Love Duet but were eventually excised; Boito paraphrased them much later, in December 1886, at Verdi's request, and transferred them to the end of the Act II Homage Chorus, where they stand in the final version.[25]

In the margin of p. 269, to the right of "Si après chaque tempête" Boito made a problematic entry that at first seems to read "parafe 6." The word could be the Italian "parafa," translating as the English cognate "paraph," a formal embellishing flourish at the end of a signature (and the lines to the left of the sign are among the last lines of Otello's first stanza in the Love Duet) or an official signature of initials meant to authenticate a formal document; it could also be a contraction of "parafrasare," to paraphrase. What looks like a "6" is not a number, but a sign that Boito used to highlight lines that he found essential for understand-

[25] See the letters exchanged by Verdi, Ricordi, and Boito on 15 December, c. 16–17 December, and 18 December 1886, in *Carteggio Verdi-Boito*, II, 356; I, 117–18.

DESDÉMONA.

∧   A quoi?

IAGO.

∧   A faire téter des niais et à tenir un
compte de petite bière.

DESDÉMONA.

Oh! quelle conclusion boiteuse et
impotente !... Ne prends pas leçon de
lui, Émilia, tout ton mari qu'il est... Que
dites-vous, Cassio? Voilà, n'est-ce pas?
un conseiller bien profane et bien li-
cencieux.

CASSIO.

Il parle sans façon, Madame: vous
trouverez en lui le soldat de meilleur
goût que l'érudit.

Cassio parle à voix basse à Desdémona et
soutient avec elle une conversation ani-
mée.

IAGO, à part, les observant.

Il la prend par le creux de la main...
Oui, bien dit ! Chuchote, va ! Une toile
d'araignée aussi mince me suffit pour
attraper cette grosse mouche de Cassio. Oui, souris-lui, va : je te garrotterai
dans ta propre courtoisie... Vous dites
vrai, c'est bien ça. Si ces grimaces-là
vous enlèvent votre grade, lieutenant,
vous auriez mieux fait de ne pas
baiser si souvent vos trois doigts,
comme sans doute vous allez le faire
encore pour jouer au beau sire !

Cassio envoie du bout des doigts
un baiser à Desdémona.

Très-bien ! bien baisé ! excellente
courtoisie ! c'est cela, ma foi. Oui, encore vos doigts à vos lèvres ! Puis-
sent-ils être pour vous autant de ca-
nules de clystère !...

Fanfares.

∧   Le More ! je reconnais sa trompette.

CASSIO.

C'est vrai.

DESDÉMONA.

Allons au-devant de lui pour le re-
cevoir.

CASSIO.

Ah ! le voici qui vient !

Entre Othello avec sa suite. La foule se
presse derrière lui.

OTHELLO.

–O ma belle guerrière!

DESDÉMONA.

Mon cher Othello!

OTHELLO.

— C'est pour moi une surprise
égale à mon ravissement — de vous
voir ici avant moi. O joie de mon âme!
–Si après chaque tempête viennent
de pareils calmes, — puissent les   *par*
vents souffler jusqu'à réveiller la mort!   €
— Puisse ma barque s'évertuer à gra-
vir sur les mers des sommets — hauts
comme l'Olympe, et à replonger en-
suite aussi loin — que l'enfer l'est du
ciel ! Si le moment était venu de mourir, —ce serait maintenant le bonheur
suprême; car j'ai peur, — tant le contentement de mon âme est absolu, —
qu'il n'y ait pas un ravissement pareil
à celui-ci — dans l'avenir inconnu de
ma destinée !

DESDÉMONA.

Fasse le ciel — au contraire que nos
amours et nos joies augmentent avec
— nos années !

OTHELLO.

Dites amen à cela, adorables puissances ! — Je ne puis pas expliquer ce
ravissement. — Il m'étouffe, c'est trop
de joie. — Tiens ! Tiens encore !

Il l'embrasse.

Que ce soient là les plus grands dé-
saccords — que fassent nos cœurs !

IAGO, à part.

Oh ! vous êtes en harmonie à présent ! — Mais je broierai les clefs qui
règlent ce concert, — foi d'honnête   ∧
homme!

ing Othello's character. It is an "Othello sign," in fact, and in nearly every case where it appears the sign flags neighboring lines that were included in the Love Duet: on pp. 251, 252, 255, and 269. The sign is also found alongside four "non-Love-Duet" passages in Act I, all of which similarly characterize Othello's personality. It may be that these four "extra" passages may at one time have been considered as potential lines for inclusion into the Love Duet. In any event, Boito's underlinings and the related sign make it clear that the principal dramatic function of the Love Duet was to sketch the contours of Otello's character—just as the "Credo" would ultimately trace out those of Iago. The four additional Act I passages with the "Othello sign" are:

1. p. 241: "si je n'aimais pas la gentille Desdémona, – je ne voudrais pas restreindre mon existence, libre sous le ciel, – au cercle d'un intérieur, – non, pour tous les trésors de la mer." (I.ii, 25–28: "But that I love the gentle Desdemona, / I would not my unhousèd free condition / Put into circumscription and confine / For the sea's worth.")

2. p. 249: "Je suis rude en mon language, – et peu doué de l'éloquence apprêtée de la paix" (I.iii, 81–82: "Rude am I in my speech / And little blessed with the soft phrase of peace"; cf. Otello's lines in the Act II Quartet: "Forse perchè gl'inganni / D'arguto amor non tendo" [158/2/1ff]).

3. p. 249: "et je sais peu de chose de ce vaste monde – qui n'ait rapport aux faits de guerre et de bataille" (I.iii, 86–87: "And little of this great world can I speak / More than pertains to feats of broil and battle").

4. p. 254: "Très graves sénateurs, ce tyran, l'habitude, – a fait de la couche et de la guerre, couche de pierre ed d'acier, – le lit de plume le plus doux pour moi." (I.iii, 226–28: "The tyrant custom, most grave senators, / Hath made the flinty and steel couch of war / My thrice-driven bed of down.")

Boito has been attracted here to lines that address the central problem of Othello's character, his gullibility. He has underscored those lines suggesting that Othello, as a rough-hewn, expansive man of war—accustomed to solving issues swiftly through rugged physical action—is glaringly naive in the ways of the world, quite unprepared for non-military intrigues. This seems important, and although Boito did not place most of these lines directly into the libretto, we may assume that they contain important "background" information for him about the hero.

This conclusion is reinforced by Boito's other annotations and markings. For instance, we find ten individual, horizontal lines drawn across the page, and five of them, all but one in blue pencil, are similar in function.[26] The significance of three of these is immediately evident: they represent operatic "curtains," the moments that will become the end of the opera's Act II (p. 314, after Iago's "quelques sanglants que soient ses ordres!"; III.iii, 470, "What bloody business ever"), the beginning of Act IV (alone among the five a black-pencil line, p. 352, before Emilia's "Comment cela va-t-il à présent?"; IV.iii, 10, "How goes it now?"), and the end of Act IV (p. 383, after Othello's "qu'à mourir en me tuant sur un baiser!"; V.ii, 355, "Killing myself, to die upon a kiss"), under which printed line Boito has written "Fine." The two other similar horizontal blue-pencil lines are probably also "curtain"-related. The first (p. 285) designates the point in the play where, after the Duel, Othello leads Desdemona offstage (pp. 284–85, Othello's "Allons, Desdémona; c'est la vie du soldat – de voir ses salutaires sommeils troublés par l'alerte," II.iii, 237–38; "Come, Desdemona," etc.—in effect, minus the Love Duet, the end of the operatic Act I, or, conversely, a marking of the moment immediately preceding the operatic Act II). The second (p. 339) occurs at the very end of the play's Act IV, scene i—that is, shortly after the climactic moment in which Othello has struck Desdemona, shocking all onlookers, especially Lodovico, who ends this scene in brief dialogue with Iago. We may perhaps see here the outlines of Boito's original 1879 ending to Act III, now lost: a short ending that had apparently concluded efficiently after the "Eavesdropping" Terzetto, without any large interior-finale concertato ensemble; an ending that Verdi would find too brief and ineffective and that would, after numerous revisions requested by the composer, be expanded into the mammoth non-Shakespearean ensemble that now ends Act III.[27]

Somewhat related to the horizontal "curtain"-lines (or to the "Othello sign") are four marginal capital-letter codes, "A," "B," "C," and "D." For the most part, the four letters seem to refer to the beginnings of or

---

[26] The remaining five lines, less obviously interrelated, occur on p. 329 (in black pencil, before the equivalent of IV.i, 106, Cassio's "Alas, poor caitiff!", that is, near the beginning of the opera's Act III Terzetto); p. 338 (two somewhat casual black-pencil lines surrounding IV.i, 252–54, Othello's "Cassio shall have my place. . . . Goats and monkeys!"—also, perhaps, as a possible ending for the original operatic Act III?); p. 341 (in black pencil, above IV.ii, 24, Othello's "Let me see your eyes," isolating a point within what would become the Act III Desdemona-Otello Duet); and p. 367 (in red pencil, above V.ii, 48, Othello's "That handkerchief which I so loved and gave thee," within the Murder Scene; this line also marks the onset of Boito's marginal blue-pencil stars, mentioned above).

[27] The problem of ascertaining the ending of Act III in Boito's initial libretto is discussed in Hepokoski, *Giuseppe Verdi: Otello*, 32–33. That it did not contain an extended *concertato* seems clear from the composer's insistence that one be added: see Verdi to Boito, 15 August 1880, *Carteggio Verdi-Boito*, I, 1–2.

inclusions in individual acts, "A" referring to the first act, "B" to the second, and so on. "A" occurs only once, on p. 273 (before the brief scene for the Herald, "C'est le bon plaisir d'Othello"; II.ii, "It is Othello's pleasure"): this is clearly an *aide-mémoire* for Boito, reminding himself that the Herald's words of celebration on Othello's victorious return (pp. 273–74, "les uns en dansant, les autres en faisant des feux de joie") suggest operatic first-act Victory and Fire Choruses. Boito's marginal "B" occurs most notably on p. 285 (beside Iago's "Quoi! êtes vous blessé, lieutenant?"; II.iii, 239, "What, are you hurt, lieutenant?"), directly below a horizontal blue line (see above): this is to be the beginning of the opera's second act. Two earlier passages are also flagged by the marginal "B" code. Both of these are important soliloquies for Iago—and it is therefore evident that Boito is planning a solo piece for Iago near the opening of Act II. The first of these earlier letters is on p. 260, beside Iago's remarks that conclude Act I (much of it also underlined, from "Je hais le More," "I hate the Moor," onward). The second "B," entered, then erased, is on p. 273, alongside Iago's soliloquy concluding II.i. Both passages stress Iago's suspicions of being cuckolded by Othello, a "motivation" ultimately ignored in the text of the opera.

The "C" marginal sign, the most frequent, occurs six times, five of which clearly indicate large passages to be used for the Act III Desdemona-Otello Duet. One occurs on p. 315, "Où puis-je avoir perdu ce mouchoir, Émilia?" (III.iv, 19, "Where should I lose that handkerchief, Emilia?"). Although the actual source of the beginning of the opera's Act III Duet occurs a few lines later, at III.iv, 31 (unflagged by Boito), the "C" on p. 315 surely refers to the ensuing Shakespearean scene (which Boito did mark off with vertical pencil lines and carets). Four other Duet-related "C"s are to be found on pp. 341, 342, 343, and 344: the passage is the equivalent of *Oth.* IV.ii, 23–93, beginning "My Lord, what is your will?" The remaining "C" indicates a prior reference to the handkerchief on p. 308, Iago's "Je veux perdre ce mouchoir chez Cassio" (III.iii, 322, "I will in Cassio's lodging lose this napkin"), words ultimately given to the operatic Iago after the Act II Quartet (170/1/1–170/3/1). Boito's single marginal "D," on p. 352 below the black-pencil horizontal "curtain"-line mentioned above, clearly indicates the beginning of the opera's fourth act. Also similar in function to the letter-codes and the "Othello sign" is a shower of blue-pencil stars—both functional grouping-stars and sheer explosions of Boitian excitement—during the murder scene (see also n. 26 above). This set of pages (pp. 367–83) is among the most moving in Boito's copy of Hugo's first edition.

There are dozens of other details within the Hugo volume to confirm its centrality to Boito's libretto-making. Some of them refer to musical or poetic and metrical features. In Act V, as Othello enters Desdemona's bedchamber and embraces his still sleeping wife (p. 365, at Othello's "il faudra qu'elle se flétrisse! Je veux la respirer sur la tige!"; V.ii, 15, "It needs must wither. I'll smell it on the tree") Boito writes in a very light, red pencil: "reminisc[en]za del I° atto" (reminiscence of the first act)—a critically important musical and dramatic feature of the opera (the return of the Act I "Bacio" theme, 343/3/3ff, evidently envisaged by Boito before the music had been written), but not of the play. And of special concern to those interested in the techniques of libretto poetry are Boito's numerous metrical suggestions or designations in the margins: the many entries of "lir" or "liric" that may stand for *versi lirici*, rhymed, regular verse; "due volte" (twice) in the Eavesdropping Scene, on p. 330 (at the point of IV.i, 113, "She gives it out that you shall marry her") to indicate an expansion of the action into the structurally formal first two stanzas of the Act III Terzetto; "mart. lir." (*martelliani lirici*, Italian alexandrines or *doppi settenari*, 2 × 7 syllables per line) on p. 312 for the Cassio quotations within Iago's narrative of the dream (III.iii, 420, "In sleep I heard him say, 'Sweet Desdemona,' " etc.); and "14 sdrucciolo" on p. 313 to indicate the unusual meter, an antique "trochaic catalectic tetrameter," of the pseudo-cabaletta at the conclusion of Act II, "Sì, pel ciel."[28]

II

Once it is established that Boito did rely on this copy of the Hugo translation, several other issues emerge. To what extent, for instance, could it have affected the librettist's word choices? For the most part, though the majority of Boito's lines are textually faithful to those in the play, the idiosyncrasies of Hugo's language do not often echo in the operatic text: much of the verbal texture of *Otello* seems Boito's own. Still, on occasion it is clear that Boito based this or that line directly on Hugo's translation. The reader may have noticed above, for example, that Hugo's translation of the lines of the Herald bidding the people to celebrate Othello's victory, "les uns en dansant, les autres en faisant des feux de joie" (pp. 273–74) immediately suggests Boito's wording, "Fuoco di gioia!", for the leading image of the Act I Fire Chorus (36/4/1ff). Indeed, Boito is unlikely to have borrowed the word "gioia" (joy) from any other source. The original reads "some to dance, some to make bonfires" (II.ii, 3–4); Rusconi's translation is the misleading "e s'intreccino danze, e s'imbandiscano mense"; Carcano's is "con danze, fuochi d'allegrezza"; Maffei's is "Sia

---

[28] Boito's metrical designations in the Hugo volume are also mentioned in Harold S. Powers, "*Otello* I.2.3: A Case Study in Multivalent Analysis" (unpublished typescript); and Hepokoski, *Guiseppe Verdi: Otello*, 26–27.

con balli e con fochi artificiati." Here and in a few other instances the textual basis in Hugo is clear. On the other hand, Boito did from time to time re-use a phrase or line from the Italian translators. Maffei's "breccia mortal" was included in the Love Duet, for instance (98/3/1; "deadly breach" in I.iii, 135), and Carcano's and Maffei's translations of Othello's "And this, and this" (II.i, 190) provided Boito with one of the key phrases of the same duet—and of the opera: in Carcano, "Un bacio, e un altro!"; in Maffei, "Un bacio ... un altro!" (As will be seen below, this "bacio/baiser" wording also appears at a crucial point in Hugo's introduction to the play.)

There is one instance, however, in which the impact of words found in Hugo is undeniable. This concerns not the 1879 libretto draft but one of the subsequent revisions of the text: Boito's 1885 refashioning of the Act IV Willow Song.[29] In this case it was not Hugo's Shakespearean text that was the inspiration; rather, it was his scholarly commentary, located in the notes at the end of the play. This is one of the clearest instances of a non-Shakespearean source for a portion of the *Otello* libretto. On p. 411 Hugo—ever the thorough scholar—cites as n. 51 what he considered to be the source of Desdemona's Act IV, scene 3 Willow Song ("l'original de la romance répetée ici par Desdémona"): an English ballad reprinted in Thomas Percy's 1765 *Reliques of Ancient English Poetry*—curiously, a ballad to be sung by a man, not a woman. Hugo does not mention that Percy's version contains twenty-three stanzas, and he translates and prints only stanzas 1, 5, 6, and 7, allowing the implication that they constitute the complete poem. This endnote, concluding with Hugo's four stanzas translated from Percy, is the real source of the operatic Desdemona's interrupted three-stanza Willow Song, "Piangea cantando":

Un pauvre être était assis soupirant sous un sycomore,
   O saule! saule! saule!
Sa main sur son sein, sa tête sur son genou.
   O saule! saule! saule!
   O saule! saule! saule!
Chantez: Oh! le saule vert sera ma guirlande.

Les froids ruisseaux couraient près de lui; ses yeux pleuraient sans cesse.
   O saule! saule! saule!
Les larmes salées tombaient de lui et noyaient sa face.
   O saule! saule! saule!
   O saule! saule! saule!
Chantez: Oh! le saule vert sera ma guirlande.

[29] A complete, but slightly inaccurate, version of Boito's 1879 version of the song may be found in Luzio, II, 118.

Les oiseaux muets se juchaient près de lui, apprivoisés par ses plaintes.
O saule! saule! saule!
Les larmes salées tombaient de lui et attendrissaient les pierres.
O saule! saule! saule!
O saule! saule! saule!
Chantez: Oh! le saule vert sera ma guirlande.

Que personne ne me blame, je mérite ses dédains.
O saule! saule! saule!
Elle était née pour être belle, moi, pour mourir épris d'elle.
O saule! saule! saule!
O saule! saule! saule!
Chantez: Oh! le saule vert sera ma guirlande.[30]

Like the operatic song, Hugo's Percy translation includes repeated utterances of "O saule! saule! saule!" in each stanza (notice the word "O" instead of Shakespeare's "Sing willow, willow, willow," IV.iii, 41ff; cf. 329/1/4), and each of its stanzas concludes with the "Chantez" refrain. Even more to the point, the beginning of Hugo's third stanza does not appear in Shakespeare but nevertheless begins Boito's third stanza, "Scendean l'augelli a vol dai rami cupi" (332/4/1ff). Boito marked off Hugo's n. 51 (as he had several others) with a blue-pencil caret, and he was particularly attracted to one of its phrases, "attendrissaient les pierres," which he underlined and retained prominently in his own third stanza in the libretto ("impietosir le rupi," 333/3/2–5). (The words "softened the stones," of course, also occur in Shakespeare, IV.iii, 44.)

Apart from the question of word selection, Hugo's work helped Boito to form general conceptions of the play and of its main individual characters. As mentioned before, this French translation was remarkable in its scholarly apparatus, which included a thirty-five-page critical introduction to the play, primarily concerned with analyzing the characters of Othello and Iago. That Boito read—and perhaps even pondered—this introduction is evident, once again, from his marginal signs and remarks.

The issue that this observation raises—that of general influence or, stated otherwise, the intellectual and interpretive context within which the libretto was created—is admittedly a complicated one. It was by no means exclusively Hugo's analysis of the play that led to Boito's *Otello*. Rather, it was a confluence of three Continental streams: Hugo; the earlier, deeply influential *Othello* criticism of Schlegel, available in nearly all

---

[30] The poem may be found in Thomas Percy, *Reliques of Ancient English Poetry* (1765; rpt. New York, 1961), 199–203. The sources of Shakespeare's Willow Song are given a more thorough, modern treatment in Peter J. Seng, *The Vocal Songs in the Plays of Shakepeare: A Critical History* (Cambridge, Mass., 1967), 191–99.

Italian translations; and the Italian *Othello* acting tradition from the mid-1850s onward, most notably the famous "primitive" interpretation of Ernesto Rossi and the more "elevated" interpretation of Tommaso Salvini.[31] In brief, the librettist selected from Hugo what he found useful; for other views he turned elsewhere. Yet Hugo's arguments were often persuasive. His criticism was erudite, boldly provocative, and skillfully argued. But its flaw was that his devotion to the cause of Shakespeare occasionally lacked objectivity and common sense: this was a commentary committed to praise, one that suppressed potentially negative judgments.[32] Although Boito read Hugo's remarks with great interest, he exercised his own critical judgment about the translator's conclusions.

We begin with an example of Boito's actively considering, but ultimately rejecting, Hugo's advice—an instance in which even Boito's rejection tells us much about his understanding of the play. Much of Hugo's introduction is devoted to a strained defense of Othello's actions and, above all, to controverting Schlegel's view that Othello's central flaw is racial. Schlegel had praised Shakespeare's "happy error" in creating Othello as a "real Ethiopian" and argued that the hero's adopted Venetian virtues amounted to little. According to his widely disseminated interpretation, only a thin coating of European constraints and values covered the inner savage; only "one drop of [Iago's] poison" was needed to release within Othello the inevitably lurking "tyranny of the blood."[33] Hugo's protracted counter-argument, an uncomfortable one for modern readers, begins by citing Coleridge's remark in the *Literary Remains* that it was self-evident that the virtuous, pure Desdemona would never have married a truly black man; and by the time Hugo's elaborate socio-historical-linguistic argument is finished Othello has been transformed into a light-skinned Middle Eastern noble of the Arab-Saracen race—an unusual point of view for nineteenth-century Continental criticism.[34] The following are representative excerpts:

It is also very true that [within the play] the Moor of Venice is frequently designated as "black". . . . But did the word "black" . . . have in Shakespeare's time the absolute sense that the American and German critics have attributed to it? I do not think so. . . . [Consider: in Sonnet 130, including the line "If snow be white, why then her

[31] Rossi's practice is closer to Schlegel's Othello; Salvini's to Hugo's. See *Giuseppe Verdi: Otello*, 163–89.

[32] Guille, 190–92.

[33] From the Italian translation of Schlegel in Maffei, 3–4. Subsequent references in the text are to this translation.

[34] Guille, 185.

51

breasts are dun,"] one sees that Shakespeare is enamored of a brown woman [d'une brune]. . . . And later [in Sonnet 131] . . . he declares "Thy *black* is fairest in my judgment's place". . . . (p. 54) Thus it is certain that the word "black" did not have an absolute sense, and it could, by extension, designate a "brown" man or woman. . . . (p. 55) [Consider also the stage directions found at the beginning of the second act of *The Merchant of Venice*:] "Enter Marochius [sic], a tawny Moor, all in white". . . . Here no more doubt is possible. . . . No, the seducer of the doges' daughter was certainly no black, even though the German and American critics have said so. Shakespeare was able to throw a bit of dusk on the noble face of Othello; but he did not put night there. He did not commit the unjustifiable mistake for which Schlegel congratulates him. He did not confuse a Moor with a black. . . . (p. 56)

The daughter of the senator Brabantio therefore did not lower herself in marrying the son of the Saracen kings. Othello's and Desdemona's union is no misalliance; it is the sympathetic fusion of these two primordial types of human beauty, the Semitic type and the Caucasian type; it symbolizes before all eyes the legitimate rapprochement of the two great rival races who, throughout the entire Middle Ages, disputed about the civilization of the world. . . . (p. 58)

Upon arriving at these last points, Boito disagreed with Hugo in the margin of p. 58: "eppure è un negro" (and yet he *is* a black), he wrote. Four more pages of Hugo's argument follow on the "interior" qualities of Othello's true, noble race:

In his drama Shakespeare wished to show us the omnipotence of jealousy. To make this demonstration conclusive, should he have chosen (as Schlegel claims) a creature inferior to other creatures, a poorly reared barbarian, a being half-conquered by his instincts, in whom the savage has dominated the moral man? No. . . . [On the contrary,] Othello's intellectual and moral superiority is intimately linked with the very idea of the drama. It is essential. . . . It alone can explain Iago's fierce hatred and Desdemona's fierce love. "I saw Othello's visage in his mind," exclaims the beautiful Venetian woman before the Senate. (pp. 61–62)

At this point of the argument, Boito seized upon the quotation and closed the case: again penciled in the margin one finds "dunque poteva anche essere un negro" (So, then, he could also be a black). One should also notice that Boito was careful to place this line from I.iii, 248, "I saw Othello's visage in his mind," in a pivotal position within the middle of the Act I Love Duet (the opera's principal Otello-definer), although there its wording is characteristically Boitian—florid, structurally intricate, and palpably (even disturbingly) physical: "Ed io vedea fra le tue tempie oscure / Splender del genio l'eterea beltà" ([101/3/1ff]; "And I saw the ethereal beauty of genius shine between your dark temples"). As if with their summarizing utterance all merely "social" obstacles to Otello's and Desdemona's marriage dissolve, they function as the trigger for the climactic, repeated final lines of the central set piece: "E tu m'amavi per le mie sventure" (102/1/1ff, "And you loved me for my misfortunes"). With these final lines we arrive at the sole moment of the opera in which the musical styles of Otello and Desdemona are explicitly fused, rendered identical. Desdemona's strategically delivered "Ed io vedea" becomes the gateway to the musical image of their union.

Despite Boito's skepticism about Hugo's racial point, there are aspects of Hugo's conception of Otello that seem to be more directly reflected in the opera, even though Boito did not mark them off in his copy of the French translation. Apart from the matter of race, Hugo's main argument is that Othello's drama was essentially one of deep love and high honor:

> Othello is a murderer, but he is an honorable murderer. He did nothing for hatred's sake; rather, he did everything for honor! . . . Do not forget . . . that Othello believes that he is obeying honor when he strikes down his wife. . . . Ah! Weep for the victim, but pity also the executioner. Desdemona suffers, but do you not think that Othello also suffers? . . .
>
> Othello never loved his wife so much as the moment when he is about to kill her. Never has she seemed more beautiful, more seductive, more desirable, more irresistible! . . . He leans over the condemned woman. He listens to the last harmonies of that breath that is about to cease [!]. . . . *Un baiser, un baiser encore*, one more, and that will be the last! . . .
>
> [With regard to Othello's suicide:] Desdemona's murder is there crying for revenge, and Othello is not the man to grant a reprieve to a murderer. Should he bring it to the Venetian courts? He finds the formalities of social justice to be too slow-moving. . . . Just as moments ago he condemned Desdemona, now he condemns himself. (pp. 76–78)

Such ideas are important strands of Boito's libretto. They suggest, for example, the centrality of "un bacio, un bacio ancora"—words also attributable to the Italian translations, as mentioned earlier—and they suggest a mode within which the operatic Otello's suicide might be understood. Still, in the libretto—particularly as set by Verdi—all of this is

53

curiously intertwined with its Schlegelian opposite, the drama of primitive uncontrolled jealousy. Boito's Otello alternates between two distinct countenances: that sketched by Schlegel and that prescribed by Hugo.

Notwithstanding its thorough discussion of Othello, Hugo's introduction gives little attention to Desdemona. Her selflessness, her chastity, and her elevated position are taken for granted, and the translator is content to refer to her evocatively as "la Vénitienne" (pp. 59, 64, 67, 68, 70, etc.), "la belle Vénitienne" (pp. 53, 60, 62, etc.), "la noble enfant" (p. 63), "la fille du sénateur Brabantio" (p. 58), and so on. In this one-dimensional conception of Desdemona, characteristic of the nineteenth century, Hugo follows Coleridge and, even more directly, Schlegel, who had robed Desdemona in celestial or mystical garments as "Othello's good angel":

> Desdemona is a victim without stain. . . . She is sweet, humble, simple, and so innocent that she cannot even conceive the idea of infidelity. She seems to have been created precisely to be a tender and affectionate wife. The need to consecrate her life to another, this natural instinct in women, brought about her only error, marrying without her father's knowledge. . . . [That which touched her heart in choosing Othello] as her protector and her lord [was] admiration for his courage, pity for the dangers he had faced. . . . In order to place the purity of this angelic being in even higher relief, Shakespeare has given her in Emilia a companion of rather equivocal behavior. . . . (Maffei, p. 5)

Hugo, too, sees Desdemona as "spiritualiste et presque mystique" (p. 67, spiritual and almost mystic). For him she is "éprise d'idéal" (p. 67, in love with an ideal), and in a brief earlier passage, noted by Boito with a vertical black-pencil line, Hugo clarifies his position:

> In her passion for the Moor the noble child has renounced all her liberty, all her initiative, all her critical thought [à tout examen]. Her enthusiasm is cultish; her affection is a superstition. Illuminated by love, she [even] finds in the harsh treatments that she undergoes a certain unidentifiable pleasure of mortification. Her master's caprice is for her an article of faith; his will is her fate. (p. 63)

Boito's—and Verdi's—Desdemona, likewise, is passive, adoring, and very nearly beatified in scenes such as the Act II Homage Chorus.[35] In his revealing character sketches in the preface to the 1887 *disposizione scenica* (production book) Boito, like Hugo, had little to say about the char-

---

[35] See especially the discussions of Desdemona in Degrada, "*Otello*: da Boito a Verdi"; and in Kunze, 29–30.

acter of Desdemona. But he does provide the predictable list of virtues: "A feeling of love, purity, nobility, docility, ingenuousness and resignation should pervade the most chaste and harmonious figure of Desdemona in the highest degree."[36] More trenchant, and most Schlegel- and Hugo-like of all, however, are Verdi's remarks about the heroine. As early as 1876 he had described her, along with Cordelia (*King Lear*) and Imogen (*Cymbeline*), as one of Shakespeare's "angels."[37] And in a celebrated letter dated 22 April 1887 Verdi insisted that she is "not a woman [but] a type! She's the type of goodness, of resignation, of sacrifice [cf. Hugo]! They are creatures born for others [cf. Schlegel], unconscious of their own *ego*!"[38] While not uniquely linked with the criticism of Hugo, then, the opera's Desdemona, an unproblematic—even relatively empty—figure, is conceived squarely within a tradition of nineteenth-century Continental criticism.

It is primarily in the delineating of Iago that Hugo most helped Boito— primarily, it would seem, because Hugo agreed so totally with Schlegel's earlier assessment of Iago as diabolical, "an evil Genius": "There was never put on the stage," Schlegel had asserted, "a more cunning villain than Iago" (Maffei, p. 4). The issue here is doubly provocative because the sources for the opera's Iago-definer, the Credo, have seemed so elusive. As is well known, there is no clear Shakespearean equivalent for Iago's "Credo in un Dio crudel."[39] This has been viewed as one of the problematic texts of the opera, and Boito has been arraigned by more than one critic for including such an overtly Mephistophelean, glaringly *scapigliato* text. The discomfort of English and American critics has been particularly acute. Julian Budden, for instance, judges it to be "a piece of high-flown nonsense which has its entire justification in the musical setting,"[40] and the tradition of treating the Credo condescendingly goes back a century, extending to the year of the opera's premiere. Thus, Blanche Roosevelt's initial reaction in 1887:

In the second act a credo for Iago is most noble music, but M. Boïto's poetry here is weak. If I understand it rightly, it is a very free adaptation of Iago's last speech with Cassio, act ii. of [the] original. Iago

[36] Budden, 329.

[37] Letter to Clarina Maffei, 20 October 1876, in Franco Abbiati, *Giuseppe Verdi* (Milan, 1959), IV, 17.

[38] In Abbiati, IV, 331–32. The translation used here is that of Martin Chusid, "Verdi's Own Words: His Thoughts on Performance, with Special Reference to *Don Carlos*, *Otello*, and *Falstaff*," *The Verdi Companion*, ed. William Weaver and Martin Chusid (New York, 1979), 161.

[39] See, for instance, the fragmentary sources suggested in Dean, 88 and 90.

[40] Budden, 318.

speaks of devils, etcetera—you know the lines—and here M. Boïto gives him a tirade about what he believes and does not believe.[41]

It now seems clear, however, that the real sources for the Credo lie in Hugo's discussion of Iago. Once again, we are guided by Boito's pencil marks—carets and vertical lines—in the margins. What caught his attention on pp. 64 and 65 was the explanation of why Iago hated Othello, those very causes that Boito seems to have downplayed in the opera. Boito's first "motivation" caret, toward the bottom of p. 64, signals a passage dealing with Iago's resentment at having been passed over for promotion in favor of Cassio: "First of all, his military service has been ignored. . . ." Another caret on p. 64 flags the often-mentioned infidelity issue: "Next, Iago's wife, Emilia, is very much a flirt, and—rightly or wrongly—rumor has circulated that she has had an affair with [*des complaisances pour*] Othello. . . ." But what follows is crucial. Hugo now proceeds to go beyond the text of the play—and beyond Coleridge's celebrated "motive-hunting of motiveless malignity"—to explain the underlying source of Iago's hatred. Boito took special note of this, and on p. 65 he marked the following passage with a series of three black-pencil vertical lines and a single caret:

But the principal cause, the true cause of Iago's hatred must be sought in his own nature [that is, not in the text of the play]. Iago is a man who is unable to accept or endure any kind of superiority. He admits it somewhere [V.i, 19–20] with cynical frankness: another's *daily beauty makes him ugly*. Now, it is not only by rank that Othello is above Iago; it is also by character, by talent, and by the respect that he inspires; it is by the glory that shines around him; it is above all by his goodness. . . .

Here are the real crimes of the Moor. Iago envies Othello for being everything that he is not. He resents him for being powerful; he resents him for being great; he resents him for being honest; . . . heroic; . . . victorious; . . . loved by the people; . . . adored by Desdemona. And that is why he wants revenge. Ah! Othello is genius! Well then, let him be careful! for Iago is envy.

A reading of Hugo, in short, must have suggested to Boito that he go beyond a listing of motivations and concentrate on a more fundamental, psychological motivation: envy, a covetousness that preys on the aspects in which others shine, the positive turned negative through envy. This point had been at the center of the Act II solo that Boito had first written for Iago, the 1879 text that would be abandoned and replaced in 1884 by

[41] Roosevelt, 195.

the Credo.[42] The 1879 text was a four-quatrain structure in *doppio quinario* that begins, "Tesa è l'insidia—ho in man le frodi, / Ti gonfia, Indivia—che mi corrodi" (The trap is set—I have the deceptions in hand, / Swell up, Envy,—you who corrode me!). Clearly an apostrophe to Envy, the text had included such similar, Hugo-based sentiments as "D'Otello il fato—io guido, io nomo, / *Son scellerato—perchè son uomo*, / Perchè ho la scoria—dell'odio in cor, / Mentr'ei di gloria—vive e d'amor" (I guide, I worship Otello's fate. / I am wicked, because I am a man [The only line that would be retained in the 1884 Credo]. / Because I have the dross of hatred in my heart / While he lives on glory and love).[43] Here the conceptual source in Hugo is transparent, and we are reminded of it once again eight years later, in Boito's summary descriptions of the operatic characters in the preface to the *disposizione scenica*; there Boito's first words about Iago are "Jago è l'Invidia" (Iago is Envy).[44]

Hugo's exegetical point is obviously also a main source of the 1884 Credo, which relies so heavily on the reversal of values—the ridiculing of positives into negatives. But even further, some of Hugo's subsequent expansions of the idea of pervasive envy seem to have contributed to the tone and imagery of Boito's 1884 Credo. The most telling of these expansions occurs on p. 67. That it is unmarked by Boito is perhaps explainable by the later date of the substituted text; most of the markings in the book date from 1879, the year of the initial draft:

Iago himself is convinced of it; *il n'est qu'un critique*, "I am nothing if not critical." But this is a critical faculty that never sees anything but the bad sides. He is incapable of admiration and enthusiasm. Morally he has the hypocrisy of Tartuffe. Intellectually he has the skepticism of Don Juan. He lacks only supernatural power to be Mephistopheles. Poetically—for Iago sometimes improvises—he never produced nor could have produced anything but epigrams. Lyricism is thus denied him, as is faith, and for him the sublime is only the neighbor of the ridiculous. Thus, in reality, he regards such a grand passion as Desdemona has conceived for the Moor as perfectly grotesque. Desdemona, spiritual and almost mystic, sees only the soul of the Moor and admires it; Iago, a materialist and almost a nihilist, sees only the body of the Moor and laughs.

---

[42] The replacement of the earlier text with the Credo is documented in Boito's letter to Verdi, shortly after 26 April 1884, in *Carteggio Verdi-Boito*, I, 74–76.

[43] The complete text may be found in Luzio, II, 110. A few lines of the text seem indebted to Iago's soliloquy at the end of II.i. For example, "(*Toccandosi la fronte*) L'idea qui regna— salda, segreta," the beginning of the second quatrain, recalls Iago's " 'Tis here, but yet confused."

[44] See, e.g., the translation in Budden, 328.

Boito's Credo may be understood as a series of potent images illustrating Hugo's ideas. One recognizes Iago the materialist, both in "sento il fango originario in me" (115/2/3ff, I feel the primal mud within me) and in the embracing of the idea of birth "d'un germe o d'un atòmo" (114/5/1ff, from a germ or an atom). All noble ideas, "il giusto", "Lagrima, bacio, sguardo, / Sacrificio ed onor" (117/1/2, 117/3/2ff, justice, tears, kisses, glances, sacrifices, honor), are subject only to ridicule. The "positive" attributes that Iago invokes are evidently selected to refer to recognizable characteristics of Otello and Desdemona. One scarcely need be reminded that Otello's "onor" and Otello as "il giusto" have been the specific topics of the previous act, and that the words "lagrime" and the crucial "bacio" have been uttered in the immediately preceding Love Duet. Iago insists that the sincerities witnessed in Act I be ascribed to "un istrïon beffardo" (117/2/1, a derisive actor), that their seemingly positive substance is "bugiardo" (117/3/2, mendacious or false). Similarly, the "nihilist" element mentioned by Hugo is probably the most potent image in the Credo: Iago as God-denier. And, finally, Hugo's reference to Iago's penchant for "epigrams" may in part have led to Boito's choice of (or Verdi's desire for) the unusual "metro rotto e non simetrico" (broken, non-symmetrical poetic meter) of the Credo—a seemingly anarchic, jagged mixture of rhymed *quinari, settenari*, and *endecasillabi*.[45] It is from such considerations as these that Verdi was moved to write to his librettist that he found the new Credo "potentissimo e shaespeariano [sic] in tutto e per tutto."[46]

One may conclude that in his operatic monologue Iago is not concerned with expounding a philosophy of action or even with revealing his true beliefs, except as those beliefs happen to be casually provoked by circumstance. The circumstance at hand is the condition of Otello and Desdemona, and Iago's unstated envy of them: "envy," the key word, but one never uttered in this more subtle form of Iago's soliloquy. To restate this another way, the two central ideas that generate the Credo—envy and the mere existence of a wondrously happy Otello and Desdemona—never appear as verbal images. Iago hides them from us (and perhaps from himself); or at least he refrains from expressing them bluntly, for his essence is subtlety and deception. Rather, they must be inferred by the astute reader—or the astute spectator—as providing what Hugo called "the *true* cause of Iago's hatred." In sum, the Credo may be understood by the psychoanalytically inclined as a kind of psychopathological reaction of Iago: a smokescreen of private rationalizations; a web of psychic

[45] See Boito to Verdi, after 26 April 1884, *Carteggio Verdi-Boito*, I, 74.
[46] Verdi to Boito, 3 May 1884, *Carteggio Verdi-Boito*, I, 76.

distortion that shields him from the burden of confronting himself more directly. Or, as the footlight staging of the 1887 *disposizione scenica* suggests, it may be understood as little more than sheer audience manipulation. As we spectators are being distracted and toyed with by the consummate deceiver, we may perceive as little of his "true self" as do Otello, Roderigo, and Cassio.

This helps to solve the perennial problem of Boito's minimizing of Iago's motivations—above all, of his taking away of the issue of Emilia's supposed infidelity. Doubtless after reading Hugo and reflecting on the "true cause," envy, Boito saw little need to stock his libretto with peripheral, lesser causes. A knowledge of Boito's sources not only helps us understand why he made the textual choices that he did but also points the way toward a line of critical interpretation that, at least, is supportable by historical demonstration.

III

Similar investigations into the genesis of Boito's *Otello*, of course, could be carried on here at further length. But the essential point is clear: when confronting the text and images of the *Otello* libretto, a knowledge of the rich tradition of English-language criticism, an awareness of the English *Othello* acting tradition, a comparison of Boito's *Otello* with the text of Shakespeare's play, a study of the contrived libretto structures—all of these things may be valuable, but the evidence that we ought to begin with is the nineteenth-century Continental understanding of Shakespeare, and the details of certain key Shakespearean translations, commentaries, and interpretations (Schlegel, Hugo, the Italian translations, and the Italian acting traditions). As part of our initial textual-analytical strategy, we need to immerse ourselves in that portion of the reception history of Shakespeare with which Boito and Verdi actually intersected, particularly because the Shakespearean lands in which they dwelled can be quite foreign to our own, very differently conditioned minds. There is much evidence that remains to be uncovered. Speculation, analysis, and textual parsing are all very well—indeed, this work must proceed—but such study, when possible, needs to be grounded firmly in real source documents.

SUSAN YOUENS

An Unseen Player: Destiny in
Pelléas et Mélisande

The most important member of the dramatis personae in Maurice Maeterlinck's *Pelléas et Mélisande*, as in all eight of his Symbolist dramas, is
"La Destinée." She, or It, never utters a word or appears, but her insistent
presence is conveyed by every means at Maeterlinck's command. The
hallmarks of the text—the *Märchen*-like milieu, sparse actions, and tragic
denouement—are conceived in accord with an unknowable and all-pow-
erful Fate. The visible and audible world of the text is, in its stylized un-
reality, a symbol for another plane of existence, more "real" than the
human and material spheres but barred forever from comprehension.
Against these mysterious powers, intellect and rationality are not only
ineffectual but irrelevant; wisdom is re-defined as passivity—why struggle
uselessly?—and as the instinctual knowledge that we neither act autono-
mously nor understand our marionette-master. Even Love, curiously devoid of passion, comes into being as an amoral agent of Destiny, as Fate's
favorite route to catastrophe and death. And yet, this depressing *fin-de-
siècle* proposition invites music as few texts have been able to do; it issued
a clarion call for composers, including Debussy, Fauré, Sibelius, and
Schoenberg.[1] How and why a flawed play could make such a good libretto demonstrates the special nature of libretti, although *Pelléas* must
also be understood as a special case. Most operatic texts do not originate
in philosophical concepts given aesthetic life, but *Pelléas* does.

When Maeterlinck's Symbolist plays first appeared, the eminent critic
Octave Mirbeau proclaimed them better than Shakespeare,[2] but—a No-

---

[1] Schoenberg's tone poem *Pelleas und Melisande* (1902–1903) is contemporaneous with
but independent of Debussy's finishing touches on the opera. Fauré's incidental music to the
play, Op. 80 (1898), precedes the completion of Debussy's opera. Sibelius's incidental music, Op. 46, and suite were composed in 1905.

[2] When Maeterlinck's first play, *La Princesse Maleine*, appeared in 1889, Maeterlinck
sent a copy to Mallarmé in Paris, who in turn gave it to Paul Hervieu, who relayed it to
Octave Mirbeau for review in *Le Figaro*. Mirbeau responded with enthusiasm, saying that
the play was "the most original work of this time and the most extraordinary and the most
naive also, comparable—do I dare say superior in beauty?—to what is most beautiful in
Shakespeare." See Maeterlinck's reminiscences, *Bulles Bleues* (Monaco, 1948), 210. Maeterlinck was strongly influenced by Shakespeare and other Jacobean dramatists; he translated John Ford's *'Tis Pity She's a Whore* into French. The Shakespearean references

60

bel Prize not withstanding—they had a short-lived run. Symbolist gloom and doom in the theater dated quickly. Maeterlinck defined his theatrics of Destiny as a radical re-fashioning of *spoken* drama, but the centrality of immaterial forces in these works constituted a demand for services that could only be supplied outside of language. As impressed as Debussy was with the drama he saw performed at the Théâtre de l'Oeuvre in 1893, he could not set it all to music, as he had intended at first, and his elimination of the dramatist's numerous redundancies suggests that Maeterlinck was attempting to fill a void only music could fill. The unmusical Belgian, who grimaced and dozed behind the composer's back as Debussy played the score for him, did not appreciate Debussy's achievement on his behalf until almost twenty years later; Maeterlinck's belated praise contains at heart the realization that his play was a "libretto in search of a composer."[3]

Maeterlinck wrote on 28 January 1920 to Mary Garden:

> I had sworn to myself never to see the lyric drama *Pelléas et Mélisande*. Yesterday I violated my vow, and I am a happy man. For the first time I have entirely understood my own play, and because of you.
>
> I saw there many things which I had never perceived or which I had forgotten. Like every great artist, more than any other perhaps, you have the genius to add to a work or to vivify in it those things which I omitted or had left in a state of sleep.[4]

He writes to Mary Garden as if to the dead Debussy, but no matter: his recognition that words alone could not convey his intended aesthetic of Destiny as well as the combination of words and music is clear. Henri Peyre has written of the antagonism between Symbolist poets and Belle

---

in *Pelléas* are generally muted. Although there is no Iago to create and then enflame Golaud's jealousy, there is at least one reminiscence of *Othello*: both wives lie to their husbands about the loss of a love-token, Desdemona's handkerchief with "magic in th' web" and Mélisande's wedding ring. Both Othello and Golaud claim special significance for the tokens, Golaud's less specific and detailed than Othello's: "J'aimerais mieux avoir perdu tout ce que j'ai plutôt que d'avoir perdu cette bague . . . tu ne sais pas ce que c'est. Tu ne sais pas d'où elle vient."

[3] Edward Lockspeiser, *Debussy: His Life and Mind*, I (1962; 2nd ed. Cambridge, 1978), p. 202.

[4] Mary Garden and Louis Biancolli, *Mary Garden's Story* (New York, 1951), p. 116. See also David A. Grayson, *The Genesis of Debussy's "Pelléas et Mélisande"* (Ann Arbor, Michigan, 1986), p. 56. Georgette Leblanc, *Souvenirs (1895–1918)* (Paris, 1931), p. 169, wrote that Maeterlinck did not understand music and "did not like musicians any more than music" (pp. 174–75). To a reporter for the *New York Sun* (28 January 1920) Maeterlinck "confessed a musical deafness" after attending a performance of *Pelléas* by the Chicago Opera Company in New York.

Époque composers,[5] but Maeterlinck is the exception. He needed Debussy.

The tyranny of Fate in *Pelléas et Mélisande* is given expression in music that closely reflects Fate's peculiar nature: she can be heard, if not seen. The history of Debussy's setting makes clear again and again the composer's increasing comprehension of what was required in order to set the play in accord with Maeterlinck's aesthetic. For example, at later stages of his compositional labors Debussy extended several of the orchestral interludes, interludes in which Destiny conducts her wordless operations bearing the drama from one incident to the next.[6] The opera is not merely the happy conjunction of a text and a musical style, although Debussy had already demonstrated in his earlier songs a liking for certain general aspects of the play: the rarefied, aestheticized, sensuous treatment of love; the pessimism; and the other-worldly atmosphere. Debussy, with his complex love-hate feelings for Wagner,[7] must also have been attracted both by the play's similarities to *Tristan* and, even more, by its divergences. Love, Death, and Fate are differently defined in Wagner's and Maeterlinck's worlds; the composer who made parodic fun of the *Tristan* chord in "Golliwog's Cakewalk" would have recognized and appreciated the inversions of Wagnerian aesthetics in *Pelléas*.

Maeterlinck must be numbered among the many writers concerned with the untrustworthiness of language at the end of the century. The belief that "Words do not say it" engendered one literary experiment after another, experiments in which poetry, plays, and novels are created from the perception that language is inherently mendacious. The thread that links the inward state to the external system of language is always tenuous at best, but Maeterlinck defines the gulf between inner life and Hamlet's "words, words, words" in his own way, distinct from the *Problematik* of language as articulated in Austria, England, or Joyce's Ireland: the "it" unavailable to language is Destiny.[8] The philosophical premise

---

[5] Henri Peyre, "Poets Against Music in the Age of Symbolism," in *Symbolism and Modern Literature: Studies in Honor of Wallace Fowlie,* ed. Marcel Tetel (Durham, N.C., 1978), pp. 179–92.

[6] Grayson, pp. 174–76, proves that Debussy tended to begin with a more purely musical conception which he then refined, altered, and directed to a more text-conscious conception of the vocal lines. Although he was not entirely consistent in doing so, the earlier stages of composition have to do more with the orchestral working-out than with the vocal parts.

[7] See Grayson's chapter *"Pelléas* and the 'Wagnerian Formula' in the Light of Source Evidence," pp. 225–75; and Carolyn Abbate, *"Tristan* in the Composition of *Pelléas,"* in *19th-Century Music,* 5 (1981), pp. 117–41.

[8] One can easily assemble a *fin-de-siècle* and early twentieth-century lexicon of statements about the untrustworthiness of language: Karl Kraus's aphorism "In keiner Sprache kann man sich so schwer verständigen wie in der Sprache" (There is no language in which it is so

that informs and shapes his new drama entailed a self-conscious use of non-naturalistic dialogue that stems from a fundamental belief in the inadequacy of language to express Destiny's presence in human existence. This view of words as severely limited in power opens wide a door for music.

THE "ETERNAL LAWS" ON THE SYMBOLIST STAGE

Maeterlinck once told a German reporter that he had studied all of Schopenhauer,[9] and one can well believe it. His "Destinée" resembles Schopenhauer's concept of "Will" as the underlying cosmic reality, unavailable to any possibility of cognition and identifiable only as a blind, universal impulse. The world as human beings perceive it is inadequate to the demands of the Will, and therefore Life is a mirage-like passage through despair, with death as the sole alleviation for the hopelessness of existence. Maeterlinck declared a particular liking for the essays of the *Parerga and Paralipomena*; although he did not mention specific titles, he presumably would have known the "Transcendent Speculation on the Apparent Deliberateness in the Fate of the Individual." Schopenhauer's insistence in that essay that "a secret and inexplicable power guides all the turns and changes of our lives," that an "invisible guidance, showing itself only in a doubtful form, accompanies us to our death,"[10] is given *fin-de-siècle* garb in Maeterlinck's Symbolist plays, but with one crucial difference. Schopenhauer locates the occult powers of determinism within the human soul; in *Pelléas et Mélisande* and its seven sisters, Destiny is something Other, outside of the soul and therefore best expressible in a sign-system other than words.

The plays originating in this quasi-Schopenhauerian determinism unfold according to theories elaborated both in Maeterlinck's dramas of the

---

difficult to communicate as in language); the Lord Chandos Letter of Hugo von Hofmannsthal, in which a fictional Elizabethan nobleman abandons poetry because words and inner experience are no longer congruent; or the passage from T. S. Eliot's *Four Quartets* that begins "Words strain, / Crack and sometimes break, under the burden, / Under the tension, slip, slide, perish, / Decay with imprecision." Maeterlinck on several occasions wrote about "Le Silence" as the truest medium for perception of the inner life of the soul: where words only veil or distort what exists in the psyche, silence allows an intuitive access to its existence. Maeterlinck's Symbolist plays are punctuated with frequent silences.

[9] Paul Gorceix, *Les Affinités allemandes dans l'oeuvre de Maurice Maeterlinck* (Paris, 1975), p. 144. Maeterlinck stated, in an interview in the *Rheinisch-Westfälische Zeitung* for 29 November 1903, that he had "Schopenhauer ganz studiert."

[10] Arthur Schopenhauer, "Transcendent Speculation on the Apparent Deliberateness in the Fate of the Individual," from *Parerga and Paralipomena: Short Philosophical Essays*, I, trans. E. F. J. Payne (Oxford, 1974), pp. 214–15, 223.

1890s and in a series of essays, including "The Evolution of Mystery," "Silence," "Everyday Tragedy," and "Apropos of King Lear."[11] The sole purpose of drama is to make apparent the invisible forces at work in life, particularly the two most formidable mysteries of all—Death and Fate. Exterior human traits such as actions and "personality" are only distant emanations of Fate: deeds, history, and psychology are of no importance. (Maeterlinck detested psychology, which he believed had wrongfully usurped the beautiful name of Psyche.) The best artists no longer depict scenes from history, memorializing human actions, but instead paint a seemingly inconsequential village road or a house lost in the country-side—"these simple images can add something to our awareness of life."[12] His proposed "tragique quotidien" would bring playwrights up to date, in accord with the radical conceptual advances made by musicians and painters. Maeterlinck believed that "an old man seated in an arm-chair, simply waiting under the lamp, listening without knowing it to all the eternal laws . . . leads a life more profound, more human . . . than the lover who strangles his mistress, the captain who wins a victory, or the husband who avenges his honor"[13]—the last clause a trifle ironic meas-ured against the plot of *Pelléas et Mélisande*. Drama should move both more deeply inward, into the soul, and outward into the cosmos beyond humanity; it should become a drama of metaphysics, without hope and without God. When the traditional deity is invoked—Arkel says in Act IV, scene 2 of *Pelléas* "Si j'étais Dieu, j'aurais pitié du coeur des hommes" (If I were God, I would have pity on the hearts of men)—it is clear that God is ineffectual in comparison to Fate, the true ruler of the universe. It is the dramatist's task to reveal not the secret of Destiny itself—that can-not be known—but the fact that we are briefly animated and then de-stroyed by a mystery. As Maeterlinck defines it, the purpose of drama is

[11] Maurice Maeterlinck, "Le Silence" and "Le Tragique quotidien," from *Le Trésor des humbles* (Paris, 1904), pp. 7–25 and 179–201. See also the related essays "La Beauté inté-rieure," pp. 283–309, "La Vie profonde," pp. 253–79, and "L'Évolution du mystère" from *Le Temple enseveli* (Paris, 1902), pp. 103–67.

[12] "Un bon peintre ne peindra plus Marius vainqueur des Cimbres ou l'assassinat du duc de Guise, parce que la psychologie de la victoire ou du meurtre est élémentaire et exception-nelle . . . Il représentera une maison perdue dans la campagne, une porte ouverte au bout d'un corridor, un visage ou des mains au repos; et ces simples images pourront ajouter quelque chose à notre conscience de la vie." Maeterlinck, "Le Tragique quotidien," 184.

[13] "Il m'est arrivé de croire qu'un vieillard assis dans son fauteuil, attendant simplement sous la lampe, écoutant sans le savoir toutes les lois éternelles . . . ce vieillard immobile vivait en réalité d'une vie plus profonde, plus humaine . . . que l'amant qui étrangle sa maîtresse, le capitaine qui remporte une victoire ou 'l'époux qui venge son honneur.' " "Le Tragique quotidien," pp. 187–88. Cf. "Novalis," *Le Trésor des humbles*, p. 156: "Une vérité cachée est ce qui nous fait vivre."

paradoxical: to represent the unrepresentable and make known the un-knowable.

Dramas of Fate are nothing new; the ancient Greeks wrote much better ones, but Maeterlinck's idea of Destiny is different. "La Destinée" is im-personal, vague, and unformed—it cannot be anthropomorphized or worshipped. Although it oppresses everyone, frailty and innocence, youth and incapacity are its preferred prey. Maeterlinck's predilection for Des-tiny's torment of children and half-formed adolescent women can seem downright sadistic, although the theoretical justifications are clear enough. The kings and commanders struck down for their hubris in Greek tragedy are not found in Maeterlinck because human achievement of any kind is non-existent, interdicted by a Fate whose inhuman pitiless-ness is more obvious when the likes of Mélisande die. Furthermore, the spectacle of youth incites a false sense of hope in the older dramatis per-sonae, who grieve all the more when their visions are dashed. Arkel looks at Mélisande in Act IV, scene 2 and dreams of a "new era":

Maintenant que le père de Pelléas est sauvé et que la maladie, la vieille servante de la mort, a quitté le château, un peu de joie et un peu de soleil vont enfin rentrer dans la maison . . . Il était temps! [He then speaks of his pity for Mélisande, who arrived at Allemonde in troubled times.] Mais à présent tout cela va changer. A mon âge, et c'est peut-être là le fruit le plus sûr de ma vie, à mon âge j'ai acquis je ne sais quelle foi à la fidélité des événements, et j'ai toujours vu que tout être jeune et beau créait autour de lui des événements jeunes, beaux et heureux. Et c'est toi, maintenant, qui vas ouvrir la porte à l'ère nouvelle que j'entrevois.

(Now that Pelléas's father is saved, and illness, the old servant of death, has left the castle, a little joy and a little sunlight are finally going to re-enter the house . . . It is time! . . . But now all that is going to change. At my age, and perhaps this is the most certain fruit of my life's experience, at my age I have gained a sort of faith in the fidelity of events, and I have always noticed that all young, beautiful, crea-tures create around them young, beautiful, and happy events. And now it is you who are going to open the door to the new era that I foresee.)

I have not quoted the entire speech, but it is the longest retained in De-bussy's opera and one of the most important, because Arkel is so disas-trously wrong.

Debussy's music for this passage exemplifies a classic dual function for operatic music both to express and to contradict the words, to tell where delusions, lies, unrevealed motivations and the like exist. However, the suggestion that the truth is other than Arkel proclaims is subtle and ambiguous, not an outright contradiction but a lack of confirmation. Debussy surrounds the old man's words about light and joy with two previously heard figures. The first, played by a solo horn, is associated with Mélisande, who Arkel believes will usher in the new age of light. The second is a triplet (occasionally quadruplet) "wave" figure introduced in Act I, scene 1 at Golaud's first words, "Je ne pourrai plus sortir de cette forêt!" (I will never be able to leave this forest!), in the context of a whole-tone scale passage, and heard later as an ostinato in the sailors' chorus; in a chromatic variant in the grotto scene, Act II, scene 3; in Act IV, scene 3 as Yniold discovers the flock of sheep; and in the last act, as Golaud confesses his guilt to Mélisande and attempts one last time to wring "the truth" out of her. The scale functions rather like a "Geh'-Figur," perhaps analogous to the "flow" of Fate, carrying all of the characters to something quite distant from joy and sunlight. In Golaud's speech, the metrical change to a broader 9/8, after the 4/4 of the sparsely accompanied opening lines about illness and death, and the duplet eighths in the vocal line at the words "vont enfin rentrer dans la maison," in slight but effective emphasis, all bespeak Arkel's hope. However, the tritone bass line beneath a rhythmically augmented fragment of the wave figure as Arkel speaks of the "most certain fruit of my life's experience" (Ex. 1) negates any sense of certainty. When Arkel says that Mélisande will open the door to a new era, the orchestra delivers a fortissimo statement of Mélisande's motive, deliberately over-emphatic, but at the word "entrevois" the entire house of cards comes tumbling down, and the crescendo evaporates within four measures (Ex. 2).

A description in words, however, both sounds more exaggerated and lasts longer than the music. Arkel's cautious hope ("*un peu* de joie et *un peu* de soleil") is not directly illuminated as false: Fate never shows her hand, never speaks clearly. The composer's attention throughout the work to nuance, to small inflections of prosody and changes in the musical atmospheric pressure, does not clarify the larger mysteries, whether of the music or of existence. Explanation is interdicted; rather, the music allows one to "sense" intuitively that hope is wrong.

Musique des mots: THE LANGUAGE OF DESTINY

Both plays and libretti are constructs of language, but they are directed to different ends. All writers choose their words in order to exclude certain possibilities and include others, but Maeterlinck entraps language in an unusually thorny hedge of restrictions. His theoretical justifications

EXAMPLE 1. ACT IV, SCENE 2

amount to a profound mistrust of language, a doubt that words can do or express anything adequately. Ordinary discourse that accompanies and explains actions, or "dialogue of the first degree," should at the same time imply the more solemn dialogue between a soul and destiny, or "dialogue of the second degree."[14] The challenge to the playwright is to present both in symbolically charged language. Maeterlinck sharply criticized earlier drama for its lack of attention to Destiny's speech, or rather, the echo of that non-verbal dialogue filtered through words:

> If you came to me, you the "outraged husband," "deceived lover," "abandoned woman," with the intention of killing me, it would not be my most eloquent and impassioned supplication that would halt your arm. But it would happen that you would encounter one of these unforeseen forces and that my soul, knowing that they keep watch around me, would say a secret word to you, disarming you. It is in these spheres that adventures are decided; it is this dialogue whose echo one must hear.[15]

[14] "A côté du dialogue indispensable il y a presque toujours un autre dialogue qui semble superflu. Examinez attentivement et vous verrez que c'est le seul que l'âme écoute profondément parce que c'est en cet endroit seulement qu'on lui parle. Vous reconnaîtrez aussi que c'est la qualité et l'étendue de ce dialogue inutile qui détermine la qualité et la portée inéffable de l'oeuvre." "Le Tragique quotidien," p. 193. Cf. ibid., p. 194: "On peut même affirmer que le poème se rapproche de la beauté et d'une vérité supérieure, dans la mesure où il élimine les paroles qui expliquent les actes pour les remplacer par des paroles qui expliquent non pas ce qu'on appelle un 'état d'âme' mais je ne sais quels efforts insaisissables et incessants des âmes vers leur beauté et vers leur vérité."

[15] "Si vous êtes venu, vous 'l'époux outragé,' 'l'amant trompé,' 'la femme abandonnée,' dans le dessein de me tuer; ce ne sont pas mes supplications les plus éloquentes qui pourront arrêter votre bras. Mais il se peut que vous rencontriez alors l'une de ces forces inattendues et que mon âme qui sait qu'elles veillent autour de moi, vous dise un mot secret qui vous désarme. Voilà les sphères où les aventures se décident, voilà le dialogue dont il faudrait qu'on entendît l'écho." Ibid., pp. 195–96.

EXAMPLE 2. ACT IV, SCENE 2

Maeterlinck's wish was clearly for "ordinary" words symbolically charged with omens and portents to suggest the presence of other-worldly forces; in the opera, music becomes in large part the carrier of "second-degree dialogue."

Were that the only charge, the task would be difficult enough, but there are other strictures regarding the means to that end. Since a soul does not truly communicate in words and has no commerce with the intellect, its "speech" cannot be that of ratiocination; nothing like Tristan's third-act Delirium Scene is possible because the sustained strength of self-inquiry he displays is beyond the grasp of Allemonde's inhabitants. The delineation of reasoned thought is out of bounds, and so too is poetry. Although Maeterlinck's first published volume was a collection of Symbolist poetry, in the plays he largely avoids poetry, with the exception of a few interpolated songs, notable for their strangeness and "withheld information."[16] The imagination that produces poetry (a word stemming from the Greek *poiein*, "to make") is, after all, a human faculty. However one defines poetry, it has to do with the assumption that language can convey personal or universal experience in the most compressed, evocative way. But for Maeterlinck truth is Destiny, and Destiny is beyond words. Its effects can be suggested by devices such as the two degrees of dialogue, but its essence is inaccessible to verbal conceptualization. It becomes the writer's task to convey in words the insufficiency of words, avoiding poetry's implications of completeness and the power of language.

It is easiest to distinguish between Maeterlinck's first- and second-degree dialogue when he contrasts the two by an abrupt change of subject. At the end of the first act of *Pelléas*, the lovers look out at the sea in a scene that concludes with two sentences of second-degree dialogue (italics mine):

> PELLÉAS: Entendez-vous la mer? . . . C'est le vent qui s'élève
> . . . Descendons par ici. Voulez-vous me donner la main?
> MÉLISANDE: Voyez, voyez, j'ai les mains pleines de fleurs.
> PELLÉAS: Je vous soutiendrai par le bras; le chemin est escarpé
> et il y fait très sombre. *Je pars peut-être demain . . .*
> MÉLISANDE: *Oh! pourquoi partez-vous?*

(PELLÉAS: Do you hear the sea? The wind is rising . . . let's go down this way. Will you give me your hand? MÉLISANDE: Look, look, my

---

[16] James L. Kugel, *The Techniques of Strangeness in Symbolist Poetry* (New Haven, 1971), points out that attempts to define Symbolism are compromised by the lack of a consistent aesthetic program. Where these writers can be grouped together as possessing a common ideal, it is in pursuit of a self-conscious quality of strangeness and a dependence on withheld information.

hands are full of flowers. PELLÉAS: I'll support you by the arm . . .
the path is steep, and it is very dark. *I'm perhaps leaving tomorrow.*
MÉLISANDE: *Oh! why are you leaving?*)

Even the first-degree dialogue, the more "ordinary" discourse, is saturated with symbolic meaning. A spiritual element—fated love—rises
along with the wind, while the darkness and the steep descending slope
of the path they take together foreshadow catastrophe. When Maeterlinck turns to second-degree dialogue, there is, significantly, no answer to
Mélisande's question. Pelléas can no longer speak of Marcellus as a reason for departure. He has instinctually recognized Mélisande as the instrument of his fate, and his first impulse is to flee; like Mélisande at the
end of Act IV, he has no courage. The uncertainty of his intent is apparent
in the word "peut-être," and Mélisande's dismay guarantees his continued presence at court.

The change of subject implies the existence of unspoken undercurrents
of feeling of which the main characters are unaware; their unconscious
words and actions issue not from autonomous human wills but from the
external agency of Fate. To say more and other than the words actually
spoken is a characteristic of all human speech, according to Maeterlinck
(and legions of present-day deconstructionists).[17] What Debussy does
with Maeterlinck's levels of literal and symbolic discourse seems at first
suspiciously close to the "psychologizing" the playwright so despised,
that is, heightening aspects of characterization by means of musical gestures, especially prosodic and harmonic nuances. Debussy sets Pelléas's
final line of the scene to a slight rising gesture, more like a question than
a statement, while Mélisande's emphasis on the tonic accent of "pour-
quoi" and, even more telling, the harmonic inflection at the word "*vous*"
(a progression from G major to F♯ major, over an F♯ pedal) reveal that
this is more than the disinterested or polite query of a new sister-in-law
(Ex. 3). The sum total of many such prosodic refinements and harmonic
inflections, however, is not characterization in the traditional sense, not a
depiction of particularized human beings; we do not know or understand
the fated pair any better for the telling musical gestures. Rather, the nuances are Destiny's *modus operandi*. The same mysterious force—Fate as
expressed by the asymmetries, non-resolving seventh and ninth chords,
unconventional tonal motion, etc. of Debussy's compositional style—that

---

[17] "En tout ce que l'homme dit, il dit autre chose que ce qu'il dit; en tout ce qu'il lit, il lit
autre chose que ce qu'il lit; en tout ce qu'il fait, il fait autre chose ce qu'il fait; et lorsqu'il
prie, il fait autre chose que sa prière." Maeterlinck, "Menus Propos" (1891) in *La Jeune
Belgique* (Brussels, 1891), 40.

EXAMPLE 3. ACT I, SCENE 3

later denies Arkel musical affirmation of his fantasies also shapes the lovers' colloquy at the end of Act I.

The characters in *Pelléas et Mélisande* live at a frontier where language falters because it is unsuited to express the knowledge that matters most; one commentator said that Maeterlinck used words to find "that precious moment when the breath from the word pushes open the door" behind which lies the silence of true being.[18] Nor does Destiny permit grandiloquence in its subjugated human puppets. A richer speech would indicate a vitality at odds with the passive resignation of an Arkel or a Mélisande, an individuality or personality outside of the playwright's metaphysical system. Maeterlinck therefore chose to work with "les mots inutiles," ordinary words lacking richness, which he felt could best suggest an extralinguistic significance. Aglavaine in *Aglavaine et Selysette* summarizes the

---

[18] Roger Bodart, "Actualité de Maeterlinck," in *Europe* (July–August 1962), p. 55: "Maeterlinck ne cherchait les mots que pour trouver cette minute précieuse où le vent de la parole pousse cette porte derrière laquelle se taît ce qui est. Sa patrie véritable était derrière cette porte."

aesthetic of limited speech and ordinary words deployed in un-ordinary ways when he says to his beloved, "Nous n'avons prononcé que des paroles à peu près inutiles, des paroles que tout le monde eut pu trouver, et cependant, ne sommes-nous pas tranquilles, et ne savons-nous pas que nous nous sommes dit des choses qui valent bien mieux que nos paroles?" (We have only said words that are almost useless, words anyone in the world might find, and yet, are we not content? Don't we know that we have said to each other much more worthy things than words?).[19]

The proposition is risky business, although Maeterlinck often uses commonplace vocabulary ("no more copious than a peasant's" was one critic's summation) in dialogue saturated with lyrical similes; he expressly wanted to write dialogue that would be "lyrical, eloquent in a simple manner, and unrealistic."[20] In one example of this strange simplicity, Golaud cries out in the fourth act of *Pelléas*, "Ah! misère de ma vie! Je suis ici comme un aveugle qui cherche son trésor au fond de l'océan! Je suis ici comme un nouveau-né perdu dans la forêt et vous . . ." (Ah! misery of my life! Here I am like a blind man that searches for his treasure at the bottom of the ocean! Here I am like a newborn babe lost in the forest, and you . . ."). The outbreak of despair is, typically for Maeterlinck, phrased like a litany. But elsewhere the lyrical similes are absent, and the dialogue is deliberately both non-naturalistic and rhetorically impoverished. Fate is not in abeyance at those moments but is more than ever distant from human speech. When Mélisande in Act III, scene 1 speaks to Pelléas in typical Maeterlinckian commonplaces, "J'ai ouvert la fenêtre . . . il fait trop chaud dans la tour . . . il fait beau cette nuit" (I opened the window . . . it is too warm in the tower . . . the night is beautiful), Debussy makes the subterranean wells of feeling more apparent by giving chromatic inflections to the viola ostinato, by sinking deeply in the bass just before she sings those words, by transferring the ostinato to the harp at the words "Il fait beau cette nuit," and by making the vocal line descend chromatically at those same words. But the ambiguity remains in full force, evident in the continuing lack of tonal orientation.

"NE ME TOUCHEZ PAS! NE ME TOUCHEZ PAS!"— REPETITION IN SYMBOLIST DRAMA

Maeterlinck's characters can only distantly approach the reality of Fate through the poor medium of words; in dim recognition of the futility of language, they repeat what they say without coming any closer to the

---

[19] Maeterlinck, *Théâtre*, III (Paris, 1929), pp. 23–24.
[20] Maeterlinck, *L'Intelligence des fleurs* (Paris, 1907), p. 207.

heart of the mystery. The reiterated phrases were also intended to create the incantatory rhythms of a non-naturalistic world, although Maeterlinck courted derision in so doing. The audience at the dress rehearsal of the opera laughed at Yniold's repeated cries of "Petit père!" (twenty-eight times in Act III, scene 4) and at Mélisande's propensity to say everything twice ("Ne me touchez pas! Ne me touchez pas!", "Ce n'est plus elle . . . ce n'est plus elle," "Mais ce n'est pas cela . . . ce n'est pas cela," "Je ne suis pas heureuse! Je ne suis pas heureuse!"—significantly, she proceeds by negation, revealing only what she is not).[21] Music admits—in fact demands—repetition on a scale inadmissible in the verbal arts unless thoroughly musicalized: Mozart's Countess can repeat the words "di cangiar l'ingrato cor" seven times at the end of "Dove sono" without provoking either laughter or a call for straitjackets because the text is so thoroughly subsumed into the aria structure. Debussy, by banishing conventional operatic forms and by expending such pains on the musical prosody, actually exacerbates the effect of Maeterlinck's repeated lines, although there are far fewer repetitions than one would find in any number opera.

These brief textual phrases assume a varied musical color when they are repeated—Debussy's attention to the changed inflections of Symbolist speech repetitions is one of the great delights of the score. In Act III, scene 1 Pelléas again speaks of leaving the next day, and again Mélisande prevails on him to stay. When she confirms her victory by asking, "Tu ne partiras pas?" (You won't leave?), Pelléas replies, not "I will stay, I will stay," but more symbolically, "J'attendrai, j'attendrai" (I will wait). The octave descent and the small falling inflection back to the pitch D for the tonic accent of the word "atten*drai*" invest the repetition with a seriousness the more ecstatic first statement lacks (Ex. 4). Much the same thing happens later in the scene as Pelléas sings, "Mais donne-moi ta main d'abord; d'abord ta main" (But give me your hand first), while Mélisande reverses the downward direction as she replies "Voilà . . . voilà." Again, when Mélisande loses her wedding ring in the well and sings, "Ce n'est plus elle . . . ce n'est plus elle," the musical statements are related, but the increased gravity of the repetition is manifest in the longer note values of

---

[21] Concerning the public dress rehearsal of the opera on 28 April 1902, Albert Carré, André Messager, and others testified to the audience's reaction to the text. Carré wrote, "Soon, poor Mélisande could no longer utter a word without unleashing hilarity," and Messager said, "It was in the second tableau of the second act at Mélisande's reply 'I am not happy!' that the storm burst forth." Messager, "Les Premières représentations de *Pelléas*," in *Revue Musicale*, VII/7 (1 May 1926), p. 208, reprinted in *Revue Musicale*, no. 258 (1964), pp. 57–60, and Carré, "La Bataille de *Pelléas*," in *Figaro Littéraire* (23 September 1950), p. 281. See also René Peter, "Ce que fut la 'Générale' de *Pelléas et Mélisande*," in *Inédits sur Debussy*, ed. Arthur Hoérée (Paris, 1942), pp. 3–10, and Grayson, pp. 78–88.

EXAMPLE 4. ACT III, SCENE 1

EXAMPLE 5. ACT II, SCENE 1

EXAMPLE 6. ACT II, SCENE 2

the anacrusis pitches ("ce n'est plus") and the lower pitch level (Ex. 5).[22] The same is true of her lines at the end of Act II, scene 2, "Je ne suis pas heureuse, je ne suis pas heureuse" (I am not happy), with a telling change of prosodic emphasis. Only in the repetition is the mid-measure accent stressed for the tonic accent of "heu-*reu*-se," while the slight emphasis produced by placement of a syllable on the first subdivision of a beat in 6/4 shifts from "suis" in the initial statement to the negation "ne" in the second statement (Ex. 6). The textual repetitions are given a *raison d'être* more specific than is possible in spoken drama.

Maeterlinck creates his heavily fatalistic atmospheres in part by means of textual leitmotifs. When a character repeats the same gesture enacted earlier by others, when the same images recur, when a significant word is repeated several times in close proximity, chance and accident become improbable, insufficient to explain so many coincidences. As the dramatis personae echo earlier words and actions, they unwittingly demonstrate the inexorability of Destiny's designs. The recurrences serve another pur-

---

[22] David Michael Hertz, *The Tuning of the Word: The Musico-Literary Poetics of the Symbolist Movement* (Carbondale, Illinois, 1987), p. 198, points out that symbols familiar from Wagnerian opera and elsewhere are altered in meaning when they reappear in Maeterlinck's play; for example, "Wagner's ring . . . signifies absolute power, and it comes from and returns to a mighty river, whereas Mélisande's ring merely stands for her unfortunate marriage to Golaud and it falls into a little fountain."

pose as well: in the teleology of dramatic determinism, the present moment contains the future. Fate, for all its mystery, foreshadows the disasters to come dozens of times before the axe falls, in a manner impossible for the characters themselves to discern. But very few of Maeterlinck's parallelisms invite or receive similar musical treatment. When the clock strikes twelve as Mélisande loses her wedding ring in the well, and Golaud hears a clock strike noon as his horse bolts and runs away with him in the forest, Maeterlinck is suggesting that the two events are simultaneous. Debussy states the simultaneity and the symbolic connection more explicitly when music associated with the loss of the wedding ring returns as Golaud sings, "Mais je ne puis m'expliquer comment cela s'est passé" (But I can't understand how it happened). The reference is fleeting, however, and not didactic in purpose. The recurring music passes before the listener can register the implications of the link between the two passages. Connection is not causality; neither event is "explained" by the brief reappearance of an earlier figure.

Debussy's understanding of Maeterlinck is especially evident in his refusal to mimic the dramatist's textual leitmotifs with a superficially similar apparatus in the musical design. For the characters, the echoed statements and occurrences are isolated and independent, and so they must be in the music, if the opera is to remain faithful to a conception of existence-as-enigma. The network of coincidences in the play is not synonymous with knowledge, but rather acts to increase the sense of mystery. Thus, when Pelléas wants to take Mélisande's hand in order to guide her down at the end of Act I, Mélisande says that he cannot because her hands are full of flowers; in Act II, scene 2 Golaud takes her hands and says that he could *crush* them like flowers, her beauty and frailty and his capacity for violence apparent in the echoed motif. Act III, scene 2 is linked to Act I, scene 3: just as Pelléas supports Mélisande by the arm as they descend the path, so Golaud supports Pelléas by the arm, refusing his hand, when he forces his half-brother to peer into the chasm at the grotto. Pelléas does not recognize the symbolic correspondence to the abyss of murderous violence in Golaud's heart, and so fails to heed the warning. In Act I, scene 1 Golaud remarks that Mélisande never seems to close her eyes, and in the spying scene, Act III, scene 4, Yniold insists that neither Mélisande nor Pelléas ever close their eyes. The owl-like peculiarity the lovers share confirms their fated attraction. Leaning over the edge, in danger of falling—symbolically, in love or to death—is another recurrent motif. In the second act Pelléas warns Mélisande not to lean so far over the well, but in Act III, scene 1 he ecstatically bids her lean farther out of the tower. At the end of that same scene, Golaud tells Mélisande not to lean out of the window lest she fall. In Act III, scene 2 Golaud bids Pelléas to lean from

75

the great rock by the grotto pool; on his release, Pelléas says that he was on the point of falling. The sense of wavering on a precipice of disaster is heightened each time the motif recurs. Mélisande five times in the first scene warns Golaud, "Ne me touchez pas!" (Don't touch me), while the enraged Golaud in Act IV, scene 2 tells Mélisande, "Je ne veux pas que tu me touches, entends-tu? Va-t'en!" (I don't want you to touch me, do you hear? Go away!). Pelléas asks Mélisande in Act II, scene 1, "C'est au bord d'une fontaine *aussi* qu'il vous a trouvée?" (It was *also* by a fountain that he found you?). "Also" is the telling word: without yet realizing what he does, Pelléas finds and claims Mélisande just as his brother had done earlier, while Mélisande too repeats her prior action of losing the symbol of marriage. When Mélisande asks Pelléas at the end of Act II, scene 1 what to tell Golaud about the lost ring, he replies, "La vérité! la vérité!" (The truth! the truth!), while Golaud in Act V desperately pleads with Mélisande to tell him "The truth! the truth!" Mélisande can only dazedly repeat the words after him, as if they were a foreign language, so little do concepts of Truth, Good, Justice, and the like have to do with Fate. But these coincidences—and there are many more—paradoxically increase the sense of disorientation and Symbolist *mystère*. The echoes are empty of meaning, and Debussy's music rightly refuses to confirm conventional expectations that these repeated textual patterns signify anything known.

One of the foremost examples of a familiar symbolic element repeated through the play but rendered diffuse and ambiguous in its signification is the opposition of light and dark. The superficial similarities between Maeterlinck's play and Wagner's *Tristan und Isolde*—what one writer has called the "divorce-court" scenario[23]—usually reveal an underlying antinomy, the most crucial one summed up in Tristan's cry that he himself brewed the fatal potion. The symbolism of light and dark, day and night, is more directly central to the Wagnerian alliance between Love, Death, and Night, and there its meaning is clear. Wagner's characters consciously seek the realm of death/darkness; Maeterlinck's characters, on the other hand, fluctuate from one realm to the other in a way that calls the Wagnerian meaning into question. "Nous aussi, nous cherchions la clarté" (We too were searching for light), Geneviève says in Act I, scene 3, and so they do, at the same time that they seek the shadows of Fate and its ultimate goal, Death. When the ship that brought Mélisande to Allemonde departs, she notices that it is in the light and points out the beacons visible in the distance when the mist lifts, like a precursor of love

<hr>

[23] Robin Holloway, *Debussy and Wagner* (London, 1979), p. 60: "The outer events of *Tristan und Isolde* and *Pelléas et Mélisande* are far from dissimilar—or, to put it differently, the two love-affairs whose progress they relate would appear much of a muchness in a divorce-court."

that can be seen when the Fate-induced fog clears away for a time. At the tower, Pelléas begs Mélisande not to remain in the shadows; shortly after, the doves vanish into the darkness, followed by Golaud's entrance as Pelléas says, "Il fait noir" (It is dark). Maeterlinck seems to imply that Golaud has brought darkness with him, a presence to inspire anxiety and fear. In Act IV, scene 4 Pelléas and Mélisande cannot decide whether they should stand in the light or in the shadows:

> PELLÉAS: Viens ici, ne reste pas au bord du clair de lune . . .
> Viens ici dans l'ombre du tilleul.
> MÉLISANDE: Laissez-moi dans la clarté. [. . .]
> PELLÉAS: Nous sommes déjà dans l'ombre . . . Viens dans la
> lumière . . .
> MÉLISANDE: Non, non, restons ici . . . Je suis plus près de toi
> dans l'obscurité.

> (PELLÉAS: Come here, don't stay on the edge of the moonlight . . .
> Come here into the shadow of the lime tree. MÉLISANDE: Let me
> stay in the light. . . . PELLÉAS: We are in the shadow . . . Come into
> the light. MÉLISANDE: No, no, let's stay here . . . I'm closer to you
> in the darkness.)

According to Yniold, the lovers have quarreled about the light and wept in the dark; as the child watches them in Act III, scene 4, they look at the light. Possibly Maeterlinck is suggesting their hope that love might indeed be illumination, not a confederate of Fate's malevolence; possibly that hope is engaged in unknowing battle with an intuitive sense of Destiny as darkness; but we cannot be certain. At the end of the opera, is light symbolic of life? Mélisande, even though Death means release from "toutes ces inquiétudes" (all these anxieties), nevertheless wants to watch the sun until it has sunk into the sea. But the familiar symbolic attribution is only hinted at. We never know if the fragmented echoes cumulatively spell anything knowable, and Debussy rightly avoids any hint of musical definition.

One of Maeterlinck's principal textual leitmotifs becomes not a single identifiable figure in music but—appropriately—a compound of musical gestures. Destiny first makes fearful those she intends to kill, and muted fear permeates the play; *peur* and *mal* are the words most often repeated. Golaud, who inspires fear in everyone, constantly speaks of it. He threatens Mélisande in Act I, scene 1 with the fear of being alone in the forest at night; he coerces and terrifies Yniold until the child cries out, "J'ai terriblement peur!" (I'm terribly frightened); and he tells both Pelléas and Mélisande "N'ayez pas peur" in Act I, scene 1 and in Act III, scene 2.

The major characters all invoke *mal* (hurt or harm) as the twin to Fate-inspired fear. Golaud asks Mélisande in the first scene, "Qui est-ce qui vous a fait du mal?" (Who was it who harmed you?), to which she revealingly replies "Everyone"; Mélisande says to Pelléas, "Oh! oh! tu m'as fait mal!" (You've hurt me) when he caresses her hair; Yniold protests Golaud's hurtful grasp in the spying scene, "Ah! ah! petit père, vous m'avez fait mal"; and at Mélisande's death-bed Golaud says remorsefully, "Je t'ai fait tant de mal" (I have done you so much harm), just before he begins another round of interrogation. Life itself is *mal* in Allemonde, and the *maladie* that afflicts the characters is unhappiness, often unexplained, seemingly causeless unhappiness.

However, the atmosphere of *mal* in the opera is the result not only of insistent repetitions of the word, but also of changes in musical atmosphere specific to the moment. To cite one example, the lovers' rapture near the end of Act IV, expressed in scale figures centered on C major, is twice broken by the awareness, first tentative, then certain, that someone else is there—Golaud. The ominous trombone and double-bass figures that combine to form an augmented triad on G♭ alternate on their second appearance with a chromatic fragment in the cellos (Ex. 7), reminiscent of the chromatic scalar underlay to his last words in Act IV, scene 2 ("Vous ferez comme il vous plaira, voyez-vous" [You shall do whatever you like]). Possibly the short-lived C major of Golaud's words "J'attendrai le hasard" (I will wait for chance) in that same scene is echoed in the two C major passages of the rendezvous, interrupted by musical *mal* and Golaud's presence, but the lack of tonal definition, of goal-oriented progressions through defined tonalities, makes such connections tenuous at best. The recurrent augmented triad G♭-B♭-D in this portion of the scene is used in a way that evokes its identity as a point of tension, but the context, especially the meandering chromatic bass line, defies certain analytical definition.

What is most striking about this example is the way in which the renewed onset of the twin evils *mal* and *peur* negates the brief moment of musical clarity and replaces it with the ambiguous atmosphere that pervades the opera in constantly changing guises. It seems paradoxical at first that Maeterlinck relies so heavily on textual repetition to create atmosphere while Debussy avoids analogous musical procedures, but the seeming paradox is in fact another index of the composer's insight. When Maeterlinck's characters repeat themselves, they do so unknowingly. The echoes enhance the sense of mystery: the more the word "mal" is repeated, the more it seems to point to something beyond, to an unknown, and the same is true of the other echoed words and actions in the play. Reminiscence motives or leitmotivic parallels to the textual repetitions would have produced a comprehensible formal pattern, a network of re-

EXAMPLE 7. ACT IV, SCENE 4

lationships at odds with Maeterlinck's central contention that Fate is
wholly unpredictable in its power; the repeated musical figures that Debussy does use are small motivic threads woven into a much larger fabric,
obscuring the connectives from view.

NATURE AND THE *mise-en-scène*

One attraction of Maeterlinck's play for Debussy was surely the playwright's reliance on a secretive, obsessional atmosphere and a legendary
world as far removed as possible from the realism of Gustave Charpentier
and his ilk; many of the same elements that Debussy found so much to
his taste in *Pelléas et Mélisande* later attracted him to Poe's tale of the

House of Usher.[24] Maeterlinck, who borrowed several of his favorite concepts from German Romanticism, translated the philosophical *Fragments* of Novalis into French and must have found there corroboration for his premonitory landscapes: Nature, according to Novalis, should be the "bearer of ideas," "dead descriptions of dead nature" serving no purpose unless they had symbolic content, as Nature was symbolic.[25] Since Fate cannot be objectified, Maeterlinck relied on the stage designer's craft and on words and situations that would imply a symbolic connection between Nature and Fate, as when Golaud in the spying scene tells Yniold, "J'ai vu passer un loup dans la forêt" (I saw a wolf go by in the forest). Maeterlinck suggests that this is no coincidence, that the forest and the wolf are objects emblematic of Fate's menace. Debussy translates the menacing atmosphere into a pianissimo bassoon figure that suddenly appears, dies away, and then vanishes, leaving behind the silence in which Golaud asks Yniold, "Ils s'embrassent quelquefois? Non?" (Ex. 8a). (Golaud's hope for a negative answer is painfully apparent in the way he coaxes/coaches the child, who obediently responds, "Non, non," then remembers otherwise.) Despite the common-tone relationship formed with the B of the seventh chord on C immediately preceding Ex. 8a, and the relationship between the bassoon figure and the subsequent sixteenth-note figuration (Ex. 8b), the impression is one of an isolated event. Things come and go in the music, as in the forest, without explanation.

In particular, Maeterlinck uses the *selva oscura* from romance and epic fiction to his own ends. (Edvard Munch's oil painting and engravings entitled *Eifersucht [Jealousy]* could be an illustration to *Pelléas et Mélisande*, with the deep forest by the ocean, the two lovers on the shore, the looming, dark-bearded face of the jealous husband in the foreground, and the simplified shapes emblematic of archetypal areas of experience.)[26] Debussy omitted Maeterlinck's first scene, but the second, set in the depths

---

[24] Debussy did not want to duplicate the manner of *Pelléas et Mélisande* in his Poe projects and stated in an interview in 1910 that he was pleased with his two Poe subjects (*Le Diable dans le beffroi, La Chute de la Maison Usher*) precisely because "one cannot find a more complete contrast than between Poe and Maeterlinck." See Robert Orledge, *Debussy and the Theatre* (Cambridge, 1982), p. 119. However, Orledge points out (p. 120) that both *Usher* and *Pelléas* are set in ancestral homes in a stifling atmosphere, subterranean vaults, with pale, suffering maidens.

[25] See Friedrich von Hardenberg, *Les Disciples à Sais et les Fragments de Novalis*, trans. Maurice Maeterlinck, 2nd ed. (Brussels, 1895), and Novalis, *Gesammelte Werke* (Zurich, 1945), pp. 193–94. See also Werner Vordtriede, *Novalis und die französischen Symbolisten* (Stuttgart, 1963).

[26] For *Eifersucht* (1895) and subsequent works on the same theme, see *Edvard Munch. Liebe. Angst. Tod. Themen und Variationen: Zeichnungen und Graphiken aus dem Munch-Museum Oslo*, ed. Ulrich Weisner (Düsseldorf, 1980), pp. 103–14.

EXAMPLE 8a. ACT III, SCENE 4

of the forest, establishes even more strongly the symbolic bonds that unite Nature, Humanity, and Fate. Post-Freudian audiences are inclined to interpret the dark forest as the unconscious and the wild beast as the id, but Maeterlinck intended a different reading, divorced from considerations of human personality; his forests are Nature's accomplices to Fate because of their shared obscurity and hostility to human beings. After Golaud's horse falls on him at the moment Mélisande loses her wedding ring, Golaud says "Je croyais avoir toute la forêt sur la poitrine" (I believed the whole forest was on my chest); he identifies the weight of fatality with the forest. Mélisande exclaims to Geneviève in Act I, scene 3 about the forests that surround the palace, and Geneviève replies that this astonishes everyone ("et cela étonne tout le monde"). Again and again, Nature is described as impenetrable, hostile, sunless: the two bottomless lakes in the grotto, the linden tree where the sun's rays never enter, the darkness that

EXAMPLE 8b. ACT III, SCENE 4

makes the mouth of the grotto indistinguishable from the surrounding night.

The opening bars of Act I are sometimes identified as the leitmotif of the Ancient Forest, objectionably so to those who dislike trafficking in leitmotivic labels. Whether or not one affixes a name to the passage, Debussy establishes the timeless other-worldly milieu of the music in just four bars—this is the listener's entrance to the world of Fate. The measured half-notes and whole-notes of the first two bars, in conjunction with the "antique" open fifth and the quasi-modal sound of the harmonic progression, seem like a conjuration to banish the real world and lull the listener into an enchanted, receptive state. The unique atmosphere created so quickly by this opening "spell" is due in part to orchestral wizardry, to the timbre produced by the combination of muted *divisi* cellos, *divisi* basses, and bassoons; harmonic adventure and shifting coloristic possibilities combine. The succeeding bars (mm. 5–6), commonly associated with Golaud, reveal an aspect of the forest world of Fate similar to the musical moment in which the wolf passes Golaud's line of sight. Golaud's figure begins on the D so unforgettably sounded in m. 1, but we hear the two-bar phrase as a discrete event, distinct from the modal spell just preceding. (It is tempting to interpret the tritone D-A♭ in the cellos at mm. 5–6, along with the A♭ in the timpani, bassoons, and basses, as Golaud's vain attempt to pull away from entrapment in Allemonde's environs. Certainly the non-functional ninth chords and the rejection of tonal clarity in this figure are the initial indices of Debussy's harmonic language in *Pelléas*.) The stream of music embeds within it fragments isolated by the lack of emphasis on derivation from what precedes it (Ex. 9).

The various *mises-en-scène* of *Pelléas* nearly always symbolize something invisible, either Fate or a subset of Fate. The stagnant water with its

Example 9. Act I, scene 1

"smell of death" symbolizes the fumes of fermenting jealousy, Fate's instrument of death. The window in Act V is opened onto another world, the realm of Death, and Mélisande's intuition that winter is coming implies the traditional, death-related interpretation. Rings, crowns, beggars, sheep to the slaughterhouse *à la* Holman Hunt—these are easily deciphered. In other instances, one can know that the physical object has symbolic significance, but the signified is unclear. Does the great ship that leaves the harbor in Act I to voyage toward inevitable shipwreck symbolize the lovers' destiny? The doves that fly away from Mélisande, never to return, perhaps signify the loss of peace, while the three white-haired beggars asleep in the grotto (Fates?) are possibly symbolic of the three principal figures in the drama, Pelléas, Mélisande, and Golaud, all of whom descend into the grotto as a premonitory descent into the Underworld of Death. The great boulder in Yniold's solo scene perhaps symbolizes Fate itself, which cannot be moved by puny human power. Is the child's golden ball, wedged between two rocks where Yniold cannot reach it, emblematic of human happiness? We sense that nothing in the milieu is fortuitous, that every detail of the surroundings exists to aid or foreshadow Destiny's designs, to mimic its hostility in tangible form; but the imbalance between known and unknown is carefully calculated so that mystery prevails.

The inhabitants of Allemonde

Destiny's place in the play is so disproportionately large that the dramatis personae dwindle by comparison, deprived of autonomy, will, and reason, of all but instinct and emotion. All the characters except Golaud seem to know instinctively that Reason has nothing to do with their lives, and Golaud, with his Othello-like insistence on proof and a spurious "truth," is too overcome by violent jealousy for any kind of understanding. In two of his Symbolist plays, *L'Intruse* (The Intruder) and *Les Aveugles* (The Blind Ones), Maeterlinck dispenses with names and almost entirely with personalities; he does not go that far in *Pelléas et Mélisande*, but neither is this a drama of personality. Debussy wrote of the "nothingness" that is Mélisande in a letter to Ernest Chausson and once considered casting a woman as Pelléas, so little virile did he find the young prince.[27] Though the characters are neither allegorical nor purely archetypal, Maeterlinck arranges them along a continuum of age to show the different conditions Fate imposes at different stages of life: Elderly Blind Grandfather, Young Ingenuous Prince, Older Violent Half-Brother, Small Child, Rapunzel-like Princess, the Mother who appears briefly and then vanishes, the entire cast reminiscent of the Brothers Grimm, *Kunstmärchen*, and Andrew Lang's color-coded fairy-story collections. The three principal characters, especially the two lovers, are shadowy creatures whose somewhat blank personalities are inhabited for a time by a strong emotion—love, jealousy, fear—before Death intervenes. They are only minimally connected to the external world, disengaged from any epoch or place, from material necessity or social responsibilities. Their existence is pure feeling, "en attendant l'inattendu" (in waiting for the unexpected).

The extreme artificiality of characterization, the non-naturalistic focus on emotion alone, is a consequence of the deterministic premise of the play. Fate, in the form of unlooked-for emotion, descends on the characters, invading and overwhelming them like an alien army of occupation.

[27] From an undated letter to Ernest Chausson, possibly written in late December 1893 or early January 1894: "I have spent days in pursuit of the 'nothingness' that she [Mélisande] is made of . . ." See "Deux lettres de Debussy à Ernest Chausson," in *Revue Musicale*, VII/7 (1 May 1926), pp. 183–84, and Grayson (see n. 4 above), p. 27. For the 1902–1903 season, Carré thought of making Pelléas a *Hosenrolle* for Jeanne Raunay. In a letter to Messager, Debussy declared his willingness to try the idea: "On the whole, Pelléas has none of the amorous ways of a Hussar, and his sluggish manly decisions are so abruptly mowed down by Golaud's sword that perhaps there would be no drawbacks to this substitution?" See *L'Enfance de Pelléas: Lettres de Claude Debussy à André Messager*, ed. Jean-André Messager (Paris, 1938), p. 31. After hearing Raunay sing, with "la voix d'un vieux monsieur passionné et un peu éssouflé" (p. 35), he decided against it.

Maeterlinck isolates and magnifies the incomprehensibility of universal human experience: the inability to locate the source of feeling or account for its intensity. The tighter Destiny's grip on the principal figures, the less they are able to explain what they do or say, and the more Maeterlinck relies on bewildered or defeated expressions of incomprehension. The characters obsessively reiterate that they are compelled and do not act of their own will. "C'est quelque chose qui est plus fort que moi" (It is something stronger than myself), Mélisande says to Golaud in refusing to explain her unhappiness and her wish to leave Allemonde. When the doors of the chateau are bolted and chained shut near the end of Act IV, Mélisande cries, "Tant mieux!" (All the better), and Pelléas, similarly grateful that the last false vestiges of volition are gone, tells her, "Ce n'est plus nous qui le voulons" (Things no longer depend on our wish). As a result of Destiny's domination, both the emotional states and the sense of powerlessness are enacted as if in a dream, the result at times an etiolated and emotion-drained appearance at seeming variance with an existence of incomprehensible feeling. Maeterlinck did not include the following fragments in his translations of Novalis, but many of his characters in the 1890s exemplify life as a "disease of the spirit," lived out in a dream-like atmosphere and culminating in Death:

Life is a disease of the spirit, a working incited by passion. It is only the weakness of our organs and our self-obsession that prevent us from seeing ourselves in a fairy world. All *Märchen* are merely dreams of that home-world, which is everywhere and nowhere.[28]

Golaud is the only character in the opera who attempts to deny Destiny's subjugating power, the only one who thinks that answers are possible and that reasons exist. Therein lies his slight degree of individuality, beyond the jealousy that increasingly possesses him, and this is why wisdom as defined in Allemonde eludes him to the end. He is more right than he knows when he cries out in Act V (his last words), "Ce n'est pas ma faute! Ce n'est pas ma faute!" (It isn't my fault), but the exclamations originate in guilt, not in the perception of Fate's operations. In a deterministic universe, Golaud's wrongdoing—the oppression of Mélisande, the murder of Pelléas—could not have been prevented. But Golaud proves his utter incomprehension in his words to Mélisande, "Mais je le vois, je le vois si clairement aujourd'hui . . . depuis le premier jour. . . . Et tout est de ma faute, tout ce qui est arrivé, tout ce qui va arriver" (But I can see it all, see it so clearly today . . . ever since the first day. And it's all my fault, everything that has happened, everything that is going to hap-

[28] Friedrich von Hardenberg/Maeterlinck (see n. 25 above), no. 196, p. 56.

pen). He does not, of course, see anything at all, and his frenzied demands that Mélisande confess a meaningless culpability prove it. Catharsis and fatalistic determinism cannot co-exist, so the one character most in need of it is denied Arkel's knowledge of the soul. If this makes Golaud the most *malheureux* of all the *malheureux* who populate Allemonde, it also distinguishes him from the others and gives him a quasi-personality that his beloved "nothingness" lacks.

The characters in this play could have posed a problem for other composers. From Monteverdi on, operatic music has served, in part, as the sonorous rendering of personality. Poppea's long, sensuous melodic sequences and chromatic underlay, just enough overdone for the listener to perceive their calculated quality; the adolescent impetuousness with which Cherubino charges into "Non so più cosa son" without an introduction; Iago's linear chromatic figures, descending straight into the pit—these are representations of personality in music. But musical characterization would not be appropriate in *Pelléas et Mélisande*, whose players avoid questions and guard their mysteriousness and their isolation from one another. At their traditional registers (Golaud a baritone, Arkel a bass, Pelléas tenor, Mélisande soprano, Geneviève contralto, etc.), the inhabitants of Allemonde sing of different things—Golaud rages and, Othello-like, demands proof; Mélisande flirts timidly, lies, and withdraws; Arkel speaks gravely of pity and sorrow; Pelléas waxes rhapsodic in the moonlight—but none of them, not even Golaud, is given a musical room of his own, deliberately so. Debussy wanted to fuse what he called the musical emotion on one hand, the characters' emotions on the other,[29] and did so by banishing conventional melody, substituting for it a subtle, flexible prosody devoid of the traditional periodicity of dramatic melody. Since conventional expectations belonging only to music do not intrude, the vocal part and orchestra can fuse in order to reflect each nuance of feeling. And yet, because of the speech-like reliance on repeated pitches in the vocal lines and the close attention to speech rhythms, the vocal parts share those elements in common, the composer abjuring the melodic individuality that distinguishes, for example, Zerbinetta from Ariadne in Strauss's opera. Debussy instead creates a unique kind of "characterization" perfectly in accord with the nature of Maeterlinck's dramatis personae.

[29] "À l'audition d'une oeuvre, le spectateur est accoutumé à éprouver deux sortes d'émotions bien distinctes: l'émotion musicale d'une part, l'émotion du personnage de l'autre; généralement il les ressent successivement. J'ai essayé que ces deux émotions fussent parfaitement fondues et simultanées." Claude Debussy, *Monsieur Croche et autres écrits* (Paris, 1971), p. 134.

CONCLUSION

Every element of Maeterlinck's play stems from the premise of an unknowable Destiny whose effects can be suggested by a thicket of theatrical devices but whose essence lies beyond grasp. The fundamental disbelief in the powers of language that results from this aesthetic is almost unbearably pessimistic. When the equation "Word represents Concept" becomes "Word represents Effect of the Unknowable," then those characters closest to the heart of Destiny can only say what the dying Mélisande says in Act V:

> Je ne comprends pas non plus tout ce que je dis, voyez-vous. Je ne sais pas ce que je dis. Je ne sais pas ce que je sais. Je ne dis plus ce que je veux.

> (I no longer understand all that I say, you see. I don't know what I'm saying. I don't know what I know. I don't say what I want to any more.)

The defeat of language and knowledge alike resonates in these words. And yet, despite the premise that language is inadequate, this is a very wordy play, its characters both talkative and inarticulate. The ideal of lyrical simplicity became Symbolist logorrhea in practice, and Debussy accordingly made numerous deletions, including four entire scenes (the first and last scenes of Maeterlinck's Act I, and the first scenes of Acts III and V—Maeterlinck became too explanatory and heavily symbolic at the beginnings and ends of acts). In Act II, scene 3, Pelléas waxes garrulous in the grotto, which Maeterlinck fills with the ruins of ancient shipwrecks, stalagmites resembling plants and men, the ghosts of explorers who never returned but who—mercifully—say nothing, and hints of great treasure in the depths. Debussy retains only the most evocative elements of Pelléas's description—the bottomless lakes, blue shadows, star-studded vault—and sets the scene to music filled with tritone figures and whole-tone ostinati, creating a more haunting impression of menace than words alone could do.[30] Debussy's editing of the text, however, does not alter—indeed it enhances—the fact that in Allemonde "Words don't say it."

[30] David Grayson, "The Libretto of 'Pelléas et Mélisande,' " *Music & Letters*, 66 (1985), pp. 34–50, speculates on the reasons for Debussy's omissions. In Maeterlinck's Act V, scene 1, for example, the servants gossip for the transparent purpose of telling the audience that Golaud threw Pelléas's body down Blindman's Well and that Mélisande has borne a child. Debussy also eliminates much of Golaud's prosy explanation in Act III to Pelléas that Mélisande might become pregnant and that he should take care not to disturb her, and cuts a brief scene for Arkel and Pelléas alone in a room of the chateau, in which Arkel explains at length that Pelléas must remain in Allemonde.

Music is ideally suited to express Maeterlinck's notion of Fate because it is inherently anti-verbal. Schopenhauer's belief that music enjoys the unique privilege of penetrating to the essence of things—music as a *Ding an sich* that resounds directly from the heart of the cosmos—becomes the assertion that music is the voice of Fate. If Maeterlinck really did read all of Schopenhauer, he must have encountered the philosopher's attempt, in "Zur Metaphysik der Musik," to establish music as a contradiction realized, a representation of the unrepresentable that emanates from the World-as-Will, the force that expresses not phenomena but inner nature.[31] Maeterlinck's premise that the emotive life issues from a Fate both foreign and inimical resembles aspects of Schopenhauer's metaphysics and, as with Schopenhauer, this leads to a perception of music as the means of expression closest to Fate's own workings—in Novalis's words, music as the "Akustik der Seele."[32] And yet, because Fate's powers are of a special kind, the text *is* vitally important. Debussy treats it as such when he traces so meticulously the speech-rhythms of French, and when he devises an orchestration of a transparency that allows the text to come through clearly. In fact, music withdraws almost entirely at times, as in Act IV when the lovers sing "Je t'aime" or at the end of Act I, scene 1 when Mélisande asks Golaud "Où allez-vous?" (Where are you going?) and he replies "Je ne sais pas . . . je suis perdu aussi" (I don't know . . . I am lost too). These lines have a dual meaning (Mélisande asks, "Where are you taking me?"; Golaud's response is more existential than geo-

---

Debussy attended the first performance of the play on 17 May 1893. The original edition of the play, printed in 1892 by Paul Lacomblez of Brussels, was the only available source for Debussy's first version of the opera, completed in 1895. For the "sixth" edition (there is some question about a possible fifth unnumbered edition), Maeterlinck revised the play in 1898, the revisions possibly stemming in part from the performances at the Théâtre de l'Oeuvre in 1893. For a three-volume collection of his plays in 1901–1902 (actually, two editions, one published by Edmond Deman in Brussels and the other jointly by Paul Lacomblez of Brussels and Per Lamm in Paris), Maeterlinck again revised the work. The revisions are minor; Maeterlinck explained in the preface to his collected plays that "the best and the worst . . . have entwined roots, and often in trying to disentangle them one risks losing the special emotion."

[31] "Weil die Musik nicht, gleich allen andern Künsten, die Ideen oder Stufen der Objektivation des Willens, sondern unmittelbar den Willen selbst darstellt; so ist hieraus auch erklärlich, dass sie auf den Willen, d.i. die Gefühle, Leidenschaften und Affekte des Hörers, unmittelbar einwirkt, so dass sie dieselben schnell erhöht, oder auch umstimmt." Schopenhauer, *Zur Aesthetik der Poesie, Musik und der bildenden Künste*, ed. Moritz Brasch (Leipzig, n.d.), p. 33. Schopenhauer considered only instrumental music as the direct voice of Will, as does Novalis in Fragment no. 3054, p. 302: "Tanz und Liedermusik ist eigentlich nicht die wahre. Nur Abarten davon. Sonaten, Symphonien, Fugen, Variationen: das ist eigentliche Musik" (see n. 25 above).

[32] From Novalis, Fragment no. 2584, p. 196.

graphic), and the musical reticence allows the implications to come through.

The correlation of Maeterlinck's text and Debussy's music is perhaps most striking on the structural level. If there is a distinction between the rational, mathematically proportioned *structure* of music and its non-logical, non-rational *meaning*, then Debussy also succeeded in making the structure independent of "rational" analysis of a traditional kind. He reinforces the impression that these sounds emanate from the sphere of Destiny, that this work is a model of another world whose laws are a mystery. The harmonies and references to key centers clearly stem from the tonal system, but cannot be explained in its terms; the fact that a musical design, an interrelatedness of events, exists is apparent but eludes articulation. It is precisely this fundamental elusiveness that makes the music such an apt representative of Destiny's being, augmenting Maeterlinck's halting words, symbolic images, and fateful silences as the true language of the *au-delà*.

Ironically, by the time Debussy completed the composition of *Pelléas et Mélisande* Maeterlinck was no longer able to sustain belief in absolute determinism. There were perhaps only so many dramatic changes that could be rung on the metaphysical premises of plays such as *La Mort de Tintagiles, Pelléas et Mélisande, L'Intruse, Les Aveugles,* and the rest; by 1896, Maeterlinck had reached an impasse with his *drames de fatalité*. Nor could Allemonde have been a comforting place to inhabit, despite its aesthetic confines within the theatre—the psychology behind both Maeterlinck's emergence from that world and Debussy's attraction to it for music-drama is an intriguing subject for further investigation but one that lies beyond the scope of this study. The world in *Pelléas et Mélisande* has no larger horizons; it is a prison to be endured: "One can only come the same painful cropper over and over again and draw from it the same bitter moral."[33] Mélisande's child, after what is surely the most discreet pregnancy in literature, exists solely to point out that the same cycle of misery is beginning again. The opera ends with outlined tritone figures whose ethereal harp and string timbres do not disguise the fundamental similarity to the sounds issuing from the ancient forest and the grotto. No wonder we sympathize with Golaud's desperate wish in Act II, scene 2 for "la joie, la joie." Debussy sets "joie" first to a wide-swinging interval of a seventh, unusual after the more restrained prosody that has preceded it, and then repeats the word to a more cramped, questioning/rising inflection, while the seventh chord on F with its flatted fifth evaporates to a

[33] Edmund Wilson's statement about A. E. Housman, *The Triple Thinkers* (1938; rpt. New York, 1976), p. 71, applies as well to Maeterlinck's play.

EXAMPLE 10. ACT II, SCENE 2

single unharmonized sustained D♭ in the the second bassoon—this is what happens to joy in Allemonde (Ex. 10).

In *La Sagesse et la Destinée*, written after the completion of his eight Symbolist plays, Maeterlinck wrote: "Resignation is good and necessary in the face of life's inevitabilities, but where struggle is possible, then resignation is no more than ignorance, weakness, or disguised laziness."[34] Had Maeterlinck begun his career as a dramatist with such views, had he not espoused determinism in his youth, his plays of the 1890s would

---

[34] "Oui, la résignation est bonne et nécessaire devant les faits généraux et inévitables de la vie, mais sur tous les points où la lutte est possible, la résignation n'est que de l'ignorance, de l'impuissance ou de la paresse déguisées." Maeterlinck, *La Sagesse et la Destinée* (Paris, 1898), p. 164. Maeterlinck emerges as a moralist in these essays and in the plays from *Monna Vanna* (1902) on. The change is radical: characters have definite personalities; events no longer suggest a transcendent plane; human actions appear as determining forces; the *enfants-femmes* figures disappear from the scene. Claims other than those of Death and Death-allied Love assert sovereignty, and the twilight atmosphere of Symbolism gives way to daylight and the realization of earthly happiness.

surely have been very different, and we might now be deprived of an operatic rarity: the perfect conjunction of a composer and a text. By limiting life to flare-ups of inexplicable emotion, by insisting that existence and life are mysteries of Fate, Maeterlinck directs attention to psychic and cosmic forces that are ultimately beyond words but not beyond music. In this sense, music asserts its primacy over words, as in so many operas, but I know of few other instances in operatic history of such fundamental interdependency between the two forces.

The Origins of Italian *Literaturoper*:
Guglielmo Ratcliff,
La figlia di Iorio, *Parisina*,
and *Francesca da Rimini*

> *Oh meraviglia delle meraviglie! D'Annunzio mio libret-*
> *tista! Ma neanche per tutto l'oro del mondo.*
>
> (Puccini to Luigi Illica, 15 May 1900)

It is generally acknowledged that a profound crisis afflicted the venerable occupation of libretto-writing at the beginning of the twentieth century. Signs of this crisis become obvious before 1900, and involve mostly Russian, French, and German opera. Its origins have been carefully studied in relation to the musical language in various European cultures—but with the seemingly natural exception of Italy, where the art of libretto-writing and the tradition of texts conceived exclusively for musical setting were more firmly rooted than anywhere else. Studies concerned with the phenomenon generally called *Literaturoper* understandably concentrate on musical theater in Russia, France, and Germany;[1] understandably because, for reasons I hope to describe below, Italian operas set directly to a pre-existing play seem always to fall short of the best examples from these other countries.

The present study tries to restrict the term *Literaturoper* to a narrow but precise definition: opera based on a text that existed as a play before it was set to music by another person. This definition excludes many borderline cases in which the term is often used to indicate the literary value of the libretto itself, or of the source play, novel, or poetry.[2] Thus, Victor Hugo's libretto for *La Esmeralda* by Louise-Angélique Bertin, the adaptation for the operatic stage of his *Notre-Dame de Paris*, could not be

---

[1] See Jürg Stenzl, "Heinrich von Kleists *Penthesilea* in der Vertonung von Othmar Schoeck (1923/25)," *Dichtung und Musik*, ed. Günther Schnitzler (Stuttgart, 1979), 224–45; *Für und wider die Literaturoper*, ed. Sigrid Wiesmann (Laaber, 1982); Carl Dahlhaus, *Vom Musikdrama zur Literaturoper: Aufsätze zur neueren Operngeschichte* (Munich and Salzburg, 1983); Jürgen Maehder, "Anmerkungen zu einigen Strukturproblemen der Literaturoper," *Aribert Reimanns "Lear"—Weg einer neuen Oper*, ed. Klaus Schultz (Munich, 1984), 79–89.

[2] See Karl Dietrich Gräwe, "Halbgestaltete dichterische Materie," in Wiesmann, 233–43.

considered *Literaturoper*, despite the fact that the libretto is based on a work of literature, because the poet himself prepared the adaptation.[3] Our definition also excludes poet-composers in the tradition of Richard Wagner. To be sure, the poem of the *Ring des Nibelungen* was published several decades before the entire score was finished, but mere distance in time does not entitle us to apply the term.

Since most musico-dramatic works of the nineteenth century are based on novels or plays, a broader concept of *Literaturoper* inevitably fails when applied to the operatic culture of nineteenth-century Europe. It could only distinguish a small minority of operas based on an original plot from the large majority with a pre-existing plot (one very often taken from a different literary culture). The distinction between pre-existing texts and texts conceived for musical setting, however, includes the intrinsic structure of the work itself. A libretto by Scribe based on a play by Schiller and a libretto by Scribe of the author's own invention would not differ significantly in structure, whereas a libretto by Arrigo Boito differs completely from a contemporary play like *Nerone* (1872) by Pietro Cossa, which was set to music by Mascagni more than sixty years after its premiere as a drama.[4]

I

It has been observed that the phenomenon of *Literaturoper* is in some sense an intrinsic sign of decadence or lack of tradition. This may indeed apply to Russian, French, or German *fin-de-siècle* operatic culture, but it is hard to believe that Italian opera, at the moment of its greatest worldwide diffusion, should have undergone a serious crisis. As the continuing tradition of writing original opera libretti even during the 1930s suggests, the métier of the librettist continued as if nothing had happened in other musical cultures. A libretto such as Zangarini's and Civinini's text for Puccini's *La fanciulla del West*, however, already shows a serious decline, especially with regard to the use of Italian verse and meter. In the midst of one of the most flourishing periods of Italian operatic culture, the signs of an end to Italian *melodramma* seem to have appeared suddenly.

Our discussion of four major operas written between 1893 and 1915 necessarily proceeds in chronological order because the period saw a

---

[3] See Anselm Gerhard, "Die Macht der Fatalität: Victor Hugo als Librettist," to appear in the proceedings of 1985 Bad Homburg symposium "Perspektiven der Opernforschung" ed. Albert Gier and Jürg Stenzl.

[4] It is interesting to note that for his last opera, *Nerone* (1935), Mascagni reverted to a librettist, the same Giovanni Targioni-Tozzetti who had prepared the libretto for *Cavalleria rusticana* (1890). See Mario Morini, *Pietro Mascagni* (Milan, 1963), I, 413–26.

rapid change in the nature of international libretto-writing. For example, the susceptibility of *fin-de-siècle* Italian literature to foreign influence makes it likely that French or German *Literaturopern* (such as *Pelléas et Mélisande* or *Salome*) were important to Italian composers of that period. But while this argument applies to the collaboration between d'Annunzio and Franchetti, Mascagni, Zandonai, and Montemezzi, works such as Mascagni's *Guglielmo Ratcliff* (1895) as well as the quotation of entire poems by Angelo Poliziano and Lorenzo de' Medici in Leoncavallo's *I Medici* (1893) must be due rather to an autonomous tendency toward greater literary quality in opera libretti, since the chronology rules out foreign influence. On the other hand, Puccini's attempts to have d'Annunzio write him a libretto and his brief enthusiasm for Oscar Wilde's *Florentine Tragedy*[5] seem to indicate that he was fully aware of the possibilities of a pre-shaped opera libretto, and this was very probably due to the influence of Richard Strauss's early works for the stage.

The theory of a crisis in *fin-de-siècle* Italian opera libretti becomes more tenable if we investigate the choice of subject, the creation of local color, and the metrical structure of contemporary opera libretti. Libretti of this period gradually become more independent of the schemes that tied musical rhythm to the metrical structure of Italian poetry.[6] Even the outward appearance of published libretti reveals how the tradition of poetic meters was gradually wearing out. To take one famous example, Rodolfo's aria "Che gelida manina" from Act I of Puccini's *La bohème* appears in the first printed editions as a group of seven stanzas of three *settenari* each. Puccini's setting, however, overruled the symmetrical poetic structure of the libretto in a way that made publication in regular stanzas useless.[7] Similar differences of structure in libretto and music are by no means uncommon even in Puccini's earlier operas. Another example is Des Grieux's aria "Donna non vidi mai," basically a recomposition of an aria that formed a portion of Puccini's final examination at the Milan Con-

[5] See Marco Beghelli, "Quel 'Lago di Massaciuccoli tanto ... povero d'ispirazione!' ", *Nuova Rivista Musicale Italiana*, 20 (1986), 605–25; *Carteggi pucciniani*, ed. Eugenio Gara (Milan, 1958), 332.

[6] See Julian Budden, "Aspects of Poetry, Metre and Music in the Operas of the 'Giovane Scuola,' " and Peter Ross, "Note sulla struttura, le caratteristiche e la funzione del verso in Puccini nel confronto con Verdi," *I libretti di Puccini e la letteratura del suo tempo*, Atti del IIº Convegno Internazionale sull'Opera di Puccini, Torre del Lago 1984, ed. Jürgen Maehder (Pisa, in preparation).

[7] Puccini's working copy of *La bohème* Act I, in the hand of Giulio Ricordi, has recently been discovered in the town hall of Castell'Arquato (Piacenza). The manuscript presents on pp. 24f the same characteristic subdivision into stanzas as in the first edition of the libretto. See Jürgen Maehder, "Paris-Bilder—Zur Transformation von Henry Murgers Roman in den 'Bohème'-Opern Puccinis und Leoncavallos," *Jahrbuch für Opernforschung*, 2 (1986), 109–76.

servatory. The original featured regular strophes in *ottonari*: "È la notte che mi reca / le sue larve, i suoi timori."[8] Puccini shaped his melody for the score of *Manon Lescaut* to fit a new text, one that offers a rather untidy mixture of *quinari* and *settenari* and that perhaps reveals the handiwork of those many authors who tried to prepare a manageable libretto out of Prévost's novel. Puccini's device of separating the melodic line (given to the orchestra) from the vocal declamation (based on repeated notes at the same pitch) was commonly used by Italian composers of his generation. The amount of "musical prose,"[9] however, is generally larger in Puccini's operas than in the works of his contemporaries, although the composer often insisted on having a predetermined verse structure filled with words by his librettists.[10]

In contrast to Puccini's more practical approach, Leoncavallo's *I Medici* (1893) and *La bohème* (1897), both to the composer's own libretti, foreshadow a central characteristic of *Literaturoper*: the use of textual as well as musical quotation. In *I Medici*, the first part of a planned trilogy (*Crepusculum*) that was to have included the operas *Gerolamo Savonarola* and *Cesare Borgia*, Leoncavallo tried to achieve a more authentic local color by introducing Angelo Poliziano's *ballata* "Ben venga maggio" and three stanzas from Lorenzo de' Medici's "La nencia di Barberino."[11] This incorporation of some of the greatest poetry of the Italian *quattrocento* induced some reviewers to make comparisons from which the composer emerged the loser.[12] Nevertheless, Leoncavallo's next libretto, *La bohème*, written in open competition with Puccini, continued to use the device, adapting original poetry by Alfred de Musset and Henry Murger to contribute Parisian local color. While the Italian translation of these texts preserves as far as possible their original meter and poetic form, most quotations serve as the basis for closed musical numbers with a strophic structure, and consequently their musical treatment relies heavily on traditional schemes.[13] An interesting example of this technique is Musette's aria "Mimì Pinson, la biondinetta" (Act I), a transformation of Musset's poem "Mimi Pinson est une blonde." Leoncavallo kept the ar-

---

[8] Felice Romani, *La solitaria delle Asturie*, music by Carlo Coccia (Milan, 1837). Puccini's autograph is in the Biblioteca del Conservatorio, Milan; see Mario Morini, "Il Puccini minore," *Discoteca*, 16 (1975), 27; and Michael Kaye, *The Unknown Puccini* (New York, 1987), 33–44.

[9] See Hermann Danuser, *Musikalische Prosa* (Regensburg, 1975).

[10] Puccini's "versi maccheronici," which roused Illica's indignation, were an easy way of transmitting requirements of verse meter and rhythm to his librettists.

[11] *I Medici*, Azione storica in quattro atti (Milan, 1893), 29f and 32f.

[12] Romualdo Giani and Abele Engelfried, *Rivista Musicale Italiana*, 1 (1894), 86–116, esp. 88–94.

[13] Maehder (see n. 7 above).

tificial rhyme scheme of the French original in his Italian version, but the periodic structure of his music tends to mask the inserted *quinari* verses.

The sense of friction between poetic and musical form is even more prominent in Rodolfo's aria "Scuoti o vento fra i sibili," which contains as its central section a poem that Rodolfo is about to write. The fourteen stanzas of Murger's "Ballade du désespéré" were condensed into six stanzas of regularly rhymed *novenari piani* and *tronchi*; the relatively rare meter of the *novenario*, introduced into the Italian *ottocento* libretto by Arrigo Boito,[14] probably reflects the metric structure of the French original. The text is set to music in a style that reminds the listener of dialogues in the German Romantic Lied—Schubert's "Der Tod und das Mädchen" could have been its model. Leoncavallo breaks the regular meter into pieces of dramatic dialogue between two fictional characters, the artist and his Muse, the latter of whom reveals her true identity as Death, come to end the artist's sufferings. The aria is among the outstanding moments of Leoncavallo's score, surpassing by far the more conventional episode of Mimì's death (not to mention the imitation of the *Tristan* prelude that opens Act III):

> — Chi batte a la porta a quest'ora?
> — La gloria son, vieni ad aprir!
> — Va via: ne la mia casa ancora,
> Larva bugiarda, osi venir?
>
> — Apri, son io, son la Ricchezza
> De la tua bella io posso ancor
> Renderti il bacio e la carezza,
> — Va, non puoi rendermi l'amor!
>
> — L'arte son io, la Poesia!
> Vo' darti l'immortalità!
> — Pace sol bramo.—E tu, va via
> Più illusioni il cor non ha.
>
> — Ebben, dischiudi a me le porte
> Poichè la pace brami sol—
> Apri, son io, sono la Morte
> E guarir posso ogni tuo duol.
>
> — Entra. Il tugurio a te dischiudo;
> Perdona a tanta povertà.—
> È la miseria, o spettro ignudo
> Che t'offre l'ospitalità.[15]

---

[14] See Ross (n. 6 above).
[15] Cited from the edition of the libretto (Milan, 1897), 69f.

Although Leoncavallo's libretto shows how much a poet-musician could be concerned with the literary quality of his libretto, doubts about the average Italian opera text seem to have arisen earlier. The craftman-ship of Italian librettists of the nineteenth century gradually faded as the generation of the *Scapigliati* established new standards of individuality for an opera libretto. The collection of essays entitled *In teatro* that Ferdinando Fontana published in 1884 provides an outstanding example of self-criticism (one to which the author of the hapless libretti for Puccini's *Le villi* and *Edgar* seems fully entitled). Although Fontana's theoretical position may no longer seem convincing, his criticism of the poetic qualities of contemporary libretti is striking:

> In fact, an opera libretto, however carefully prepared, cannot be other than a degradation of poetry and poets. If you want to convince yourself of the absurdity to which a libretto can reduce a poet, even a great one, you have only to read the libretti of Augier or even of Victor Hugo.—The libretto must serve no one but the composer and the singers; to the public one should give the poem, that is, the poetry; and if here and there in the libretto, as sometimes occurs, there are lines that are true poetry, the poem (I repeat) can be presented to them, and the rest rejected.[16]

II

In 1889 Pietro Mascagni decided to set aside Andrea Maffei's translation of Heinrich Heine's tragedy *William Ratcliff* in favor of *Cavalleria rusticana*, a libretto that would enable him to win the Sonzogno competition for the best one-act opera and make him famous overnight. But he then returned to his first project, which was completed and performed for the first time in 1895. Mascagni maintained throughout his life that *Guglielmo Ratcliff* was his best opera.[17] The first printed editions of the libretto are unique in Italian publishing practice. The libretto of a *Literaturoper* normally presents the abridged text as it was set to music by the composer; but Mascagni insisted on publishing Heine's complete text, in Maffei's translation, with deleted passages underlined to show where excisions had reduced the drama to manageable length. Mascagni's cuts are surprisingly few and serve mainly to focus the interest of the audience on the central conflict.

A crucial problem, however, arose in the rhythmic structure of Maffei's translation of Heine's meter, the traditional blank verse of German clas-

---

[16] *In teatro* (Rome, 1884), 112.
[17] See his letters to Vittorio Gianfranceschi in Morini, *Pietro Mascagni*, I, 255–84.

sical drama. Following a well-established Italian tradition, Maffei used the *endecasillabo sciolto* throughout, with the exception of a few passages—mostly in Margarita's part—that are also in a different meter in the German original. The syllable-counting basis of Italian verse thus necessitated a text in which virtually all the lines show a high degree of similarity in both metrical structure and individual rhythm. In his review of the opera's Milanese premiere, Luigi Torchi pointed out that the uniform verse structure of Maffei's translation created a very difficult task for the composer, with repercussions for the musical declamation of the text and its formal structure.[18]

Since the theory of Italian verse structure allows for the *endecasillabo* a variety of subdivisions into smaller units, as well as a relatively free distribution of accents (something absent in other Italian meters),[19] the *endecasillabo sciolto* easily acquires the character of a prose text. Despite the resulting variety in rhythm, *Guglielmo Ratcliff* is probably the only example of an Italian opera libretto that features one meter throughout, and the special nature of the text demonstrably influenced Mascagni's music. A comparison of two examples from Act I of Mascagni's score reveals the structural difference between "normal" libretti and a metrically homogeneous text. In the first example, Count Douglas tells his future wife Maria and her father MacGregor about life in London. The music depicts the idea of continuous activity, the ceaseless life of a big city as seen from the solitude of a Scottish castle:

> È sempre il vecchio andazzo.
> Vi si corre a cavallo ed in calesse,
> Un premere, un calcar per ogni via;
> Di giorno vi si dorme, e della notte
> Vi si fa giorno; e sale all'uso aperte
> De' lottatori; e quel non mai sospeso
> Succedersi di crocchî e di banchetti.
> Drurilàn, Coventgarda han sempre folla
> Di spettatori, e l'opera vi romba.
> Note di banca d'una lira, in cambio
> Di note musicali; e: "Dio—vi s'urla—
> Salvi il Re!" Nelle mèscite più buje
> Stanno politicando i patrioti,
> Soscrivono, scommettono, bestemmiano,

[18] *Rivista Musicale Italiana*, 2 (1895), 294f.
[19] W. Theodor Elwert, *Italienische Metrik* (Munich, 1968), 54–65. I am indebted to Peter Ross for an exchange of ideas on the relationship between verse and music that has substantially influenced the following discussion.

Sbadigliano, e fan molle il gorgozzule
Alla prosperità dell'Inghilterra.[20]

The first line, "È sempre il vecchio andazzo," appears as a *settenario* but is only the second part of an *endecasillabo*, since traditionally lines in Italian operatic recitative can be divided between two or more speakers: the final words of Maria's question about life in London ("nulla ne giunge") constitute the first part, thus creating a regular *endecasillabo a minori*.[21] Douglas's third line employs *dialefe*: the normally elided "premere un" are separated in order further to emphasize "premere" and "calcar," and the musical consequence is the triplet on the first quarter of m. 6 in the Allegretto ritenuto section (see Ex. 1). The caesura in line 4 is placed after the seventh syllable, as in any regular *endecasillabo a maiori*. Mascagni's music follows the metrical structure closely and underlines the juxtaposition of day and night in Heine's text. The remaining three and a half lines are set to music in a continuous flow of words, interrupted only by the long note on "sospe...so," which depicts the delay of time expressed in Douglas's text. By this point, Mascagni has set out the underlying model of movement; he leaves the region of the tonic in order to reach an extended dominant section that starts with the word "Drurilàn" (the Italian spelling of the Drury Lane Theatre).

Mascagni's musical prosody rarely follows the subdivision into semantic units that would be used by a normal speaker; but neither does his setting of Maffei's verse respect the intrinsic structure of the *endecasillabi*. While the lines of text are kept together by an accompaniment pattern that dictates the speed of musical declamation, several techniques keep the stresses of single words in line with the rhythm of the accompaniment: triplets, the subdivision of one sixteenth into two thirty-second-notes ("notte vi si fa giorno"), artificial dieresis ("ma–i") not prefigured in Maffei's text, and the separation of musical and speech accent ("Drúrilan"). Although Mascagni manages to set very long lines of text with great skill, the impression of an indefinite rhythmic declamation prevails, because the more prose-like structure of *endecasillabi sciolti* does not meet with an equivalent structure in the music itself, while the rhythmic structure of the musical declamation appears as a mere consequence of the rhythms of the accompaniment to which it is subordinated.

The second example, another narrative that informs the audience about the personal history of the characters onstage, occurs in MacGregor's part. Induced by events to tell Douglas the history of Maria's unhappy former lovers, her father begins by describing William Ratcliff's

---

[20] Libretto of *Guglielmo Ratcliff* (Milan, 1905), 11.
[21] Elwert, 54–58.

EXAMPLE 1. MASCAGNI, *Guglielmo Ratcliff* (MILAN: SONZOGNO, 1895), PP. 20–22

not- te vi si fa gior- no; e sa- le al- l'u- so a- per- te de' lot- ta-

-to- ri e quel non ma- i so- spe- - - so suc-

-ce- der- si di croc- chi e di ban- chet- ti.

Ex. 1 (*cont.*)

unrequited passion for her and then goes on to tell how, since Ratcliff's departure, each of Maria's suitors has been found dead on his wedding-day, killed at the "Negro Sasso" (Schwarzenstein). The following passage, taken from the first edition of Mascagni's libretto, shows how the composer canceled half-lines regardless of their structure as *endecasillabi sciolti*:

> *Con animo tranquillo il luttuoso*
> *Racconto udite.*—Il sesto anno già corre
> Che nel nostro castello uno studente
> Pellegrino arrivò. Venìa costui
> D'Edimburgo, e chiamavasi Guglielmo
> Ratcliff. Io conosciuto un tempo avea,
> —E ben, ben conosciuto!—il padre suo,
> Di nome Edvardo; e quindi accolsi il figlio
> Ospitalmente, *e di tetto e di mensa*
> *Per un quindici dì gli fui cortese.*
> Egli vide mia figlia e troppo addentro
> Negli occhi la fissò; poi die' principio
> Ai sospiri, ai languori, alle querele,
> Tanto che la fanciulla aperto e netto
> Comprendere gli fe' che l'era uggioso.[22]

A comparison of Maffei's text with Mascagni's setting reveals that the inversion of the first words immediately destroys the metrical structure of the *endecasillabi* (Ex. 2). The first lines establish a sequence of pseudo-meters completely different from the verse structure created by Maffei:

Già corre il sesto anno	(7)
che nel nostro castello	(7)
uno studente	(5)
pellegrino arrivò	(7)

Obviously, the first line has to be read with *dialefe* in order to appear as a *settenario*; in this context of artificially created *quinari* and *settenari* one *senario* would have destroyed the rhythmic fluency of the musical declamation. But despite Mascagni's artificial re-ordering of verse lines, the impression of a prose-like configuration prevails. The feeling of true *endecasillabi* is re-established only by the line "E chiamavasi Guglielmo Ratcliff," which was not a metrical unit in Maffei's text. The following line, an *endecasillabo* that Mascagni deprives of its first two syllables ("Ratcliff"), is artificially stretched by dieresis ("I–o") and *dialefe*

---

[22] *Guglielmo Ratcliff*, 15f.

EXAMPLE 2. *Guglielmo Ratcliff* (MILAN, 1895), PP. 47–49

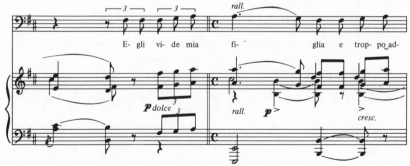

Ex. 2 (*cont.*)

("conosciuto / *un*") in order to form a regular *endecasillabo*. As a result, the crucial syllables "E ben, ben conosciuto!" are completely isolated. They are further stressed by a declamation that makes them seem artificially unimportant; only during Act IV will the drama reveal that "conosciuto" here takes the meaning of "killed." The following lines, "il padre suo, di nome Edvardo" and "e quindi accolsi il figlio ospitalmente," seem to form a couplet, musically treated as one *quinario doppio* and one *endecasillabo*. In the next verse, Mascagni composed the first straight *endecasillabo* of this section; but by cutting the whole verse into irregular sections he created out of this *endecasillabo* and the first half of the following line three autonomous verse lines, which seem to fit perfectly into the modern tradition of Italian recitative verse:

Egli vide mia figlia	(7)
e troppo addentro	(5)
negli occhi la fissò,	(7)

The underlying rhythmic model is kept for the setting of the next lines of verse in order to provide a metrical scheme for the word-setting; Mascagni's intention is obvious from the inversion of the words "languori" and "querele," which provides him with rhythmic units of speech of the necessary length. The resulting meter, as perceived by the listener, appears to be a combination of *quinari* and *quaternari*, an alternation that corresponds to the regular change between eighth-note triplets and normal eighth-notes at the beginning of each verse:

poi die' principio / ai sospiri,	(5 + 4)
alle querele, / ai languori,	(5 + 4)

Only in the following two lines does Mascagni attempt to create two normal *endecasillabi* in his musical setting. The first one benefits from the traditional caesura that separates the verse line into two unequal halves, one *settenario* and one *quinario*, whereas the second line is pronounced rapidly in order to reach the final cadence of the section. In the further development of MacGregor's arioso, the melody of the beginning of this section recurs frequently. Meant to underline the parallelism of events, it creates a uniformity of meter that was certainly prefigured by the metrical structure of the underlying poem.

As this analysis suggests, Mascagni treated Maffei's *endecasillabi* as if they were a prose text, establishing his subdivisions in pseudo-meters of his own. In other words, Mascagni's method of word-setting seems to neglect the frame of Maffei's poetic structure, a frame that does not reflect the semantic units of the text; instead he develops a metrical structure that imparts a quasi-natural declamation, thus building his own system of rhythmic and referential correspondences. Nevertheless, the problem of setting to music an endless chain of *endecasillabi* was not fully solved; the harmonic basis of the composer's language still relies heavily on a regular cadence structure, and this creates recurrent symmetrical groups of bars that sometimes contradict the metrical implications of the text. A peculiar example of the artificial regularity of Mascagni's musical language is provided by Willie's "Padre nostro" at the beginning of Act II. The only prose passage in the entire libretto of *Guglielmo Ratcliff* is reduced by its musical setting to a chorale-like structure of surprisingly regular shape. The music outlines a form that could be represented by the scheme:

$$A - A - B - B' - A' - A'' - A''$$

in which A'' stands for the closing cadential phrase—underlining the words "e non lasciarci tentar dal male!"—that Tom sings twice with special emphasis. The whole structure is then repeated, and Willie's inability to sing the final sentence directs the interest of the audience to the peculiar character of Guglielmo Ratcliff.

III

The next attempt at the direct composition of a pre-existing play was made eleven years after the premiere of *Guglielmo Ratcliff*. After setting one libretto by Fontana (*Asrael* [1889]), a mixture of *Mefistofele* and *Lohengrin* in terms of plot and local color, and two by Luigi Illica (*Cristoforo Colombo* [1892] and *Germania* [1902]), which were to remain his greatest successes, Alberto Franchetti decided to tackle the recently published "pastoral tragedy" *La figlia di Iorio* (1904), written by d'Annunzio for Eleonora Duse. The opera (though it remains virtually unknown) opens a new chapter in the history of Italian *Literaturoper*, if only because the tradition of setting texts by d'Annunzio was to continue for more than a decade and includes Mascagni's *Parisina* (1913), Riccardo Zandonai's *Francesca da Rimini* (1914), Ildebrando Pizzetti's *Fedra* (1915), and Italo Montemezzi's *La nave* (1918).

We can only speculate on why Franchetti became the first composer to use a play by d'Annunzio as an opera libretto. Settings of earlier plays by d'Annunzio would certainly have been possible; the fact that they did not occur should probably be attributed to a structural feature of his early plays: *Sogno d'un mattino di primavera* (1897), *Sogno d'un tramonto d'autunno* (1899), *La città morta* (1898), *La Gioconda* (1898), and *La Gloria* (1899) are all written in prose, a form that had little attraction for composers still used to an elaborate verse structure as the basis for the rhythmical shaping of musical phrases. But perhaps it was merely that Franchetti was very wealthy, and thus able to pay the exorbitant fees that d'Annunzio regularly asked from composers wanting to use his texts—fees which inspired doubts even in so successful a composer as Puccini.[23]

Whatever the case, it is certainly significant that most of the dramas by d'Annunzio that were to provide the text for an opera were set in a well-defined period of Italian history. The imaginary beginning of Venetian culture during the barbarian invasions ("negli anni della fruttifera Incarnazione del Figliuolo di Dio 552"), which constitutes the dramatic kernel of *La nave* (1908), belongs to the most impressive creations of local color in Italian drama of the *fin de siècle*, as does the epoch of Dante that serves as historical background in *Francesca da Rimini* and *Parisina*.[24]

A comparison between two opera libretti based on the story of Francesca da Rimini in Dante's *Divina Commedia* will reveal the extent to which d'Annunzio's imagination provided the opera composer with a highly original vision of scenic events and local color. Antonio Ghislanzoni's libretto, set by Antonio Cagnoni in 1878, describes the setting for the crucial encounter between Francesca and Paolo il Bello in a very down-to-earth way:

Large courtyard with colonnades.—To the right, backstage, a practicable grand staircase, completely decorated with flags and rich canopies.—To the left, to the far side of the colonnade, a chapel.—On the right wing of the colonnade, in center stage, the great door of the palace.—Two tables furnished with food and wine.[25]

A comparison with d'Annunzio's elaborate setting for a love scene amid war between the Ghibelline and Guelf factions may seem unfair, but one should keep in mind that only fourteen years separate the two descriptions:

---

[23] The moment at which Italian composers choose to set d'Annunzio's tragedies coincides, strangely enough, with a profound crisis in the libretto-writing of Luigi Illica, for over twenty years a central figure in Italian opera. Illica's correspondence with the firm of Ricordi, preserved in the Biblioteca Passerini-Landi in Piacenza, reveals how much he suffered during the last years of his life from a sense of being outdated by the increasingly numerous settings of original plays by d'Annunzio. However, Illica's correspondence with Ricordi and with Puccini gives some hints of the difficulty of obtaining permission to use one of d'Annunzio's plays.

[24] The influence of "dannunzianesimo" on stage was by no means limited to Italy; Thomas Mann's *Fiorenza* (1911), as well as the early stage works of Hugo von Hofmannsthal, bear the mark of d'Annunzio's vision. See Jürgen Maehder, "Bühnenvision und Stoffwahl in der italienischen Oper des Fin de siècle," *Perspektiven der Opernforschung I* (n. 3 above).

[25] *Francesca da Rimini* (Turin, 1888), 7.

There appears a piazza with a round tower, in the houses of the Malatesta. Two lateral staircases of ten steps rise from the piazza to the stone floor of the tower; a third staircase, between the other two, descends to the lower floors, passing through a trap door. One sees the square battlements of the Guelf faction fortified with turrets and openings for pouring down molten lead. A powerful catapult lifts its head out of its supports and stretches out its framework of twisted ropes. Heavy crossbows with large-headed, short, and square bolts, ballistas, arcoballistas, and other rope artillery are placed here and there, with their cranks, pulleys, wheels, wires, and levers. The summit of the Malatesta tower, crowned with engines and arms that stand out in the murky air, overlooks the city of Rimini, where the wing-shaped battlements of the highest Ghibelline tower can dimly be seen. On the right is a door; on the left, a narrow, fortified window looking out on the Adriatic.[26]

If we add to this description elements of the stage action, the Greek Fire displayed by Francesca at the beginning of the battle, actual fighting with arrows striking the soldiers, the firing of a huge siege catapult, and—in between—the tenderness between Paolo Malatesta and Francesca, then the vast difference between Ghislanzoni's and d'Annunzio's visions becomes even more obvious.

However, the task of setting to music a play by d'Annunzio required not only extraordinary insight into the timing of actions on stage, an insight that had to dictate the inevitable cuts in his plays, but also a capacity for creating musical ambience—in the double sense of *couleur locale* and *couleur historique*—that could match the individuality of d'Annunzio's vision. It was perhaps inevitable that Franchetti, the first composer to set a play by d'Annunzio to music, failed in both respects. The choice of *La figlia di Iorio* may seem today less understandable than it was at the time; but the shortcomings of his score, especially the lack of any definite local color other than a traditional exercise in vaguely "pastoral" style, are much more obvious after the experiences of twentieth-century opera.[27]

The technique of cutting a play by d'Annunzio acquired particular importance in the three operas that will now be treated in more detail. While Tito Ricordi's adaptations of *Francesca da Rimini* and *La nave* for the operatic stage perfectly reflected both the needs of the music and the necessity to reduce the personnel of a prose play to the more limited number

[26] Libretto of *Francesca da Rimini* (Milan, 1914), 21.

[27] Jay R. Nicolaisen, *Italian Opera in Transition, 1871–1893* (Ann Arbor, 1980), 12, draws attention to the little-known tradition of Italian "pastoral" operas, mostly by composers from southern Italy.

of singers normally available, d'Annunzio's adaptation of his own *La figlia di Iorio* rarely met Franchetti's musical and dramatic needs. D'Annunzio removed several secondary characters, but he was certainly mistaken in changing the course of the action in Act II, where Mila di Codra's attempt to commit suicide and her violence against Anna Onna were necessary ingredients in the psychological constellation of love and violence so typical of his work. What remains of d'Annunzio's archaic cruelty in Franchetti's score may appear to a modern audience as the sordid incest between Lazaro di Roio and Mila di Codra, the daughter of the sorcerer Iorio and mistress of Lazaro's son Aligi, who kills his father in an attempt to protect her.[28] The composer's musical language, still firmly rooted in the traditions of the *ottocento*, lacked the capacity to express d'Annunzio's psychological characterization of a pre-rational society in which superstition and the absolute authority of the older generation substitute for any coherent system of ethics. This fundamental misunderstanding of d'Annunzio's dramaturgy doomed the opera. After the expiration of Franchetti's exclusive rights in 1934, d'Annunzio offered his tragedy to Ildebrando Pizzetti, who was to compose his opera only after World War II.[29] A commemorative article on d'Annunzio and the music of his time (written in 1939) succinctly sums up the critical reaction to Franchetti's score: "As a whole, the music of Alberto Franchetti unequivocally spoils *La figlia di Iorio* and makes it into a really dreadful *melodramma*" (*un assai brutto melodrammaccio*).[30]

IV

Of the two subsequent operas based on plays by d'Annunzio, Mascagni's *Parisina* was written in direct collaboration with the poet, then in exile at Arcachon.[31] Although it may seem strange to include in this study a text explicitly written to be set to music, the complicated history of its creation as well as the structure of d'Annunzio's drama, which was also performed from 1921 on as a play, confirm the fact that the poet did not take the

---

[28] Only Franchetti's autograph score and copies of the piano-vocal score survived the bombing of the Ricordi Company in World War II. I wish to thank Mimma Guastoni, Luciana Pestalozza, Fausto Broussard, and most especially my friend Carlo Clausetti for their assistance during my work in the Ricordi archives.

[29] See d'Annunzio's letter to Pizzetti in Guido M. Gatti, *Ildebrando Pizzetti* (Milan, 1954), 49f.

[30] Luciano Tomelleri, "Gabriele d'Annunzio, ispiratore di musicisti," *Rivista Musicale Italiana*, 43 (1939), 198.

[31] A vivid account of the collaboration between the two during Mascagni's stay at the villa Castel Fleury (Bellevue, near Paris) has been given by Mascagni's daughter, Emilia Mascagni, *Si inginocchi la più piccina* (Milan, 1940).

musicability of his work into consideration. Neither in dramatic structure nor in poetic language does *Parisina* differ significantly from *Francesca da Rimini*. Announced in 1902 as the continuation of the trilogy *I Malatesta* that began with *Francesca da Rimini*, *Parisina* was offered first to Puccini (in 1906), then to Franchetti.[32] It thus seems probable that d'Annunzio was actually offering Mascagni a text written several years previously. The most important reason for including *Parisina* among *Literaturopern*, however, is the role assumed by Mascagni during the composition of the opera. His approach, cutting and changing the text of a pre-existing play according to his specific musical needs, did not differ substantially from that of any other composer:

> The opera lasts about three and a half hours, played continuously, without breaks. There are exactly 1400 verses, of which I have cut 330. The cuts were made by me, and they cost me hard work and thought because, more than cutting, I stripped the poet's excessive wordiness from the tragedy. I did not touch anything essential to d'Annunzio's whole work. But in order to do this, I had to treat the verse form in such a way that no cut would leave a single line defective. Therefore I had to reconstruct the verses with d'Annunzio's own words, and I had the great satisfaction of seeing myself completely approved of by the poet, and of receiving sincere congratulations for my "literary and poetic labor." Re-examining *Parisina* I believe that, if nothing else, it represents a rare example of fidelity in the interpretation of the word.[33]

The fact that the cutting of d'Annunzio's text and the reconstructing of its verse structure were left to Mascagni leaves the poet's role in their collaboration uncertain. As Mascagni and his biographers have indicated, d'Annunzio's task was apparently limited to reading his drama to the composer who, following the poet's declamation, was able to create three and a half hours of music in vocal score within 134 days. It is certainly important that Mascagni's work took shape under the direct influence of d'Annunzio's reading; suddenly his skill in handling free rhythms and continuous chains of *versi sciolti* corresponded to the most advanced standards of composition that his Italian contemporaries had developed. Although the central conflict of *Parisina* is basically static,[34] the work

[32] See Beghelli (n. 5 above), 610f, and Morini (n. 17 above), I, 363.

[33] Morini, I, 375. On Mascagni's treatment of d'Annunzio's verse, see Luigi Baldacci, "Quattro libretti per Pietro Mascagni," *Rassegna Musicale Curci*, 28 (December 1975), 16f.

[34] See Tomelleri (n. 30 above), 214–17; Rein A. Zodergeld, "Ornament und Emphase. Illica, d'Annunzio und der Symbolismus," *Oper und Operntext*, ed. Jens Malte Fischer

contains several dramatically vigorous and effective scenes. The following example, La Verde's solo passage, is taken from the very beginning of the opera and fulfills the function of an introductory chorus. D'Annunzio's opening lines are conceived as a series of rhymed *endecasillabi* with changing caesura, the resulting *settenari* and *quinari* alternating freely:

> Oimè grido il mattino, oimè la sera,
> oimè la notte, oimè da mezzo giorno,
> oimè di verno, oimè di primavera,
> oimè quando la state fa ritorno,
> oimè se il cor si strugge, oimè se spera,
> oimè s'io poso, oimè se vado a torno,
> oimè se dormo, oimè da tutte l'ore,
> oimè pena, oimè doglia, oimè 'l mio core![35]

The musical rhythm (see Ex. 3) seems to assure a natural declamation of d'Annunzio's verses but, as the insertion of one bar in 4/4 meter shows, the resulting regularity is created by depriving the musical structure of its autonomy; the second and second-to-last syllables of each *settenario* or *quinario* act as fixed points that guarantee the symmetrical appearance of the musical declamation. The intermediate syllables are free; following the dictates of the text, Mascagni used eighth-notes or eighth-note triplets in order to fill the space between the two stressed syllables of the line. The last line emphasizes that a particular rhythmic pattern is maintained throughout the piece: the words "oimè pena, oimè doglia" cover virtually the same span as one longer section that starts with "oimè" in each of the other verses, so that an identical length for the first half of each line is maintained.

In contrast to the relatively closed structure of these first lines, the ensuing example demonstrates the extent to which Mascagni allowed freedom of declamation. The dialogue between Stella dell'Assassino and Ugo d'Este, her illegitimate son by the Duke Niccolò d'Este, centers on the jealousy Stella feels for the Duke's new mistress, Parisina Malatesta. She reproaches her son for accepting the new situation and not defending the interests of his mother against Parisina, whom she sees as an immoral intruder. Mascagni slightly shortened d'Annunzio's text without affecting its verse structure; its regular recitative-like structure is composed of *endecasillabi*, *settenari*, and *quinari*, as any recitative section in an opera from the later nineteenth century would have been:

(Heidelberg, 1985), 160–62; Cesare Orselli, "Panneggi medievali per la donna decadente: *Parisina e Francesca,*" *Chigiana*, 37 (1985), 135–50.

[35] Libretto of *Parisina* (Milan, 1913), 8.

Example 3. Mascagni, *Parisina* (Milan; Curci, 1974), pp. 8–9

-mè, se il cor si strug-ge, o-i-mè se spe-ra, o-i-

-mè s'i-o po-so, o-i-mè se va-do a tor-no, o-i-

-mè se dor-mo, o-i-mè da tut-te l'o-re, o-i-mè

pe-na, o-i-mè do-glia, o-i- mè_____ 'l mi-o co-re!_____

STELLA: Sogni di leonessa,	(7)
se protesa è la branca	(7)
non per morire ma per dar la morte.	(11)
Tanto non sai? Se vivere non vuoi	(11)
come tu vivi,	(5)
non osi tu guardare la vergogna	(11)
nostra e l'ammenda?	(5)
UGO: Ah, che vuoi dunque? Di': ch'io mi ribelli	(11)
al mio padre? ch'io tagli il nodo? }	(11)
STELLA: No.	
Sofferitore sei. Sei paziente.	(11—dieresis)
Ti curvi al giogo, ruminando l'odio,	(11)
come il vitello rumina il suo strame,	(11)
Ugo bastardo.	(5)
UGO: Hai il pungolo crudele,	(7)
madre. }	(7)
STELLA: Non hai più madre.	
Hai la matrigna	(5)
che ti dà'l pane e rigna.	(7)
E tu t'appaghi di menar la vita	(11)
del bastardello,	(5)
e i suoi cani di seguito tenerle	(11)
a guinzaglio, e portare al collo l'arpa;	(11)
chè Maestro Domenico Calceda	(11—dieresis)
per te le fece il cordoncin di seta. . . .	(11)
UGO: Ah, leonessa, come mordi e strazii![36]	(11)

Mascagni's setting of these lines (Ex. 4) strictly follows the metrical structure imagined by d'Annunzio; the musical declamation appears tailored to the gestural content of the dialogue. If we examine the performance instructions, it immediately becomes evident that the music of this passage attempts to follow the inflections of natural speech: "Violento," "Sinistro," "Ambiguo," "Risoluto," "Freddo," "Implacabile," "Ironico," and "Furente" may seem exaggerated for a musical passage of only four pages, but these instructions convey exactly the emotions that Mascagni wanted for each phrase. Not only the frequent changes in musical meter (3/4; 2/4; 4/4; 5/4; 4/4; 3/4; 2/4; 4/4; 3/4; 2/4; 4/4; 3/4; 4/4 in the course of 47 bars!) but above all the continual changes of tempo, expressed by the above-mentioned instructions and by the changing metronome

[36] *Parisina*, 18f.

EXAMPLE 4. *Parisina* (MILAN, 1974), PP. 62–65

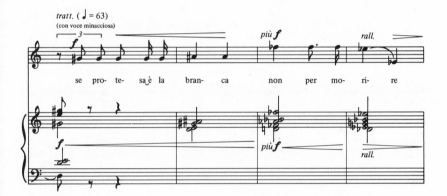

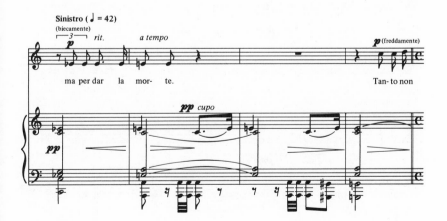

Ex. 4 (cont.)

119

Ex. 4 (*cont.*)

marks, serve to create a true sense of musical prose. Unfortunately, the overall structure of the musical syntax in *Parisina* cannot cope with the complexity of speech declamation. While individual events of the dramatic dialogue are undoubtedly impressive, no motivic or thematic links are provided by the musical structure to bind together the sequence of disconnected dramatic gestures.

The fact that *Parisina* was an almost complete failure shows that the novelty of the score lacked the counterbalance of a solid musical structure. Other passages of the work, such as the pseudo-Gregorian chants that are heard at the beginning of Act II, may be inferior in sheer musical quality, but such shortcomings do not suffice to explain why *Parisina* was denied performances granted to lesser operas. The novelty of musical declamation, especially in comparison to Mascagni's own earlier works, must have assaulted an audience expecting from the composer of *Cavalleria rusticana* a more popular score full of melodic invention.

In the history of Italian word-setting, however, Mascagni's solution appears as a gesture toward current European tendencies in musical prose and in setting prose texts to music; the influence of Strauss's *Salome* seems clear. *Parisina* and ensuing works helped create the Italian tradition of free rhythmic setting of prose texts that appears in a fully developed state in Alfano's *Leggenda di Sakùntala* (text by the composer after Kalidasa's drama [Bologna, 1921]). However, as can be seen from Alfano's later neoclassical works (*Cyrano de Bergerac*, after Rostand, originally in French, 1935), the increasing simplification of musical structure during the Fascist era did not allow further development of these tendencies until after World War II.

V

When *Francesca da Rimini* was performed for the first time at the Teatro Regio of Turin in February 1914, Zandonai was by no means an unknown composer. His *Conchita* (1911), based on a libretto discarded by Puccini, had brought him a certain measure of fame. Zandonai was favored by Tito Ricordi and greeted by the Italian musical world as the successor to Puccini, and it was Ricordi who not only introduced him to d'Annunzio but was also responsible for making the cuts in the drama. Zandonai describes the memorable encounter:

> Paris 1912–13. First meeting with the Poet. The publisher Tito Ricordi must read to him the libretto reduction of *Francesca da Rimini*. The poem has been reduced to a size identical with Boito's *Falstaff*, and we greatly fear that the enormous pruning of lines, scenes, and

characters will seem to him a cruel mutilation. I confess that my emotion was intense, because on the Poet's verdict depended the musical realization of the poem that had already occupied me for months and months. At the end of the uninterrupted reading, d'Annunzio, calm and smiling, got up, shook the hand of his friend the publisher and pronounced these exact words: "Well done, Tito; you are truly a man of the theater; your reduction is perfect and, when the libretto is published, I want your name to appear next to mine."[37]

Tito Ricordi's extensive cuts include the loss of several secondary characters, most of the references to political events in Rimini, Cesena, and Forlì, much repetitive text, and many details that fill the play with medieval color.[38] The archaic features of d'Annunzio's vocabulary and artificial grammar fulfill on the level of the poetic language a function similar to that of the *couleur historique* in Zandonai's music. Fully aware of the unique possibilities for local color that d'Annunzio's play offered the composer, Zandonai created a highly individual orchestral sound for the fictitious medieval ambience of northern Italy. *Francesca da Rimini* is also one of the first examples of a use of historical instruments onstage in order to depict the music of the past: lute and "viola pomposa,"[39] the instrument of the Giullare, provide historical timbres for d'Annunzio's medieval Adriatic setting.[40]

The best example of Zandonai's sophisticated use of *couleur historique* can be found in the women's chorus of Act I, which serves as an introduction to Francesca's first appearance onstage. A comparison of Francesca's first appearance in the play and in the opera illustrates the amount of text eliminated as well as the method according to which the cuts were effected. This scene seems prefigured by d'Annunzio's play: the exposition of the main conflict follows the rules that governed the dramaturgy of nineteenth-century opera as well as a great part of contemporary dramatic literature. In accordance with the tradition of *Grand Opéra*, the principal soloists appear gradually in the course of a great tableau, prepared by the chorus and secondary characters of the same voice range. Francesca's sister Samaritana and her maidens Biancofiore, Alda, Gar-

---

[37] Bruno Cagnoli, *Riccardo Zandonai* (Trent, 1983), 56.

[38] Tomelleri (see n. 30 above), 189f, criticized Ricordi for cutting the character of Bannino, thus destroying the balance between the children of Guido da Polenta and Malatesta da Verucchio, particularly the mirror-like function of Bannino and Malatestino within Francesca's drama. See also Orselli (n. 34 above), 144–46.

[39] See Marco Tiella, "Gli strumenti per la musica antica in 'Francesca da Rimini' e 'Giulietta e Romeo,' " *Riccardo Zandonai*, ed. Renato Chiesa (Milan, 1984), 307–10.

[40] See Piero Santi, "Arcaismi e folklorismi nella musica italiana del primo Novecento," *Chigiana*, 37 (1985), 73–80.

senda, Altichiara, and Adonella form a female chorus that acts very much like the traditional introductory ensemble in a Meyerbeer opera.

A close examination of d'Annunzio's text and its transformation into the libretto reveals that more lines in Francesca's part were cut than were preserved. The single line "Amor le fa cantare!" serves to underline the caesura between two stanzas of the chorus; Francesca's voice is combined only rarely with the voices of the chorus in order to allow the soloist's timbre to be heard alone. The following text shows Tito Ricordi's cuts in italics and indicates Zandonai's changes in brackets, but excludes all the stage directions, which were also reduced:

CORO: Oimè che adesso io provo
 che cosa è troppo amore. Oimè.
 Oimè ch'egli è uno ardore
 che al cor mi coce. Oimè.
FRANCESCA: Amor le fa cantare!   [Zandonai:]
CORO: Oimè penare atroce   Oimè che doglia acerba
 ch'al tristo cor si serba. Oimè.   alla mia vita. Oimè.
FRANCESCA: *Son come inebriate dagli odori!*
 Non le odi tu? Con melodia dolente
 cantan le cose
 della gioia perfetta.   [Zandonai:]
CORO: Oimè che doglia acerba   Oimè penare atroce
 alla mia vita. Oimè.   ch'al tristo cor si serba. Oimè.
FRANCESCA: *Come l'acqua corrente*
 che va che va, e l'occhio non s'avvede,
 cosí l'anima mia . . .
                                        [Zandonai:]
                                        CORO: Oimè che doglia acerba
                                         alla mia vita.Oimè.[41]

The creation of a coherent musical form from d'Annunzio's alternating stanzas for chorus and soloist must be interpreted as a product of the collaboration between Tito Ricordi's shaping of the text and Zandonai's rearrangement of the chorus lines. The logical sequence from "troppo amore" through "doglia acerba" to "penare atroce" confers on the chorus a unity lacking in d'Annunzio's version. The repetition of the first stanza closes the entire chorus and helps to integrate Francesca's most extended solo passage. In his adaptation of d'Annunzio's text, Tito Ricordi retained only the phrases that contained important information for

---

[41] Gabriele d'Annunzio, *Tragedie, Sogni e Misteri*, I (Verona, 1942), 514f; Libretto of *Francesca da Rimini* (Milan, 1914), 13f; Riccardo Zandonai, *Francesca da Rimini*, Riduzione per canto e pianoforte (Milan, 1914), 39–47.

the drama. In this passage, the synaesthetic vision of scents that are "heard" must have seemed superfluous to the composer and his collaborator. The phrase "Con melodia dolente cantan le cose della gioia perfetta" was certainly considered redundant: Francesca absorbs the song of the women's chorus into her own feelings and gradually reveals the sensations of her own soul. A more extended description of her maidens' and sisters' feelings would have diverted attention from her own emotions, which form the kernel of the drama. The adaptation of the stanzas for chorus obviously follows Zandonai's predilection for closed musical structures. The fact that the differences between the piano reduction, which reflects the shape that the text actually took in Zandonai's composition, and Tito Ricordi's libretto version are as large as those between the latter and d'Annunzio's original confirms the active part taken by Zandonai.

Zandonai's own account of an important change in Act III, to which the poet acquiesced without hesitation, underlines the composer's active role in the shaping of *Francesca da Rimini*:

> Second meeting. I wanted to ask the Poet for several modifications to lines and the replacement, in Act III, of the passage in which Paolo narrates to Francesca his Florentine meetings with Casella, Guido Cavalcanti, and "a young man of the Alighieri named Dante." These historical remarks, at the climactic point of the love duet, chilled my fantasy; and I considered it better, for the lyrical appearance, to replace them with a beautiful poetic flight that would not restrict the free rise of the music. My request, which stemmed from a purely musical criterion, might have seemed exigent, since it required the invention of a new section in the tragedy. D'Annunzio understood me immediately, approved, and promised that he would set to work that day. And he kept his word in an unexpected manner: three hours later he had composed and written out on seven sheets, in the most beautiful calligraphy, the marvelous lines that appear in the third act of the libretto to *Francesca* [. . .] and culminate in that divine "Ahi, che già sento all'arido fiato / sfiorar la primavera nostra!" in which is compressed the entire tragedy.[42]

VI

Zandonai's *Francesca da Rimini* established the standard for Italian *Literaturoper*, and was followed in 1918 by Italo Montemezzi's setting of *La nave*, again on a text adapted to music by Tito Ricordi. Another composer of the *generazione dell'Ottanta*, Ildebrando Pizzetti, developed a

[42] Cagnoli (see n. 37 above), 56f.

method of setting d'Annunzio's verse to music that left the rhythm of speech nearly unaltered, but had to sacrifice the traditional links joining verse structure, musical meter, and melodic as well as rhythmic contours of declamation that had governed Italian opera for centuries. The following example, taken from Act I of d'Annunzio's *Fedra* (1909), which Pizzetti set to music without textual changes in 1909–12,[43] reveals a metrical structure very similar to the passage from *Parisina* discussed above in connection with Ex. 4:

LA SUPPLICE: Ma perché, s'egli ha vinto e se si torna, (11)
perché t'adiri nel tuo cuore senza (11)
gioia? e perché la tua bocca è terribile (11)
come gli archi curvati nella tua (11)
Cnosso, o Minòide?
FEDRA: Li conosci tu   } (11)
i grandi archi cretesi? Tu che parli (11)
con la parola a doppio taglio ascosa (11)
nella guaina pallida (7—dieresis)
non sei la madre tu d'Ippomedonte (11)
ch'ebro mandasti di combattimento (11)
e urlante come Tìade alla Porta (11)
Onca?
LA SUPPLICE: Son quella.   } (11)
FEDRA: Te l'uccise l'asta
cadmèa di bronzo.[44]

Pizzetti's setting of Fedra's words (Ex. 5) shows a frequent change of musical meter similar to Mascagni's in Ex. 4; but while Mascagni's setting tries to capture the emotional expression of each phrase through a sequence of vocal gestures, Pizzetti creates a continuous flow of words, monotonously declaiming on fixed pitches, the music deprived of thematic substance and rhythmic individuality. His score abounds in triplets, quintuplets, sextuplets, and similar rhythmic devices that were introduced in order to correlate the accents of text and musical meter after an uneven number of syllables. As thematic construction and the choice of pitch material also suggest, Pizzetti's *Fedra*—and his earlier incidental music for *La nave*[45]—were created with a conscious attempt to limit the music,

[43] Guido M. Gatti, *Ildebrando Pizzetti* (Milan, 1954), 16, states that Pizzetti, in collaboration with d'Annunzio, cut more than half of the poet's verses in his score.
[44] Gabriele d'Annunzio, *Fedra* (Milan, 1909), 20; libretto of *Fedra* (Milan, 1934), 13f; Ildebrando Pizzetti, *Fedra*, Riduzione per canto e pianoforte (Milan, 1959), 44–46.
[45] See Cesare Orselli, "Primo incontro di Pizzetti con l'estetismo dannunziano: Le musiche per 'La nave,'" and Piero Santi, "La funzione ideologica del modalismo pizzettiano," *Chigiana*, 37 (1985), 51–62 and 81–104.

EXAMPLE 5. PIZZETTI, *Fedra* (MILAN: SONZOGNO, 1959), P. 45

which serves the drama exclusively, depriving itself of any autonomous structure.

The fact that after World War I mainstream Italian composers abandoned setting pre-existing plays to music can be explained only in part by an innate tendency of composers of the *generazione dell'Ottanta* to prefer closed formal structures and return to a clear distinction between dynamic ("recitative") and static ("aria") sections. Certainly, their neoclassical aesthetic favored a return to what was thought to have been the past *grandezza* of Italian opera. Above all, the defensive position taken by conservative composers such as Pizzetti and Zandonai against the musical revolution begun in Vienna and Paris by Schoenberg, Stravinsky, and their pupils and friends isolated Italy from the mainstream of contemporary composition for the stage.[46] On the technical level of musical language adopted by the Italian neoclassicist generation, no musical declamation was conceivable that could have combined the quasi-natural declamation of a prose or prose-like text with a sound structural basis for its pitch construction.

For a few years, Italian *Literaturoper* of the *fin de siècle* opened perspectives on avant-garde music theater and created the musical and technical basis for a fusion of poetry and music that could have rivaled that of other European musical cultures. But after the deaths of Leoncavallo and Puccini an interest in plot rather than in the literary value of texts was reinforced by the pervasive influence of Fascist ideology on the choice of subjects for Italian opera.[47] Propaganda operas such as *Palla de' Mozzi* by Giovacchino Forzano and Gino Marinuzzi (1932), *Guido del popolo* by Arturo Rossato and Igino Robbiani (1932), *Caracciolo* by Rossato and Franco Vittadini (1937), and *Ginevra degli Almieri* by Forzano and Mario Peragallo (1937) returned to traditionally written libretti; even Gian Francesco Malipiero's anti-Fascist *Favola del figlio cambiato* (1933), based on a play by Luigi Pirandello, made no attempt to renew the structural basis of speech composition. A reluctance and inability to accept a new, atonal concept of musical language reduced Italian opera of the Fascist era to a provinciality from which it recovered only after World War II with the dramatic works of Luigi Dallapiccola.

[46] Pizzetti and Zandonai, together with Gian Francesco Malipiero and other composers of the conservative wing, signed the famous manifesto of 17 December 1932 against contemporary music on Italian soil. See Fiamma Nicolodi, *Musica e musicisti nel ventennio fascista* (Fiesole, 1984), 141–43.

[47] See Jürgen Maehder, "Il libretto patriottico nell'Italia della fine del secolo e la raffigurazione dell'Antichità e del Rinascimento nel libretto prefascista italiano," to be published in the Proceedings of the International Musicological Society Congress, Bologna 1987.

Erik's Dream and Tannhäuser's Journey

In the second scene of Wagner's *Der fliegende Holländer*, the hunter Erik tells Daland's daughter Senta of an "ill-fated dream": how Erik dreamt of a sea-captain, how the sea-captain and Senta departed together "over the ocean." In Act III of *Tannhäuser*, Wolfram von Eschenbach demands from Tannhäuser the full story of his pilgrimage to Rome; Tannhäuser obliges.

Erik's Dream, which foreshadows the denouement of the opera, invokes a familiar Romantic topos: a representative of the supernatural intrudes upon humanity. Freud regarded this myth as a representation of repressed fears and their disorienting surges into ordinary thought.[1] Nineteenth-century librettists and dramatists cast the myth in many forms; if it was debased by being taken literally in Marschner's *Der Vampyr* (whose protagonist seems more at home in the penny-dreadful than the unseen realm), it was elevated in *The Lady from the Sea*. Tannhäuser's journey belongs to another genre of Romantic myth. The "Rome Narrative" tells the story of a journey, not a lesson in geography but a depiction of the protagonist's inner wanderings through repentance to a state of grace.

As stories, Erik's Dream and Tannhäuser's Rome Narrative may represent common Romantic types, but as scenes in opera they are unusual. Narrative exposition is commonplace in spoken drama but less common in opera before 1850. Narrative halts dramatic time. So does lyric meditation, but lyric is better suited to life as an operatic aria. Lyric text in opera arias must be denatured by fragmentation and nonsensical repetition, and is calculated precisely to bear such distortions, to be expanded or compressed as needed to fill up aria's musical volume. Few of us care

---

[1] Sigmund Freud, "Das Unheimliche," *Studienausgabe*, IV (Frankfurt am Main, 1982), 243–74; see esp. the analysis of Hoffmann's "Der Sandmann," 250ff. Freud argues (272–73) that not all supernatural personages seem *unheimlich* (sinister/uncanny); in fictional worlds where magical beings belong to the invented everyday (most fairy tales, the doomed souls of *Inferno*, Shakespeare's ghosts), the supernatural figures may be gloomy, pitiful, or frightening, but not profoundly disturbing. *Das Unheimliche* depends in part on this very notion of intrusion, the creation of a fictional world allegedly and convincingly human, into which the sinister, the uncanny, can drift.

how often the Queen of the Night says, "So sei sie dann auf ewig dein," or how she mangles the words and their syntax; as she sings we are listening for musical sense and structure, not literary meaning. But narrative text cannot be twisted into a verbal mass and spread indiscriminately under a musical structure, for narrative must tell its story, in order, and the story must be heard by the listeners. The inviolability of narrative text thus places heavy constraints on any accompanying music; for operatic composers it was easier to avoid the occasion of sin by avoiding narrative exposition. Narrative in early Romantic opera had two traditional modes of presentation: recitative (story told as briskly as possible, with scant musical underpinning), and inserted storytelling song, which might be called a "Ballade," "Romanza," "Lied," "Aria," or "Canzone." Narrative song appeared in opera in many languages, from Pedrillo's "Romanze" in *Die Entführung* to the "Bell Song" in *Lakmé* and beyond. But outside this realm of operatic convention, even in the early nineteenth century, were various experiments, such as the dramatic narrative duet sung by Orestes in Rossini's *Ermione*, or the *Melodram* liberally supplied with musical symbolism in Schubert's *Fierabras*. Erik's Dream and Tannhäuser's Rome Narrative belong to this other realm; one might even say they were intruders from realms of poetry, spoken drama, and novel, which brought with them intimations of other worlds.

I. Erik's Dream

Romantic opera's most common narrative mode is the inserted song, sung to an attentive onstage audience.[2] *Der fliegende Holländer*, of course, includes Senta's famous Ballad, but strophic narrative songs also appear in Marschner's *Vampyr*, Meyerbeer's *Robert le Diable*, and Boieldieu's *La Dame blanche*. These four operas also share a dramaturgical conceit. All invoke the myth of intrusion. The vampire needs no introduction; Meyerbeer's Robert is the half-human child of Satan, bent on contracting his own earthly marriage; the white lady is a betrayed female ghost, an ectoplasmic Donna Elvira, who returns to earth to stalk philandering baritones. The myth in all four operas is both played out onstage and narrated at a critical juncture by one of the characters, who sings a narrative song not knowing he will be an actor in the tale he tells. The four ballad-like narratives are dropped into the surrounding opera like a play-within-the-play, enacting in microcosm the drama that is its context.

The balladic song, an operatic topos of the early nineteenth century, has its roots in Romantic ballad poetry and in musical settings of that

2 Siegfried Goslich, *Die deutsche romantische Oper* (Tutzing, 1975), 249–66.

poetry as Lieder. "Ballad" is used here loosely to refer to the brief, strictly strophic narrative art-poetry typical of the German Romantic tradition.[3] Narrative in the ballad unwinds over multiple verses of identical prosodic and structural design, whose identity is often reinforced by a refrain that repeats at the close of each verse.

The epic formula, or repeated refrain, was typical of the poetry that art-ballad contrived to evoke; that is, of traditional folk-ballad. In folk-ballad, of course, the repeated formula has a critical mnemonic function in the composition, performance, and transmission of the repertory. Yet the refrain is more than this. The repeated text also presages and interprets the events narrated, its recurring sound an ominous thump that articulates the story's progress.[4]

In a sense the repetitive structure of ballad is at war with the narrative its words describe. The narrative, Goethe's poetic "Ur-Ei" with its mixture of dialogue, epic (objective) description, and lyric, represents the passage of time, represents history both played out and commented upon.[5] But this forward-moving pageant is realized within an eternally repeating sonorous structure, and trapped in the unvarying strophic beat. The dialectical tension between narrative metamorphosis and structural repetition is itself a poetic device. The monotony of rhyme, meter, and strophe forces the reader-listener to fix on the meaning of the words and not their sound: to listen to the story. In poetry whose sonorities are more elaborate, whose syntax and strophic design are more baroque, we begin to hear the music of the words rather than their meaning.

But beyond this, the monotony of balladic poetry is used to heighten narrative effects. Goethe's "Der Zauberlehrling"—the story of the sorcerer's apprentice—is a *locus classicus*. We are lulled by the pattern established in the first two stanzas:

> Hat der alte Hexenmeister
> Sich doch einmal wegbegeben!

---

[3] Hegel wrote in 1835 of the ballad as a lyric genre brushed by the narrative mode of epic: "andererseits aber bleibt der Grundton ganz lyrisch; denn nicht die subjektivitätslose Schilderung und Ausmalung des realen Geschehens, sondern umgekehrt die Auffassungsweise und Empfindung des Subjekts . . . ist die Hauptsache," *Aesthetik*, ed. Friedrich Bassenge (Berlin, 1985), II, 474. Goethe regarded the poet-singer, in making his ballads, as mixing epic, lyric, and dramatic elements as needed to realize his "prägnanter Gegenstand," yet the strict strophic structure of such poetry is a hallmark of the lyric: "der Refrain, das Wiederkehren ebendesselben Schlußklanges, gibt dieser Dichtart den entschiedenen lyrischen Charakter." "Ballade, Betrachtung und Auslegung" (1821), *Goethes Werke: Hamburger Ausgabe*, ed. Erich Trunz, I (Hamburg, 1949), 400.

[4] See Otto Holzapfel, "Winterrosen: A German Narrative Love Song," *The Ballad as Narrative* (Odense, 1982), 103–10.

[5] "Ballade, Betrachtung und Auslegung," 400.

Und nun sollen seine Geister
Auch nach meinem Willen leben.
Seine Wort' und Werke
Merkt' ich und den Brauch,
Und mit Geistesstärke
Tu' ich Wunder auch.
　Walle! walle
　Manche Strecke,
　Daß, zum Zwecke,
　Wasser fließe
　Und mit reichem, vollem Schwalle
　Zu dem Bade sich ergieße.

Und nun komm, du alter Besen!
Nimm die schlechten Lumpenhüllen;
Bist schon lange Knecht gewesen:
Nun erfülle meinen Willen!
Auf zwei Beinen stehe,
Oben sei ein Kopf;
Eile nun und gehe
Mit dem Wassertopf!
　Walle, walle
　Manche Strecke,
　Daß, zum Zwecke,
　Wasser fließe
　Und mit reichem, vollem Schwalle
　Zu dem Bade sich ergieße.

(For once at last the old magician / Whom I serve has gone away, / And his spirits, ghostly beings, / Now it's I whom they'll obey. / All his words and sayings / I've made sure to hear, / So with my new-found powers / I'll make miracles appear. / Flowing, flowing, / To its courses, / Magic forces / Water pouring, / And resounding, waves unending / To the well in torrents roaring.

So, old broomstick, come before me, / Take these rags, your tattered cloak, / Long you've been my master's servant, / Obey instead the spell I spoke. / Legs you'll need for walking, / And a head up top, / Take the bucket, hurry, / March, and don't dare stop. / Flowing, flowing / To its courses, / Magic forces / Water pouring, / And resounding, waves unending, / To the well in torrents roaring.)

The narrative unfolds in the long strophes (the wizard has gone away, the broom sprouts arms and legs and marches off with the bucket), while in the shorter sestets descriptons of events give way to a narcotic, hieratic spell ("Walle! walle / Manche Strecke"), the refrain text. But the poem thwarts our complacency; events begin to seep into the "refrain" position, into the sestets. The broom is set in motion, it fetches water, it fetches too much water, the apprentice can't remember the counter-spell, in desperation he chops the broom into pieces. What follows is truly magical and terrifying. The pieces of the broom spring back to life, and each resumes its task:

> Seht, da kommt er schleppend wieder!
> Wie ich mich nun auf dich werfe,
> Gleich, o Kobold, liegst du nieder;
> Krachend trifft die glatte Schärfe.
> Wahrlich! brav getroffen!
> Seht, er ist entzwei!
> Und nun kann ich hoffen,
> Und ich atme frei!
>> Wehe! wehe!
>> Beide Teile
>> Stehn in Eile
>> Schon als Knechte
>> Völlig fertig in die Höhe!
>> Helft mir, ach! ihr hohen Mächte!

(Dragging buckets, he's returning, / Ha! just look at how I throw / Myself upon you; goblin, perish! / Feel the axe's crashing blow. / Mighty strokes to fell him! / Look, he's split in two! / Now my breath comes freely, / Hope has been renewed! / Help me! Help me! / Both the pieces / Quick as lightning / Stand and lower, / Loom above me, ready servants! / Rescue me, eternal powers!)

It is within the sestet that the broom rises from the dead; the description is devised to echo the sound of the non-narrative refrain: "Walle! walle" becomes "Wehe! wehe!"; "Zwecke" and "Strecke" resound in assonant rhyme with "Knechte," "Mächte"; "reiche" is linked to "beide" and "Eile." Expectations of a pattern repeated (actions in the long strophe, spells or outcries in the sestet) are thwarted to dramatic effect; we are compelled to experience with the apprentice a tremendous surprise.

Goethe preferred strictly strophic settings of his ballads, in which the single musical unit was repeated without variation for the singing of all verses.[6] His stance is not surprising. If the same music runs under each

---

[6] Jack Stein, *Poem and Music in the German Lied* (Cambridge, 1971), 63–65; Werner-

verse of text, then the music merely echoes the repeated phonetic and prosodic cycle of meter, rhyme, and verse-length; it effaces itself, and is merely the patterned sonority of words made louder. Music does not interpret the poem, introduces no alien element—a reading—but rather collaborates with the poem, helping the words to shout out their own sounds. Artful collisions of formal structure and narrative events, like those in the "Zauberlehrling," can survive the addition of such music. Goethe's notorious distaste for Schubert's "Erlkönig" setting (and his preference for the original setting by Corona Schröter) is thus not simply a mark of musical philistinism. Schröter's setting was hardly more than a bit of patterned melody for the recitation of each verse.[7] In Schubert's setting, music reacts to the progress of the story and imposes an interpretation. Each verse is set to different music, reflecting the unwinding narrative. But by turning its eyes to meaning, the music obscures the strophic structure, and so overwhelms and destroys the tension between meaning and formal design.

"Erlkönig" was in fact written as a text for an opera, *Die Fischerin*, a Singspiel first performed in 1782, with music by Schröter. The heroine sings the ballad as a curtain-opener. When she has finished she announces that she has now sung all the songs she knows; the action begins. Ballad and Romanze settings in early nineteenth-century opera were (like most inserted songs) invariably strophic and, like Schröter's "Erlkönig" music, were calculated as artful imitations of folksong's simplicity.

Emmy's strophic song from *Der Vampyr* (Ex. 1), is typical. The soprano tells her listeners that she knows a "fairy story" about the vampire: would they like to hear it? She describes in her Romanze how the "sad glance" of a mysterious stranger lures a young girl to her unfortunate end. The repeated refrain, "Denn still und heimlich sag ich's dir, / der bleiche Mann ist ein Vampyr! / Bewahr' uns Gott auf Erden / ihm jemals gleich zu werden" (For I whisper to you in secret: / the pale man is a vampire! / May God be by your side / that you never become his like!), is echoed by the chorus at the close of each parallel verse.

Senta's Ballad in *Der fliegende Holländer* is a relative of Emmy's song. Wagner had conducted *Der Vampyr* in Würzburg in 1833, and for that occasion had revised (and partly retexted) Aubry's aria in Act II.[8] In *Der Vampyr*, Emmy's Romanze seems to conjure up the vampire himself, who makes his entrance a few moments later; this dramatic conceit was

---

Joachim Düring, *Erlkönig-Vertonungen: Eine historische und systematische Untersuchung* (Regensburg, 1972), 108–109.

[7] Düring, 10.

[8] See John Deathridge, Martin Geck, Egon Voss, *Verzeichnis der musikalischen Werke Richard Wagners und ihrer Quellen (WWV)*, (Mainz, 1986), 120–21.

echoed by Wagner in *Holländer*.[9] Fragments of text, familiar Romantic formulae—the "bleicher Mann" and the "bleicher Seemann," the "trauriger Blick" and (in Erik's Dream) the "düsterer Blick"—appear in both texts. The two numbers are similar formally, for Senta's Ballad is strophic, with a non-narrative refrain doubled by the chorus. The same verse, the same motivic sequence, recur for different words, and the calculated monotony of the musical domain diverts the listener's ear from music to story. What sets this ballad apart, of course, is the explosion at its end, as Senta interrupts the third choral refrain and identifies herself with the redeeming heroine, "ich sei's, die dich durch ihre Treu' erlöse" (I am the one whose faith shall redeem you)—an apotheosis of Hegel's definition of balladic "content and coherence . . . borne by the subject himself."[10]

But Senta's Ballad cannot be interpreted simply as a "number," in isolation from the opera around it. Wagner's famous comments in *Eine Mitteilung an meine Freunde* (1851) make this clear: he reported in the essay that in writing the music for *Der fliegende Holländer* he had begun with Senta's Ballad, and when setting the rest of the libretto he found that

the thematic image I had created [in the Ballad] spread itself out involuntarily over the entire drama like a continuous web; without further effort on my part, I had only to continue with and complete the development of the various motivic cells contained in the Ballad.[11]

This characterization of the opera as an interrelated "web of themes" is an exaggeration, and reflects a vision in 1851 of yet-uncomposed music for the *Ring*, a vision projected in retrospective interpretation of the earlier work.[12] *Holländer* itself is of course a rather conventional score: separate numbers strung together, each with its own thematic identity and

[9] Dieter Borchmeyer, *Das Theater Richard Wagners* (Stuttgart, 1982), 182. The entire ballad scene was in fact an afterthought for Wagner; in the early surviving prose draft for the opera, the French text sent on 6 May 1840 to Scribe (Bibliothèque Nationale N.a.fr. 22552; published in *La Revue hebdomadaire*, 33 [9 August 1924], 216–19), Senta's obsession with the portrait is presented as only one element in a narrative that describes the past history of her relation with her lover, the young man (later to be called first Georg, then Eric). See Isolde Vetter, *Der fliegende Holländer von Richard Wagner—Entstehung, Bearbeitung, Überlieferung* (Diss. Berlin, 1982, microfiche), 10.

[10] "Gehalt und Zusammenhang . . . vom Subjekte getragen." *Aesthetik*, II, 473.

[11] "Es breitete sich nur das empfangene thematische Bild ganz unwillkürlich als ein vollständiges Gewebe über das ganze Drama aus; ich hatte, ohne weiter es zu wollen, nur die verschiedenen thematischen Keime die in der Ballade enthalten waren, nach ihren eigenen Richtungen hin weiter und vollständig zu entwickeln." *Sämtliche Schriften*, IV, 323.

[12] Carl Dahlhaus, "Zur Geschichte der Leitmotivtechnik bei Wagner," *Richard Wagner—Werk und Wirkung* (Regensburg, 1971), 17–20.

12

EXAMPLE 1. MARSCHNER, *Der Vampyr*, ACT II: EMMY'S ROMANZE

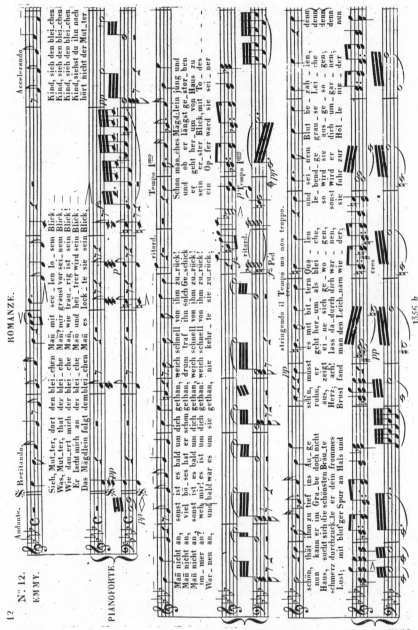

1356 b

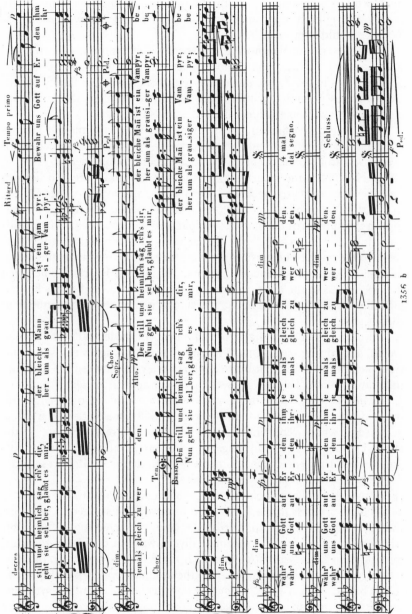

1356 b

(despite the patina of musical transition that connects one number to the next) with its own tonal and gestural closure. The *Holländer* numbers are beads jostling each other on a string, not the net of interwoven threads Wagner would later place before us.

Yet his description was not entirely specious; certain beads are streaked with spots of identical color. No listener can possibly miss the signals. Several times in the course of the opera a strongly marked family of musical motives is quoted within some individual number; the family includes the main thematic ideas used in Senta's Ballad.

In creating these thematic cross-references, Wagner exploited music's most familiar and least interesting narrative competence: the leitmotif, the association of musical motive with a specific textual idea. In *Der fliegende Holländer*, the recurrences of the motivic family are tied both to onstage enactments of the legend (such as the appearance of the Dutchman's ship "with blood-red sails" in scene 1), and to the legend's retellings in the mouths of the many participants in that enactment—in Senta's Ballad, or Erik's Dream, or the Dutchman's own confession in the final scene of the opera. The musical motives, then, are defined from the outset as signs for certain elements in the story. The famous association between the open fifths of the horn-call motive (the first motive in Senta's Ballad) and the physical presence of the Dutchman is only the most familiar of these signs.

In evoking the motivic signs for enactments of the legend in the human world, and for the narrations of legend as fiction, Wagner devised a musical metaphor for the link between the two levels, between the play and the play within it. This is what sets *Holländer* apart from *Der Vampyr* or *La dame Blanche*, where there are no such musical symbols for the dramatic device. Senta's Ballad, considered formally in isolation, is a three-verse song whose repeating musical verse cannot read or react to the changing images of an unfolding story. In context, however, the Ballad's music reacts to the drama in another way, with the leitmotifs that saturate the monotonously repeated musical verse.

But we must not overlook one critical point. When Senta casts her story as a Ballad, she tells it in a formal and historically distanced tongue. She thereby interprets her own words; she denies their verisimilitude. This (she implies) is a fairy tale, meant to divert, without the power to determine human fate. No matter how rich the Ballad's musical color, how terrifying the calculated plunge from the Spinning Song's girlish idiocies to the Ballad's empty fifths, no matter how genial the use of the symbolic motives, the singing of a strophic narrative song invokes convention and the historical archetype. And the convention carries a meaning.

Senta of course represents the legend as fiction only to deny its fictional status: *"ich sei's,* die dich durch ihre Treu' erlöse." In confirming her identity as the Ballad's heroine—in saying that the Ballad will come true—she paradoxically rejects the Ballad as ballad. Yet how firm is her conviction? A few moments later, she denies her denial, telling Erik "ich bin ein Kind, und weiß nicht, was ich singe" (I am a child, and don't know what I sing); here the Ballad is represented again as a fairy tale, sung by a child. Into the Ballad, its denial, and its reconfirmation (as the child's fairy tale) Wagner wove his representation of Senta's hysteria and spiritual chaos. She wavers between belief and disbelief, and between human and transcendent destiny. But to grasp the representation we must grasp the significance of the Ballad, and look past its alluring (unconventional) musical *tinta* to see convention and historical context.

Erik rushes in upon Senta's great outburst at the Ballad's close, and a few moments later he retells the legend in a new guise, his dream narration. The Ballad and the Dream are two focal points in the long second scene, different versions of the same story.[13] The Dream, in a sense, also denies the Ballad as fiction, in confirming Senta's momentary identification of herself with the Ballad's heroine.

Erik's Dream (Ex. 2) is meant for a warning but, as the stage directions indicate, Senta falls into a "magnetic slumber" as Erik speaks and "appears to be dreaming the very dream he is relating to her."[14] At times Senta's foreknowledge of the dream narration enables her to anticipate Erik's words; he allows her to usurp small fragments of the unfolding story, and the verse lines are split between them:

ERIK: Du stürztest zu des Fremden Füßen,
     Ich sah dich seine Knie umfangen,
SENTA: Er hub mich auf ...
ERIK: ... an seine Brust.

(ERIK: You threw yourself at the stranger's feet, / I saw you clasp his knee, / SENTA: He raised me up ... ERIK: ... into his arms.)

[13] Reinhold Brinkmann, "Sentas Traumerzählung," *Bayreuther Programmheft* (Bayreuth, 1984), 4, writes of "Kristallisationspunkte" (the Ballad, the Dream Narration, and the opening of the Senta-Dutchman duet) alternating with banal and typical operatic conceits (the Spinning Song, the Erik-Senta dialogue-duet, Daland's aria, the final trio). Borchmeyer's reading (see n. 9 above) of scene 2 as a smooth progression from "Dichtung" (ballad) to "Wirklichkeit" (Senta's explosive final line) to "Wahrheit" (the appearance of the Dutchman) is too neat (183); it passes over ambiguous lines like "ich bin ein Kind, und weiß nicht, was ich singe," and hence over Wagner's delaying tactics in the play of fictional against real.

[14] Brinkmann (11–16) links the conceit of Senta's prescience, her "magnetic slumber," to contemporary philosophical and medical speculation on Mesmer's theories of "animal magnetism," and the nature of hysterical ecstasy.

Example 2. Wagner, *Der fliegende Holländer*: Erik's Dream

(Senta sits down exhausted in the arm-chair; at the beginning of Erik's recital she sinks into a kind of magnetic slumber, so that she appears to be dreaming the very dream he is relating to her. Erik stands leaning on the arm-chair beside her.)

Fluth; die Brandung hört' ich, wie sich schäumend am U- fer brach der Wo- gen

Wuth: ein fremdes Schiff am na- hen Stran- de er- blickt' ich,—

selt- sam, wun- der- bar: zwei Män- ner nah- ten sich dem

141

Ex. 2 (*cont.*)

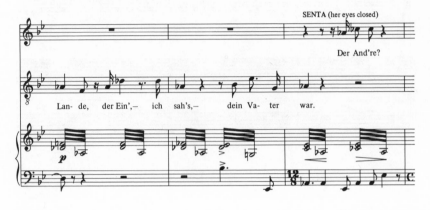

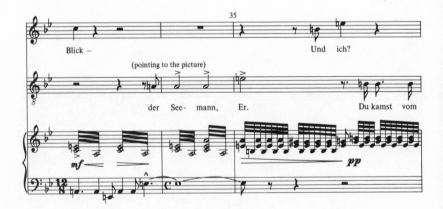

Hau- se her, du flogst den Va- ter zu be- grü- ssen;

40

doch kaum noch sah' ich an dich lan- gen, du

stürz- test zu des Frem- den Fü- ssen, ich sah_____ dich sei- ne

Ex. 2 (*cont.*)

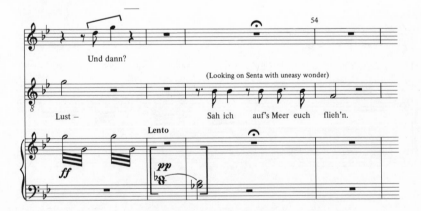

But her prescience fails: she cannot see how the dream ended. Erik's reply to her last "und dann?" (and then?)—"sah ich auf's Meer euch flieh'n" (I saw you depart over the sea)—is ambiguous. He seems not to say what he really saw after Senta embraced the stranger. What follows is an outburst by Senta, set to the music that had accompanied her explosive line at the close of the ballad ("ich sei's, die dich durch ihre Treu' erlöse"). And Senta's outburst here—"er sucht mich auf" (he is searching for me)—is perhaps the grimmest line in the libretto. She envisages the unreal, the fictional, searching for her and in her for its portal into the human world.

Despite Senta's prescience, her hysterical "magnetic slumber" and its intimations of medical pathology, Erik is the key to the Dream's meanings. In weaving this dream, the Hegelian Wagner whispers to us to distrust Senta for her prim operatic narrative, for her selection of an historically pedigreed archetype, to distrust its implications of the legend's fictionality. When Erik is granted his dream, the legend draws ominously closer to its enactment in the real world. Senta's Ballad tells a story in general terms and at a distance, while Erik's version of the same story is peopled not with abstractions like the "true woman," but with characters from the opera: Daland, Senta, himself. Dreaming, which can foreshadow reality, has a privileged status far more secure than that of ballad poetry, mere exposition of supernatural events. Erik's own banality only enhances the force invested in the intruder he describes, whose shadow, seemingly, can touch anyone. When Erik declares at the end of his scene that his dream has come true, the legend is at last dislodged from fiction, and Erik's line "Sie ist dahin! Mein Traum sprach wahr!" (She is gone! My dream spoke true!) lays a bridge over which the Dutchman can walk, to appear at last before Senta a few moments later.

In short: Senta narrates conventionally, then denies the implications of that conventionality, then retracts her denial. But Erik's narrative is the turning point, after which Senta understands that the legend *will* become real. This is an ironic reversal, wherein access to the magical tale's reality is transmitted by a bourgeois character to an hysterical "genius." The ironic reversal has a musical presence. Senta's Ballad, with its threefold repetition of a single closed musical unit, is rigidly structured into music's most elementary and predictable formal type. The formality of the balladic mode is challenged by Erik as he makes the music for his dream; where Senta's Ballad is representative of a genre, Erik's Dream is *sui generis*.

This is the story of the dream. The last sounds Erik hears in the waking world are a pair of thirds, B♭-D♭ falling to G♭-B♭ (Ex. 2, mm. 2–6), scored for combinations of woodwinds. Over this, Erik sings his prefacing recitative line, "I had a dream; listen to its warning." The first sound in the dream world is that of the low bass F, the A-C in the winds, and the muffled hunting-horn calls, a sonic reference to Erik-as-hunter, as a man set apart by this profession from the briny individuals that otherwise populate the opera. The hunting horns define the narrator's presence at the opening of the dream, which begins with Erik himself, watching and hearing the sea, the world set apart, from the high cliff that is his own domain. For these first four lines, Erik intones his lines over a two-note horn figure repeated monotonously in the bass registers as one element in the motivic wallpaper backing his words. In this limited sonic world, the musical turns at "a strange ship" (measure 21ff)—marking Erik's first glimpse of the Dutchman—have tremendous force. The initial tonal realm of B♭ minor is abandoned, as is the original accompanimental figure. Indeed, the two-note horn call that had rumbled under the first four lines (bracketed in the example) is transformed into the iconic three-pitch horn call (mm. 24–26) that is associated with the visual presence of the Dutchman; thus Erik's presence as narrator recedes and we are transported from his cliff to the drama below. From this moment on, the musical substance of the narrative will be spun out of ascending sequential repetitions of the Dutchman's horn call, through the pitch areas G♭, A♭, A, C, D♭, D, E♭, E, F, G♭, G: a juggernaut that could continue infinitely, and that defines no harmonic center.

Erik and Senta do not sing so much as intone; the open fourths and fifths of the Dutchman's horn call infiltrate and come to dominate their vocal idioms as both are drawn into the vision. At the end, when Senta sings "und ich?" (m. 35), "er hub mich auf" (m. 45), "und dann?" (m. 52), she merely drones the open fourth, the opening interval of the motive, as if the musical icon has robbed her of any other melodic tongue. There is no musical closure to the dream, for Senta's last question ("und dann?") is answered not by music but by silence: the ascending harmonic series simply stops. Erik's ambiguous reply, "sah ich auf's Meer euch flieh'n," is set to the peculiar falling thirds, B♭-D♭ to G♭-B♭, the last music heard outside the dream, before we fell into Erik's narrative landscape. The *sound* calls Erik out of the dream and back into real time; we hear it as the resumption of a D♭-B♭-B♭-G♭ oscillation that had been ringing out, and that was interrupted for a few instants by a dream, a state of unconsciousness. But while the sound signals the dream's end, Erik's words apparently contradict the signal: he tells the end of his dream, "sah ich auf's Meer euch flieh'n." The sound, then, actually interprets Erik's enigmatic reply, by revealing that this vision did not lie within the Dream, hence revealing that Erik has told a lie. We cannot know what—if anything—he really saw.

The music for Erik's Dream on many levels takes the measure of the story narrated where the Ballad did not. The Dutchman's horn call is drawn from the two-note motive that anticipates it: a musical process of motivic transformation, but it happens at the moment that Erik sights the Dutchman's ship. The vocal lines are progressively saturated with the intervals of the Dutchman's horn call: a musical dynamic that also acts as metaphor for the dream's waxing power over the dreamers; the ascending harmonic sequence has the same force. Finally: the Dream has no formal shape, no structural repetition of thematic periods, no harmonic closure. Its beginning and end are marked off by the odd Db-Bb-Bb-Gb thirds that define no single key. We cannot understand it as a musical object (like a ballad, a song, an aria), for it is an assemblage of musical impulses that underline the narrative's progress, and that in so doing also undermine music's very fabric, undermine formality and coherence. This is Erik's reply to Senta.

Wagner's ironic reversal, granting Erik a dream of the legend's real power over the human actors, is thus given its musical presence in the contrast between the Dream and the Ballad. Senta's musical narrative is conventional, invoking a balladic aesthetic wherein structured music is merely a prosodic background for words. Erik's musical narrative addresses the semantic content of his text, and in so doing relinquishes its purely musical meaning, becoming unstructured and vagrant. Indeed, the myth of intrusion, the archetype behind the drama, is played out in the musical aesthetic of Wagner's setting: into the ordered world of number opera and its historically entrenched formal types Wagner brings a musically enigmatic language that is born of narrative exposition, and that is a musically anarchic principle. Wagner's willingness to devise music that narrates proved a means of liberation from an historical imperative.

II. TANNHÄUSER'S ROME NARRATIVE

Erik's Dream tells a story heard before, and a story soon to be enacted onstage. Tannhäuser's Rome Narrative is different: it tells of events not presented on stage or previously described, for Tannhäuser is telling the story of his pilgrimage from Thuringia to Rome, in a time between spring at the end of Act II and autumn in Act III. Where Erik's Dream could draw upon motives established *a priori* as symbols in creating analogies for narrative, Tannhäuser's Rome Narrative, in dealing with a fresh-minted tale, cannot. The world Tannhäuser describes has no musical identity except that which he creates for it from moment to moment.[15]

---

[15] In "Richard Wagner der Erzähler," *Österreichische Musikzeitschrift*, 37 (1982), 299,

In a sense, then, the musical world of the Rome Narrative is like that of any number: self-sufficient, with its proper thematic ideas and harmonic design. The aesthetic presence of the strophic narrative song, of the ballad, undoubtedly broods over the Rome Narrative, but in the manner of an inattentive parent whose offspring grows into delinquency. The text, for instance, preserves remnants of balladic structure. Lines 3–8, alluding to Tannhäuser's wish to atone for the "angel's sweet tears," are echoed in 21–22:

Inbrunst im Herzen, wie kein Büßer noch
sie je gefühlt, sucht' ich den Weg nach Rom.
    Ein Engel hatte, ach! der Sünde Stolz
    dem Übermütigen entwunden;
    für ihn wollt' ich in Demut büßen,   (5)
    das Heil erfleh'n, das mir verneint,
    um ihm die Träne zu versüßen,
    die er mir Sünder einst geweint!

Wie neben mir der schwerstbedrückte Pilger
die Strasse wallt', erschien mir allzu leicht.   (10)
Betrat sein Fuß den weichen Grund der Wiesen,
der nackten Sohle sucht' ich Dorn und Stein;
ließ Labung er am Quell den Mund genießen,
sog' ich der Sonne heißes Glühen ein;
wenn fromm zum Himmel er Gebete schickte,   (15)
vergoß mein Blut ich zu des Höchsten Preis;
als im Hospiz der Müde sich erquickte,
die Glieder bettet' ich in Schnee und Eis.
Verschloss'nen Aug's, ihr Wunder nicht zu schauen,
durchzog ich blind Italiens holde Auen.   (20)
    Ich tat's, denn in Zerknirschung wollt' ich büßen,
    um meines Engel's Tränen zu versüßen.

Brinkmann argues that the Rome Narrative's tendency away from the formally structured musical *Satz* toward the through-composed motivic web in a sense presupposed a (nonexistent) collection of symbolic leitmotifs: "Die Formidee der Romerzählung setzt überdies, um zu voller Wirkung zu gelangen, im Grunde das entwickelte Leitmotivgewebe bereits voraus . . . das Fehlen dieser Technik—beziehungsweise ihre musikhistorisch und innerhalb der Entwicklung Wagners erklärbare erst rudimentäre Form—bezeichnet den Bruch zwischen Konzeption und Realisierung des epischen Stils im *Tannhäuser.*" Brinkmann also deals at length with an issue passed over here, the intersection of the Rome Narrative with its orchestral mirror image, the Act III prelude, and the degree to which musical signs created within the prelude, as well as the structure of the prelude itself, impinge on our hearing of Tannhäuser's narrative (299–302).

(With burning heart, more penitent / than all others, I sought the way to Rome. / An angel had driven out / the pride that used to rule me; / for her I wished to do penance, / to pray for salvation denied me, / to dry the tears she wept / because of me, a sinful man. / The most heavily burdened pilgrim / seemed to me to carry but little. / If he walked on soft meadows, / I trod barefoot on thorn and rock. / If he drank to quench his thirst, / I sought the sun's hot glow. / If he sent prayers to heaven, / I offered up my blood; / when he rested in the inn, / I made my bed in snow and ice. / Eyes closed, so to ignore their beauty, / I went blind through Italy's meadows. / I did this, for in contrition I wished to atone, / to sweeten my angel's tears.)

This seems a gesture toward the imperative of refrain. Lines 11–20 are a second verse that parallels a first verse in lines 1–2; but the huge second verse, with its long litany of antithetical juxtapositions, dwarfs the first verse, just as the first refrain in 3–8 outweighs its less loquacious relative in 21–22. The cyclic verse-refrain-verse-refrain design remains, but its proportions have gone awry.

The memory of recurring musical strophe is present alongside the remnants of the balladic verse structure. Both text "verses" begin with the identical eight-measure phrase (an ostinato theme: see Ex. 3, mm. 1ff, 22ff); both end similarly with a cadence to F major cast in the ecclesiastical sounds of sustained woodwind chords (mm. 17ff, 52ff) The interior expansion in the second verse (mm. 30–51) is a tonal and motivic digression between these two pillars of ostinato phrase and F major cadence. The strophic song still haunts this passage (up to line 22), but imperfectly.[16] And so formality is used self-consciously and mockingly. When Tannhäuser narrates with a faint balladic accent he is condescending to his bourgeois listener by speaking in that listener's own conventional operatic tongue. He makes a terrible history palatable to ears easily outraged. In this, Tannhäuser's balladicisms are like his sneer in the preceding dialogue, "sei außer Sorg', mein guter Sänger! Nicht such' ich dich, noch deiner Sippschaft Einen" (have no fear, my dear singer! I seek neither you nor one of your company), a lash at the self-righteous society that exiled him. At the same time, however, Tannhäuser serves himself, for he must cloak his tragedy in artifice in order to keep it at a distance,

[16] The first sketch for the Rome Narrative, labeled "Tannh. Pilgerlied," was made on the final sheet of the first (Composition) draft for Act II of *Tannhäuser* (Bayreuth, Richard-Wagner-Gedenkstätte der Stadt Bayreuth, Hs 120/IV 2a). This sketch, as well as the Composition draft for the Narrative (Hs 120/III/3a, III/3b, and III/1a), point to an earlier, more formally strophic concept that metamorphosed into a freer form. The very word "Lied"— synonymous for Wagner with strophic design—is an indication of this strophic concept.

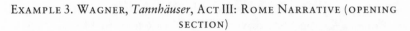

EXAMPLE 3. WAGNER, *Tannhäuser*, ACT III: ROME NARRATIVE (OPENING SECTION)

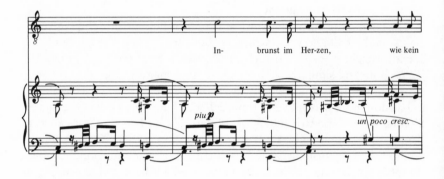

Ex. 3 (*cont.*)

Wie ne- ben mir der schwerst- be-drück-te Pil- ger die Stra- sse wallt', er-schien mir all- zu leicht: be-trat sein Fuss den wei- chen Grund der Wie- sen, der nack-ten Soh- le sucht' ich Dorn und Stein; liess

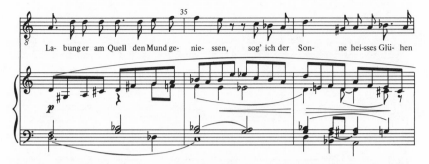

La- bung er am Quell den Mund ge- nie- ssen, sog' ich der Son- ne hei-sses Glü- hen

ein; wenn fromm zum Him-mel er Ge- be- te schick-te, ver-goss mein

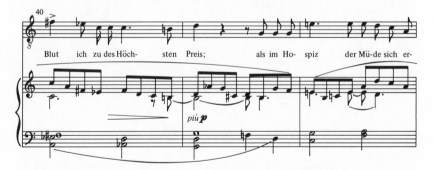

Blut ich zu des Höch- sten Preis; als im Ho- spiz der Mü-de sich er-

- quick- te, die Glie- der bet- tet' ich in Schnee und Eis; ver-

153

Ex. 3 (*cont.*)

-schloss'- nen Aug's, ihr Wun- der nicht zu schau- en, durch-zog ich blind I- ta-

- liens hol- de Au- en. Ich that's, denn in Zer- knir- schung wollt' ich

bü- ssen, um mei- nes En- gel's Thrä- nen zu ver- sü- ssen!

and by starting with this limping ballad he tries to brush his tale with fictitiousness. In this way, he can confront it.

But the pretense of strophic order and balladic distance begins to crumble after his cry "nach Rom," a quotation from the end of Act II and the words that sent him into exile:

> Nach Rom gelangt' ich so zur heil'gen Stelle
> lag betend auf des Heiligtumes Schwelle.
> Der Tag brach an: da läuteten die Glocken, (25)
> hernieder tönten himmlische Gesänge;
> da jauchzt' es auf in brünstigem Frohlocken,
> denn Gnad' und Heil verhießen sie der Menge.
>
> Da sah' ich ihn, durch den sich Gott verkündigt,
> vor ihm all' Volk im Staub sich niederließ. (30)
> Und Tausenden er Gnade gab, entsündigt,
> er Tausende sich froh erheben hieß.

(I came to Rome, the holy city, / lay praying at salvation's gate. / Dawn came: the bells rang, / heavenly songs rang from above, / a cry of joy broke forth, / the songs told of mercy and grace. / Then I saw him through whom God speaks; / in the dust, the throng fell prostrate. / And to thousands he gave mercy, / he pardoned them, bid them rise.)

The words "nach Rom" represent the moment of arrival after the journey through Italy depicted in the first part. The narrator, traveling through Italy's meadows with eyes shut fast, first perceives Rome as sound: bells, anthems, shouts of joy. His blind eyes open to a divine figure who is only "him": "da sah ich ihn, durch den sich Gott verkündigt."

The moment of the journey's completion "nach Rom" breaks the imperfect formality of the opening, with an odd effect of tonal shift from the F major woodwind cadence of the refrain to a distant D♭ (Ex. 4, mm. 59–63). Tannhäuser abandons the thematic and tonal realm of the initial verses. Lines 23–28 (mm. 62–85) and 31–32 (mm. 97–105) are set similarly to music derived from the "Dresden Amen" tune. The music for the two passages is parallel; only scoring and key are changed in the second passage, and the effect of a cleared sonic palette at "nach Rom" is repeated at "da sah ich ihn" (compare mm. 59–63 with 88–91).

The music's own tongue and the conversation of the narrative now intersect on many levels, and uneasily. The broad—musically illogical— tonal shifts for "nach Rom" and "da sah ich ihn" are certainly metaphorical, calculated in the first instance to represent the sudden transportation of the narrator's presence to a distant scene, as Tannhäuser com-

EXAMPLE 4. *Tannhäuser*, ACT III: ROME NARRATIVE (CENTRAL SECTION)

be- tend auf des Hei- lig- thu- mes Schwel-le.

Der Tag brach an, da läu- te-ten die Glo-cken, her- nie- der tön-ten

himm- li-sche Ge- sän- ge: da jauchzt' es auf in

brün- sti- gem Froh- lock- en, denn Gnad' und Heil ver-

Ex. 4 (*cont.*)

-hie- ssen sie der Men- ge.

Da sah ich

ihn, durch den sich

Gott ver-

-kün- digt, vor

pp *cresc.-* - - - -

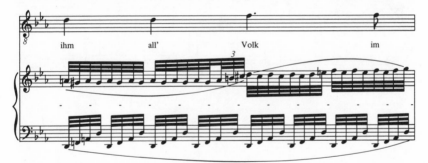

ihm all' Volk im

Staub sich nie- - der-

f *dim.-* - - - - - - - - *p*

159

Ex. 4 (*cont.*)

presses his weeks of wandering into a moment of arrival; in the second instance to underline a different motion: the motion of the mind when a blind eye opens to a single image. The "Dresden Amen" tune is a sonic icon whose meaning is defined outside *Tannhäuser*; its associations with sanctity and Catholicism could be taken for granted. Here, the "Dresden Amen" is also used in a piece of musical mimesis, depicting bells, hymns, and anthems so that we can hear them with Tannhäuser.

The basic parallelism of the two passages (mm. 59–87 and 88–105) is a piece of musical-formal structuralism that disregards the changing events depicted by the continuing narrative. Yet even while the thematic formal parallelism is at odds with the narrative's progress, a critical re-scoring (from winds to brass) and the tonal change (from D♭ to E♭) take account of this progress. Wagner has contrived a situation in which the narrative's demand that it be symbolized, a demand for musical unrelatedness, affects tonality and scoring, and yet is contradicted by the musical coherence and relatedness which find their expression in the thematic-formal repetition. Music only half listens to the story being told.

In the final part of Tannhäuser's narrative, there is a fundamental change in the music's stance toward the story. Tannhäuser has been motionless since his cry "nach Rom"; now he once again begins a physical journey. Duplicating in microcosm his entire pilgrimage, he approaches the Pope, and begins his confession. In accompaniment, the ostinato theme of the narrative's first verses returns, but now its function has been transformed. There, it was semantically neutral, a thematic item used as the building material for a neat eight-measure phrase. Here, it is given a completely different musical presence (Ex. 5, mm.105ff). The motive is stated; there is a pause; Tannhäuser says, "da naht' auch ich"; the motive is stated again, dissonant, presented as a hesitant fragment punctuated by long silences.

When Tannhäuser calls again on the ostinato, presents it as a fragment, and pauses to say, "then I too drew near," he makes out of that ostinato motive a musical symbol: the ostinato motive mimics the halting resumption of motion as Tannhäuser takes his first steps towards the Pope. This is an extraordinary moment. The motive's symbolic meaning is revealed to us; and at once we rehear and reinterpret the Rome Narrative's opening verses: what had seemed merely a "theme," a recurring ostinato motive that could not comment on the text it accompanied, is revealed as a secret sign with a secret meaning appropriate to those first verses. The motive is an audible metaphor of physical motion, of the progess of a journey.

In transforming the ostinato motive from purely musical idea to musical sign, Tannhäuser arrives at the threshold of a new musical aesthetic

EXAMPLE 5. *Tannhäuser*, ACT III: ROME NARRATIVE (FINAL SECTION)

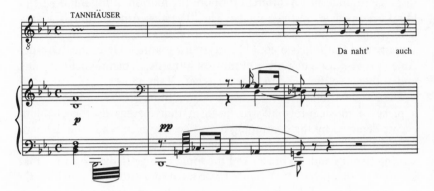

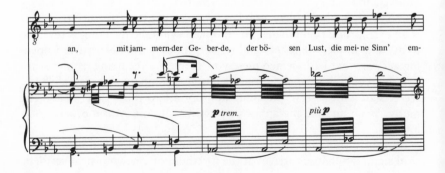

163

Ex. 5 (*cont.*)

that will govern the Rome Narrative's final moments. Now, as in Erik's Dream, all formality is abandoned, and the music is created from an assemblage of unrelated, fragmentary moments that react to the events in the narrative. The diminished sevenths associated with Venus are cited at Tannhäuser's confession of his liaison (mm. 106–12). The diminished fifth A-E♭ scored for brass and low strings and the chromatic bass motive that accompanies the Pope's curse (mm. 129–43) also have a previous association, with Tannhäuser's ominous entrance following Wolfram's aria. Several seconds of silence mark Tannhäuser's loss of consciousness (m. 149); an iconic quotation of the "Dresden Amen" music (mm. 150ff) sounds at his "von fern her tönten frohe Gnadenlieder" (in the distance happy songs of grace resounded)—once more he hears the music of the hymn, now far away.

The journey to this musical world from the strophic feint of the Rome Narrative's initial moments has been as long as Tannhäuser's pilgimage, and is a metaphorical journey as well. In contemplating his past, in approaching his memory of the Pope's words, Tannhäuser cannot maintain his ironic pose; he becomes entangled in his tragedy and abandons the artifice of convention. In the end, Tannhäuser begins to compose music as a translation for the events he narrates, and in so doing his composer's voice becomes a voice of musical anarchy.

"TANNHÄUSER composes music": the phrase is deliberately artificial. But it resonates from others that have occurred before. Emmy asks her onstage listeners whether they would like to "hear" her fairy-tale; Senta announces that she will "sing a song"; Erik admonishes Senta to "hear" the dream; Tannhäuser sings, "hör an, Wolfram, hör an" (Listen, Wolfram, listen). Operatic narrative begins with an exhortation, an invitation to listen, not only to words but also to a musical performance. When a character in opera sings "hör an" and launches into a narrative song, he creates a special illusion. First, he and his onstage listeners know that he is singing a song; they know that music is sounding around them. Operatic characters, of course, do not normally "hear" the music that is their natural ambiance and their only language. But when he sings a narrative, the singer creates another illusion, a magical illusion: that he has himself created what he sings, that, for a few moments, he is both a poet and a composer, be he sea-captain's child, or hunter, or like Tannhäuser in truth a maker of songs.

But—surprisingly—in the Rome Narrative we do not lose this illusion of Tannhäuser as both narrator and composer when the strophic opening begins to dissolve. Put another way: at a certain point, Tannhäuser is no longer singing a narrative song, and yet he still *sings*; the sounding world of the opera comes from him, he hears the music he creates. A border that is usually clearly marked—the border between music the characters do not hear and are not aware of singing, and songs they can hear—has been dissolved.

Wagner's dissolution of this border created opera in which the characters live in a realm animated by music that they at times seem to hear, at times to invent. Of course he thereby insinuated himself into his imaginary realms, for these listening and composing characters with their various professions—knights, princesses, courtiers, Valkyries, gods, shoemakers—thus stand for the poet-composer behind them all. Elusive as it is, the illusion of the character who *hears* is a characteristic element of Wagner's language. Act III of *Tristan* is born of this illusion; when the "alte Weise" passes into the orchestra during the second part of Tristan's narrative, we are aware that the music we hear comes from Tristan, that we are hearing what he hears as he lingers at the edge of our world. And this illusion was one element of Wagner's language which (unlike leitmotifs) few later composers could mimic. Perhaps only a very few recognized it for what it was. The capacity of the characters to hear every sound around them is the truly Wagnerian aspect of *Pelléas*; when Chrysothemis tells Elektra of the joyous singing at Orestes' return, Elektra replies, "ob ich nicht höre? ob ich die Musik nicht höre? sie kommt doch aus mir" (as if I don't hear? as if I don't hear the music? but it comes from me).

But in the case of *Tannhäuser* the illusion of the listening and composing singer carries with it a final irony. The purely musical sense of the Rome Narrative, the more periodic, tonally closed structuralism of its beginning, begins to dissolve at the very moment that the music begins to *represent* the story Tannhäuser's words describe. If Tannhäuser has composed the Rome Narrative, with its many musical representations of narrative, if Wagner presents himself, through Tannhäuser, as the composer, then the Rome Narrative itself becomes a warning.

This is the story it tells: if music should begin to hear the story told by poetry, if music narrates with poetry, then music welcomes incoherence— a dangerous, seductive intruder—into an ordered musical world.

NELLY FURMAN

The Languages of Love in *Carmen*

OVERTURE, FOREPLAY

In August 1983, the French weekly magazine *Le Nouvel Observateur* devoted its lead article to the figure of Carmen, thus acknowledging the return of the nineteenth-century gypsy as a genuine news item in our time. *Le Nouvel Observateur* was taking note of the fact that in 1983 there had been four major revivals of the story of Carmen: Italian director Francesco Rosi's screen version of Georges Bizet's opera; a Spanish film based on a reworking of Prosper Mérimée's story and Bizet's opera by Carlos Saura in collaboration with choreographer Antonio Gades; *First Name: Carmen*, an interpretation of the Mérimée story by the New Wave "enfant terrible" of French cinema, Jean-Luc Godard; and *La Tragédie de Carmen*, Peter Brook's adaptation of the Bizet opera as an uninterrupted eighty-minute musical play, produced first in Paris and later at the Vivian Beaumont Theater in New York City. Perhaps the number and range, the international and multimedia variety of these Carmen revivals should not surprise us, since they only reflect the continuing and constant fascination exercised by the tale of the gypsy and the soldier. Enjoyed by generations of readers, produced countless times by opera companies for its box-office appeal, the story of Carmen has also inspired more than thirty film makers, including Charlie Chaplin, Lotte Reiniger, Ernest Lubitsch, Raoul Walsh, Cecil B. de Mille, Charles Vidor, Jacques Feyder, Christian-Jaque, and Otto Preminger.

Like the stories of Don Juan, Tristan and Isolde, Heloise and Abelard, or Romeo and Juliet, the tragedy of Carmen and Don José exemplifies a certain expression of desire, a certain code of love. Through its many revivals and adaptations, the story has become legendary; and in each of its versions, differing inflections mirror the shifting values of society. *Carmen* may be the only story of operatic origin to have attained the status of myth: for the *Carmen* we know best is not the Mérimée novella of 1845; the legendary *Carmen* is the love story enacted in Georges Bizet's opera of 1875.[1]

Mérimée's Carmen is a recruiter of young and able men for a band of

---

[1] Dominique Maingueneau, *Carmen: Les racines d'un mythe* (Paris, 1984), 11, and Jean Roy, *Bizet* (Paris, 1983), 3.

gypsy smugglers; she spies on the English merchants and tourists of Gibraltar and sets them up to be robbed. She is, in her own way, an entrepreneur. The story thus reflects concerns of the July Monarchy at the beginning of the industrial revolution: international trade, economic growth, commercial development, and colonial expansion; values best expressed in Prime Minister Guizot's famous dictum, "Enrichissez-vous!" (Get wealthy!). Thirty years later, after the "ignominious" defeat of the French army in the Franco-Prussian War of 1870, during which the Emperor Napoleon III and his armed forces were taken prisoner at Sedan, Bizet's opera shows us a well-meaning but naive soldier beguiled by an enticing foreigner. Napoleon III had married a Spaniard, Eugénie de Montijo, whose mother was a close friend of Mérimée. According to Mérimée, who was an habitué of the imperial court, it was the Countess of Montijo, mother of the Empress, who first told him the story of Carmen. By implying that the woman causes the soldier's downfall, as traditional interpretations of the opera suggest, Bizet and the librettists, Henri Meilhac and Ludovic Halévy, seem to propose a psychological explanation for a political and military event.[2] One could perhaps infer that Bizet, who had called Napoleon III "un grand homme" and "un homme merveilleux,"[3] could neither accept the Emperor's downfall nor credit him with full responsibility for his actions. Because it presents the consequences that befall those who, in the thrall of passion, abandon duty and honor, *Carmen* lends itself to being used for nationalistic purposes; and because it shows a woman and a man negotiating their relationship, it can easily be appropriated for gender issues. The "Carmen mania" of the early 1980s may well have been triggered by the contemporary feminist debate.

Carmen: THE OPERA

After becoming disenchanted with his musical idol Richard Wagner, Friedrich Nietzsche found in Georges Bizet's *Carmen* the "art of the future," the antithesis to Wagner's decadent modernism. For Nietzsche, both Bizet's music and the realism of the story were worthy of enthusiastic praise. Wagner's exemplar of tender devotion, Senta, the heroine of *The Flying Dutchman*, evokes an idealized vision of love, whereas Bizet's concept of love as a deadly struggle for possession reflects, in Nietzsche's view, the reality of gender relations:

[2] In *Opera and Ideas: From Mozart to Strauss* (New York, 1985), 263, Paul Robinson reminds us that "opera appears to respond vigorously to ideas that might broadly be called psychological."

[3] Michel Cardoze, *Georges Bizet* (Paris, 1982), 131–32.

Finally, love—love retranslated into *nature*! *Not* the love of a "cultured maiden!" No Senta-sentimentality! But love as fate, as *fatality*, cynical, innocent, cruel—and thus true to *nature*! Love, which in its expedient is the war of the sexes, and in its basis their *mortal hatred*. I know of no case where tragic humour, which forms the essence of love, has expressed itself so strenuously, has formulated itself so terribly, as in the last cry of Don José, with which the work concludes:

> "Yes! I *myself* have killed her;
> Oh my Carmen! my Carmen adored!"[4]

The sentimental relationship represented in Wagner's *Flying Dutchman* is, according to Nietzsche, essentially a product of culture, while the passionate feelings expressed by Carmen and José are truer to nature. Leaving aside the question of love's connection to "nature" as opposed to "culture," what has clearly changed between Wagner's Senta and Bizet's Carmen is the essence of love, its very character. The ideal of complementarity of the sexes played out in Wagner's opera has been replaced in Bizet's by a concept of equality. For in *Carmen* the dramatic tension is created by the necessity for each of the two lovers to satisfy his or her essential need—even though it may be opposed to the other's.

The entry for *Carmen* in the *Larousse* encyclopedia describes the plot of the opera as follows:

> For the love of Carmen, a gypsy, Don José, who is a corporal in the dragoons, deserts and becomes a smuggler; in the end, he kills his mistress, who had left him for a matador.[5]

If we are to believe the *Larousse*, it would seem that the story of the opera is really about a soldier named Don José. But one could just as well describe the events from Carmen's perspective:

> To thank him for letting her escape, Carmen, a gypsy, bestows her favors on José, a corporal in the dragoons. He falls in love with her, abandons the army, and joins the gypsies. When Carmen tires of him and his jealousy, she breaks off their relationship and becomes involved with a matador; José kills her.

Plot summary, like any retelling, is an interpretive act, a forceful muting of some voices of the text, an option between reading strategies, the evidence of an ideological stance. *Carmen*, of course, is not exclusively *his*

---

[4] "The Case of Wagner," in *The Works of Friedrich Nietzsche*, ed. Alexander Tille and trans. Thomas Common, XI (New York, 1896), 8.

[5] *Larousse du XXe siècle en six volumes* (Paris, 1929).

story, any more than it is *her* story; nor is it simply *their* story, for it is also *my* story of his, her, and their story.

The synopsis proposed by the editors of the *Larousse* has often been reproduced with added details in theater program notes. It reflects the traditional view of José as a victim: victim of his own naiveté, of his upbringing, of his obsessional passion; or, conversely, victim of Carmen's beguiling beauty, her enticing manner, her supposedly demonic nature. In this conventional argument, José is often seen as the dupe of a woman who uses her attraction to reduce her lover to a debased and impoverished condition: she is a female vampire and he is her prey. In *The Romantic Agony*, for example, Mario Praz includes Carmen in a long list of *femmes fatales* because her "diabolical feminine fascination" brings about "a violence of passion that makes the man lose all regard for his own social position."[6] The corollary of this psychological argument is that when José stabs Carmen, his murder is seen as an act of self-defense, the means by which he regains his manhood. For Michel Leiris, there is no doubt that Carmen's death appears as a just retribution:

> Carmencita—who stabs one of her companions in the cigar factory and ridicules the wretch whom she has forced to desert until he kills her; mistress of a matador who dedicates the beast he is about to kill to her, as to a bloodthirsty goddess for whom he must risk death— the lovely Carmencita, before being murdered, is indeed a murderess.[7]

If, however, we read the opera not as the story of poor Don José but as Carmen's struggle for freedom, then the roles of victim and torturer become reversed. It is no longer José but Carmen who is the sufferer. Irritated by José's authoritarian behavior, Carmen tells him in Act III: "Je ne veux pas être tourmentée ni surtout commandée. Ce que je veux, c'est être libre et faire ce qu'il me plaît" (I won't be pestered and ordered about. I want to be free and do as I please).[8] A case could thus be made to show that, psychologically, Carmen is as much the victim of José's possessiveness and jealousy as he is the victim of her charms. When she chooses to confront José and force the issue in the last act, her gesture of self-affirmation acquires the dimensions of a political act. In *Opera or the Defeat*

---

[6] 2nd ed., trans. by Angus Davidson with a new foreword by Frank Kermode (London and New York, 1970), 207.

[7] *Manhood: A Journey from Childhood into the Fierce Order of Virility*, trans. Richard Howard (New York, 1963), 54.

[8] The original libretto is reproduced by Dominique Maingueneau (n. 1 above). My translations rely at times on the English version by Nell and John Moody in *Carmen: Georges Bizet*, English National Opera Guide no. 13 (London and New York, 1982).

of Women, Catherine Clément calls Carmen "the most feminist, the most stubborn of those who perished," the one who embodies "the dark and revolutionary proclamation of a woman who chooses to die before a man decides it for her."[9] But one could then respond that Carmen's death, seen as a suicide, could be interpreted as a victory for Don José, for his definition of love and social values.

Despite the conflicting interpretations that Carmen's death may elicit, her struggle for personal freedom has assured her a place in the pantheon of feminist idols. Yet there is still much to say about *Carmen* from a feminist viewpoint. In the raised consciousness of the 1980s, even José is no longer merely a victim, for he too is now seen as fighting for individual recognition. Thus, in a recent opera guide, Michel Rabaud seems to consider José an example for men's liberation:

Rather than the weak soldier who renounces his duties to follow a dangerous seducer (which is how he too often appears), Bizet's Don José is a man whose fatal vocation compels him to abandon a pale sentimental love and banal occupations, and to plunge into what he does not know—the outlaw world of passion. [. . .] Don José begins to live when he meets Carmen: love acts as a second birth, transforming a rather ectoplasmic character into a full-blooded man. One could argue that if he shows any weakness it is not by following Carmen, but by being unable to follow her completely. He returns to his dying mother instead of responding to Carmen's vital challenge; he is not a free man and he loses her.[10]

In this analysis, José's mother rather than Carmen has a destructive hold on the poor soldier. Whether it is José's attachment to Carmen or to his mother that spells his doom, the function of the woman remains the same—that of man's torturer.

Whether we see José as victim or Carmen as martyr, we are forever caught in the mirror image of a master/slave relationship, where the two main characters are reflections of each other. In the *corrida* of passionate love, both Carmen and José occupy in turn the position of bullfighter and bull. Beyond the psychological interpretation, the text itself suggests the interchangeability of the two roles: structurally by having Carmen wield a knife in the first act, and José stab her in the last; linguistically by having Escamillo name a bull after her; grammatically by making it impossible to determine whether the eye referred to in Escamillo's signature tune

---

[9] *L'opéra ou la défait des femmes* (Paris, 1979), 103.
[10] Michel Rabaud, " 'Carmen': A Tragedy of Love, Sun and Death," in the English National Opera Guide (see n. 8 above), 39.

belongs to the woman or the bull, "Et songe en combattant / Qu'un oeil noir te regarde / Et que l'amour t'attend" (Remember, while you are fighting, that a dark eye watches you, and that love awaits you). On the stage, the interchangeability of their positions is often indicated visually by having Carmen wear a red dress reminiscent of the bullfighter's costume and by hiding part of her face with her mantilla, while José is dressed in dark pants and a white shirt, the very color combination of the bull's markings. Bull or matador, matador or bull? It is perhaps one of the great strengths of this text that it does not permit us to choose either of these interpretations.[11] Bizet's opera thus challenges the reader who, while acknowledging the importance of the dynamics of power between the lovers, attempts to move beyond the confines of the bullfighting arena, the analogical topos that has guided most critical studies.

The master/slave dichotomy is but one of a series of oppositions that structure the opera. One could, for example, discuss numerous thematic networks in this fashion: freedom and possessiveness, northern ethics and southern mores, Spaniards and gypsies, bourgeois values and bohemian life styles, etc.[12] These oppositions have made Bizet's *Carmen* a convenient instrument for the representation of political ideologies. In Frank Corsaro's 1984 staging for the New York City Opera, the story is set during the Spanish Civil War, and Carmen is portrayed as a freedom fighter who falls in the struggle against fascism. However, in a similar staging of the opera presented at Pforzheim during the Third Reich, Carmen, I imagine, personified the danger awaiting innocent fascist youth bewitched by a member of a racial group designated as inferior by the Nazi regime.[13]

Because of its oppositional structures, Georges Bizet's opera would seem particularly well suited to illustrate the war of the sexes. Yet, interestingly enough, in the area of sexual difference the polarities are not between the sexes but within each gender; the opposition is not between male and female, but between characters who embody traditional middle-class standards of femininity and masculinity and protagonists who appear as less perfect representatives of their sex: Micaëla in contrast to Carmen, the virgin versus the whore; or Escamillo compared to José, virility versus muliebrity. The figures of Micaëla and Escamillo do not appear in Mérimée's story. Invented by the librettists Henri Meilhac and Ludovic Halévy, they are stock characters in the *opéra comique* tradition. Micaëla represents the model of chaste femininity, Escamillo the paragon

---

[11] This is also the argument made by Maingueneau (see n. 1 above), 80.
[12] Other oppositional poles have been noted by Cardoze (see n. 3 above), 245–46.
[13] See Henry Malherbe, *Carmen* (Paris, 1951), 305.

of masculinity; in terms of gender, they serve as foils to the main characters. But although Micaëla and Escamillo occupy the same space at the same time in Act III, there is no interaction between them. Micaëla's lack of interest in the famous toreador from Granada is commensurate with his failure to notice the charms of the young woman from Navarre. Indifference, not war, characterizes the relationship between these exemplars of the two sexes.

Compared to Micaëla and Escamillo, Carmen and José are both equally far from the gender ideal. From the beginning of the opera, we face a world divided according to gender. Across from the cigar factory—which no man may enter—stands the guardhouse, a male enclave that Micaëla does not enter. Only in the public square between these two buildings are men and women free to mingle.[14] José pays with his virility for having entered the prohibited area, and Carmen steps into a male circle when the soldiers form a barrier around her, effectively separating her from the other women. From a psychological viewpoint, an argument could also be made that by wielding a knife and by showing disdainful courage in the face of death Carmen exhibits supposedly manly characteristics, whereas José's dependence on a woman as well as the simple fact that he is in love make him seem a lesser man. As Hélène Cixous remarks, "being possessed is not desirable for a masculine Imaginary, which would interpret it as passivity—a dangerous feminine position";[15] and Roland Barthes notes that "a man is feminized not because he is inverted, but because he is in love."[16]

Through Micaëla and Escamillo, Meilhac and Halévy affirm sexual differences, while simultaneously blurring gender differentiation in Carmen and José. In Andalusia, where our story takes place, a *carmen* is a villa or country house, a residence between town and country, between culture and nature. One could thus argue against Nietzsche that Bizet's opera does not represent the war between the sexes, but rather that it skillfully illustrates the polarities within each gender, and the congruence of identity between the two.[17]

For Nietzsche, the war of the sexes is only an expedient for depicting love in its violent cruelty. The greatness of Bizet's opera—and Nietzsche insists upon this—is due to its vision of love:

Such a conception of love (the only one that is worthy of a philosopher) is rare; it distinguishes a work of art among thousands of

---

[14] Maingueneau, 28.
[15] *The Newly Born Woman*, trans. Betsy Wing (Minneapolis, Minn., 1986), 86.
[16] *Fragments d'un discours amoureux* (Paris, 1977), 20.
[17] Nietzsche's argument (see n. 4 above) has been reiterated by many commentators, including the latest biographer of Bizet, Jean Roy (see n. 1 above), 146.

others. For, on an average, artists do like all the world, or worse even—they *misunderstand* love. [. . .] People imagine they are unselfish in love because they seek the advantage of another being, often in opposition to their own advantage. But for so doing they want to *possess* the other being [. . .] Even God himself is no exception to this rule. [. . .] he becomes a terror, if he is not loved in return. (9)

Placed here between the philosopher, the superior artist, and God, José finds himself in distinguished company. In the opera, however, José is the only one who feels that his love is a proprietary right. Escamillo, for example, patiently waits his turn. Even Micaëla has no desire to hold on to José, for in Act III she refers to him as "celui que j'aimais jadis" (the one I once loved). Nor is José always possessive. As soon as Carmen enters the picture, he easily lets go of Micaëla, his mother's messenger. While possessiveness is the characteristic feature of José's love for Carmen, the opera itself presents the tragic outcome of the lovers' liaison as a conflict between divergent concepts of love, between contradictory emotional needs, between antithetical forms of desire.

CARMEN AND JOSÉ: A DUET

Incapable of choosing an object of love for and by himself, José acts and reacts in terms of others. It was at his mother's suggestion that he looked on Micaëla as a love object. Whereas all the soldiers court Carmen, José at first shows no interest in her. It is she who, intrigued by his indifference, forces him to notice her. If it were not for the unexpected return of Lieutenant Zuñiga at the end of Act II, José would leave Carmen to return to his barracks. And at the end, his words to her are revealing; it is not love but regret at having forgone his salvation and fear that she will laugh at him in the arms of his rival that prompt him to kill her:

> Ainsi, le salut de mon âme,
> Je l'aurai perdu pour que toi,
> Pour que tu t'en ailles, infâme!
> Entre ses bras, rire de moi.
> Non, par le sang, tu n'iras pas!
> Carmen, c'est moi que tu suivras!

(And so, the salvation of my soul / I shall have lost for you, / for you to go running, you harlot, / into his arms, laughing at me. / No, by the saints, you shall not go, / Carmen, it is I that you shall follow.)

For José, desire is always triggered by someone else, determined by another, inscribed therefore in a mimetic system. In the triangle of mimetic desire, as René Girard defines it, "it is the rival who should be accorded the dominant role," for "the subject desires the object because the rival desires it."[18] Carmen, whose charms are not powerful enough to keep José when the bugles sound, becomes irresistible when she is coveted by another man. For Girard, mimetic desire is the operating principle of human relationships, and this of necessity leads to violence, a violence that is averted through the ritual sacrifice of some scapegoat. In the Girardian model, Carmen occupies the position of the bull, a sacrificial animal immolated for the common good on the altar of violence. But in the triangle of mimetic desire, Carmen stands only as the sign of José's bonding to other men. Or, to quote Luce Irigaray, in such a system, "woman exists only as the possibility of mediation, transaction, transition, transference between man and his fellow-creatures, indeed, between man and himself."[19] As the medium between two men, Carmen is neither the matador nor the bull—she is the matador's cape, the lure with which the matador goads his opponent and behind which he hides his sword until the moment of truth. Once lifted, the cape reveals the likeness of the two combatants, unveils a subject trapped in its own gaze. In the triangle of mimetic desire, the triad becomes a dyad, the dyad a one.

José is possessive, not because he is possessed by some Other, but because the other is himself. The chaste Micaëla can be abandoned because a widowed mother, no matter how phallic and fetishized she may be, is no match for the father, for another man's gaze. As another man's object of love Carmen cannot be abandoned or rejected, for she is the sign of José's self-image. In José's case, love is a narcissistic eroticism, the specular bond of a man caught in his own reflection.

For Carmen, however, it is not the lover—he is not a mirror for her own image—but the freedom to love that matters, to love without constraints. Her object of desire is desire itself, not simply to be desired, but herself to be desiring. In the Habañera, an aria that stands as her *ars erotica*, she describes love as unpredictable, uncontrollable, absent when you want it, present when you no longer await it, appearing when and where you least expect it. The Habañera is composed of free-floating stanzas of varying lengths, with three different voices skillfully interlaced.[20] There are descriptive passages in the impersonal, collective third person:

[18] *Violence and the Sacred*, trans. Patrick Gregory (Baltimore, Md., 1977), 145–46.
[19] *This Sex Which is Not One*, trans. Catherine Porter (Ithaca, N.Y., 1985), 193.
[20] According to Charles Pigot, *Georges Bizet et son oeuvre* (Paris, 1911), 211–12, Bizet composed the lyrics and the music of the Habañera during rehearsals. The song was rewritten thirteen times before the composer and Galli-Marié, the first interpreter of Carmen, agreed on a final version. Ulrich Weisstein seconds the opinion of Paul Landormy, *Bizet* (Paris, 1950), 167, when he writes of the Habañera: "Bizet appears here, at any rate, if

L'amour est un oiseau rebelle
Que nul ne peut apprivoiser,
Et c'est bien en vain qu'on l'appelle,
S'il lui convient de refuser.
[. . .]
L'amour est enfant de Bohême,
Il n'a jamais connu de loi.

(Love is a rebellious bird / no one can tame; / if love refuses to appear, / it is in vain that one calls it. / [. . .] / Love is a child of Bohemia / who follows no laws.)

The last two lines are repeated twice. After the impersonal third person, Carmen switches to the first person:

Si tu ne m'aimes pas, je t'aime;
Mais si je t'aime, prends garde à toi!

(If you don't love me, I love you; / but if I love you, watch out!)

Finally, the second person comes into the song:

L'amour est loin, tu peux l'attendre;
Tu ne l'attends plus . . . il est là!
Tout autour de toi, vite, vite,
Il vient s'en va, puis il revient;
Tu crois le tenir, il t'évite;
Tu veux l'éviter, il te tient.

(Love is far away, you can await it; / you give up waiting—here it is! / All around you, fast, fast, / it comes, goes, and then comes back; / you think you hold it, and it escapes you; / you want to avoid it, and it holds you.)

When she sings this stanza, Carmen is almost always seen addressing some young man. Although she says "you," her words are part of a monologue; this feigned dialogue is but a rhetorical figure, an apostrophe. She acts as if she were addressing an interlocutor, but the "you" is also herself. In Carmen's vision of love, there is a specular "I"/"you," a streak of narcissism, but there is also an impersonal third pronoun, at once singular and plural, the "one" present in the first stanza: "It is in vain that *one*

---

compared with Meilhac and Halévy, as the one collaborator with the soundest intuition and the deepest understanding of the subject under consideration. The words he wrote are among the best in the entire libretto and may be regarded as the only ones that really enable one to fully understand Carmen's character." Weisstein, *The Essence of Opera* (London, 1964), 226.

calls it." Carmen's conception of love is founded on a triadic structure, but the three positions are not in a mimetic relationship. If "I" and "You" are reflections of each other, the pronoun "one" is the signifier of the Other. By introducing a possible third position, an impersonal third voice, Carmen explodes the specularity of the "I" and "you." The "I," the "you," or the "Other" can be tamed no more than love itself. All are always free, and this is why Carmen is in love with love itself, and enjoys loving as much as being loved, loves herself as well as others. Love is Bohemian because Bohemians are free. A gypsy without freedom has ceased to be a gypsy. Her vision of love is that of a bird in flight. Twice a child, of love born and born to love, twice a gypsy, twice free. Not necessarily mutually shared or even reciprocated, love nonetheless happens; it is an energy in constant motion. Lovers play out, in turn, each and every role. They are plural and yet one, free in their identity and ethnicity, giving and receiving without restraint. Carmen's vision bears a striking resemblance to the libidinal economy, the feminine *jouissance* that Hélène Cixous exalts in *The Newly Born Woman*. For Cixous, the feminine Imaginary allows "self-constituting a subjectivity that splits apart without regret,"[21] and to this divided subjectivity corresponds an emancipated, dispossessing form of love:

> The new love dares the other, wants it, seems in flight, be-leaves, does some stealing between knowing and making up. She, the one coming from forever, doesn't stand still, she goes all over, she exchanges, she is desire-that-gives. Not shut up inside the paradox of the gift-that-takes or in the illusion of onely uniting.[22]

"The test of love," Julia Kristeva tells us, "is a test of language, of its univocity and its referential and communicative powers."[23] When José and Carmen speak of love they are not speaking of the same thing; as Carl Dahlhaus remarks, "there is not a single duet in the work in which the pair express unanimity of emotion."[24] Carmen never says "Je t'aime"—at least she never lets the words "Je t'aime" stand alone, as a self-sufficient and self-contained phrase. In the Habañera, for example, she says: "Si tu ne m'aimes pas, je t'aime," a statement that can be read in two different ways. "If you don't love me, I will love you" expresses a causal relation—after all, José caught her interest precisely because he seemed uninterested in her. But this sentence can also be translated, "I will love you whether you love me or not," love being for her unpredict-

---

[21] Cixous (see n. 15 above), 90.
[22] Cixous, 99.
[23] *Histoires d'amour* (Paris, 1983), 10.
[24] *Realism in Nineteenth-Century Music*, trans. Mary Whittall (London, 1985), 89.

able and uncontrollable. She speaks of love in the future tense or inscribes it in indirect discourse. In Act III she tells José, "Ce qui est sûr, c'est que je t'aime beaucoup moins qu'autrefois" (what is certain is that I love you a lot less than I used to); in Act IV she uses a negative construction, "Je ne t'aime plus" (I don't love you any more). And when in the last act she sings of her love for Escamillo, her "je t'aime" is an answer to his conditional question, and is couched in a long and complex sentence with several clauses:

> ESCAMILLO: Si tu m'aimes, Carmen, tu pourras tout à l'heure
> Etre fière de moi.
> CARMEN: Ah! je t'aime, Escamillo, je t'aime et que je meure,
> Si j'ai jamais aimé quelqu'un autant que toi.

(ESCAMILLO: If you love me, Carmen, you will very shortly / be proud of me. CARMEN: Oh! I love you, Escamillo, I love you, and may death take me / if I have ever loved any man more than you!)

Unlike Carmen, José incessantly repeats "je t'aime" and "je t'adore." Roland Barthes argues that "Je t'aime" (I love you) is only what linguists call a holophrastic expression.[25] That is to say: although it is composed of three words, the components of "je t'aime" come together as if they were only one. The popular French pronunciation "j't'aime" more adequately reflects the merging of these three words. In the conflation of these terms, the "I" and the "you" disappear into each other, become each other, and fuse with "aime," united, as it were, in "love." "Je t'aime" is the signifier of specular love, and thus—appropriately—the verbal expression of José's love. His aria "La fleur que tu m'avais jetée," which recounts his days in prison and tells of his desire to see (*revoir*) Carmen again, is a poem composed of two parts, structured by the alternation of the first and second persons, "je" and "tu," in either the subjective or the objective case. The interchangeability of their positions is underscored by the thematic development that starts with an object once belonging to Carmen, the flower, and ends with José's declaration that he was now her object: "Et j'étais une chose à toi" (And I was a thing belonging to you). Whether triggered by the smell of her flower, the recollection of her first appearance, or the memory of her glance, for José the mechanism of seduction is linked to sight, the limited vision of narcissistic self-reflection. José sings of *his* days in prison, *his* thoughts, *his* desire. His aria seems less a cry of selfless surrender, as Paul Landormy would have it,[26] than the expression of egotistic pride. Carmen is not blind to his words: "Non,

---

[25] *Fragments* (see n. 16 above), 175–83.
[26] *Bizet* (Paris, 1950), 185.

tu ne m'aimes pas," she answers him, "non, car si tu m'aimais / Là-bas, là-bas, tu me suivrais." (No, no, you don't love me, for if you loved me, / over there, over there, you would follow me.) José's *ars erotica*, as Carmen senses, is but an ode to himself. As a signifier, the flower not only denotes Carmen but is also a reminder of Narcissus, the beautiful Greek youth who died contemplating his own image mirrored in a pool and who is remembered by the flower that bears his name. In Greek myth, the nymph Echo pines away attempting to catch Narcissus' interest until there is nothing left of her corporeal being but her voice;[27] in José's romance, Carmen's bodily reality is reduced to a lingering scent. No wonder the cigarette girls laugh at the young men's loving words and vows of passion as just so much smoke!

Carmen's last word is "Tiens!," which she utters as she throws the ring, symbol of their relationship, back at José. "Tiens!" translates as "Here! Have it!" In French "Tiens!" has several meanings; it is the nexus of several intertwined signifieds. First, it is simply an exclamation, a cry, a sound. Secondly, it is the second person of the imperative form of the verb *tenir*, "to hold, to possess." In French, as in English, the second person pronoun, the marker of the addressee, is dropped in the imperative. Thirdly, *tien*, spelled without the mute "s," is also the form of the second-person possessive pronoun, "yours." Thus, in Carmen's utterance the "you" is simultaneously invisible and visible, at once absent and present, taken and given in the same breath. Finally, "Tiens!" brings back to mind the Habañera and its closing lines:

> Tu crois le tenir, il t'évite;
> Tu veux l'éviter, il te tient.

(You think you hold it, and it escapes you; / you want to avoid it, and it holds you.)

To love and be loved, as her aria reminds us, are beyond the scope of one's wish or power. Not merely a gesture of refusal, as Michel Cardoze suggests,[28] Carmen's final word is at one and the same time an assertion of freedom and a recognition of enslavement. In its explosive plurality, "Tiens!" comes to be the signifier of her love story, the trace of her *jouissance* at once affirmed and denied, the graphic remains of her voice.

Love, as the libretto indicates, hinges on the fictions that mask the iden-

---

[27] For a study of the Echo myth and the question of reading strategies, see Caren Greenberg, "Reading Reading: Echo's Abduction of Language," in *Women and Language in Literature and Society*, ed. Sally McConnell-Ginet, Ruth Borker, and Nelly Furman (New York, 1980), 300–309.

[28] Cardoze (see n. 3 above), 50.

tities of the pronouns "I" and "you." Love is but the movement, the flow, the energy of their eternal and yet impossible dialogue.

ACT III: CARMEN, LA CARMENCITA

"What is your name?" Escamillo asks. She answers: "Carmen, la Carmencita, as you please." Escamillo understands her answer as meaning that he has the option of calling her by one or the other name, and he replies: "Eh bien! Carmen ou la Carmencita" (Very well, Carmen *or* la Carmencita).[29] For Escamillo, one name seems to exclude the other. But Carmen presents both names in apposition, one echoing the other. Her answer leaves Escamillo, as well as us, free to choose or not to choose between two identities: her formal public name and her intimate diminutive. As the etymology of the former implies, Carmen means poetry, magic, and music; and she performs these arts, which are her own, with dazzling skill. At her arrest she does not refuse to answer the lieutenant's questions, but merely gives him a non-answer and dismisses his authority with a simple "tra la la." It is through a song seemingly addressed to no one in particular that she makes a rendezvous with José at the tavern of Lillas Pastia. For her, only tarot cards speak the language of truth; words are merely objects that can be fashioned to suit her purposes. Breaking a plate to make castanets when she cannot find her own, Carmen reveals herself to be what Claude Lévi-Strauss would call a *bricoleuse*, a tinker, a gypsy in every way.[30] A similar inventiveness characterizes her speech. When José tells her that he is repairing the chain of his priming pin, his "épinglette," she calls him "épinglier de mon âme," that is to say, "fastener of my soul"—an appropriate description and a startling metaphor. Later, when José expresses his jealousy, referring simultaneously to his bile and his yellow uniform, she tells him that he is a real canary in coat and character: "Canari va . . . tu es un vrai canari d'habit et de caractère." In this figure of speech (zeugma), two phrases or words belonging to sep-

---

[29] Act II, at the tavern of Lillas Pastia:
ESCAMILLO: Dis-moi ton nom, et la première fois que je frapperai
le taureau, ce sera ton nom que je prononcerai.
CARMEN: Je m'appelle la Carmencita.
ESCAMILLO: La Carmencita?
CARMEN: Carmen, la Carmencita, comme tu voudras.
ESCAMILLO: Eh bien! Carmen ou la Carmencita . . .
(ESCAMILLO: Tell me your name, and when I first strike the bull, it will be your name that I pronounce. CARMEN: My name is la Carmencita. ESCAMILLO: La Carmencita? CARMEN: Carmen, la Carmencita, as you please. ESCAMILLO: Well, Carmen or la Carmencita . . .)
[30] *The Savage Mind* (Chicago, 1966), 16–30.

arate registers are joined together: José's uniform with his jealousy, the concrete with the figural.

José is no *bricoleur*. In his world everything has a set function. His is the engineering mind: repairing a chain to restore it to its original purpose, keeping the file Carmen sent him to sharpen his lance, returning money for which he found no use. And in comparison with Carmen's repertoire of rhetorical devices, José's verbal skills are noticeable only for their indigence. His speech is commonly prosaic, flat, trite. Whereas Carmen relies on a variety of tropes, the only figure of speech José uses is the simile. He tells us, for example, that Carmen's flower hit him "like a bullet," a fitting metaphor for his tragic story, but hardly an original image for a soldier. When he recounts the scene in the cigar factory, he describes Carmen as "rolling her eyes like a chameleon," adding that afterwards she was "sweet as a lamb." José's analogies are stereotypes: they do not add new meaning, they add intensity and elongation, they are simply syntagms of contiguity, their function is metonymic.

Both Carmen and José seem to share a predilection for animal imagery. But whereas in José's speech they are comparative clichés, in Carmen's the animals appear only as metaphors. In the Habañera, she calls love "a rebellious bird"; to describe her relationship with José, she uses a proverb: "Chien et loup ne font pas longtemps bon ménage" (Dogs and wolves don't live together for long). The metaphoric and metonymic aspects of language are reproduced in Carmen's and José's arias about love. For her, love is expressed through a Habañera, a dance, the enactment of a movement; for him, desire is represented by the flower she once wore, an extension of herself.

METAPHOR and metonymy, the very stuff of literature, form one more dichotomy in the long inventory of oppositions that structure Bizet's opera. How then can one practice a feminist reading of *Carmen* that does not limit itself to a mere reversal of oppositions, but alludes to the possibility of some deconstructive displacement? It is of course only a rhetorical question, a mimetic gesture; in other words, an apostrophe. One could easily denounce Bizet's opera as another example of a work showing that a woman's expression of her *jouissance* has to be stifled; or one could put these oppositions in a dialectical process and hope to arrive at some synthesis, an analytical third stance that would erase all differences. For my part, however, I prefer simply to follow Carmen's lead (*Lied*), to read the libretto through Carmen, to follow her moves, to be attentive to her speech and to listen to her voice. Like Carmen's dual name, "Carmen, la Carmencita," these are readings not in opposition but in apposition, set side by side, echoing each other, in which I attempt both to delineate the arena of the visual and to modulate the phrasing of a song. A zeugmatic process, if you will, that joins the concrete with the figural, the metonymic with the metaphorical, the masculine of the text with its feminine, its exteriority with its interiority.

Having pinned (*épingler*), as it were, the fictions of the critical discourses of my modernity on the libretto, it is now time to release *Carmen* from its and my textual hold: to let the libretto turn into opera, and by giving up control be free to enjoy the spectacle, and open to the seduction of the performance.

Opera! A world uniquely Carmen's own: Poetry, Magic, Music. An extravagant assemblage of drama and music; a bizarre mixture of voices, dances, decors, costumes, and extras with orchestral accompaniment; and yet, this peculiar, queer, often grotesque coming together in unison of different art forms creates an indescribable theatrical happening, a fantastic experience, a visual as well as an aural enchantment! And so, in lieu of a bouquet of flowers to the *prima donna* of the opera house, for the *diva* of the libretto, an academic offering of ink, paper, and words: a postscriptum.

P.S.   To Carmen, la Carmencita
                        The echo of a voice
                        With love.

183

KATHERINE BERGERON

How to Avoid Believing (While Reading Iago's "Credo")

The "text of pleasure," imagines Roland Barthes at the start of his *Le Plaisir du texte*, "is a sanctioned Babel," a place where the reader "gains access to bliss by the cohabitation of languages *working side by side*."[1] If such confusion of tongues be the stuff of pleasure, one could hardly find a greater source of gratification than the text of an opera. More than just the libretto, the complete text of an opera represents an animated encounter of words, music, and spectacle: a coming together capable of arousing the reader through its very excess.[2] With different languages competing for attention at every turn, the reader is pulled now here, now there, until the moment of the last word, the closing sonority, the final curtain.

One subject willing to take operatic pleasure in this manner is surely the opera "buff" (we recall that this word originally denoted an enthusiast about going to fires),[3] a reader for whom the competition inherent in the total text is cause not for distress but delight. The opera buff needs no justification for his enjoyment; he takes in all manner of details purely for their own sake: the greater the number, the greater his enthusiasm. But there is another type of reader—the so-called specialist—who seems to find in the text of opera an altogether different experience. William Weaver reveals something about this reader in the introduction to his *Seven Verdi Librettos*. Although he, too, speaks of pleasure, there is implied a certain reserve: "to the ordinary reader a volume of librettos in translation, divorced from their music, may seem a peculiar enterprise . . . Only specialists sit down to read a libretto for pleasure."[4]

One imagines that there cannot be much pleasure in this reading—not, at least, in Barthes' sense of the term. For the specialist practices reading

---

[1] Roland Barthes, *Le Plaisir du texte*, trans. Richard Miller, *The Pleasure of the Text* (New York, 1975), 4 (emphasis as in the original). See also Jonathan Culler, *On Deconstruction* (Ithaca, N.Y., 1982), for a discussion of Barthes' views on readers and reading.

[2] Barthes' discussion, 8, of Severo Sardury's *Cobra* presents a brief but tantalizing account of excess in the text.

[3] This usage apparently evolved from the buff leather coats worn by volunteer firemen in New York City during the first quarter of the nineteenth century. See *Webster's New Collegiate Dictionary* (Springfield, Mass., 1977), s.v. "buff."

[4] William Weaver, *Seven Verdi Librettos* (New York, 1975), xii.

of an informed sort: a reading that reduces confusion, limits competition, because it knows in advance what the text is *supposed* to mean. What this specialist knows, of course, is the music. He reads the libretto fully aware of that music now "divorced" from the words; he uses music to smooth the rough edges of the text, to answer the difficulties that might arise as he reads. His pleasure comes from control, rather than from letting go: it issues from the knowledge that everything is just as it should be.

My interest in Barthes' reader—a reader he dubs "anti-hero"—is thus motivated in some part by a perverse curiosity about one who could find gratification in incongruity, who could, as Barthes puts it, "live in contradiction without shame."[5] But beyond professional voyeurism there lies a further motivation which has to do with the very nature of the operatic text—a text defined by the contradictions inherent in its three distinct signifying systems. While such a text is a pleasure for Barthes' reader, it seems to pose problems for the specialist, whose often-defined task is to affirm not confusion but coherence—the ultimate "readability" of the text—and, further, to define that coherence in terms of a single code of signification: music.[6] Yet this type of reading appears to undermine the very features that distinguish the genre and all that might be pleasing about it. Does not Barthes' "anti-hero," taking his pleasure as it comes (in whatever form), then constitute the better reader of opera?

I should like to pursue this question through a reading of Iago's "Credo" from Act II of Verdi's *Otello*. This unusual piece—an elaborate trope on the Shakespearean text which served as the opera's model—has been explained in various ways by Verdi scholars: explained away by some, scrutinized and argued over by others.[7] Dismissive or not, this body of criticism reveals a general view of the piece as somehow problematic. Certain tonal "perversions" have been pointed out; and the flagrant archaisms of its literary style (a kind of trademark of the librettist, Boito) have been commented on by more than one reader. Indeed, Julian Budden

[5] Barthes (see n. 1 above), 3.

[6] Frits Noske's concern over this practice of opera specialists is expressed succinctly in the preface to his *The Signifier and the Signified* (The Hague, 1977), v: "Musicologists have treated opera as a musical object, analysing its component elements as if they were consecutive movements in a symphony or a string quartet. Questions concerning both verbal and musical drama . . . are almost always ignored in scholarly writings on opera. Even specific operatic problems (e.g., what is the exact function of a libretto?) are evaded or overlooked."

[7] In his chapter "Otello: Drama through Structure," Noske (despite what he said in his introduction) seems to view the "Credo" as little more than an effective characterization of Iago's wickedness—his "self-revelation" as an evil man—and focuses the major part of his discussion on its supply of melodic motives. For a more detailed analysis of the piece as a whole, see James A. Hepokoski's review of Budden, *The Operas of Verdi*, III (see n. 8 below), *Journal of the American Musicological Society*, 35 (1982), 577–85.

has gone so far as to judge the text "nonsense—a conglomeration of sentiments which Shakespeare's villain would not have thought worth formulating."[8]

Such descriptions obviously point to conflicts within the text, to inconsistencies that have thrown readers off course. And while contradictions like these can serve to justify the dismissive readings, they may also encourage new readings. If we return to Barthes for a moment, this "Credo" may begin to appear not so much problematic as essentially gratifying—like some version of his "text of bliss" that "unsettles the reader's historical, cultural, [and] psychological assumptions, the consistency of his tastes."[9] The pleasure of the "Credo," then, lies in the way it resists an easy reading, thwarting expectations, defying logic. And the pleasure of the reader comes when he allows himself thus to be unsettled—to be taken in by a text that advises, like Shakespeare's Iago, "I am not what I am."[10]

THE poetic structure of the "Credo" could of itself cause a reader some discomfort. Its unconventional design—the work of a librettist whose ingenuity has been both admired and condemned by critics—represents something of a novelty in operatic verse. For while the text shows formal articulations at its surface, every expectation of regularity is denied: the verses yield neither reliable metrical patterns nor conventional strophic divisions.[11] Complete sentences, marked off in the text with dashes (as if they needed to be made more recognizable), are the only strophe-like units apparent in the form, and even these escape regularity by outlining segments of changing proportions.[12]

—Credo in un Dio crudel che		I believe in a cruel God who
m'ha creato	a	created me

[8] Julian Budden, *The Operas of Verdi*, III: *From Don Carlos to Falstaff* (New York, 1981), 359.

[9] Barthes (n. 1 above), 14.

[10] Iago's admission may give us insight into Verdi's enthusiastic response to Boito's text of the "Credo," a text obviously unlike anything the original *Othello* has to offer: "bellissimo questo credo . . . e shaespeariano [sic] in tutto e per tutto." Perhaps it was the slippery character of this "Credo" that seemed so "wholly Shakespearean" to Verdi, rather than any protracted expression of evil sentiment. For the complete text, see Mario Medici and Marcello Conati, ed., *Carteggio Verdi-Boito* (Parma, 1978), I, 74–76.

[11] In view of the text originally conceived for Iago at this point in the drama—four quatrains cast in regular *doppi quinari*—this alternative form seems especially significant. For a transcription of the earlier text, complete with commentary, see Alessandro Luzio, ed., *Carteggi verdiani*, II (Rome, 1935), 110.

[12] Such dashes (presumably in Boito's hand) appear in the original text, a facsimile of which is reproduced in Evan Baker, ed., *Giuseppe Verdi: Vicende, problemi e mito di un artista e del suo tempo* (Colorno, 1985), Tavola 71. The translation here is adapted from Weaver (n. 4 above), 448–51.

Simile a sé, e che nell'ira io nomo.	b	Similar to himself and whom I name in my wrath.
—Dalla viltà d'un germe o d'un atòmo	b	From the meanness of a seed or particle
Vile son nato.	a	I was born evil.
—Son scellerato	a	I am wicked
Perché son uomo	b	Because I am a man
E sento il fango originario in me.	c	And I feel the primordial mud within me.
—Sí! Questa è la mia fé!	c	Yes! This is my faith!
—Credo con fermo cuor, siccome crede	d	I believe with a firm heart just as
La vedovella al Tempio,	e	The little widow in Church believes
Che il mal ch'io penso e che da me procede	d	That the evil I conceive, that comes from me,
Per mio destino adempio.	e	I fulfill through my destiny.
—Credo che il giusto è un istrion beffardo	f	I believe that the honest man is a lying actor
E nel viso e nel cuor,	g	In his face and in his heart,
Che tutto è in lui bugiardo,	f	That everything in him is lies,
Lagrima, bacio, sguardo,	f	Tears, kiss, gaze,
Sacrificio ed onor.	g	Sacrifice and honor.
—E credo l'uom gioco d'iniqua sorte	h	And I believe man the plaything of an unjust fate
Dal germe della culla	i	From the babe of the cradle
Al verme dell'avel.	j	To the worm of the grave.
—Vien dopo tanta irrision la Morte!	h	After all this mockery comes Death!
—E poi?—La Morte è il Nulla,	i	And what then? Death is Nothing
E vecchia fola il Ciel.	j	And Heaven an old wives' tale.

The disruption of formal expectations seems to be indicated in the very label Boito affixes to this novel verse form: *metri rotti*, "broken" or "fractured" verses. It is not the division of sentences into lines of unequal length that makes these verses unusual, but their exploitation of rhyme.[13] Whereas a reader would expect to find rhyme operating in metrically regular *versi lirici*, he is startled to find it in these more freely conceived lines.

[13] While the construction of long operatic monologues without a regular meter (generally, using lines of 7 and 11 syllables) was incontestably a well-established practice by the time Boito conceived of this "Credo," his occasional use of 5-syllable lines might also be considered something of a novelty.

In *versi sciolti*—the conventional alternative to rhymed and metrically uniform verse—the absence of rhyme defines an aspect of the speaking style associated with operatic recitative. Rhymed poetry, on the other hand, signals the formally expressive (and powerful) domain of aria. Thus what appears to be "broken" in these verses is the autonomy of form. By combining the force of end-rhyme with the freedom of blank verse, the "Credo" presents itself neither as recitative nor aria, but as some kind of form suspended between.

The use of rhyme in these *metri rotti* also causes the form to appear a good deal less arbitrary—giving rhyme *and* reason, so to speak, to the apparently haphazard internal divisions of the text. For the individual sentences within the "Credo" are generally arranged in longer or shorter sections according to the distribution of rhymes. And through this minimal scheme, the reader can perceive some motivation behind the contour of individual lines and the shapes of the sentences themselves. The point where this rhyme "scheme" fails to observe the basic structural unit of the sentence, then, appears to have interesting consequences for this already marginal form. A full stop in the third stanza, for example, following the assertion "E sento il fango originario in me" (And I feel the primordial mud within me), draws attention not only to the strong sonic difference between "*me*" and the preceding rhymes, but also to the line's abrupt *tronco* ending.[14] The rhythmic caesura would seem to impel the reader toward the next line, "Sí! Questa è la mia fé!" (Yes! This is my faith!), an exclamation that completes the rhyming pair at the same time as it signals closure. The explosive affirmation of faith also stands out structurally, for it marks a complete section with but a single line of text. It is thus interesting to observe a similar effect in the only other single-line stanza in the "Credo," also an exclamation: "Vien dopo tanta irrision la Morte!" (After all this mockery comes Death!). As before, the verse follows a sentence whose rhyme is left dangling; and its entry appears to complete both the rhyme and the structural unit. But this time the resolution is ineffective, transformed immediately into a question: "E poi?" (And what then?).[15] Turned back on itself, "la Morte" is ironically redefined, its apparent strength reduced to "Nulla"—Nothing—by a lingering couplet that thwarts any possibility of a strongly rhymed ending.

Ingenious as this form may be, it is not the only image the "Credo" presents of itself. To confront this text not as poetry but as a piece of

---

[14] *Tronco* refers to a line of verse ending (in "truncated" fashion) with a stressed syllable; such an ending is distinct from the more typically Italian trochaic ending, called *piano*, in which the strong syllable is followed by a weak one, e.g. "cre-*a*-to," "*na*-to," "*no*-mo," "*uo*-mo," etc.

[15] Note that in Boito's original "E poi?" is followed by another dash, a signal that this question is unique within such an apparently "assertive" form.

music (a task perhaps now long overdue) is to find its formal conception entirely altered. Following musical declamation only, for instance, a reader (or listener) finds the form of these broken verses "broken" once more, recast into a new shape whose difference cannot be measured in terms of any conventional standard of value. This is the beginning of pleasure in the text: no sooner has one configuration passed across the reader's imagination than another comes to attract him—appearances are never what they seem. The musical setting of the "Credo" thus becomes a musical "unsettling," an inflecting of the text that alters not only its formal appearance but also its force:

Credo in un Dio crudel che m'ha creato simile a *sé*,	a
E che nell'ira io nomo.	b
Dalla viltà d'un germe	c
O d'un atòmo	b
Vile son nato.	d
Son scellerato perché son uomo	b
E sento il fango originario in *me*.	a
Sí! Questa è la mia *fé*!	a

Credo con fermo *cuor*,	e
Siccome crede la vedovella al Tempio,	f
Che il mal ch'io penso e che da me procede	g
Per mio destino adempio.	f
Credo che il giusto è un istrion beffardo e nel viso e nel *cuor*,	e
Che tutto è in lui bugiardo, lagrima, bacio, sguardo,	h
Sacrificio ed *onor*.	e
E credo l'uom gioco d'iniqua *sorte*	i
Dal germe della culla	j
Al verme dell'avel.	k
Vien dopo tanta irrision la *Morte*!	i

E poi?	l
E Poi?	l
La Morte è il Nulla	j
E vecchia fola il Ciel.	k

Such an unsettling is apparent in the very first line. In the momentum of its recitation the voice passes over the first end-rhyme observed by the poetry ("creato") and comes to rest on the word "sé." The presence of a comma in the text may in fact prescribe this type of phrasing; but one can see the impact that this musical figure has on the overall operation of rhyme: by bringing "sé" to the musical surface—with the help of a prominent diminished chord—the first line of text now articulates the same *tronco* ending that had earlier signaled the entrance of the text's first exclamation ("Sì! Questa è la mia fé!"). With the truncated measure thus brought forward, the music seems both to foreshadow the announcement and to prepare for an even stronger close than that achieved in the poetry. This musical preference for strong ("masculine") poetic endings emerges at another significant moment, immediately following the exclamation of faith. The new line of text (marked in the poetry by an initial "Credo" and a final "crede") is musically shortened this time to highlight the word "cuor," a rhyme that serves to establish, as before, the sense of a larger formal unit extending to the word "onor." It may even mean to extend further; for the declamation of the next lines, in honoring the segmentation of the original poetry, brings out the important words "sorte" and "Morte," a pairing whose sonic correspondence to "cuor" and "onor" can hardly be missed.

Less significant formal arrangements are also altered under the influence of music; in fact, the contour of almost every sentence appears to yield to musical fancy, sections being lengthened or shortened with no apparent motivation beyond the music's power to do so. Yet among the most interesting of these formal changes is the treatment of the text's one interrogative statement: "E poi?" This moment represents the only point where a line of poetry is musically reiterated—as if the voice were unequipped to transmit the force of a question in the space of a single musical utterance. And the slowing down of the declamation at this point seems to lead in turn to a kind of poetic disintegration. For in the setting of these final lines, beginning with the repeated question, the words are increasingly overwhelmed by their musical surroundings—orchestral sounds and silences take over. The role played by poetry in marking formal closure thus strains to be acknowledged, upstaged now by a bombastic musical figure whose formal purpose appears also to have given way to the pleasure of sheer sound.

THIS subtle shifting of the textual form, a result of the "cohabitation" of words and music, represents only one of the ways in which the "Credo" embodies contradiction. Beyond external appearances, the text takes on other problematic identities, which may be just as "unsettling" to a reader's assumptions. For example, the very fact that Iago sings a "Credo"—a profession of belief having apparently little to do with Shakespeare—

raises questions about the text's true function, as well as its proper relationship to prayer.

Iago's piece is frequently described as a "mock" Credo, suggesting that one might read this piece as an imitation of the Credo from the Roman Mass, or, alternatively, as "mockery"—a parody of prayer. Certainly, aspects of the structure recommend it as imitation: four prominent repetitions of the verb "credo" appear to signal the presence of four "articles of belief," to correspond (however obliquely) with the same structure in the Roman Creed.[16] Even more significant, the initial affirmation, "Credo in un Dio crudel," bears a likeness to the Latin "Credo in unum Deum" that is unmistakable. But they are not the same. The adjective "crudel," playing on the very sound of the opening verb ("credo"), clearly upsets the identity—marking Iago's text as unique, and calling the whole idea of "traditional" belief into question. And this crucial (and cruel) turn sets into motion a whole series of statements which increasingly disrupt order in this profession of faith.

The first disturbance in the "Credo" follows immediately after the modifier "crudel." Following the apparent form of a Creed, the speaker— the subject of the verb "credo"—makes a move to describe the God in whom he professes belief.[17] But the relative clause "che m'ha creato simile a sé" (who created me similar to himself) seems only to direct itself back toward the speaker, an action that gives way to yet another clause which forcefully completes the reversal. With the end of the first complete sentence, the cruel God—once an object of belief—is reduced to an object of the speaker's action: he is the God "whom *I* name in my wrath."

This empowering gesture on the part of the first person seems to remove the text even further from a traditional statement of faith. For a true Creed, we recall, is built around the action of a single verb, "credo," a verb whose subject bears some consideration. To say the Creed's "I believe" is to perform an act of speech in some way distinct from ordinary

---

[16] A text also based on four articles of belief, the first of which is cast in the formula "Credo in . . ." All other statements use a shortened form, "Et in . . . ," whose conjunction obviously refers to the original verb. The four articles begin as follows:

> Credo in unum Deum . . .
> Et in unum dominum, Jesum Christum . . .
> Et in Spiritum Sanctum, Dominum . . .
> Et in unam . . . ecclesiam . . .

The fact that Boito himself called his text "a sort of Evil Credo" seems to suggest his identification with this type of prayer, for which the traditional Roman form would be the obvious paradigm.

[17] Just as in the Roman Creed "Credo in unum Deum" is followed by a list of attributes— "patrem omnipotentem," "factorem caeli et terrae," and so forth.

discourse. The "I" who utters these words speaks not as an individual, but as a member of a larger community of believers: he is the same as every other "I" that professes the faith. Having no individual voice, no separate presence, the speaker who says "I believe" performs an act that is fundamentally social; his voice merges with the voices of all the faithful in order that they might speak as one. Indeed, it seems especially significant that in its liturgical usage the opening formula of the Creed ("Credo in unum Deum") is not even spoken by the community: it is intoned only by the priest—the one speaker who is present, in some sense, for all. The subject of the verb "credo" appears then to be blurred, if not entirely effaced, by the very structure of the text. To perceive this subject speaking out—saying "I name," as in the opening lines of Iago's text—is thus to signal an unprecedented moment for the act of faith, a moment that causes the reader to wonder who this subject is and whether his "Credo" can really be a Creed after all.[18]

Having come forward, the speaker (shall we call him Iago now?) then proceeds to describe himself, completing his bold "I am" with predicates ("scellerato," "uomo") that ever affirm his presence and lead to a more excessive claim—his acknowledgment of primordial mud flowing within him. And here, in the midst of confusion, the speaker hastens to confirm all that he has said. Yet by the time his impassioned announcement "Yes! This is my faith!" appears in the text, the first person speaks with so much personal authority that the exclamation seems no longer to govern the original act of "I believe" ("credo") but rather "I feel" ("sento"). The subject's individual voice has made impassive belief sensual—primordial mud ("fango originario"), the symbol of this speaker's constitution not as a believer but as a man.

What is a reader now to believe? The remainder of the text hardly settles the question. To read on is to become more tangled in feelings, eluded

[18] In his chapter "The Nature of Pronouns," the French linguist Émile Benveniste presents a brilliant exposition of the special function of the pronoun "I" in discourse, an exposition that may shed light on the problematic role of the first person in Iago's text. Benveniste defines "I" simply as "the person who is uttering the present instance of discourse containing *I*," providing the following explanation: "if I perceive two successive instances of discourse containing *I*, uttered in the same voice, nothing guarantees to me that one of them is not a reported discourse, a quotation in which *I* could be imputed to another." For Benveniste, "I" is definable only in the moment of utterance; every time it is spoken, the possibilities for signification change. Iago's Creed thus presents a dual problem: the reader must first cope with the presence of a speaker saying something other than "I believe"; then, having acknowledged this second "I," he must determine its relationship to the original. See Émile Benveniste, *Problems in General Linguistics*, trans. Mary E. Meek (Coral Gables, Fla., 1971), 217–22. I am grateful to James Siegel for bringing this text, and his own careful *explication*, to my attention.

by beliefs. For while the three reiterations of the word "credo" certainly hark back to the authority of the text's first word, the presence of a clearly defined speaker cannot help inflecting these repeated verbs, giving each new "I believe," as it were, Iago's voice and body, an identity the first utterance did not yet have. Indeed, even the syntactical arrangement has changed. The verb "credo" is presented here not in the form "I believe *in* . . ." but as part of the construction "I believe *that* . . . ," making the statements more like personal opinions than impassive beliefs. It becomes difficult to view the "Credo" now as any kind of "evil" imitation of the Roman Creed, or even as a simple parody of it; a more serious conflict confronts the reader: whether to read the text as a Creed or not. The contradiction played out in the opening lines is thus fulfilled in the verses that follow, brought to an ironic conclusion in Iago's final exclamation: "After all this mockery comes Death!" Is this to be the fate of the speaker? the believer? the reader? Or is it simply the fate of a text that turns on itself again and again?

THE only answer the text seems to offer comes in the form of another question, "E poi?"—"And what then?" (or perhaps, even more simply, "So?"). The response reminds us once again that nothing has been settled, a conclusion that is borne out further when we examine more of the musical setting of the "Credo." Those conflicting intentions contained in Iago's opening lines are played out through the music at a number of structural levels, with a similar result: music offers no easy solutions to the problem of what to believe.

Music is, however, effective in setting up the problem. The opening vocal gesture—stark recitation over an orchestral trill played by violas and low clarinets—gives the impression not so much of operatic recitative as of a liturgical reciting tone, a simple melodic formula structured around a single pitch. It is as if the solo voice meant to imitate the voice of the priest, intoning those first words of the Creed ("Credo in . . .") with all the solemnity proper to such a profession of faith. But this illusion does not last long. With the end of the first phrase, the voice ceases its recitation, shaping the words that follow ("e che nell'ira io nomo") into a line at once more melodic and tonally directed, articulated by a sudden cadence to E♭ major in the full orchestra. This contrast of orchestral textures, of vocal effects, and of tonality (the onslaught of the full orchestra causing E♭ major to sound somehow unexpected) fills the brief space with a profusion of mixed signals—oppositions which prove the "Credo" to be as difficult to pin down musically as it is textually.

The strategy of these opening measures might be seen as a kind of musical representation of the problem of "speakers" inherent in the first

193

lines. Interrupting the recitation, the fragment of melody that starts the second phrase (and completes the entire thought) is a form of musical subversion: the established aura of prayer is undermined by this vocal gesture—this new "voice"—that now takes control. The shift toward melody might be read, then, as a shift of intentions, a sign that marks the moment when prayer is given up for another type of speech. But to consider melody in this piece is also to consider the larger problem of form. As we observed earlier, the "Credo" can be classified neither as recitative nor as aria; and while it appears to function more like a real "set piece" than other numbers in the opera,[19] it tends to avoid expansive melodic lines, presenting vocal melodies instead in short bursts—terse phrases that seem more like motives than fully developed tunes.[20] Such a reductive approach to melody indicates something about the problematic form of the piece, so that "tunelessness" appears at another level to be a sign of this Creed's equivocal nature.

These observations may enhance our understanding of portions of the piece where melodic lines are featured. Among the most obvious are the settings that introduce the three other articles of faith presented in the "Credo."[21] Each of those phrases begins, predictably, with the word "credo," and each outlines a similar vocal gesture (a stepwise ascent of a third) whose repetition provides a kind of rhetorical emphasis; the melodic treatment of the statements is certainly to be distinguished from the plain recitation of the first "Credo." But what is particularly interesting in the repeated "I believe" is a unifying motive—a fragment that derives from the very melody which subverted the opening recitation (Ex. 1). The use of this melodic "sign" may suggest that the later statements of belief are also to be considered subversive, as if to utter "I believe" through melody were to speak in a tone of voice that undermines meaning.

Cadences appear to function in a similar way. For if melody, as we have observed, represents a shift of intention in the opening measures—a shift to a new speaker—the strong cadence that follows in the full orchestra only makes this shift more compelling. The "I" that says "I name" rather than "I believe" is made authentic through the power of cadence; and this effect appears all the more significant when one notes the relative scarcity

---

[19] Joseph Kerman does not shrink from calling Iago's "Credo" the "single great aria" of Act II, and "the most sensational number in the score." *Opera as Drama* (New York, 1956), 140–41.

[20] Budden (n. 8 above), 357, uses the term "canto declamato" to describe the piece.

[21] Credo con fermo cuor . . .

Credo che il giusto . . .

E credo l'uom . . .

194

EXAMPLE 1. MELODIC DERIVATIONS

IAGO

Cre- do in un Dio cru-del che m'ha cre- a- to si-mi- le a sé,   E   che nell'i-ra io no-   mo

Cre-   do con fer-mo cuor__

Cre-   do che il giusto

E   cre- do l'uom

of true cadences in the piece. Authentic ones are, for the most part, avoided; melodic gestures either are left unresolved or, at best, are resolved deceptively. Thus it is striking that the only points of strong closure in the "Credo" can be linked directly to the presence of a first-person speaker. Following the E♭ close on "io nomo," the next forceful cadence is a confident arrival on C minor, which occurs at the assertion "And I feel ("sento") the primordial mud within me." And C is articulated once again with the verb "adempio" (I fulfill), although this time the resolution is more temporary, in the form of a half-cadence that leads straight on to the next phrase (Ex. 2).

The selective use of these most common of musical signs thus seems to invite questions about the real identity of the "Credo": which voice are we to listen to? the conventional voice that speaks through melody and cadence? or the one that resists such conventions? Which of these, in the end, is the truly subversive voice? The signs are as elusive in the music as they are in the poetry. Yet there is one further musical effect—perhaps the most significant aspect of the setting—that plays on this problem more directly. For the texture of this "Credo" is dominated by the interjection of two purely orchestral subjects: moments when music seems to speak for itself. It is the first of these subjects, in fact, that establishes when the "Credo" actually begins. A blast of octaves from the full orchestra marks the end of Iago's preceding words without any pause in the musical action; the angular path traced by this orchestral statement clears the stage,

195

EXAMPLE 2. CADENCES

so to speak, for the first words of his "Credo." And it is the orchestra again that signals the end of his dramatic opening sentence, with full ranks articulating the cadence to E♭, followed by strings alone outlining another, more elaborate musical figure whose tunefulness and rhythmic character stand in direct contrast to the first (Ex. 3).

There is no doubt that these interruptions from the orchestra serve as important articulations for Iago's opening assertion. But even more significant, they heighten the sense of conflict contained within that assertion, a conflict embodied in its first and last words: "credo" and "nomo." Enfolding this sentence with difference, these orchestral subjects function in much the same way the two verbs do: presenting two distinct "voices"—two "I"s—that are destined to remain separate. The themes thus become the emblem of a crisis of identity, a crisis that is the basis for the problem of belief in this piece.

The orchestral statements, furthermore, return continuously: the first, though somewhat ambiguous, always associated with F minor; the second, usually harmonized, restated in several different tonal configurations. Such a recurrence of the two subjects (often at close range) leaves the reader in a constant state of tension between the ideas they represent.[22] And the tension is never resolved. While the second orchestral mel-

[22] One striking example occurs at the middle of the piece, with the words "Sí! Questa è la mia fé!" The first orchestral theme accompanies this exclamation of faith, which is intoned

EXAMPLE 3. ORCHESTRAL "RITORNELLOS"

ody might appear to be the last word, settling the conflict once and for all, it is not conclusive: it enters just at the point where music has given way to silence, where confident assertion has dissolved into one reiterated question. Even a brilliant sweep of the full orchestra cannot completely obliterate the element of doubt introduced by that question—"E poi?"—with its chorale-like final restatement of the first theme. The piece seems to end without ever making clear whether it was really a "Credo" or not.

MY final point involves an aspect of the text that is neither linguistic nor musical. It is often said that "seeing is believing"; and indeed, to consider even the smallest feature of the spectacle presented by Iago's "Credo" is to understand more fully its problem of belief. In the tradition, for example, of embellishing the final orchestral flourish with a burst of mocking laughter, we have an aspect of performance that relates directly to spectacle, a dramatic detail that is both visible and audible. Through this tradition the reader is offered, at last, a conclusive solution to the unanswered question of the "Credo"—the laughter moving beyond words, beyond music (and beyond doubt) toward a definitive view of the text as mockery.

---

on a single pitch much like the opening line. And immediately upon this affirmation follows the second theme—fully orchestrated this time—whose presence seems to undermine the effect of the first, calling the statement into question.

But this settling of the question might actually tell us more about the inclinations of readers than it does about any real intention of the piece. For, as more than one Verdi scholar has commented, there is no warrant for this addition to the score.[23] The tradition thus reflects, I would suggest, a desire on the part of performers to end the piece with a vocal gesture as bold as the orchestral conclusion: to sum up the Creed in an act of defiance recalling the power of the opening words. It is even likely that such a performance practice has arisen not so much from a reading of the words as from a predetermined view of Iago's cynically sinister character, a view supported by many critics. The laughter is thus heard as part of the dramatic voice of Iago, described by two commentators as that "villain direct, complete, and terrible,"[24] a demon "far more positively evil than he is in Shakespeare."[25]

Yet such conclusive readings of Iago's character are at odds with the suggestions sketched by Boito and Verdi for the *disposizione scenica*, the production book of *Otello* released by Verdi's publisher Ricordi. The view of Iago set forth in that text is far more equivocal than most modern commentators would have us believe.[26] One telling passage advises that

> the crassest of mistakes, the most vulgar error into which any artist attempting this role can possibly fall is to play him as a kind of human demon; to give him a Mephistophelian sneer and make him shoot satanic glances everywhere. Such an artist would make it all too plain that he had understood neither Shakespeare nor the drama which we are discussing.[27]

This advice is carried out through the very specific stage direction designated for Iago upon finishing his Creed: "at the final words 'e vecchia fola il Ciel' he shrugs his shoulders, turns away and moves upstage."[28]

Hardly a bold conclusion. Such a casual gesture, in fact, seems to represent a concept of the piece quite at odds with one that would finish with derisive laughter; for the shrug utterly fails to sum up the "Credo." It acts instead more like a question, extending the influence of that unexpected

[23] See David Rosen, "The Staging of Verdi's Operas: An Introduction to the Ricordi *Disposizioni sceniche*," in Daniel Heartz and Bonnie Wade, ed., *IMS Report of the Twelfth Congress* (Basel, 1981); and Budden, 359.

[24] Kerman (n. 18 above), 140.

[25] Benedict Sarnaker, "*Otello*: Drama and Music," in *Otello*, English National Opera Guide no. 7 (New York, 1981), 13–22.

[26] Indeed, the Ricordi production book, as Rosen writes (n. 23 above), flatly "contradicts the received opinion that Boito, composer and librettist of *Mefistofele*, conceived Jago as a satanic figure."

[27] As translated in Budden, 328.

[28] Budden, 359.

and inconclusive "E poi?" to the very end. It extends the problem of knowing what to believe. Through this noncommittal sign, a shrug, the reader is faced with the one option he would have preferred to avoid—the suspension of his disbelief. The difference between laughing and not laughing thus points to the central problem of reading Iago's "Credo," a problem outlined in another context by Jonathan Culler, through a story about reading that seems useful to cite here. Culler describes reading "as an attempt to understand writing by . . . removing obstacles in the quest for a coherent result." But the moral of this story is that:

> the construction of texts . . . may block this process of understanding
> . . . The reader may be placed in impossible situations where there is
> no happy issue but only the possibility of playing out roles drama-
> tized in the text.[29]

Iago's "Credo" seems to be constructed in just this way—as an "impossible" text that thwarts the possibility of a truly coherent reading. Believing in this "Credo" (believing in that subject who says "I believe") or avoiding belief altogether is thus the reader's choice: either he proceeds on faith, removing the obstacles, or he takes them in as a part of the total textual drama. Those who would choose to believe, holding the "Credo" to be the definitive expression of Iago's evil nature (unequivocal like all good Creeds), must read like specialists—past the obstacles, past all signs of question or doubt. Those choosing to read for pleasure would avoid reading this Creed as if it ever needed to be believed.

[29] Culler (n. 1 above), 81.

CHRISTOPHER WINTLE

The Numinous in *Götterdämmerung*

I

In his *Reflections of a Non-political Man*, that loyal but unfaithful Wagnerian Thomas Mann gave an account of an embattled open-air concert held in Rome in the late 1890s. The music was Wagner's "lament for the fallen Siegfried," and the players the municipal orchestra under "the champion of German music in Rome," Maestro Vessella:

> The piazza is crammed with people, every balcony is packed. The piece is heard out in silence. Then all around the square the battles begin between defiant applause and national protest. One faction cries "Bis" and claps furiously. The other shouts "Basta" and whistles. It looks as though the opposition will win the day; but Vessella goes for the encore. This time the protestors carry on without regard for the performance. The *piano* passages are shattered by whistles and loud calls for Italian music, while shouts of approbation from the Wagnerian camp dominate during the *forte* passages.[1]

The continuation of the riot, moreover, showed that the Piazza Colonna had nothing to learn from Old Nuremberg:

> I shall never forget how the Notung motif welled up for the second time, amidst cries of "Evviva" and "Abbasso!," unfolding its mighty rhythms above the brawling factions, and how, when it reached its mighty climax in that shattering dissonance that precedes the twice-repeated C major chord, a great howl of triumph broke forth, engulfing the helpless, broken opposition, and cowing them into discomfited silence for some considerable time [. . .][2]

Nevertheless, the cadence that followed the climactic "shattering dissonance" proved only temporarily triumphant, and the riot soon resumed with even greater intensity.

For us, the passions roused here seem mainly amusing, even if their description leaves us wondering, with a certain regret, what new works of art would have to do to provoke comparable reactions. Yet for Mann,

[1] From Mann, *Pro and Contra Wagner* (London, 1985), 56.
[2] Mann, 57.

200

writing about his own experiences in the light of the Great War, this account was important in furnishing occasion for an unsolicited apology:

> I am not deluded. Even if the intense experience of that art did become a source of patriotic feelings for that young man, it was a spiritual experience of supra-German significance, an experience that I shared in common with the European intelligentsia [. . .]

Indeed, it was an apology that he advanced with disconcerting insistence:

> what fascinated me was not the German nationalist element in his art, nor its specifically German poeticism or romanticism [. . .] but rather the all-powerful European appeal that emanates from it. [. . .] No, I was not so German that I failed to see the profound psychological and artistic affinity between his artistic devices and those of Zola and Ibsen [. . .][3]

Important though these issues were for Mann, my concern here is not with Siegfried's national or supra-national significance, nor with the political or even anti-political identities he has come to assume. Although these arguments may be relevant to a consideration of the creative motivation for *The Ring*, they must not be allowed to set the boundaries of discussion. Rather, it is with the intra-musical or intra-musico-dramatic question of how one moment could have unleashed, and with different effects can still unleash, feelings that may be described as "spiritual" and "intense." For straightforwardly heroic though this "mighty climax" may seem when Siegfried's Funeral March is played in isolation, once this orchestral interlude is restored to its position within the cycle, its few bars may be heard to partake in a large-scale narrative process, the recognition of which in turn suggests new interpretations.

The impetus for such an approach to *The Ring* comes directly from the work of a living composer, Sir Michael Tippett. In "The Birth of an Opera,"[4] a justly celebrated introduction to *The Midsummer Marriage* (1955), he advances four principles, or "rules," that guided him in the formation of his libretto. These rules are predicated on the possibility of creating an "indissoluble unity of drama and music," and two of them explain the function of that unity, namely to engender the "experience of the numinous" by relating "the marvellous to the everyday."[5] Thus rule 2 asks that the librettist "wait upon the revelation of some ageless mythological tradition" (since invented mythologies may seem merely idiosyn-

---

[3] Mann, 57–58.

[4] Michael Tippett, "The Birth of an Opera," *Moving into Aquarius* (London, 1959), 31.

[5] The term "numinous" here denotes the awareness of some divine or supernatural force for the good.

cratic), and rule 3 that he work upon such traditional material "so that it may speak immediately to our own day" (otherwise the result may seem "mere fantasy"). Of course, to a certain extent these rules bespeak their time and place: Tippett's juxtaposition of the marvelous and the everyday in his opera testifies to an era when Shaw, Fry, and Eliot exerted more influence than they do today. Yet they also reveal the truth of another of Tippett's remarks, that he had been "taught by Wagner," and specifically by *Oper und Drama*.

This essay represents a quest for the numinous in *The Ring*, pursued through Act III of *Götterdämmerung*. The trail is taken up at Mann's "mighty climax" in the Funeral March, proceeds by way of Gutrune's subsequent monologue, and reaches its conclusion with the raising of the dead Siegfried's hand, a revelation of the "marvellous" that both preempts Hagen's triumphant appropriation of the ring and sets in motion the train of events that culminates in Brünnhilde's immolation. In the first instance, the issues engaged are narrative, and as such reinforce Tippett's other two "rules": the first (rule 1) urges the librettist not "to do already with his words things that really belong to music" (and thereby produce "a play set to music"), and the second (rule 4) asks the composer to "produce musical schemes which *are the situations* of the libretto" (if his music is not to seem "lovely but irrelevant"). Inverting the order of these rules, we may understand the Funeral March as a purely *musical* interlude important for effecting a *narrative* change of focus, and conversely Gutrune's monologue as part of the *narrative* unfolding significant for the *musical* effects it suggests. More deeply, though, this "quest for the numinous" will lead to an understanding of the musico-dramatic organization of the passages concerned in terms of form, tonality, leitmotif, and the large- and small-scale manipulations of harmony and counterpoint.

Before embarking on this quest, though, let us return to the Piazza Colonna.

II

Mann's description of the "lament for the fallen Siegfried" contains a tiny slip: he refers to the welling up of the "Notung motif" when, at least by modern convention, he should refer to the "Sword motif." Given the current preoccupation with the very status of such descriptions, this slip might well seem negligible. Yet it prompts the vexing question as to what exactly is signified at this late stage of the cycle, as well as the further, no less vexing, question as to whether this is in itself an appropriate question. The passage under scrutiny, mm. 24–31 of the Funeral March, is reproduced as Ex. 1. After its first three measures, which search for a harmonic

EXAMPLE 1. *Götterdämmerung*, ACT III

stability beneath the persistent leading-note B, the Sword motif rises triumphantly to a high G, beneath which sounds Mann's "shattering dissonance." The subsequent two measures introduce the first statements of the exclamatory, "twice-repeated" C major chords.

There are four immediate contexts for this passage, each drawn from a different evening of the cycle. First, and most obviously, there is the context of the Funeral March itself. As a piece of Nietzschean monumental history,[6] its fusion of lament and paean generates from the chronicle of Siegfried just that myth-within-a-myth that validates Brünnhilde's later self-sacrifice. Through a simple but brilliant exercise of narrative technique, Wagner derives these twin genres of his March from the history it unfolds: the lament broods upon the saga of Siegmund (whose mortality

---

[6] Nietzsche makes the distinction "between a *monumental*, an *antiquarian* and a *critical* species of history" in "On the Uses and Disadvantages of History for Life," *Untimely Meditations*, trans. R. J. Hollingdale (Cambridge, 1983), esp. 67ff.

has, by implication, become Siegfried's), and the paean relives the excitement of the burgeoning of its hero's themes. The transition from one genre to the other is characterized musically by a turn from the minor to the major mode at just the point when the Sword motif bursts forth. Concomitantly, there is a broad redefinition of the portentous funereal opening chords as choric cries of affirmation (the "twice-repeated C major chord"). Although these are suffused with outrage at what has been wrought upon Siegfried, they nevertheless confirm beyond all doubt the mythic efficacy of a figure who at this moment seems, in Mann's words, hardly less than the sun-god himself.

The Funeral March, moreover, forms a synopsis of action that is still unfolding. It draws to no conclusion, but dissolves into the next scene with a reference to Brünnhilde's motif, a motif that indicates her offstage visit to the Rhinemaidens just at the point when her story might legitimately have been incorporated into the chronicle of Siegfried. This merging of set-piece into action reveals the function of the March as stagecraft. Not merely does its duration permit a scene change, but it stands as a profoundly appropriate prelude to what, within the time scheme of *Götterdämmerung*, is the fourth and last night, a night that correspondingly blends the darkest and most luminous events of all.

The first context, then, establishes that mythic status of the hero so necessary for the generation of the numinous. But it may still be asked whether the Sword motif plays any greater role in the Funeral March than that of inaugurating its paean. The answer, which leads to our next context, emanates from a recognition that the themes recapitulated in the lament immediately prior to the emergence of this Sword motif have been exposed in Act I of *Die Walküre*. Indeed, the dramatic extremes of the later stages of this act are marked by two contrasting presentations of the Sword motif. At the end of the second scene, the minor-mode version shown in Ex. 2 follows various statements of the themes associated with the Volsungs (just as did the major version in Ex. 1). To its furtive sound

EXAMPLE 2. *Die Walküre,* ACT I

(With a last look at Siegmund, she goes into the bed-chamber, closing the door behind her.)

Sieglinde "deutet mit ihrem Blicke andauernd und mit sprechender Be-
stimmtheit auf eine Stelle am Eschenstamme" (indicates with her eyes,
persistently and with an eloquent explicitness, a spot at the stem of the
ash tree). At the end of the third scene, on the other hand, the major
version blazes forth as the newly named Siegmund "zieht mit einem ge-
waltigen Zuck das Schwert aus dem Stamme und zeigt es der von Staunen
und Entzücken erfassten Sieglinde" (plucks the sword from the tree with
a mighty effort, and shows it to the astonished and enraptured Sieglinde)
(Ex. 3). Between these extremes, the Sword motif weaves its way through
the music in countless other versions, serving—metaphorically speaking—as a vehicle for Siegmund's gathering love and self-confidence. At
the same time, the narration returns constantly to the role of "der Greis,"
the old man whom we as audience understand from the motifs to be Wotan, and whom the twins come to recognize as their father. Indeed, the
confidence and love of Sieglinde and Siegmund is predicated on the act of
reparation represented by the evolution of the third scene as a whole, and
the musical and textual imagery relate the glinting of the sword in the
firelight to the gleams that flash from the eyes of the siblings and (by report) their progenitor.

Love, self-confidence, trust in the father, the capacity to effect reparation: these are the attributes that accrete to the sword and its motif in the
first act of *Die Walküre*, and that still leave their traces in the Funeral

EXAMPLE 3. *Die Walküre*, ACT I

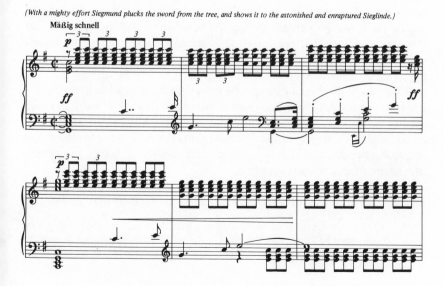

(With a mighty effort Siegmund plucks the sword from the tree, and shows it to the astonished and enraptured Sieglinde.)

March from *Götterdämmerung*. Yet there is a striking difference between these two manifestations. Although the first part of the Funeral March unfolds the Volsungs' themes, its presentation of the Sword motif is not even closely similar to anything in the first act of *Die Walküre*. For such a correspondence, we have to turn to our third context, the final scene of *Das Rheingold*.

Ex. 4 quotes Wotan's familiar apostrophe to Valhalla shortly before the entry of the gods. His claim that Valhalla is "sicher vor Bang' und Grau'n!" (secure from fear and dread) is manifestly not borne out by the conflagration with which *Götterdämmerung* closes. Yet the issue is not this simple. The first of the two statements of the Sword motif included in Ex. 4 immediately follows a passage in which Wotan recognizes, to the sound of diminished harmony, that—literally and metaphorically—"the night draws nigh" (Es naht die Nacht). It is an exclusively orchestral statement, and one that, *pace* Wagner's own production at Bayreuth,[7] articulates a thought whose substance is concealed from the audience. Indeed, the so-called Sword motif, borne from Wotan's apprehensions, has here in its first and most essential appearance more the quality of a pre-conscious feeling than of a formulation that can at once be transmuted into expression and action.

However, it is the second of the two statements of the Sword motif in Ex. 4 that approximates most closely to the motif's presentation in the Funeral March, and that also reveals rather more of Wotan's intentions. It includes a descending scale from C to G in the bass, a high G in the melody beneath which is heard Mann's "shattering dissonance," and a harmonic close into C major. Ex. 5 shows that most of these characteristics derive from the Valhalla music first heard in the second scene of *Das Rheingold*, a fact that reinforces the listener's sense that in the fourth scene Wotan has related the feelings represented by the Sword motif to the defense of his newly constructed citadel.

What, then, do these observations from *Das Rheingold* suggest for our interpretation of the passage from *Götterdämmerung*? Hardly that the Sword motif's appearance in the Funeral March is intended to bring to mind Siegfried's origins in the defensive fantasies of Wotan: for the effort of the *Ring* cycle is assiduously to foster the myth of its hero's autonomy, his independence from his creator.

Such an allusion to origins, coming *after* the Volsungs' themes, would appear to disrupt the chronological progression of motifs that the Funeral

---

7 "As the new theme is sounded, signifying a new deed to be accomplished in the future [. . . ,] Wotan, seized by a great thought, picks up the sword left by Fafner and, pointing to the castle, cries 'So grüss ich die Burg . . .' " Heinrich Porges, *Wagner Rehearsing the "Ring"* (Cambridge, 1983), 39.

EXAMPLE 4. *Das Rheingold*

Ex. 4 (*cont.*)

EXAMPLE 5. *Das Rheingold*

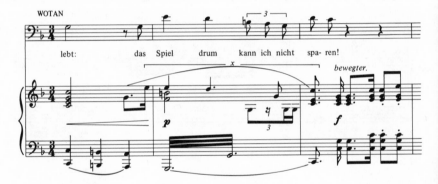

March unfolds. Rather, what is invoked is Wotan's instinct for self-preservation, and his conviction of the intrinsic worth of this feeling. Indeed,
this pre-conscious disposition is signified by the Sword motif, whose conventional label, as is so often the case, falls far short of what is denoted.
Whereas in *Das Rheingold* the motif arose in response to the threat to
Valhalla, in *Götterdämmerung* it rises to proclaim the integrity of its
fallen hero. What was intended to guard the self-interest of one of the
protagonists at the opening of the cycle now characterizes the selfless concerns of the orchestral narrator, who assumes the role of classical chorus.
The implications of such a fundamental shift in narrative stance are

208

thought-provoking. But before pursuing them we must deal briefly with the fourth of our contexts, which suggests that in the Funeral March Wagner sought to reduce the earlier associations of the Sword motif with the defense of Valhalla.

Ex. 6 contrasts four passages, each of which is concerned with a cadence into C major (three of these have already appeared in previous examples). The first, from Ex. 5, shows the Valhalla music from the early part of *Das Rheingold* concluding with the melodic formula E-D-G-C ("x" in the example); the second passage, from Ex. 4, shows this formula extending the Sword motif at the point toward the end of the same work where, as we have seen, Wotan solemnly invites Fricka to follow him into the fortress. The third passage is new, and is taken from the second scene of Act III of *Siegfried*. Here the eponymous hero finds Wotan, disguised as the Wanderer, barring his way to Brünnhilde's rock. In the exchange that follows, Wotan hints at their blood relationship, and deploys the melodic formula "x" to lend Valhalla-like authority to his observation that one of Siegfried's eyes compensates for his own missing one. To the fearless Siegfried, however, Wotan's words are merely ludicrous and, with a callow laugh, he turns the music brusquely away from the tonic that Wotan has tried to establish.[8] Valhalla has lost its efficacy—irrevocably, as later events prove. The fourth passage reproduces mm. 28–30 of the Funeral March once more. Despite its similarity to the earlier passages, and to the second especially, we can see at once that the melodic formula "x" has been suppressed, and only its harmony, Mann's "shattering dissonance," has been retained. For Wagner to have made an overt reference to Valhalla at this point would have been inimical to the generation of the Siegfried myth.

Let us summarize what the four contexts evoked by the Sword motif tell us. Placed in chronological order, they affirm the intrinsic worth of the instinct that gave rise to the sword and its two bearers (Siegmund and Siegfried); they associate the motif with burgeoning love, self-confidence, and trust; they cast aside its local associations with the defense of a discredited Valhalla, and use it in the March to establish the Siegfried myth, as lament turns into paean. From these perceptions follow two extreme reactions that we as audience may adopt to this musical passage. We may, like some in the Piazza Colonna, cry "Evviva," and celebrate the inauguration of a process that will lead in the final scene of *Götterdämmerung* to the clinching, numinous moment. Or alternatively we may cry "Abbasso," and consider the dissociation of the Sword motif from the defense

---

[8] The matter is discussed more fully in my article "The Questionable Lightness of Being," *Twilight of the Gods*, English National Opera Guide no. 31 (London, 1985), 39–48.

EXAMPLE 6

of an untenable Valhalla, together with the transformation of Wotan's point of view into the narrative stance of the entire work, as an unpardonable sleight-of-hand. Put another way, we may celebrate a myth-making that has a certain resonance with what Mann described as Romantic Christianity (since Siegfried's slaughter at the hands of the forces of darkness has endowed his image with the brightness of a Redeemer); or we may decry an inherently disingenuous instinct for self-preservation, of a kind that brings to mind the charge that D. H. Lawrence leveled against Goethe, that of perverting himself "into perfection and God-likeness."[9]

We do not necessarily have to choose between conflicting feelings: our quest for the numinous will reveal that within the processes of the work the possibility of both attitudes is at least acknowledged. This being so, let us move on to Gutrune's monologue and the musical organization of its text.

III

The soliloquy that opens the final scene of *Götterdämmerung* runs as follows:

(*Es ist Nacht. Der Mondschein spiegelt sich auf dem
Rheine.
Gutrune tritt aus ihrem Gemache in die Halle hinaus.*)
War das sein Horn?
(*Sie lauscht.*)
Nein! Noch
kehrt' er nicht heim.
Schlimme Träume
störten mir den Schlaf.
Wild wieherte sein Ross;
Lachen Brünnhilde's
weckte mich auf.
Wer war das Weib,
das ich zum Ufer schreiten sah?
Ich fürchte Brünnhild'.
Ist sie daheim?
(*Sie lauscht an der Thüre rechts und ruft:*)
Brünnhild'! Brünnhild'!
Bist du wach?
(*Sie öffnet schüchtern, und blickt in das innere Gemach.*)

[9] D. H. Lawrence, *Selected Literary Criticism*, ed. Anthony Beal (London, 1967), 148 (letter to A. Huxley, 27 March 1928).

Leer das Gemach.
So war es sie,
die ich zum Rheine schreiten sah?
(*Sie erschrickt und lauscht nach der Ferne.*)
War das sein Horn?
Nein!
Öd' alles!
Säh' ich Siegfried nur bald!

([*It is night. Moonlight is reflected from the Rhine. Gutrune emerges from her chamber into the hall.*] Was that his horn? [*She listens.*] No! He is not yet on his way home. Evil dreams have disturbed my sleep. His horse neighed wildly; I was woken by Brünnhilde's laughter. Who was that woman I saw pacing by the shore? I dread Brünnhilde. Is she at home? [*She listens at the right-hand door and calls softly:*] Brünnhilde! Brünnhilde! Are you awake? [*She opens the door shyly and looks into the inner chamber.*] The room is empty. So it was her whom I saw walking down to the Rhine? [*She starts, and listens into the distance.*] Was that his horn? No! All is desolate! If only I could see Siegfried soon!)

At first sight, this seems no more than an introductory passage, lasting barely three minutes, and occupying a mere forty-six bars of the score. Yet, to the extent that it elaborates a key sonic event, rather than a key word or concept, it is typically Wagnerian. As early as 1876, the event was well understood by Heinrich Porges. Of the General Pause and fermata that follow Gutrune's anxious call "Brünnhild'! Brünnhild'! Bist du wach?" he wrote that they must be "lengthened so that the effect of silence is uncanny."[10] But why, we may ask, should such emptiness be necessary? Does it have symbolic significance? And how does it relate to the events that follow? To answer these questions, we need first to return to the sources at Wagner's disposal as he constructed his libretto.

Only a few of these texts recount the death of Siegfried in the open air rather than in his bed. The "Lay of Brynhild" from the *Poetic Edda* offers the following version:

> Sigurd lay slain
> On the south of the Rhine,
> High from the fair tree
> Croaked forth the raven,
> "Ah, yet shall Atli
> On you redden edges,

---

[10] Porges, 142.

The old oaths shall weigh
On your souls, O warriors."[11]

The cortège, led by Hogni (Hagen), is greeted by Gudrun, Sigurd's legitimate wife (not merely his lover, as in Wagner):

Without stood Gudrun,
Giuki's daughter,
And the first word she said
Was even this word:
"Where then is Sigurd,
Lord of the Warfolk,
Since my kin
Come riding the foremost?"
One word Hogni
had for an answer:
"Our swords have smitten
Sigurd asunder,
And the grey horse hangs drooping
O'er his lord lying dead."

At this point Brynhild, the all-wise seer, steps forward to offer her scornful rebuke for the slaughter of Sigurd:

Then laughed Brynhild—
Loud rang the whole house—
One laugh only
From out her heart:
"Long shall your bliss be
Of lands and people,
Whereas the famed lord
Ye have felled to the earth!"

In the *Saga of the Volsungs*,[12] Brynhild's laughter turns to tears as she explains to her husband Gunnar the retribution that awaits him. For it is he, and not Hogni, who has killed Sigurd:

And now none might know for what cause Brynhild must bewail with weeping for what she had prayed for with laughter: but she spake—"Such a dream I had, Gunnar, as that my bed was acold, and

[11] *The Story of the Volsungs and Niblungs*, trans. Eiríkr Magnússon and William Morris (1870; rpt. London, 1980), 209–11. As accuracy is not impugned in this instance, I have for rhetorical reasons chosen this translation in preference to the more recent *The Saga of the Volsungs*, trans. R. G. Finch (London, 1965).

[12] *The Story*, 125.

that thou didst ride into the hands of thy foes: lo now, ill shall it go with thee and all thy kin, O ye breakers of oaths; for on the day thou slayedst him, dimly didst thou remember how thou didst blend thy blood with the blood of Sigurd, and with an ill reward hast thou rewarded him for all that he did well to thee [. . .]"

In selecting from and transforming what little these narrations offer, Wagner seizes on the sonic imagery they either embody or suggest. In *Götterdämmerung* we learn from Gutrune's words, themselves drawn from the exchanges in the Eddas between Hogni and Brynhild, that it is Brünnhilde's laughter that has disturbed her sleep. (Although neither in the text nor the music does Wagner disclose the cause of this laughter, the sources reveal Brynhild's guilt to be motivated by envy.) That Gutrune's nightmares relate directly to her apprehensions about Siegfried may be understood from the orchestral distortions of his horn calls. In an addition of his own, Wagner makes Gutrune refer to the "wild" neighing of Siegfried's horse, a neighing that is linked orchestrally to Brünnhilde's laughter through the agency of the Valkyrie motif.

These, however, are relatively minor transmutations. Of far greater significance are some of the other images Wagner introduces to articulate Porges's uncanny silence. There are three sets of these, and together they introduce a further narrative ploy by playing on two different states of knowledge: that of the audience, which has borne witness to the fatal events of the previous scene, and that of Gutrune, who has not. It is by way of this narrative ploy, moreover, that we are brought back onto the trail of the numinous.

The first set of images emanates from the sonically oriented question that frames this monologue: "Was that his horn?" Whereas Gutrune experiences the answering silences in terms of thwarted expectation, the audience, recognizing the irony of the situation, reinterprets them as the stifled speech that has so often been understood as the concomitant of tragedy.[13] The evocation of the horn, furthermore, creates a powerful association between this and many other parts of the work, itself dominated by arrivals and departures, nocturnal deliberations and the uncertainties surrounding events that have taken place elsewhere. The horn calls of the hero and his hunters have, as recently as the beginning of Act III, scenes 1 and 2, rung through the theatre in a grim fusion of the pastoral and the portentous. Before that, they have been exposed on several occasions: at

[13] For example, by Walter Benjamin and Michel Foucault (I am indebted for this point to John Deathridge and Lucy Hadland). One might add that the audience also experiences these silences as the final dissolution of the momentum of the Funeral March, and as the emptiness that precedes the denouement of the drama.

the end of the Norns' scene; on Siegfried's departure for the Rhine; before his arrival at the Hall of the Gibichung; and again at his disguised return to Brünnhilde. (Gutrune will likewise experience the shock of an unexpected homecoming.) Yet in Gutrune's monologue, the horn that is paradoxically both heard and not heard is no ordinary funeral monument. From the next part of this final scene we shall come to understand that it is a symbol undergoing transformation; and as such it testifies to the absent presence of Siegfried that will become manifest when the numinous point is reached.

The second network of images reinforces the prevalent emptiness by focusing on Brünnhilde's absence. We have already noted the "uncanny silence" that follows the call "Brünnhilde! Brünnhilde! Are you awake?" Through the discovery of the empty room ("Leer das Gemach") Gutrune finds in her rival's absence a mirror of her own isolation. Indeed, her forlorn and pathetic cry "Öd' alles!" (All is desolate!) completes the conjunction of "öd' " and "leer" so familiar from *Tristan*. As Gutrune realizes, Brünnhilde is down by the Rhine, drawn there by the Rhinemaidens ("zu ihr" was their cry in the first scene of this act as they abandoned Siegfried to his fate), and deriving from them the understanding and power necessary to fulfill her own destiny and hence to resolve the conflicts of the cycle.

We know from the second act of *Götterdämmerung*, of course, that Brünnhilde already has this power: "Zauber" (magic) is one of its keywords. Brünnhilde's revelation "Unwissend zähmt' ihn mein Zauberspiel, das ihn vor Wunden nun gewahrt" (Unknown to him, my magic charms tamed him, so that he is now protected against wounds) was the remark that paradoxically both betrayed her husband and signaled her capacity to redeem him. Gunther's plea that he could no longer face his sister if he acquiesced in Siegfried's slaughter provokes Brünnhilde to a wild outburst that embodies a near-truth: "Gutrune heisst der Zauber, der den Gatten mir entzückt!" (Gutrune is the name of the magic that has spirited my husband from me). The whole truth is that Gutrune's magic derives from Hagen, and it is against his power that Brünnhilde must pit her own. That Gutrune senses Brünnhilde's magical qualities ("Ich fürchte Brünnhild' " [I dread Brünnhilde], she sings) makes the Valkyrie's absence in this scene so telling. It is no coincidence that Brünnhilde will make her final and decisive appearance in the work exactly at the numinous moment, when Siegfried reveals his magical immortality.

Although the third network of images is unspoken, it stands behind the text of Gutrune's monologue, and manifests itself to the audience by way of music. Its subject is not merely her latent fears, but rather the spirit of evil embodied in the preoccupations of the absent Hagen. The motifs that represent his insatiable desire for domination, heard at the outset of the monologue, recall his unconscious nocturnal communion with Alberich at the opening of Act II. The source harmony that derives from the Curse motif, F♯-A-C-E, hangs predatorily in various transpositions across two keyless sections of music. The chord, moreover, that precedes Gutrune's "Who was that woman I saw pacing by the shore?"—F♯-D♯-A-C-G—recalls the opening of the final scene of Act II, where the bewildered Brünnhilde has herself asked:

> Welches Unhold's List
> liegt hier verhohlen?
> Welches Zaubrer's Rath
> regte diess auf?

(What fiendish cunning / lies here concealed? / What magic counsel / stirs this up?)[14]

In the monologue, too, the same malign magic is responsible for the thematic distortions, the minor and diminished versions of the motifs associated with Siegfried, Gutrune, and Brünnhilde.

Although this spirit of evil merely underlies what Gutrune has to say, it surfaces with appalling force as Hagen returns in shameless exultation with his prize "booty," the dead Siegfried. We shall see that the numinous moment, which interrupts this grim celebration just as it draws to its climax, represents a confrontation between this evil of Hagen's and the combined magic forces of Siegfried and Brünnhilde. And although more will be said about the music of the monologue, we may now move to a consideration of this moment itself.

IV

[. . .] the greater percentage of the marvellous will allow the opera composer to present the collective spiritual experience more nakedly and immediately—the music helping to suspend the critical and analytical judgment, without which happening no experience of the numinous can be immediate at all. For example, as soon as we begin to have critical doubts of the propriety, say, of the pseudo-Christian ritual of *Parsifal*, we are provoked, not enriched.[15]

Tippett's reference to "collective" experience and his closing distinction between provocation and enrichment raise fundamental aesthetic issues. But for the time being let us draw the conclusion that nowhere in

---

14 For this point, I am indebted to Derrick Puffett.
15 Tippett, 56.

The Ring can the suspension of critical and analytical judgment be more necessary than at the miraculous raising of the dead Siegfried's hand. No image offers a more potent paradox than that of the living dead, or indeed a more persuasive testament to the power of a Redeemer. What has Wagner done to help suspend our judgment?

The passage is reproduced as Ex. 7. Once again, we find that a crucial narrative formulation is assigned to the music, and that it falls between two strongly contrasted imperatives, Hagen's "Her den Ring!" (Give me the ring!) and Brünnhilde's "Schweigt eures Jammers jauchzenden Schwall!" (Silence the exultant flood of your lamenting!). Before the first of these imperatives, a vertiginous succession of events has embraced, within a matter of seconds, the quarrel of Gunther and Hagen, their fight, the slaughter of Gunther, and Hagen's attempt to snatch the ring; between the lifting of the hand and the second imperative not only does the entire company freeze in terror but so, musically, do the dynamics, the harmonic rhythm, the texture, and the tempo.

Yet, frozen though it may be, the music of the numinous is unexpectedly rich in significance. The Sword motif in the trumpet rises ("phantasmagorically," to use Adorno's term[16]) out of the turmoil, supporting a stage action that offers concrete evidence for just that mythic power of Siegfried's asserted by the Funeral March. Hagen's lethal avarice is vanquished by a hero who is most present in his deathly absence. The D major tonality recalls a directly comparable statement of the Sword motif at the end of Act I of *Siegfried*, where the hero cried for vengeance:

> Nothung! Nothung!
> Neidliches Schwert!
> Zum Leben weckt' ich dich wieder
> [. . .]
> Zeige den Schächern
> Nun deinen Schein!

(Notung! Notung! / Sword of my need! / I restore you to life. / [. . .] Now show the scoundrels / Your gleam!)

At the numinous moment, by contrast, Siegfried is metaphorically reborn, with the instrumentation providing a kind of answer to Gutrune's "Was that his horn?" The terrestrial horn has revealed its mortality; the trumpet, which as early as *Das Rheingold* symbolized the instinct that prompted Wotan's plan for self-perpetuation, is indomitable.

The ascending Sword motif does not, however, lead to a cadence, as it did in the Funeral March, but is complemented by the descending figure in D major (the "Twilight of the Gods" motif) that solemnly introduces

[16] Theodor Adorno, *In Search of Wagner* (London, 1981), 85–96.

217

EXAMPLE 7. *Götterdämmerung*, ACT III

EXAMPLE 8. *Götterdämmerung*, VORSPIEL

Brünnhilde. This motif, together with its continuation to the Neapolitan
E♭ major harmony, recalls the words and music for the Third Norn from
Götterdämmerung's Prelude, as shown in Ex. 8.[17] The allusion reveals a
number of things: that Brünnhilde's nocturnal communion described in
Gutrune's monologue is now complete; that through her new wisdom
and maturity she has gained a hieratic authority aligning her with the
eternally feminine forces of Erda, the Norns, and the Rhinemaidens; that
she herself has entered into the mechanism of eschatology set in train at
the outset of this work; and that by virtue of all this she is now fit to act
as the redeemer of her dead husband's image.

So much, then, for Wagner's means of helping us experience the numinous. We may still ask, though, what deeper meanings might be revealed by analysis, and whether these meanings would necessarily provoke rather than enrich us.

---

[17] As Freud pointed out in his 1913 essay "The Theme of the Three Caskets," in mythology it is the third Norn, Atropos, who has the fatal role. See *The Complete Psychological
Works of Sigmund Freud*, trans. James Strachey, XII (London, 1958), 296.

EXAMPLE 9

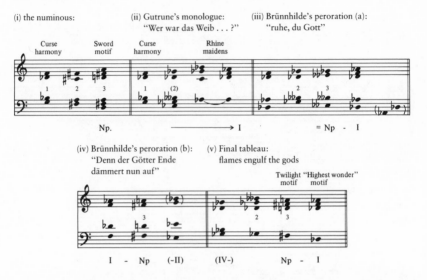

All five harmonic progressions set out in Ex. 9 derive from the last scene of *Götterdämmerung*, and each is related tonally to what in another essay I have described as the home key of *The Ring*, D♭ major.[18] The first is extracted from the numinous moment, and interprets the D major harmony as standing in a broadly Neapolitan relationship to the home key. The curse harmony with which it opens is *Götterdämmerung*'s equivalent for the ambiguous *Tristan* chord, and an alternative resolution of this harmony is shown in the second extract, which occurs earlier, in Gutrune's monologue. The libretto and motifs in this passage tell us that Brünnhilde is by the river, communing with the Rhinemaidens; the tonality reveals that their preoccupation is to bring matters to a conclusion in the home key of D♭ major (as indeed was Waltraute's in Act I of this work, as may be seen from her incomplete Valhalla cadence at the words "erlöst wär' Gott und Welt"[19]).

Significantly, no full close into D♭ is achieved until Brünnhilde's peroration (where there are in fact two such closes[20]), and none before her valediction to Wotan, the celebrated "ruhe, du Gott" cadence, from which the harmony of the third extract is drawn. The second and third chords replicate their equivalents from the first extract. From this we may infer that the numinous seals Wotan's fate, much as it had Hagen's. Of

[18] "The Questionable Lightness of Being" (n. 8 above).
[19] This cadence is completed with the "ruhe, du Gott" close in the peroration. That this was itself closely modeled on Waltraute's music is shown by the sketches included in Curt von Westernhagen, *The Forging of the "Ring"* (Cambridge, 1976), 231.
[20] The second cadence occurs after Brünnhilde's "Selig grüsst dich dein Weib."

course, this suggests that the Neapolitan relationship between D (or E♭♭) major and the home key of D♭ major, set up *between* the first two extracts but heard only now *within* the third, has a broadly portentous significance. Such a suggestion is enhanced by the remaining extracts. The fourth recalls yet again the conjunction of D♭ and D as Brünnhilde pronounces the end of the gods to the "Twilight" motif (the continuation to E♭ sounds, locally, as yet another Neapolitan); and the fifth expands the work's closing plagal approach to D♭ by incorporating the second and third harmonies from the first extract at just the moment when the flames engulf the gods. This demise of Wotan and his world is the supreme act of destruction unleashed by the numinous. However, since in the fifth extract the final tonic supports a statement of the motif proclaiming the "highest wonder" (cf. *Die Walküre*, Act III, scene 1), the magnificent resolution to which the numinous has been leading (Brünnhilde's self-sacrifice) now stands fully revealed.

At this point, various methodological objections may be raised. It could be argued that a number of widely separated details have had to shoulder an unacceptable burden of interpretation; yet the first, third, and fifth extracts in Ex. 9 manifestly represent nodal points in the drama of the final scene, and their selection entails no discontinuity with any other observations that might be drawn from the same passage. Another complaint might be that the harmonies are treated out of context, with apparent disregard for their local functions; yet it has long been clear that a necessary distinction has to be drawn between *motivic tonalities* of the kind described here and the *governing tonalities* of musical sentences, periods, scenes, acts, or even entire works. It was the latter tonalities that Alfred Lorenz attempted to map and that, in a different way, preoccupy the followers of Heinrich Schenker. One could go further, indeed, and insist that music-drama draws powerfully on the tension between these two concepts of harmony.[21]

What conclusions, though, may we draw from all these arguments? There are at least two ways of interpreting the numinous in *Götterdämmerung*: one is psychological, the other generic. Psychologically, we may understand its moment of revelation as the fulcrum in unfolding the inner drama of the quintessentially human Wotan. In *Das Rheingold* we saw his violations, compromises, and fears give rise to the vision of Siegfried, a fearless, mythic hero sanctified by the love of another of Wotan's creations, his daughter Brünnhilde. This vision represents a profound gratification of primal instincts; and so ruthless are these instincts, so contemptuous of the demands of the super-ego, that during the course of *Die Walküre* and *Siegfried* Wotan's creations rise up against their progenitor,

---

[21] These issues are amplified in the Analytical Postscript to this essay.

who has in any case distanced himself from them. Having survived many vicissitudes forced upon them by the outer world, Siegfried and Brünnhilde unite in the highest joy, laughingly defying the death that in mortal terms is, and can be, their only goal. The revelation of the numinous testifies to the extraordinary capacity of these instincts for resistance to outer threats, and the Schopenhauer-like determination they have to fulfill their destiny in extinction. Glorious to the fantasy though such fulfillment may be, to the reflective mind this extinction stands as a sombre reminder of the impossibility of meeting fully the demands of both inner and outer worlds.

A generic interpretation, on the other hand, would find in the numinous a more traditionally mythological means of introducing some *deus ex machina* to resolve the conflict between the forces of good and evil, and to draw the action to a conclusion. Of course, the conflict has psychological roots as well. To win power and gold, Alberich violently represses love; and although Wotan too has suppressed part of (his) nature's innocence for authority and knowledge, there is still another and nobler part that through miraculous events and interventions can offer exemplars of a better life. From this point of view, the numinous ushers in the most exaltedly moral part of the cycle, a part that through the self-sacrifice of Brünnhilde blends the exotic with the Romantically Christian. Within this scenario the destruction of Wotan appears tragically necessary (his violation of the World Ash Tree and all the consequences of that action have to be redeemed); and the spectacle of the downfall of the gods purges us "collectively," in the truest Aristotelian manner.

Now, there is no more need to resolve the contradictions between these interpretations than there was to choose between ambiguous attitudes at

on Freud,[22] works of art by their nature embrace the (conflicting) demands of fantasy and parable. But it is nevertheless remarkable that the numinous unleashes a greater power of vengeance, and through the union it presents of Siegfried and Brünnhilde prepares us to witness a far more voluptuous delight in self-destruction than is demanded by Classical tragedy, or for that matter is suggested by Wagner's literary sources. And indeed, it is this identification of *an excess of gratification* born out of the numinous that represents one of the goals of our quest.

ANALYTICAL POSTSCRIPT

In this additional part of my essay, I hope to show how carefully Brünnhilde's gratifying final act of self-destruction is prepared musically

[22] *The English Auden*, ed. Edward Mendelson (London, 1977), 332–42.

through the formal and harmonic organization of Gutrune's monologue, and hence how central an awareness of the numinous must be for close analysis. As the discussion here will be concerned primarily with technical issues, it need not preoccupy the general reader, who will already be aware that the broad issues raised in this essay are reflected in the deepest and most particular features of musical language.

Let us return to one of our observations about the numinous moment: the Sword motif unfolds to the sound of a sustained D major triad. The rationale for the choice of tonality has already been discussed; but no attention has yet been paid to the fact that the chord itself is a pure triad, and a major one. However simple this observation may be, it is nevertheless important for three reasons.

First, this triad forms an arresting contrast with the other relatively impure sonorities through which the anxieties and conflicts of the immediately preceding passage have been projected: minor triads, sevenths, ninths, secondary sevenths, and diminished sevenths. Since the end of Gutrune's monologue there have been no major triads of importance, apart from the brazenly contemptuous C♭ major chord accompanying Hagen's revelation of his booty to Gutrune: "Siegfried, deinen todten Mann" (Siegfried, your dead husband). Secondly, the rediscovery of the major triad at this point symbolizes the mythic rebirth of Siegfried precisely because this type of sonority has been used at the opening of the cycle as the chord of nature. And thirdly, this particular triad establishes no governing tonality in its own right, but is savoured as an isolated sonority— connected to adjoining sonorities, to be sure, but also conveying self-sufficient meanings of the kind described earlier. This capacity of Wagnerian music-drama to contract the scale of its tonal utterances to an isolated entity complements the equally important tendency of Wagner's poetic diction to surrender sense to sonority, and in extreme cases to pre-verbal formulations.

But let us return to Gutrune's monologue, shown in vocal score reduction as Ex. 10 (which includes the preceding dissolution of the Funeral March). The tension of the music obviously derives from the disintegration of the texture in terms of the silences, the volatile handling of motifs, the unsettled tempo, and the *sforzandi* that puncture the predominantly restrained dynamic level. It also stems from a harmonic language that, as in the subsequent passage leading to the numinous moment, is formed from chords (again minor triads, sevenths, ninths, diminished sevenths, and so forth), many of which yearn for resolution, for reintegration into the supreme order symbolized by the major triad.

Evidence for this last point may be demonstrated negatively: in the entire course of the monologue only two major triads are heard, and both

EXAMPLE 10. *Götterdämmerung*, ACT III

(*From this point the mists disperse, gradually*

revealing the hall of the Gibichungs, as in the first Act.)

Scene III. *(It is night. The moonlight is reflected in the Rhine.)*

Noch etwas zurückhaltend.

Allmählich etwas bewegter
(Gutrune comes out of her chamber into the hall.)

GUTRUNE

(She listens.)

War das sein Horn?

Maßig, wie zuvor.

Wer war das Weib, das ich zum U- fer schrei-ten sah?

Ich fürch- te Brünn-hild'.

ausdrucksvoll

(She listens at the door (right) and calls softly:)

Ist sie da- heim? Brünn-hild'! Brünn-hild'! Bist du wach?

(She opens the door timidly and looks into the inner room.)

Leer___ das Ge- mach.

Ex. 10 (*cont.*)

So war es sie, die ich zum Rhei-   ne schrei-ten sah?

War das sein Horn?   Nein!   Öd' — al-les!

Horn *(on the stage, in the distance.)*

Bewegt, und immer bewegter.
(She starts and listens to a sound in the distance.)

Säh'   ich Sieg- fried nur bald!

zart

228

conspicuously promise (but fail to provide) a point of dramatic resolution. On the one hand, there is the distant horn call that Gutrune imagines (m. 43), a recollection of her marriage to Siegfried, the pure C major of which is nevertheless denied by the tritonally related Curse harmony that occupies the foreground of our attention.[23] On the other hand, the D♭ major triad of m. 27 (already quoted as part of Ex. 9) is more significant for this discussion. Although this triad occurs in the context of a motif that recalls the Rhinemaidens' nostalgic plea for the return of the gold (a motif articulated by the horns), and although this context contrasts a falling whole tone B♭-A♭ with the previous menacing semitones, it nevertheless appears only in second inversion. In other words, no more than a glimpse is provided of what resolution and reintegration might be.

Yet Ex. 11 suggests that this glimpse is the most, and not the least, of

EXAMPLE 11

(a) mm. 25 - 27

(b) mm. 3 - 5   mm. 12 - 17 MODEL   SEQUENCE

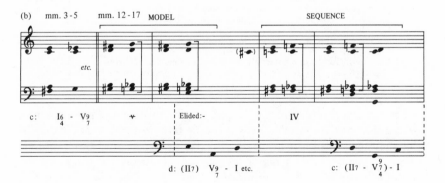

---

[23] It is worth noticing that her "War das sein Horn?" is now set to a perfect fourth, and not to a tritone as at mm. 10–11.

229

what is offered in the monologue: (a) summarizes the harmonic progression under discussion, leading from the curse harmony to the partial resolution (onto the D♭ major triad) II-V-(I); in (b), by contrast, the stave below the model and sequence of mm. 12–17 shows that after the II⁷ chords that follow on from curse harmonies, the progressions to V and I are elided, or partially so. (In mm. 3–5, of course, the curse harmony does resolve to a six-four triad [and then to V]: but here the modality is resolutely minor, as befits the final stage of the dissolution of the Funeral March.)

What does all this tell us? The answer opens up further vistas on the music. To the extent that the D♭ major triad refers to Brünnhilde's redeeming mission, and alone promises a resolution to the tensions that pervade the monologue, it has a function comparable to that of the numinous D major triad later on: both chords look outside immediate contexts to the denouement of the drama. But, equally, neither triad establishes a region of its own, and here the D♭ second inversion represents one of two motivic tonalities invoked within the broader C minor tonality that governs both the Funeral March and the monologue. Such a discussion of tonality inevitably leads to a consideration of local formal arrangements; and from this point of view we shall see that the D♭ major triad has a very particular structural significance.

Gd. III. P. 8 S. 260—265,7 [989—1032] c-moll

Gutrunes Grußmotiv	3	
Alberichs Herrscherruf mit Siegfriedhorn		HS 10 t
(eine eingestreute Pause) „War das sein Horn?"	7	
Waldknabenruf (auf Siegfried bez. Motiv)		
Walkürenruf-Figuren und Walkürenmotiv	8	
(Brünnhilde)		
Alberichs Herrscherruf.	2	MS 19 t
Rheinfahrtmotiv (auf Siegfried bez. Motiv)		
Brünnhildemotiv — Schicksalsfrage — Pause	9¹)	
Brünnhildemotiv		
Alberichs Herrscherruf mit Horn h. d. Sz.		
(eingestreute Pause) „War das sein Horn?"	8	
Gutrunes Grußmotiv verbunden mit Rachewahn, der zur nächsten		HS 12 t
P. überleitet	4	

Let us open this final part of our inquiry by turning to Alfred Lorenz's description of the monologue as a simple ternary form.[24] At first sight, this may well seem a realistic set of divisions, especially from a motivic point of view. Lorenz's period begins with Gutrune's entrance to the sound of a diminished seventh (Scene 3, m. 7), a harmonic deflection of the C minor close anticipated at the end of m. 6. The middle section co-

[24] Alfred Lorenz, *Der Ring des Nibelungen*, vol. 1 of *Das Geheimnis der Form bei Richard Wagner* (Berlin, 1924), 138.

incides with the account of her troubled night (Lorenz omits the three emptiest measures [mm. 33–35] from his proportional scheme); and the conclusion (mm. 39–46) appends to a compressed recapitulation four further measures (mm. 47–50) that link this with the subsequent period. The fact that there is restatement of elements from earlier in the monologue justifies Lorenz's positing of an overall (governing) C minor tonality, however remote the designation may seem during mm. 39–46. (Indeed, it might well be argued that the plagal [iv-I] cadence in mm. 46–47 seems a curiously unconvincing way of re-establishing C as the centre for the passage.)

But it is just this point of recapitulation that brings into question Lorenz's divisions. The harmonies that return at m. 39, for example, reintroduce a motif heard not at the outset of the period but six measures earlier, at the beginning of the scene. Similarly, the (entirely notional) C minor key signature is reintroduced not at m. 39 but at m. 27, with the establishment of the dominant (and six-four harmony) of D♭ major. But the immediately ensuing passage brings back at m. 29 a now distorted version of Brünnhilde's theme, heard last in the same (motivic) tonality during the dissolution of the Funeral March, six measures *before* the opening of Scene 3. From a harmonic point of view, then, recapitulation begins earlier than Lorenz suggests, and restates material drawn from the previous period.

Just how these relations may be represented formally is shown in Ex. 12 and 13, which offer voice-leading charts of the music included as Ex. 10. Although these charts are indebted to the work of Heinrich Schenker, the path they trace from background to foreground is uncharacteristic in that it integrates within the governing tonality of C minor two motivic tonalities, E♭ major and D♭ major. Ex. 12 maps out their deployment in the dissolution of the Funeral March. Within the context of a linear 5–4 and harmonic III-iv contrapuntal move in C minor (level 1), a V-of-V harmony within E♭ major (level 2) includes a neighbor-note G♭ to the (local) second degree F, which in turn acts as a pivotal note for the introduction (in level 3) of a dominant seventh of D♭ which, as the foreground reveals, supports Brünnhilde's motif. It is interesting to see that in this foreground, the G♭ is temporarily written as F♯ when the bass composes out the interval A to F: Wagner clearly considered that the clash of G♭ and G♮ would have been an impropriety. In the centre of the chart, notice the indication of the curse harmony, which is responsible for effecting the mixture of major and minor third degrees in C minor.

Ex. 13 reveals how, at the deepest level, a great proportion of the monologue prolongs the second scale degree of C minor over its dominant, and how it is only at the point of recapitulation that the two motivic tonalities are reintroduced. Moreover, there is no closure of the back-

EXAMPLE 12. *Götterdämmerung*, ACT III: SIEGFRIED FUNERAL MARCH: DISSOLUTION

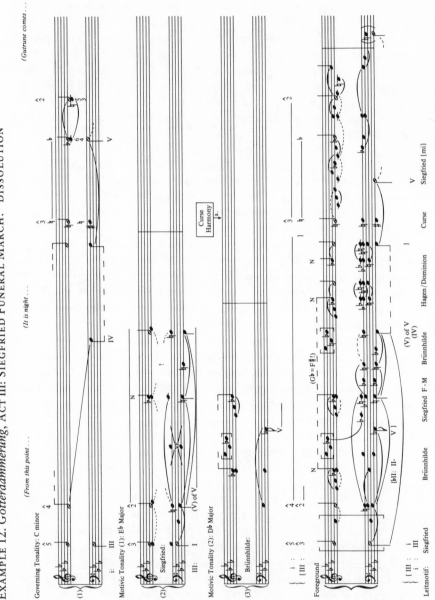

EXAMPLE 13. *Götterdämmerung*, GUTRUNE'S MONOLOGUE

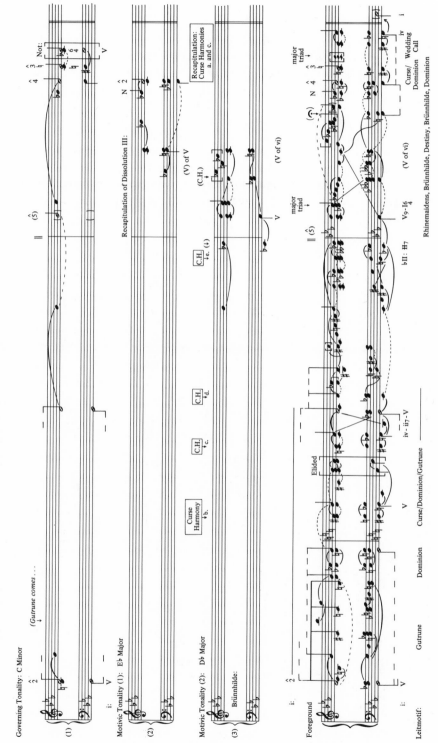

ground line (level 1), which is left open in order to effect a link with the next period. At the end of the example, the reference to the recapitulation of curse harmonies *a* and *c* (exactly the same chord in each case) denotes that Wagner has foreshortened his restatement by omitting the music lying between his original *a* (in Ex. 12) and his original *c* (in Ex. 13). The formal potential of this ambiguous harmony is thus revealed, while its other occurrences, set at different transpositional levels (*b, d, e,* and so forth) help to create the characteristic style and sonority of the passage. These harmonies throw into even greater relief the D♭ major triad which, as we have already observed, alone carries the promise of some deep resolution to the musical and dramatic issues of the entire cycle.

Musorgsky's Libretti on Historical Themes: From the Two *Borises* to *Khovanshchina*

Over one hundred years ago—in February 1886—an amateur music group in Petersburg staged the premiere performance of Musorgsky's *Khovanshchina*.[1] Both the music and the libretto in this production differed profoundly from the piano-vocal score that Musorgsky had left incomplete at the time of his death five years earlier. This fact in itself should occasion no surprise; re-doing Musorgsky's compositions is a minor industry. What is surprising, in retrospect, is that *Khovanshchina* survived at all.

After Musorgsky's death, Rimsky-Korsakov spent two years on the manuscript, cutting some 800 bars of music and orchestrating, reharmonizing, and shaping the score into a performance version.[2] The libretto passed the state literary censorship in September 1882, and Bessel published a full score the following year.[3] But in tsarist Russia, dramatic texts approved for print were then subject to another, more severe censorship for public performance.[4] When *Khovanshchina* came up for considera-

---

[1] For an account of the premiere and a brief performance history, see M. Rakhmanova, "K 100-letiiu prem'ery 'Khovanshchiny'" [In Honor of the Centennial of the Premiere of *Khovanshchina*], *Sovetskaia muzyka*, 1986 (3), 88–96. (*Sovetskaia muzyka* is cited hereafter as *SM*.)

[2] The most important cuts were: the wrecking of the Clerk's booth (Act I); Golitsyn's reading of his mother's letter, the episode between Golitsyn and the Lutheran pastor, and a substantial portion of Dosifei's dialogue (Act II); and the *streltsy*'s "Rumor Song" (Act III).

[3] The first edition of the Rimsky-Korsakov redaction of *Khovanshchina*, published by Bessel in 1883, bears a censor-stamp dated 8 September 1882. The score contains plate numbers at the beginning of clearly detachable dramatic episodes, which suggests that Bessel contemplated marketing individual arias and choruses as sheet music. I thank Robert William Oldani for information on the 1883 score and its U.S. location (the Boston Public Library).

[4] Robert Oldani, who is currently researching this stratification of censorship, has located no single statute that draws a distinction between the right to read a text and the right to perform it. But such secondary censorship indisputably existed. Three years after the *Khovanshchina* score was published, "theatrical censorship" made its presence keenly felt in the premiere performance. Konstantin Pobedonostsev, lay head of the Russian Orthodox Church and chief advisor to the Tsar, objected to the libretto's graphic portrayal of state persecution of religious dissenters, and that theme was "rewritten" in the performing ver-

tion, Russia was in a period of crisis and political reaction. Tsar Alexander II, liberator of the serfs, had been cut down by a terrorist's bomb in March 1881, the very month of Musorgsky's death; literary committees attached to the imperial theaters were understandably nervous about historical opera on political themes. "One radical opera by Musorgsky is enough," the Imperial Opera Committee reputedly said when *Khovanshchina* came to a vote, and was rejected, in 1883.[5] Rimsky-Korsakov resigned from the committee in protest. When the opera was finally brought to the amateur stage, its plot was unrecognizable: all reference to the Old Belief had disappeared (including the entire self-immolation scene at the end), and the religious dissenters had been replaced by a nondescript group of Muscovites vaguely politicking on behalf of Andrei Khovansky.[6] In an article marking the fifth anniversary of Musorgsky's death, Vladimir Stasov remarked bitterly: "Is it even thinkable that in Germany people would conceal and stubbornly forbid to be staged some still unperformed opera of Wagner's? But with us it's fully thinkable."[7]

One hundred years have passed, and Musorgsky's move from musical eccentric to mainstream classic is by now well-researched territory. Centennial celebrations in the last decade have occasioned a new round of discussions in the Soviet press on Musorgsky's peculiar skills as a librettist and on his historical sensibilities. The present essay grows out of that recent literature, and out of my own dissatisfaction at attempts to yoke together Musorgsky's two major operas under a single or continuous "philosophy of history." Several central questions remain unresolved: what changes occurred in Musorgsky's historical imagination as he moved from *Boris Godunov* to *Khovanshchina*? Is there a continuum, or

---

sion. For the problems Rimsky encountered in bringing *Khovanshchina* to the stage, see A. Gozenpud, "V bor'be za naslediia Musorgskogo" [Fighting for Musorgsky's Legacy], *SM*, 1956 (3), 88–93. On Musorgsky's earlier experience with the censorship over *Boris*, see Oldani, "*Boris Godunov* and the Censor," *19th-Century Music*, 2 (1979), 245–53.

[5] See Gozenpud, 89, and V. V. Stasov, "Po povodu postanovki 'Khovanshchiny' (Pis'mo k redaktoru)" [Concerning the Production of *Khovanshchina* (A Letter to the Editor)] in V. V. Stasov, *Stat'i o muzyke*, III (Moscow, 1977), 277.

[6] For details of the changes in the premiere, see Rakhmanova (n. 1 above), 94, and Gozenpud, 88–89. Gozenpud relates that E. Feoktistov, Chief of the Main Bureau for Printed Materials and advisor to Pobedonostsev, exhorted Rimsky-Korsakov to remove the Old Believers from the opera and "turn them into people dissatisfied with something." "But dissatisfied with what?" Rimsky asked. "There's lots to choose from," Feoktistov answered. "Ultimately, I guess, Peter's reforms" (Gozenpud, 88). The time of the opera, of course, precedes Peter's reforms by at least a decade.

[7] "Iz stat'i 'Pamiati Musorgskogo' " [From the article "In Musorgsky's Memory"], in Stasov, *Stat'i o muzyke*, III, 283. The article originally appeared in the journal *Istoricheskii vestnik* (March 1886), 644–56.

a conceptual break? Can Musorgsky's two libretti on historical themes be said to have an integrated poetics? I will argue here that Musorgsky's mode of emplotting history did indeed evolve, but in a direction uncongenial both to the progressive Hegelians of Musorgsky's own era and to the ideology of his later Soviet interpreters. Within nineteenth-century Russian culture, this evolution is not so much linear as circular, a return to the source of Musorgsky's initial inspiration in historical drama, Pushkin's *Boris Godunov*. But this return is complex and indirect. Along the way, Musorgsky appears to have developed a vision of history quite radical for historical opera—even as he embodied that vision in increasingly conventional, Italianate operatic forms. We might open the argument with a review of Musorgsky's earlier experience as a prose dramatist.

I

Although Musorgsky was librettist for all his operas, his source material came in varying degrees of literary "preparedness." His first operatic experiment drew on a novel, Flaubert's *Salammbô*; his second was a word-for-word setting of a portion of Gogol's dramatic farce, *Marriage*. At the end of his life Musorgsky again returned to Gogol, this time to the Ukrainian tales, for "The Fair at Sorochintsy." All these projects were either abandoned or left incomplete. The two great operas for which Musorgsky is remembered, *Boris Godunov* and *Khovanshchina*, do not have prose fiction at their base but rather historical drama—or the naked historical document itself. Let us first consider *Boris*.

Musorgsky's source for *Boris Godunov* was Pushkin's drama of 1825, a recognized Russian classic. Out of this source Musorgsky created two versions of the *Boris* opera, one in 1869 and a revised version in 1872–74. As Richard Taruskin has persuasively argued, these two operas are not variants of a single plan but two quite separately conceptualized wholes.[8] Musorgsky composed his initial 1869 version under the influence of a strict realist aesthetic, in which fidelity to the verbal text and the intonational patterns of Russian speech took precedence over musical form or development.[9] This first version nevertheless reflects a curious

---

[8] Richard Taruskin, "Musorgsky vs. Musorgsky: The Versions of *Boris Godunov*," in *19th-Century Music*, 8 (1984–85), 91–118 and 245–72. On Musorgsky's adaptation of Pushkin's text in the context of the musical aesthetics of the 1860s, see my *Boris Godunov: Transpositions of a Russian Theme* (Bloomington, Ind., 1986), 142–206.

[9] The libretto drew on only eight of Pushkin's twenty-five scenes, but those eight scenes follow Pushkin's text closely. Musorgsky either set the words almost verbatim, as in the Cell and Inn scenes, or he condensed and paraphrased—respecting, however, Pushkin's basic

type of fidelity. The words that characters sing, and thus the sentiments they express at any given moment, are indeed those of Pushkin's characters realized in music. Since music slows down a text, however, Musorgsky was obliged (as are most librettists who adapt an existing stage drama) to cut and simplify the plot drastically. This reduction in the number and complexity of scenes could only result in a very casual fidelity to the whole of the source. Pushkin's sense of the historical event and the relation among scenes was inevitably lost.

The 1874 version of the opera has an equally complex relation to its source. After the Theater Directorate rejected the initial version, Musorgsky returned to Pushkin and created an entire new act out of the Polish scenes. The new opera thus incorporated more of the larger shape of Pushkin's play. At the same time, Musorgsky revised both music and text of the previously composed scenes, in places radically altering the words and world-views of Pushkin's characters. Their operatic counterparts became static and less subtle, their behavior more melodramatic, their musical line less declamatory.

To this conventionalization of the leading roles Musorgsky added an unconventional ending, the mass scene of popular rebellion in Kromy Forest. This scene is neither in Pushkin's play nor in the primary source for that play, Karamzin's *History of the Russian State*. The Kromy scene is without literary prototype; Musorgsky pieced it together from chants, folksongs, Jesuit hymns, and previously composed procession music. The scene contains no extended recitative, and its sequence of events is in fact *non*-narrative. Musorgsky did not oblige himself in this instance to compose a plot; he was satisfied with musical tableaux that suggested a historical event but neither portrayed its logical progression nor created dialogue among its participants.

The inspiration for the Kromy scene—as well as its appropriateness—has been widely debated.[10] In its openness and ambivalent ideology, this

intent in plot and character. In one important respect only does the initial version differ from its literary source: the onstage prominence given to the title role. The opera favors scenes in which Tsar Boris either appears or is the immediate topic of conversation. Unlike Pushkin's drama, which minimizes Boris's grandeur, the 1869 opera magnifies the Tsar's sufferings and ends conventionally on the Tsar's death.

[10] Several forums have appeared over the last two decades in the major Soviet music journal, *Sovetskaia muzyka*. The most important are: "K izucheniiu naslediia M. P. Musorgskogo: Stsena 'Pod Kromami' v dramaturgii *Borisa Godunova*" [Researching Musorgsky's Legacy: The Kromy Scene in the Dramaturgy of *Boris Godunov*], discussants Yu. Tiulin, E. Frid, B. Iarustovskii, A. Kandinskii, P. Aravin, in *SM*, 1970 (3), 90–114; A. Tsuker, "Narod pokornyi i narod buntuiushchii" [The People Submissive and Rebellious], *SM*, 1972 (3), 105–109; I. Obraztsova, "K ponimaniiu narodnogo kharaktera v tvorchestve Musorgs-

final scene in fact recalls the ending Pushkin had devised for his version of the story. In the final scene of Pushkin's play, a government official announces the death of Boris's widow and son, and then orders the crowd to cheer the victorious pretender. In a famous final stage direction, the crowd does not respond: "The people fall silent." There is something of the same unexpected emptiness at the end of the Kromy scene, which creates an expectation of robust sonic closure in the form of competing choruses and then, at the last minute, takes the choruses away—leaving the stage empty except for a holy fool, who hops distractedly to center stage and sings of the coming destruction of Russia as the curtain falls. Both play and revised version of the opera express at their final moments a sense that historical process is capricious and often governed by chance (or by silence), and that the meaning of historical events is not to be found in the fate of the title role—who has long since departed the stage.

Thus Musorgsky in 1874 was both less and more faithful to his literary source. Although the words that characters sing and the operatic personalities that emerge depart significantly from their counterparts in Pushkin, it could be argued that the actual sense of historical process in the later opera is closer to the spirit of Pushkin's play than is the technically more "faithful" first version.

Musorgsky's strategies for adapting his source in the two *Boris* libretti can serve as a case study of problems we confront when considering a librettist's fidelity to sources—and to the larger whole of a historical event. Libretti based on literary texts will inevitably "leave something out." But the parts left in can be faithful to their source on several different planes. They can be true to the characters or true to the narration. When whole portions of spoken text are moved verbatim into the libretto, as Musorgsky chose to do in his first version of *Boris*, the first strategy obtains: the privileged fidelity is to the characters' integrity, the degree to which libretto personalities sound or behave like their literary prototypes. Their words and stories are of course condensed and simplified, but the librettist strives to respect their inner perspective on events and to preserve their images intact.

The second strategy, more characteristic of Musorgsky's revised version of *Boris*, is founded less on fidelity to the words or characters than on the spirit or narrative structure of the source. By melodramatizing Boris, adding love interest, and interpolating a number of set songs into the score, Musorgsky made the body of his opera more suited (as he him-

---

kogo" [Toward an Understanding of the People's Character in Musorgsky's Works], *SM*, 1980 (9), 95–101. See Emerson, *Boris Godunov*, 198–206.

self admitted) to the "grand stage."[11] But this operatic whole then re-addresses its source text on a higher, one might even say a "historiographical," level. The new final scene in Kromy Forest moves the focus away from the title role and into the uncertainties of the nation's fate—just as Pushkin's play had done. With the exception of that final scene, however, both strategies for libretto genesis draw on a single literary source that embodies a unified aesthetic vision of a historical period.

II

One year after the Kromy scene's composition—and two years before *Boris* was premiered—Musorgsky began work on another opera. Its libretto strategy could be said to pick up where the Kromy scene left off. Like the final scene of *Boris, Khovanshchina* drew on no single literary source text; Musorgsky created the plot out of raw historical sources, from various authors and bearing various ideologies. Thus the *Khovanshchina* libretto was not vulnerable to the charges brought against *Boris Godunov*—charges of infidelity to a source, disrespect for a canonized poet, distortion of a literary masterpiece. On the contrary, reviewers of the premiere scarcely mentioned the libretto. The fact that the opera's plot made little sense was not perceived as a weakness—and this is a good index of the conceptual distance separating *Khovanshchina* from the two *Boris* libretti. The angry reviews following the 1874 *Boris* premiere had been directed at least as much against the words as the music. The music was sufficiently dissonant and declamatory to offend professional opera critics, and the libretto (in what was surely the worst of both worlds) was faulted for being both derivative of and unfaithful to its source. *Khovanshchina* reversed this impression. Its music was unexpectedly melodious; the opera rang with fanfares, folksongs, well-behaved choruses, and arioso-style lyrical monologues. A more conventional musical structure, in short, appeared to placate the demand for a rigorously motivated libretto. The problems *Khovanshchina* presents are of another sort altogether.

There is, first, the usual difficulty in ferreting out "authorial intention" from an opera unfinished, and unpublished, during its composer's lifetime. Secondly, there are the special problems that accompany any research into Musorgsky's later period: poor documentation, the compos-

[11] In a letter to Golenishchev-Kutuzov (15 August 1877), Musorgsky explained that a composer writing for the grand stage must project characters "in bold relief," true to their "dramatic inevitability." See M. P. Musorgskii, *Pis'ma k A. A. Golenishchevu-Kutuzovu*, ed. Yu. Keldysh (Moscow-Leningrad, 1939), 69; for a translation, see *The Musorgsky Reader*, ed. and trans. Jay Leyda and Sergei Bertensson (New York, 1970), 360.

er's many evasive masks, and the personal tragedy of poverty and alcoholism. Lastly, there is the peculiar status of the libretto itself, which exists in several versions with and without its music. All these factors must become part of any interpretation of *Khovanshchina*.

Boris Godunov confuses us because it has two authorial versions; *Khovanshchina*, strictly speaking, has none. Musorgsky left only a piano-vocal score in manuscript, with completion dates for the separate episodes ranging from 1873 to 1880.[12] Select pieces from the opera had been orchestrated (and even performed) during his lifetime, but the whole was much too long for continuous performance and the finale had only been sketched. Rimsky-Korsakov's efforts to turn his friend's unfinished opera into a performable work have therefore not been castigated as have his wholesale recastings of *Boris*—which was, after all, a published and performed work. Some critics have even credited Rimsky with joint authorship of *Khovanshchina*.[13] But for that reason it has been all the more difficult to get at an "authoritative"—that is, single-authored—text. In the early 1930s Pavel Lamm "de-Rimskified" *Khovanshchina*, as he had *Boris*, on the basis of manuscript materials; Shostakovich re-orchestrated the Lamm piano-vocal score in the late 1950s.[14] But even when the Shostakovich orchestration is used in performance, Rimsky's cuts in the score and libretto are often retained—as indeed they were, by and large, in the Metropolitan Opera's 1985 production.[15] The sound might be closer to Musorgsky's, but the dramatic concept is still several editings away.

---

[12] The sequence of composition (based on Musorgsky's own dating) suggests that the opera did not unfold as a chronological whole but was sketched, revised, and then "filled in." Approximate completion dates are: for Act I: 1873 (first half) and 1875 (final two episodes); for Act II: most episodes 1875–76; for Act III: 1873 (first half) and 1876 (second half); for Act IV: most of the Act in 1876 and two episodes in 1880; for Act V: most scenes sketched during 1873 and separate episodes dated 1876, 1878, 1879, 1880.

[13] See V. Karatygin, " 'Khovanshchina' i eia avtory" [*Khovanshchina* and Its Authors], in *Muzykal'nyi sovremennik*, 5–6 (January–February 1917), 192–218. Karatygin surveys Rimsky's cuts, praising him for this most difficult task: "He not only healed the wounds, but did it in such a way that one gets the impression no operation ever took place" (194); "*Khovanshchina* has two authors, although only one spirit of genius" (218). Richard Taruskin reminds me that Karatygin's article (which appeared in a journal edited by Andrei Rimsky-Korsakov, the composer's son) was itself highly polemical, an attempt to discredit the 1913 Diaghilev production of *Khovanshchina* mounted in Paris with the collaboration of Igor Stravinsky.

[14] See Vl. Gurevich, "Shostakovich—redaktor 'Khovanshchiny' " [Shostakovich as the Editor of *Khovanshchina*], in *Muzyka i sovremennost'*, 7 (Moscow, 1971), 29–68, and Vl. Gurevich, "Shostakovich v rabote nad 'Khovanshchinoi' " [Shostakovich at Work on *Khovanshchina*], in *Voprosy teorii i estetiki muzyki*, 11 (Leningrad, 1972), 84–108. Less technical background can be found in Georgii Khubov's introductory essay to the 1963 Shostakovich score, M. Musorgskii, *Khovanshchina*, partitura (Moscow, 1963), 7–14.

[15] The libretto made available for the Metropolitan Opera production is the English ver-

241

Compounding these textual problems is the general paucity of material on Musorgsky's final years. His working methods make it almost impossible to retrieve clear stages of creation "intact" from drafts. Apparently the scenic situation, verbal text, and musical characteristics occurred to him as a unified whole, and he constructed his plot by a sort of "free improvisation."[16] Our best sources for the genesis of the libretto are not drafts at all but Musorgsky's lengthy letters to Vladimir Stasov (who differed with the composer on the direction of the plot) and a "Notebook for Khovanshchina" that Musorgsky himself compiled in 1872. Musorgsky ultimately filled twenty pages of this little notebook with citations from seventeenth-century eyewitness accounts, historical documents, and excerpts from contemporary histories, either transcribed literally or paraphrased.[17] Eventually, whole chunks of this material—mostly documents dating from 1682—were moved into the libretto almost intact: Shaklovity's denunciation, for example, and Sophia's love letter to Golitsyn.[18] Of the secondary sources cited in the Notebook (both eighteenth- and nineteenth-century), most are by authors whose allegiances were anti-Old Belief and pro-Peter. But Musorgsky did not passively absorb this framing ideology; in fact, his extracts favor historical personages speaking in their own voices. Often Musorgsky would lace these citations with his own commentary or rejoinders, so the notebook entries occasionally evolve into primitive dialogues.[19] From these quasi-dialogized fragments Musorgsky created his plot.

The actual shape of Musorgsky's intended dramatic whole has been the

---

sion by Christopher Hunt for the San Francisco Opera Company (1984). Its omissions and conflations are peculiar. Act I respects all of Rimsky's massive cuts in the manuscript; Act II omits the reading by Golitsyn of his mother's letter but inserts Dosifei's comments about his past life as Prince Myshetsky (an episode cut by Rimsky), and includes one exchange present in the piano-vocal manuscript that Musorgsky himself cut from his 1879 libretto; in Act III, the Susanna-Marfa confrontation is shortened as per Rimsky. A more complete version of the opera, with a startlingly full, multi-voiced first act, is that for the Covent Garden production (1972) under Edward Downes.

[16] Ruzanna Shirinian, *Opernaia dramaturgiia Musorgskogo* (Moscow, 1981), 170–71.

[17] The contents of this notebook have been thoroughly analyzed. For a title page and table of contents, see *The Musorgsky Reader* (n. 11 above), 195. For analysis of the entries, see esp. Galina Bakaeva, *"Khovanshchina" M. Musorgskogo* (Kiev, 1976), ch. 1 and 2; Emilia Frid, *Proshedshee, nastoiashchee i budushchee v "Khovanshchine" Musorgskogo* [Past, Present, and Future in Musorgsky's *Khovanshchina*] (Leningrad, 1974), ch. 2, esp. 74–97; also Shirinian, 152–66.

[18] For texts of the denunciation in the notebook and in the libretto, see Bakaeva, 51–52; for the texts of Sophia's letters to Golitsyn (in the source that Musorgsky most probably consulted), see Mikhail Semevskii, "Sovremennye portrety Sofii Alekseevny i V. V. Golitsyna," in *Russkoe slovo* ([St. Petersburg], December 1859), 429–30.

[19] See Bakaeva, 38.

subject of some controversy. The problem here centers neither on the confused state of the manuscript scores nor on Rimsky's reworkings, but on a document that turned up unexpectedly fifty years after Musorgsky's death. In 1931, Pavel Lamm had just reconstructed the original piano-vocal score of *Khovanshchina* from the surviving manuscripts. But no drafts of a libretto were extant in the Musorgsky archive, and none of Musorgsky's surviving letters mentions any such separate libretto-writing activity. Lamm assumed, correctly, that *Khovanshchina* had been composed without a pre-existing libretto. Then in 1932 a blue school notebook filled with Musorgsky's handwriting turned up in the Golenishchev-Kutuzov archive.[20] Kutuzov, a minor poet, had roomed with Musorgsky in 1874 and 1875, and had provided the words for Musorgsky's vocal cycles *Sunless* and *Songs and Dances of Death*. Even after Kutuzov left to get married, Musorgsky remained in correspondence with the poet, often consulting with him on matters of prosody.

The blue notebook in the Kutuzov archive contained an undated libretto of *Khovanshchina* written out entirely in prose. Compared with the manuscript piano-vocal score, this verbal text is much simplified and "accelerated"; four major dramatic episodes are cut.[21] Drawing on evidence provided by the publication dates of folksongs included in Act IV, the Soviet editor assigns the blue-notebook libretto to 1879 or 1880—making it one of Musorgsky's last literary projects.[22] And here a paradox presents itself.

If the dating is correct, Musorgsky wrote out the libretto when the concept of the operatic whole had finally settled in him. He did not live to adjust the already-composed music of his piano-vocal score to this new verbal text. And yet this text now enjoys the status of an authoritative libretto among Soviet researchers, who presume, not unreasonably, that the blue notebook was to serve Musorgsky as a guide for his final revision

[20] See M. P. Pekelis, "Musorgskii—pisatel'—dramaturg," in M. P. Musorgskii, *Literaturnoe nasledstvo/Literaturnye proizvedeniia* (Moscow, 1972), 31–34. The blue-notebook libretto (henceforth Pekelis) is reproduced in prose on 124–48, with departures from the piano-vocal manuscript indicated in notes.

[21] The four cut or shortened episodes are: a dialogue between the Moscow folk and the Clerk in Act I; the episode between Golitsyn and the Lutheran pastor in Act II; an exchange between Marfa and Susanna, and between Dosifei and Susanna, in Act III; and Act V, which is fragmentary in the piano-vocal score and in the blue-notebook libretto even more so. The blue-notebook libretto divides the text into six scenes (*kartiny*), with no markings for acts.

[22] This dating must remain a hypothesis. In personal communications, both Robert Oldani and Richard Taruskin have expressed reservations about so late a date. Oldani points out, for example, that familiarity with folksongs among folk-oriented composers in the 1870s can scarcely be limited to published editions. To my knowledge, Soviet scholars have not offered any other grounds for the attribution of an 1879 date.

and orchestration.[23] Its precise wording and division of scenes, however, are not those of the manuscript scores, nor are they those associated with the opera for most of its performance history. And such a non-coincidence of texts cannot be easily remedied by any "restoration," because no complete or continuous music exists for this libretto. The editor has suggested that the unusual prose layout of the libretto (extending even to the embedded folksongs and chants) was a deliberate attempt on Musorgsky's part to emphasize the purely dramatic concept of the opera, undistracted by the pull of musical form.[24] Kutuzov, in whose archive the notebook was found, was a writer of historical drama as well as a poet; quite possibly Musorgsky sent him the libretto for his advice and recommendations. The presence of numerous "corrections" in red pencil indicate that this was most likely the case.[25]

The blue-notebook libretto thus has a peculiar legitimacy as an independent *literary* work, an artistic unity in its own right. However provisional in Musorgsky's mind, it probably represents his final—and thus arguably most advanced—dramatic concept of the opera.[26] Its rights to performance depend, of course, on the way one resolves the competing

[23] See Pekelis, 33, and Shirinian (n. 16 above), 172–73.

[24] Pekelis, 33.

[25] Robert Oldani, in a personal communication, raises legitimate doubts about this interpretation. How do we know that the red-pencil corrections are Kutuzov's? And does the notebook's authority end there? Since many of Musorgsky's own cuts and compressions in the blue-notebook libretto are ones that Rimsky later adopted, is it not possible that Rimsky knew of this blue-notebook libretto and used it as a guide when preparing his own version of the opera? If so, Rimsky's reworking was much less arbitrary than it has appeared. One can only regret that Kutuzov's discussion of *Khovanshchina* in his *Reminiscences of Musorgsky* (written in the 1880s) is so brief. Kutuzov deals with the opera largely in musical terms, praising its wealth of song and lyricism, which pleases him "despite all the inconveniences presented by the plot, which is not only not an operatic subject but not even a dramatic one, and chosen for God knows what reason." See A. A. Golenishchev-Kutuzov, "Vospominaniia o M. P. Musorgskom," in *Muzykal'noe nasledstvo* (Moscow, 1935), 25.

[26] Only in one respect must this hypothesis be qualified. The blue-notebook libretto ends with an apparently incomplete final act, primarily choral and containing none of the dialogue among principals (Marfa, Andrei, Dosifei) that was sketched in the piano-vocal manuscript. Pekelis (n. 20 above) states simply that "here the libretto comes to an end" (200). A. Vul'fson has researched the final scene, and asserts that the love duet between Marfa and Andrei was indisputably part of Musorgsky's plan (the scene was often sung in a solo version by Daria Leonova between 1878 and 1880, but after Musorgsky's death that manuscript was lost; Andrei's part was found in 1947). The absence of this love duet in the blue-notebook libretto "should not be awarded exaggerated significance," because clearly "the work was interrupted, not completed." See "K problemam tekstologii" [*Toward Problems of Textology*] *SM*, 1981 (3), 103–10, esp. 104. Both Vul'fson and Oldani point out that Musorgsky neither signed, dated, nor dedicated the blue-notebook libretto—a significant detail for a composer who habitually signed with a flourish his completed works, even his completed scenes and segments of works.

claims of words versus music in a given operatic text, and on one's approach to the general problems of co-authorship, dating, and multiple versions. With a textual history this uncertain, what constitutes an "authoritative performance"? One in which music is devised to fit a coherent libretto, or one where words (or other transitions) are created to patch together all segments of surviving music?

Here students of the opera may simply make a choice. The 1879 blue-notebook libretto, except for its incomplete final scene, will serve as the basis for my comments on the "historical world-view" of *Khovanshchina*. That world-view has proved elusive indeed. The best students of Musorgsky are routinely embarrassed by the opera's ideological implications, and several of their solutions are relevant to my own reading.

III

The Soviet debate over *Khovanshchina* opened with the controversial thesis put forth by the Soviet musicologist Boris Asafiev in the 1930s.[27] Asafiev was concerned—as were many in the Stalinist era—to understand Musorgsky's move from the second version of *Boris* to *Khovanshchina* as linear and historically progressive. The difficulty came, of course, in deriving *Khovanshchina* from the Kromy Forest scene. In Kromy, the Russian masses on stage are inspired with a spirit of rebellion, a sense of freedom and free choice, even though they ultimately exercise it on behalf of a pretender. In *Khovanshchina*, apart from a few boastful drinking songs, there is no freedom at all. The mutinous troops in Act III instantly succumb when Prince Khovansky declines to lead them into battle against Peter's troops. Act IV ends with a pardoning of the mutineers, but only after they file meekly by with nooses round their necks, carrying their own execution blocks and axes. The famous last scene, where the Old Believers prefer to set fire to themselves rather than surrender to government troops, does indeed show resistance—but it is of a peculiarly passive and historically reactionary kind. Everywhere the people die, or are disarmed and humiliated. How can this plot qualify as "people's musical drama"? How can it be squared with "progressive" history?

Asafiev's solution is to reinterpret the very label Musorgsky devised for

[27] See "V rabote nad 'Khovanshchinoi' " [At Work on *Khovanshchina*], in B. V. Asafiev, *Izbrannye trudy*, 3 (Moscow, 1954), 160–67. Asafiev wrote the essay in 1931, in connection with his own efforts at orchestrating Musorgsky's piano-vocal manuscripts (Asafiev's score, if it exists, has not been published). During the war years Asafiev returned to the ideology of Musorgsky's opera with even more historical optimism; see "Russkii narod, russkie liudi" [The Russian Folk, the Russian People] (1944) in *Izbrannye trudy*, 4 (Moscow, 1955), 118.

his opera, "people's musical drama." The composer notwithstanding, Asafiev declares, this is not a drama of the people but a drama of the *state* (166). One social class after another is isolated and rendered powerless; the libretto unfolds as stages in the dying of Old Muscovy. And the idea of Old Russia dying is itself progressive. This reading, of course, is a Soviet extension of statist historiography in the 1870s—best exemplified by the works of Sergei Soloviev, known to be among Musorgsky's sources for *Khovanshchina*.[28] In the organic, centralizing statist view, history might indeed cause pain to some groups of people; the course of history is ineluctable and unsentimental. But Peter the Great in the wings of *Khovanshchina* is ultimately more progressive than all the self-confident joyous delusions of the Kromy scene. Asafiev almost celebrates in *Khovanshchina* the collapse of popular resistance, seeing it as something historically necessary for the growth and defense of the Russian state. Not surprisingly, this bold Stalinist reading of the opera has come under attack in recent, more liberal years.[29]

Two of these recent "revisionist" readings of *Khovanshchina* are of special interest. Both claim that Musorgsky did indeed have an artistic plan, and that the fate of the Russian people is at the center of it. But neither is "political" in the way Asafiev is. Both seek, rather, *aesthetic* precedents for Musorgsky's embodiment of history in opera, and both vaguely locate that precedent in Alexander Pushkin.

Galina Bakaeva's 1976 monograph on *Khovanshchina* is the more conventional.[30] She adopts Asafiev's basic dramatic scheme for the opera: the first two acts bring the forces of Old Muscovy on stage, and then each group is eliminated in an inevitable unfolding of historical necessity (57–61). But she stresses, as Asafiev did not, that Peter's troops—not to mention Peter himself—are forever invisible and offstage (189–91).[31] To the

---

[28] See the letter from Musorgsky to Vladimir Stasov, 6 September 1873: "I am re-reading Soloviev, to become acquainted with the epoch" (*The Musorgsky Reader* [n. 11 above], 251). Internal evidence suggests that Musorgsky drew upon and modified ch. 3 ["Moskovskaia smuta 1682 goda"] of Soloviev's *History of Russia from Ancient Times*, vol. XIII, which describes in detail several of the events in the opera (the execution of the Khovanskys, the cooperation between *streltsy* and Old Believers, the destruction of the "pillar" [*stolp*] on Red Square, etc.). See S. M. Soloviev, *Istoriia Rossii s drevneishikh vremen*, Book VII (vv. 13–14) (Moscow, 1962), 261–302.

[29] For a good example of the routine anti-Asafiev disclaimer, see S. Shlifshtein, "Otkuda zhe rassvet?" [So Where's the Dawn Coming From?], *SM*, 1971 (12), 109–13. Later editors are quick to insist that Asafiev did not mean "state" in the Marxist-Leninist sense (as something, presumably, that should wither away), but "state" in the sense of a patriotic, defense-oriented unity of the whole people. See note 5 to "V rabote nad 'Khovanshchinoi,'" *Izbrannye trudy*, III, 318.

[30] Bakaeva (see n. 17 above).

[31] The exact location of Peter's trumpeters and troops (backstage, or moving onstage as

246

participants onstage, Peter I and his men are specters, and terrifying ones. Statist historians in the 1870s idealized Peter I and strove to see in their reigning Emancipator-Tsar, Alexander II, traces of Peter's vision and boldness. Musorgsky refused to make any such gesture of the present binding on the past. The personal histories of his characters are backward-looking, locked in time, and obsessively simple. Episodes do not combine dynamically to move action forward. From this Bakaeva concludes that Musorgsky "had decisively rejected the narrative principle in the dramaturgy of a libretto" (72).

The second monograph, Emilia Frid's 1974 study *Past, Present, and Future in Musorgsky's "Khovanshchina,"*[32] also targets mode of narration as a key to the opera's peculiar stasis, and refers us back to Pushkin. But Frid then speculates at length on this radically innovative dramaturgy. If Musorgsky's operatic *Boris* departs profoundly from the spirit of its Pushkinian source, then *Khovanshchina*, oddly, returns to it. Reminiscent of Pushkin's play, *Khovanshchina* is not organized narratively, not even linearly; it is more a vertical cut through compressed time. This cross-section branches out into various plot lines, each of which is extremely simple and relatively isolated from the others. And yet the action onstage strikes us as quite complex. This complexity is achieved, Frid argues, not by development and interaction among characters but by static episodes passing through one another—strata, as it were, that move across our field of vision at arbitrary points, without clear climaxes or well-marked ends (240–43).

This time-space structure has an inevitable effect on the relationship between personality and idea in the opera (279–91). Here Frid contrasts *Khovanshchina* with *Boris*. In *Boris*, the lofty tragedic style is linked with one person: the Tsar himself. Other factors—fate, the people, history—take on importance and weight through association with his theme. In *Khovanshchina*, by contrast, the tragedic style is not linked personally with any single character, nor with the moral gravity of any one person's particular sin. Rather this lofty style "unites all those who episodically

---

the final scene draws to a close) differs in the stage directions of various versions. The blue-notebook libretto, skimpy in general with its stage directions, provides little help here, breaking off before the final episode. But Musorgsky could never have brought Peter the Great on stage, even had he wished to: censorship forbade any representation onstage of a ruler from the reigning house of Romanov. Musorgsky, it could be argued, was making a virtue out of necessity. But this does not invalidate Bakaeva's thesis that Peter's absence has ideological significance for the opera as a whole, however non-negotiable the matter was for the composer.

[32] See n. 17 above.

become carriers of the general idea" (280).[33] Frid leaves the content of this idea strangely open; what interests her is the relationship between idea and personality as a formal problem. If *Boris Godunov* is dramatic opera built up out of guilt and personal choice, then *Khovanshchina*, in its basic contours, is an epic.

But this is not, Frid hastens to add, the epic music-drama of Wagner or the fairy-tale epic of Rimsky-Korsakov. Dramatic conflict in *Khovanshchina* is too decentered; the conflict source is never localized or concentrated (306–309). And, more important, *Khovanshchina* is too closely tied to actual historical events to be mythical or lyrical after the usual manner of such operas. The originality of *Khovanshchina*, Frid concludes, lies in its bizarre fusion of drama and epic, in which lyricism— conventionally the vehicle for private and fictional fates—serves to embody generalized, extrapersonal images and historically grounded philosophical ideas (310).

Frid's extended discussion is, in my view, the most convincing conceptualization to date of Musorgsky's "people's musical drama." But the energy she must expend to make the familiar categories of epic, drama, and lyric cohere in *Khovanshchina* suggests that the opera's identity might better be sought altogether outside such labels. I would like to offer another framework for viewing the opera—one that draws upon, but modifies as it extends, the insights of this recent Soviet scholarship.

IV

My own point of departure is a question that occupied Pushkin as he worked on his *Boris Godunov*: how does one embed a historical event in artistic form so that the product is both true to history and true to art? Musorgsky, I would argue, never lost his early *kuchkist* passion for verisimilitude in art. But he became more flexible and subtle about the areas where it might apply, and less hostile to conventional operatic techniques. The *Khovanshchina* libretto does not raise questions of fidelity to a literary source; the question here, rather, is Musorgsky's desire to construct a text faithful to an era and a spirit of the time.

---

[33] This thesis would explain—to take but one example—the apparent "inconsistency" in Shaklovity's character that routinely baffles opera-goers. How can this slippery bureaucrat, who concocts a false denunciation of the Khovanskys in Act I and coldbloodedly murders Ivan Khovansky in Act IV, deliver in Act III a somber, heartfelt lament on the tragedy of Russia's violent history and internal feuding? Frid (284–85) argues that such "character consistency" is simply not part of Musorgsky's plan. Shaklovity's aria is not his own: it is lyrical, Glinka-like, a timeless patriotic sentiment that does not issue from Shaklovity's historical character but rather uses Shaklovity as *its* mouthpiece.

Late seventeenth-century Muscovy knew several times simultaneously, each with its own spirit. There were old princely families like the Khovanskys, jealously guarding what remained of their independence. Supporting them, unreliably and erratically, were the *streltsy*, garrison troops in the capital. In the cities a new bureaucratic class of scribes and clerks peddled literacy for profit. And in the Kremlin, a partial westernization had been achieved under Tsar Alexis, which was later extended by his daughter Sophia Alekseevna, regent while Peter was a child. Sophia's favorite, Prince Vasily Golitsyn, embodied that tentative impulse to learn from Western culture that would become a compulsion of the court under Peter the Great. Finally there was a massive schism in the Russian Orthodox Church, precipitated by Tsar Alexis and his autocratic Patriarch, Nikon. Nikon had decreed some changes in Orthodox ritual and iconography, and a large and vocal portion of the faithful (the so-called "Old Believers") refused to cooperate. They interpreted the reforms as an indication that the past was no longer sacred, the End of the World was nigh, and the Antichrist, posing as Peter the First, was already abroad in the land.[34]

Among the various times and degrees of change represented by these social groups, "Old Believer time" has a special status. It is not merely another way of assessing what happens in the present, or debating what social class will inherit the future. It is an end to *all* presents; in fact, it is an end to time itself, and thus inherently incompatible with other attitudes toward history. In a music-drama where Old Believers play a role, then, their understanding of time cannot really be integrated with the others. There are two options for Old Believer time: it must be rated as hierarchically superior or dismissed as superstition.

Soviet researchers, who tend to apologize for Musorgsky's tenderness toward the schismatics, have favored the latter option. Not surprisingly, they comb the sources for evidence that the composer was a materialist, a realist, and a progressive Hegelian in his understanding of historical process.[35] Dosifei is usually perceived as a fanatic—albeit an astute and noble one[36]—and Marfa as an experienced politician who predicts Golitsyn's fate not because she can read fortunes in a bowl of water but

[34] See Michael Cherniavsky, "The Old Believers and the New Religion," *Slavic Review*, 25 (1966), 1–39.

[35] See Bakaeva (n. 17 above), ch. 1, especially 36–40, 49, 139, and 188–202; Frid (n. 17 above), 156–63; M. Sokol'skii, " 'Khovanshchina' v Bol'shom teatre" [*Khovanshchina* at the Bolshoi Theater], *SM*, 1950 (6), 17–18.

[36] Aleksei Ogolevets's treatment of Dosifei is characteristic in its condescension: "The image of a religious fanatic, a partisan of the past, is completely alien to us" (*Vokal'naia dramaturgiia Musorgskogo* [Moscow, 1966], 395).

because she knows the workings of Sophia's court. The mystical and supernatural elements in the Old Belief, and in Musorgsky's own beliefs, are routinely passed over lightly or simply ignored.

My reading of the opera will pursue the first option: the possibility that Musorgsky took the Old Believer concept of time very seriously—indeed, that he structured his whole opera around it. In this view, Musorgsky created *Khovanshchina* with one particular verisimilitude in mind: he wished to be true to the world as the Old Believers saw it, and thus granted them the ultimate victory. Support for this position will accumulate gradually in the discussion that follows. To place the opera more firmly in its history, however, we should first consider various other types of verisimilitude Musorgsky might have pursued. There are, it seems, at least four: fidelity to event, character, music, and language itself.

Verisimilitude can be registered, first, in the actual sequence of events, in historical chronology itself. Musorgsky chose to compress and rearrange events, combining elements from three *streltsy* revolts between 1682 and 1698. The bulk of the action, and most of the actual historical documents embedded in the libretto, date from 1682. That year was one of constant turmoil.[37] One tsar had just died; the ten-year-old Peter and his sixteen-year-old half-brother Ivan were elevated to the throne under the regency of their older sister Sophia. The *streltsy*, restless in the interregnum and recently brought under the protection of Ivan Khovansky, joined with militant Old Believers to demand a cancellation of the Church reforms. Sophia alternately placated and repressed this complex revolt. She beheaded one leading religious dissenter and initiated severe persecution of the Old Belief throughout the Empire. In the autumn of 1682 both Ivan Khovansky and his son Andrei were executed, but when the *streltsy* rose up in protest against these deaths the Regent did not dare to carry out mass reprisals. Fearful for her own position, she pardoned the troops (this is the source of the macabre pardon at the end of Act IV, attributed to Peter).

Tucked into this basic 1682 chronology are events from much later years. In 1689 Sophia herself attempted to lead the *streltsy* (then under the command of Shaklovity, her own appointee) against her half-brother Peter and thus to secure the throne in her own name. But Peter was by then grown up, and dangerous. This is the situation reflected at the end of Act III, where Khovansky (historically seven years dead) declines to lead the *streltsy* into battle because "times are different now: Tsar Peter

[37] See Robert O. Crummey, *The Old Believers and the World of Antichrist: The Vyg Community and the Russian State, 1694–1855* (Madison, Wis., 1970), ch. 3 ("Death by Fire").

is terrifying!" The 1689 rebellion failed; Shaklovity was executed, Sophia imprisoned in a convent, and Golitsyn, Sophia's lover, exiled to Siberia (the fulfillment in Act IV, scene 2 of Marfa's prophecy from Act II).

Final retribution against the *streltsy* did not come until 1698, when Peter I returned from his European tour to suppress a third rebellion. This historical event is the source for those mass gallows on Red Square we see almost under construction in Act IV. But in history the pardon never came: Peter had 1,000 rebel troops tortured and put to death, and the surviving *streltsy* disbanded.

Retribution against the final rebellious group, the Old Believers, was more diffuse and inconclusive. But Musorgsky's choice of a self-immolation scene to end *Khovanshchina* is especially appropriate for an opera set in the 1680s. Sophia's regency ushered in an authentic inquisition. An edict from 1684 established search-and-destroy missions against Old Believer communities, with orders to take the dissenters alive. The following decade witnessed an epidemic of mass suicides by communities intent on sacrificing the body so that the soul might be saved from the Antichrist: 2,700 burned to death in a chapel on the White Sea in 1687; several thousand perished in like manner on Lake Onega in 1688, another 1,500 in 1689.

As regards verisimilitude to event, then, Musorgsky selected from the historical record both real and representative "facts" to construct his plot. But he did not observe chronological accuracy. This license with historical sequence, we should note, also freed him from the larger constraints of causality.

Verisimilitude with respect to historical character—our second category—is also observed only partially.[38] Some of the historical roles, such as Ivan Khovansky and Golitsyn, are given their "own lines" taken literally from documents written by their historical counterparts. Other characters appear to be amalgams of several historical figures—as is Dosifei, who combines features of the schismatic Prince Myshetsky, Nikita "Pustosviat" [the Bigot] beheaded by Sophia in 1682, and the most famous preacher of the Old Belief in Russian history, the Archpriest Avvakum.[39] Still other characters, including Shaklovity and Andrei Khovansky (the son), bear genuine historical names, but the events associated with them in the opera do not accord with the historical records. And a final category (including the Clerk, Marfa, Emma, and Susanna) has precedent as a social or historical type, but is modeled on no specific historical figure.

---

[38] For details on historical prototypes, see Bakaeva (n. 17 above), 29–47; Frid (n. 17 above), 127–85; Shirinian (n. 16 above), 202–22.

[39] On sources for Dosifei, see Frid, 164–78.

So character, like event, is true to history only in crude outline, intermittently and with artistic embellishment.

Two more verisimilitudes remain to be considered. The first concerns embedded musical genres. *Khovanshchina* is significantly less declamatory than Musorgsky's earlier operas: folksongs and church-style chants adorn and at times actually govern the musical texture. But these native genres do not, as a rule, embody seventeenth-century harmonies or musical forms.[40] Musorgsky's sources for folk music (both words and melodies) were contemporary anthologies—or songs making the rounds of the capital, as was the case with Marfa's famous song in Act III.[41] His settings are closer to Western European harmony than to anything in the indigenous Russian tradition. Recent work on the Old Believer texts and choruses has shown that Musorgsky did not draw upon authentic liturgical texts, nor does he appear to have been familiar with ancient church chants.[42] In sum, the musical genres in *Khovanshchina*, like its chronology and its characters, are only partially, almost impressionistically, true to their time and historical prototypes.

It remains to consider the verbal fabric of the libretto itself. Here, questions of verisimilitude are complex. Musorgsky had constructed his earlier operas, *Marriage* and the first version of *Boris*, on the principle of fidelity to spoken Russian. This "speech" was adjusted, at times stylized, and enriched with signature motifs and embedded songs, but the uttered phrase still remained the intonational touchstone of the opera, that to which it was true. *Khovanshchina* presents a significantly different picture. Here, as one Soviet musicologist has put it, "the composer does not go from word to melody (as in *Boris*) but from melody to word, from a melodic generalization to a manifestation, in words, of the approximate content of the melody."[43] If the rule for *Marriage* and *Boris* is singularity, the unique utterance unfolding through time, then the rule for *Khovan-*

[40] See Vladimir Morosan, "Folk and Chant Elements in Musorgsky's Choral Writing," in *Musorgsky: In Memoriam, 1881–1981*, ed. Malcolm Hamrick Brown (Ann Arbor, Mich., 1982), 99–131.

[41] See Frid (n. 17 above), 223. "Iskhodila mladen'ka," surely the most famous folksong melody associated with *Khovanshchina*, was by Musorgsky's time well known in musical circles. It was published in Vil'boa's folksong anthology in 1860, and Tchaikovsky included it in his own collection, *50 Folksongs Arranged for Piano Four-Hands* (Tchaikovsky also used the melody in his own "Groza" overture). Musorgsky apparently first heard the song from the actor and folklorist Gorbunov.

[42] See Morosan, 123–26. The opera as a whole contains only one Old Believer melody, sung in the final immolation scene, and even that is not a liturgical chant but a secular devotional song.

[43] Ogolevets, *Vokal'naia dramaturgiia Musorgskogo* (n. 36 above), 318. The subsequent comment on Marfa's musical line occurs on the same page.

shchina is repeatability, the single melodic unit that recurs obsessively behind many different words. Exemplary, of course, is Marfa's love theme—which occurs ten times in the opera, always to different words and in different situations.

The stability of melody in *Khovanshchina* does not mean, however, that the settings ignore the intonation patterns of a prose text. Here as elsewhere Musorgsky demonstrates an extraordinary ear: at least one student of the opera detects a different socio-linguistic rhythmic layer for each character.[44] But this linguistic differentiation is not that of the seventeenth century. Except in those places where actual documents from the 1680s are set to music almost intact—the denunciation, the pardon, and the personal letters—the language of the opera is contemporary with its composer, not with its events. To create a sense of historical verisimilitude in language, Musorgsky saturated certain roles (especially the Old Believers) with archaisms. But he did not create the libretto wholly in the language of its depicted time.

We see, then, that language verisimilitude in *Khovanshchina* is as partial and as artistically hybrid as are the other fidelities. It is this last linguistic category, however, that marks most clearly the space separating *Khovanshchina* from *Boris Godunov* as historical opera. The language in *Boris* (with the exception of several stylized portions in the parts of Pimen and Varlaam) is thoroughly modern; its source text, after all, was written in 1825. In the *Boris* operas, Musorgsky made no special effort to mark the cultural distance between his nineteenth-century present and the sixteenth-century Muscovy of Tsar Boris's time—as Pushkin had not before him. The primary verisimilitude observed (in the first version especially, but in the second as well) was the truth of Russian intonation as spoken in Musorgsky's own era, amplified and embellished into melodic recitative. *Boris Godunov*, with its 300-year-old plot, presents itself on stage as something dynamic, dramatic, and contemporary.

The events depicted in *Khovanshchina* occur a half-century after the reign of Boris Godunov, on the brink of Russia's modern era. But the verbal fabric sounds immeasurably older; text, music, and theme com-

---

[44] See Shirinian (n. 16 above), 173–74. Ivan Khovansky's language is ritualized, narrow in scope, with phrases that barely move (he has a "leitword"—"Spasi Bog!"—rather than a leitmotif); Andrei Khovansky's lexicon is full of poetic folk expressions, crudely parodied in his cynical pursuit of Emma; Golitsyn's language is "Europeanized," with fewer Russian roots, and his melodies are more changeable; the Clerk sings a public-square language of comic self-abasement. Dosifei can master many styles: to the Old Believers or in his lyrical monologues his speech is dominated by Church Slavonicisms, but to Marfa his language is lyrical and passionate. Marfa, too, has among the richest lexicons of any character in the opera, although musically her part could be described as one sustained lament.

bine to distance the opera from the audience's present. This distancing effect has led some musicologists to classify *Khovanshchina* as an epic.[45] But the "epic essence" of *Khovanshchina* is more far-reaching than most critics have suspected. I would like to offer here an alternative framework for reading the libretto, and therefore the dramatic intent, of the opera. This reading depends upon a fifth verisimilitude in addition to historical event, character, music, and language: fidelity to each character's inner vision of time.

V

Khovanshchina, I would suggest, is not merely distanced from its audience, as are all epics. In addition, each character is distanced from every other character within the opera. Each major role lives in its own time, and that time is valuable primarily for what is *past* about it. The *streltsy* mourn their lost autonomy; Marfa mourns her lost Andrei and the memory of their love; Emma mourns her exiled fiancé and Andrei—obsessively—his lost Emma; old Khovansky mourns his loss of rank vis-à-vis the upstart princes at Sophia's court; and the chief among those princes, Vasily Golitsyn, mourns the passing of his glory, both as Sophia's lover and as military commander. Nothing that is mourned in this opera ever returns, at least not on the plane of this world. For the characters within the opera, the future is as closed as epic plots generally are to later audiences. All true value remains in the past.

This might explain why Musorgsky routinely resisted Stasov's request to make the libretto more dramatic and give the characters more to do. Turn Marfa into Golitsyn's mistress, he recommended, put Marfa on trial for her illicit love, add the potential of passion to the characters' (and hence the audience's) *present*.[46] In the end, Marfa remains a vehicle of memory, and the other characters are astonishing in their unwillingness (or inability) to learn from events on stage.

The crucial emblem uniting all these isolated, bereaved fates is the Old Belief. It surely is no accident that the only loving, communicative exchanges in the opera occur between Marfa and Dosifei—because they

[45] See Frid (n. 17 above); also Shirinian, who prefers the category of "lyrical folk epic"—remarking on the unhurried pace of most scenes, the many digressions on Russia's fate, the solemn and predominantly trochaic meter of the text, and the lack of a sense of proportion among the opera's parts (166–87).

[46] See Stasov's letter to Musorgsky of 18 May 1876, in which he complains about the purposelessness of activity in the opera and the characters' strange, vacant interactions, the "jerkiness and external episodic quality of the whole" (*The Musorgsky Reader* [n. 11 above], 333–36).

have given up this world. For them, time has genuinely stopped. History is already over. The passing of time can only confirm what has already been decreed; it can introduce nothing new. As Dosifei gives us to understand at several points, the Old Believers are not *in* Russia, but have lost Russia and are seeking her. Holy Russia is in another time and space altogether, in a static future that will, in the act of martyrdom, fuse with a sacred past. Then perfect memory will triumph over change, that curse of the present.

The hypothesis that Musorgsky structured his entire opera around "Old Believer time" requires some expansion. The opera's plot is a single tissue of blind self-interest, lust, power-mongering, and murder. Only among the Old Believers does any genuine faith or love operate. Musorgsky copied into his *Khovanshchina* notebook more excerpts (fifteen) from the Archpriest Avvakum's autobiography than from any other single source, but none of these excerpts reflects the Archpriest's intolerant or aggressive side.[47] Baiting intolerance is not the province of the Old Belief in this opera. The Old Believers' function is to *stop time*. And here, it seems, is a productive way to understand Bakaeva's claim that in *Khovanshchina* Musorgsky rejects the "narrative principle." Old Believers appear whenever a debate, or self-doubt, or personal rivalry, begins—that is, whenever time threatens to change something, whenever drama invades the libretto.

Consider the general pattern of plot movement in the opera. At various points in Acts I, II, and III, the forces of Old Muscovy gather—and are deadlocked. Then Dosifei or Marfa comes onstage to disperse the tension, Marfa to save Emma from Andrei, Dosifei to save Emma from both Khovanskys; in the following scene, Dosifei arrives to separate Khovansky and Golitsyn and offer protection to Marfa. But the deadlocks are not

[47] Frid (see n. 17 above), 164–69; Bakaeva (see n. 17 above), 29–38 and 59–60. Bakaeva considers the lexical borrowings from Avvakum's autobiography so benevolent and so uncharacteristic of the historical Archpriest that she doubts that Avvakum should be considered a prototype for Dosifei. See also A. Andreev, "Zametki o soderzhanii 'Khovanshchiny' " [Comments on the Contents of *Khovanshchina*], *SM*, 1981 (3), 99, where a case is made for Dosifei's different temperament: his is one of renunciation, whereas Avvakum is decidedly free of that "consciousness of chosen martyrdom" that Dosifei assumes and that so isolates the Old Believers in the opera. Toward the same end, Musorgsky made changes in the blue-notebook libretto that lessen Marfa's dramatic and accusatory function. Omitted from Act I (Scene 1 in the libretto) is an exchange where Marfa accuses Andrei of being false to his Orthodox oath "not to fall under the charm of the Lutheran faith, a snare of the Antichrist" (Pekelis [n. 20 above], 149); likewise, the scene with Marfa, Susanna, and Dosifei is considerably shortened in the final libretto version. In an earlier variant (151) Marfa defends herself vociferously against possible condemnation by a court of her fellow schismatics; in the 1879 text, Marfa ignores Susanna's ravings about court proceedings and concentrates on saving Susanna's soul—i.e. driving devils out of it (138–40).

resolved, they are simply dissolved. Dosifei enters a scene and silences both sides. No one resists him, but no one is changed by him. The Old Believer element thus presents that odd spectacle of authority that is unquestioned but somehow is impotent to move action ahead in this world.

In the blue-notebook libretto, Dosifei appears in five of the six scenes, and his presence is much more prominent and paradoxical than in the versions of the opera familiar to us. In every appearance, Dosifei maximizes his authority with his immediate audience by sensing the tone that makes his presence most authoritative *for them*. With Marfa he is a loving father; with Susanna he drives out devils; with Golitsyn and Khovansky in Act II—a conversation severely cut and simplified by Rimsky—he teases the two men with his possible past identity as Prince Myshetsky.[48] All the squabbling factions are continually put to shame by the sophistication and dignity of Dosifei, but ultimately he owes his own moral stability to an abandonment of the social reality in which all the others live.[49]

Marfa and Dosifei, the only morally uncontaminated persons among the major heroes of *Khovanshchina*, live in "Old Believer time and space." As a genuinely apocalyptic structure, it cannot co-exist; given any credence at all in a work, it must dominate. The bleak strength of the Old

---

[48] Dosifei seeds and then confirms rumors of his princely lineage as soon as his secular counterparts place any constraint on his authority. See the lengthy passage from the 1879 libretto, omitted by Rimsky, which reads in part:

DOSIFEI: Princes! Calm your rage . . .

GOLITSYN: Dosifei! I beg you to keep within your proper limits. You have forgotten that princes have their own way of doing things, it's not your way, my good man.

DOSIFEI: I've not forgotten, I have only to remember my own past. [. . .] a forgotten past, forever buried [. . .] My princely rights, which I myself cast aside [. . .] [The princes debate the rumor, and Khovansky then chides Dosifei for disavowing his rank.]

DOSIFEI: But let's drop this empty chatter, princes. We've gathered here to advise one another: let's begin, time will not wait. (Pekelis [n. 20 above], 136)

[49] One recent Soviet commentator on Musorgsky has confronted this issue squarely. "Dramatic development in *Khovanshchina* is unusual in the extreme," she writes. "In the final analysis, the conflict between the departing 'old' and the arriving 'new' is resolved by Musorgsky in accordance with historical truth. The old order perishes in the face of the new. But at the same time all the major heroes of the opera perish" (Elena Abyzova, *Modest Petrovich Musorgskii* [Moscow, 1985], 122–23). This understates the case. In a letter to Stasov in August 1873, Musorgsky describes the confrontation of the princes in Act II: his intent was to "expose this vile conference at Golitsyn's in its true light, where they're all grabbing at the throne and scepter, and probably Dosifei is the only one with a firmly fixed conviction" (*The Musorgsky Reader* [n. 11 above], 240). True enough, and the conviction firmly fixed in Dosifei is that the new order perishes in the face of the old—and the old will be forever.

Belief is especially compelling in the blue-notebook libretto, where the (admittedly incomplete) final immolation scene contains no Marfa and no Andrei. The only surviving hero is Dosifei, exhorting the true believers to sacrifice, as the shrouded chorus responds: "We have no fear, father, our promise before God is sacred and unalterable. [. . .] The enemy of man, the prince of this world has come! Terrible are the fetters of the Antichrist!"[50]

The centrality of Old Believers to the sense of history in *Khovanshchina* is a vexed issue. In Soviet scholarship, the preferred image of Musorgsky as populist and progressive has tended to narrow the role that Old Belief plays. The schismatics are either cast as exotic and ornamental or—in an alternative move—presented as proto-revolutionaries, constrained by their religious prejudices to play a reactionary political role but nevertheless a genuine anti-government force. The centerpiece for the latter argument is always the crucial line sung by Dosifei at the beginning of Act V: "We shall burn, but we shall not surrender" (sgorim, a ne dadimsia!)—a line which, in any case, is not in any of Musorgsky's manuscripts and which Rimsky-Korsakov apparently invented.[51] The effect of both "exotic" and "revolutionary" approaches to the Old Belief has been, in my view, to domesticate the radical, and radically disturbing, historical framework that Musorgsky offers in this opera. Its events cannot be incorporated into a comfortable historical continuum of future revolutions, or even of failed attempts at revolution. The representation of "apocalyptic time and space" has more unsettling implications for historical opera grounded in real events. Musorgsky tells the story from a point of view sympathetic to the one group that did not believe in a future. This permits him to be both realistic and otherworldly at once, and true to his desire to reflect the spirit of an age. That age presents no easy transition to *our* present.

One important index of meaning in any apocalyptic structure would be its frame, its sense of the beginning and the end. *Khovanshchina* begins

---

[50] See Pekelis (n. 20 above), 147–48. At the end of this brief scene, Pekelis adds: "A dialogue between Marfa and Andrei Khovansky was projected, as well as a scene with Dosifei and the schismatics." See also n. 26 above.

[51] The line occurs in the 1883 Bessel (Rimsky) first edition, at the end of thirty measures of text and music wholly by Rimsky: "Brothers! Our cause is lost! Throughout Russia we are persecuted. Old man Khovansky is dead, Golitsyn is in exile, our hope Prince Andrei is hiding with us in the hermitage. And whose fault is it? The quarreling of the princes themselves. [. . .] The time has come to suffer for the Orthodox faith. [. . .] We shall burn, but we shall not surrender!" (Act V, scene 2, 189–90). Rimsky's text returns Dosifei vigorously to the political arena—in contrast to Musorgsky's versions, where Dosifei's final words are already abstract and liturgical, no longer of this world.

with the beautiful, but ideologically ambiguous, prologue, "Dawn over Moscow River." As luck would have it, Musorgsky left the end of Act II,[52] and also the end of the opera, unfinished—leaving to later editors and arrangers the necessity of tying up the whole. This is a delicate task, for whatever is done to the final scene of an historical opera will generate a philosophy of history retroactively applicable to the rest of the work. Unfortunately, Musorgsky himself is an uncertain ally in this project, for he expressed his views on Russian history (and on the role of the schism within it) with characteristic eccentricity. His personal ideology has been intensely, and inconclusively, debated.[53]

Among those obliged to create endings for Musorgsky, Rimsky-Korsakov has been the most influential—and he chose a progressive statist solution. He completed Act II with a recapitulation of the "Dawn" theme, thus linking Peter's final edict to "arrest the Khovanskys" with this inspiring theme of a new dawn for Russia. Rimsky then further advanced Peter's cause by adding his own aggressive finale to the closing scene: as the hermitage burns, a trumpet fanfare by Peter's troops obliterates the

[52] Apparently Musorgsky was experimenting with new ways to end his scenes, and had projected a vocal quintet to end Act II. An ensemble piece to climax the second act of an opera was "new," of course, only in the context of Musorgsky's evolution; it is a conventional ending structure, and quite in keeping with the Romantic, lyric emphasis in *Khovanshchina*. Musorgsky's failure to compose the finale was probably due to the challenge of composing a grand quintet for the unusual combination of three basses, one tenor, and one mezzo.

[53] In the 1930s, as we have seen, Asafiev popularized the idea of the people as carrier of the statist principle. Scholarship in the 1940s advanced the thesis that the "Dawn" theme opening the opera (and recurring at various points in Rimsky's redaction) was intended to refer positively to the Petrine reforms and a new day for Russia (Asafiev, "Russkii narod, russkie liudi" [n. 27 above]). In the post-Stalinist period a cautious rethinking began. M. Sokolsky suggested that the "Dawn" theme was not necessarily so optimistic; the true theme of *Khovanshchina* was not the people, but the *deception* of the people, who are forever misguided, caught off guard, and unable to rally in time ("Narod v 'Khovanshchine'" Musorgskogo" [The Folk in Musorgsky's *Khovenshchina*], *SM*, 1954 [12], 61–72). Recently A. Andreev has updated this idea, turning deception into parody: Musorgsky is giving us a parodied "Dawn" scene, he suggests, the ironic evocation of a fairy-tale to open an opera that then unfolds as one hideous disintegration after another. (See "Zametki o soderzhanii 'Khovanshchiny,' " [cf. note 47 above], 95–99). In the 1970s, the Musorgsky specialist Shlifshtein decisively separated himself from the Asafiev thesis: the Petrine reforms were *not* progressive for the people, and Musorgsky was careful to idealize no special social class— preferring to be, as Pushkin had been before him, "as dispassionate as fate" ("Otkuda zhe rassvet" [see n. 29 above], 106–17). Frid (see n. 17 above) argues an ideologically neutral position: Musorgsky was sympathetic to social movements and ideas, she writes, but "he did not have a clear-cut *system* of opinions on social matters" (72). Less persuasive is M. Rakhmanova's attempt to link Musorgsky with the *pochvenniki* of the 1860s and their "progressive" understanding of the Schism: see her "Musorgskii i ego vremia," *SM*, 1980 (9), 95–110, and 10 (1980), 109–15.

Old Believers' fragile hymn. This vigorous pro-Petrine stance fits in well with Rimsky's own statist views on Russian history as reflected, say, in his *Pskovitianka* of the same period.[54] But other reconstructions are certainly possible. For his 1958 reorchestration of the opera Shostakovich rethought the unfinished portions, ended *his* version of Act II with a martial fanfare instead of the "Dawn" (more appropriate, perhaps, but equally liable to a pro-Peter reading), and provided two alternative endings for the final scene. Between these two famous versions, Igor Stravinsky reconstructed an ending chorus from Musorgsky's manuscripts for the 1913 Diaghilev production that culminated with neither fanfare nor "Dawn" theme but simply with the hymn itself, which fades eerily offstage.[55] Stravinsky's solution would seem to be the one most honest to Musorgsky's intent. For *Khovanshchina* moves forward neither through the acts of individual heroes, nor through the massed crowds on stage, but through the otherworldly workings of fate.

Fate-based operas are common enough, of course, especially with libretti drawn from fairy-tale or myth. But what is peculiar in *Khovanshchina* is the implacability of fate combined with a concreteness of historical event. Even more startling is the absence of any genuine, sustained dramatic resistance—of the sort we get in *Boris*—to what fate has decreed. Characters do not confront their destiny so much as fuse with it. The crucial concepts in the libretto are those favorite words of Marfa and Dosifei: *sud'ba* and *nevolia*, fate and unfreedom (or "non-will"). "In God's will lies our non-will," Dosifei consoles Marfa, and all the characters still alive by the end of the opera come around to this truth. The passage of time neither adds nor removes. In an astonishing piece of advice Dosifei says to Marfa: Do not resist your sinful love, do not censure yourself. "Endure, my dear child, love as you have always loved, and all your sufferings will pass." Even the foolish Andrei Khovansky finally ceases asking for Emma and instead sings that moving melody at the foot of the funeral pyre, "Gdye moia voliushka" (where has my dear freedom gone?).

We sense here Musorgsky's own passion and terror for human history as a powerful but blind force. In the fall of 1872, just as *Khovanshchina* was first being sketched out, Musorgsky wrote Vladimir Stasov that he was reading Darwin and was in bliss: "While instructing man as to his

---

[54] See Richard Taruskin, " 'The Present in the Past': Russian Opera and Russian Historiography, ca. 1870," *Russian and Soviet Music: Essays for Boris Schwarz*, ed. Malcolm Hamrick Brown (Ann Arbor, Mich., 1984), 77–146, esp. 90ff.

[55] Stravinsky's chorus has not been recorded. See the Bessel vocal score, "Zakliuchitel'nyi khor dlia 'Khovanshchiny' " [The Concluding Chorus for *Khovanshchina*], by Igor Stravinsky (St. Petersburg and Moscow, 1913).

origin, Darwin knows exactly the kind of animal he has to deal with . . .
Without man being aware of it, he is *gripped in a vise.*"[56]
A central message in *Khovanshchina* is man's unfreedom in history.
This theme resonates variously in Musorgsky's two surviving versions of
the ending scene: the uncompleted communal farewell between Dosifei
and the Old Believers in the 1879 libretto, and similar choral passages,
enriched with dialogue between Marfa and Andrei, in the manuscript
score. In both settings lust, hate, and activity are countered by profoundly
passive sorrow and love. The reality of this world drops away before the
eternal glory of the next. Musorgsky's inability over eight years to complete the opera perhaps attests to the difficulty of transmitting this idea of
unfreedom in a format that is both dramatic and realistic. The Old Believers are the key, for they were a real historical force with an integral
world-view, and yet they expected nothing from the temporal processes
of this world but evil.

Such an apocalyptic, fate-based opera must of necessity transpose all
positive historical reality to some other realm. The features that Emilia
Frid and Galina Bakaeva note in their analyses are present in this reading
too, but with a different aesthetic rationale. Action in *Khovanshchina* is
indeed decentered and events "pass through one another," because man's
power to control the result of his activity is profoundly restricted. If the
narrative principle gives way to static lyrical digression, it is because all
important personal stories have already happened and Old Believers are
forever on guard to stop time. Emilia Frid links the "general idea" of
these lyrical digressions vaguely with Russian patriotism, for their content is universal rather than personal. But another aspect of the lyrical
interludes seems at least as significant: they are neither from nor to individuals, and they do not engender or expect any response. When the conservative music critic Hermann Laroche reviewed a performance of
Khovanshchina in 1893, he faulted Musorgsky for an inability to write
recitative. It was a complaint, Laroche admitted, that made him seem
"more of a royalist than the king."[57]
Khovanshchina thus marks a somber stage in Musorgsky's own crea-

[56] Musorgsky to Vladimir Stasov, 18 October 1872 (in *The Musorgsky Reader* [n. 11
above], 198). See also the review of the Metropolitan Opera production by Evan Eisenberg
in *The Nation* (8 February 1986), 154–56. Eisenberg locates the central force of the opera
in the hopelessness of human striving. The plot is confusing, he writes, "[b]ut one relation
is clear: the female principle that is Marfa overpowers all the men and binds them to their
fate. She is the earth they walk on, the earth that gave them birth and will take them back"
(156).

[57] H. Laroche, "Musorgskii i ego 'Khovanshchina,' " *Teatral'naia gazeta* 23 (1893); cited
in Rakhmanova, "100-letiiu" (see n. 1 above), 95.

tive evolution. The libretto represents a falling-away of dialogue—not necessarily because Musorgsky's skills had deteriorated or his tastes had changed, but because the historical material provoked a cast of characters who *no longer listen*. If one trait links all the secular heroes in this opera (collective as well as solo), it is their tendency to be caught unawares, to wake up too late.[58] Emblematic here are the opening lines of Shaklovity's aria in Act III, sung to the *streltsy* who are dead to the world at noon: "The lair of the *streltsy* sleeps. Sleep on, Russian people, the enemy is not slumbering!" The Old Believers, to be sure, are eternally alert, but they can hear or desire nothing new. The opera is thus caught in this odd unfree time where those who do not oversleep merely wait until the preordained comes to pass.

There is something of the same sense of personal helplessness and acquiescence to fate in Pushkin's *Boris Godunov*. And it is here that we must seek the essential poetics of Musorgsky's sense of history. The composer embraced that poetics most fully in his second historical opera, not his first. In the earlier work (significantly labeled an opera, not a "people's musical drama") the title role takes on all the melodramatic guilt and self-hatred that Pushkin had deliberately laid aside in his play. All sin is concentrated in Boris's personal past, in the murder of Dmitri at Uglich. Boris attempts to atone for that sin with his death—for in the opera, fate is linked with personal action and responsibility. The individual personality remains central to the resolution of the plot. And thus both versions of the opera, while drawing on historical events and featuring historical figures, remain personal dramas *in* history, not dramas about history.

Khovanshchina is structured differently.[59] Here, much as in Pushkin's *Boris Godunov*, fate is linked with personal renunciation and impotence. Nothing anyone can do will alter events, and no single character is empowered to resolve the plot. Each player merely acts his own appetite out to the end. All sin—and the opera is full of it—is in the present; the past is sacred, and the future (if we keep Peter's trumpets offstage) does not exist. The real ideology of the opera is stasis.

This reading suggests another level of meaning to Musorgsky's well-known comment on Russian history, written to Stasov at the beginning of the *Khovanshchina* period:

---

[58] See Sokolsky (n. 53 above), 64–66.

[59] The title itself shifts us away from the Khovanskys and into the realm of societal disorder; the suffix -*shchina* in Russian denotes troubled times associated with the excesses of the proper noun. But the action of the opera makes it quite clear that what Peter calls "Khovanshchina" or the "Khovansky mess" is not attributable to that family alone. Tsar Peter, too, is a historical figure looking for someone to blame.

The power of the black earth will make itself manifest, when you plow to the very bottom. It is possible to plow the black earth with tools wrought of alien materials. And at the end of the 17th century they did plow Mother Russia with such tools . . . "Where are you pushing me?" [Russia asked]. The ignorant and the confused were put to death. "We've gone ahead," you lie. "We're still here!" Paper, books, they've gone ahead—but we're still here. . . Public benefactors are inclined to glorify themselves and to fix their glory in documents, but the people groan, and drink to stifle their groans, and groan all the louder: still here![60]

The letter was written two weeks into the bicentennial celebrations marking Peter the Great's birth, launched in Petersburg at the end of May 1872.[61] The Petrine Jubilee was a confirmation of progress and historical optimism. And as if in response to this affirming chorus, Musorgsky projected *Khovanshchina* as a document to which no "public benefactor" could affix his glory.

VI

During that brief period in Soviet musicology when tsarist glorification of Peter the Great had receded and Soviet glorification of the revolutionary Russian folk had not yet become mandatory, Boris Asafiev wrote: "There is a groan that goes forth from all Musorgsky's music, and that groan stretches from the cradle to the grave."[62] But the nature of that suffering is encoded differently in *Khovanshchina* than in the other finished works of the 1870s. In both versions of *Boris*, and even more markedly in the vocal cycles *Sunless* and *Songs and Dances of Death*, private histories predominate. The dramas that unfold onstage illustrate personal loss, and terror before individual death. With those works in mind, Asafiev is probably right to call Musorgsky more of a pessimistic Romantic than a realist or a populist. For the composer of those works, death "is neither a conciliatory principle nor a natural point of finalization—it is simply a senseless, unenlightened dead end."[63]

---

[60] Musorgsky to Vladimir Stasov, 16 and 22 June 1872 (*The Musorgsky Reader*, 185–86).

[61] For a discussion of the possible dialogue between *Khovanshchina* and this Petrine Jubilee, see Sokolsky (n. 53 above), 61–62. Sergei Soloviev's public lectures on Peter the Great, delivered at Moscow University in the spring of 1872 and widely publicized, were surely known to Musorgsky and possibly supply another subtext. See S. M. Soloviev, *Publichnye chteniia o Petre Velikom* (Moscow, 1984), and esp. the interpretive afterword by L. N. Pushkarev (178–204).

[62] B. Asafiev, *Simfonicheskie etiudy* (1922; rpt. Leningrad, 1970), 212.

[63] Asafiev, 213.

Khovanshchina, however, does not indulge the anguish of personal loss. The characters of this world—the *streltsy*, the Khovanskys, Golitsyn—do not engage our sympathies sufficiently for us to mourn their fall. The only sorrow we care about belongs to Marfa, and she can nevertheless end the opera on intonations of faith and ecstasy because death is for her a reunion; she has given up on earthly history altogether. Personal death is not a senseless dead end; history is. Tragedy shifts from the individual plane to the universal, where its personal tones are muted and made less accessible.

With this move, Musorgsky emerges as a new sort of realist. He does not have the interests of the people in mind, but merely their experience. History books have gone ahead, as Musorgsky wrote Stasov; these are the books upon which historical drama must draw, but the people are *still there*. They owe the future nothing and expect nothing in return.

Musorgsky's historical stance gains special poignancy when measured against the various potential "audiences" of his opera. For educated Russians—those, that is, who wrote and read history books and believed in historical continuity—*Khovanshchina* was simply a historical opera on a period that had come to pass and that was now past. From an Old Believer point of view, however, such continuity is denied; the opera is set in time that has stopped. But this is time that nevertheless guarantees salvation, a leap from the present to the Kingdom of God. Musorgsky's project, it seems, was to present an authentically apocalyptic sense of time (time before the end of time) to an audience that did not believe in it.[64] The appropriate response would indeed simulate being "gripped in a vise": everything is already over, but nothing will follow. History does not end with Divine Judgment or any other value-producing event; it simply shuts down.

We have here, on the historical plane, the same dead-endedness that can be sensed in Musorgsky's *Songs and Dances of Death*. In the first three songs of that cycle, the touch of Death always ends both the life of the singer *and* the song; there is no place for survivors or witnesses. In the final song, "The Field Marshal," Death promises her victims on the battlefield that she will dance her dance over their bones, tamping the earth down so thoroughly that—contrary to the expectations of the deceased—they will never rise from the dead. That precisely is the effect of Old Be-

[64] For a persuasive account of changing attitudes toward time during the *Khovanshchina* era, see A. M. Panchenko, "Istoriia i vechnost' v sisteme kul'turnykh tsennostei russkogo barokko," *Trudy otdela drevnei russkoi literatury*, 34 (1979), 197–98. Panchenko notes that the new historiography did not fear the Apocalypse; beginning in the seventeenth century the Final Judgment became a literary theme, an idea, and therefore distanced and allegorical. Here was Musorgsky's audience, and his challenge.

liever time seriously presented to a nineteenth-century audience. From what perspective, indeed, can one tell the story of the end of time? To choose the Old Believer movement as vehicle for this bleak view of historical process was indeed a masterstroke, for the Old Belief was both in history and (from its own point of view) at the end of it.

THE privileged position granted in this opera to non-communication, to stasis, perhaps even to the Apocalypse itself has intriguing implications for a poetics of opera.[65] Contrary to the spirit of Wagner—and, much later, perhaps to the spirit of Joseph Kerman as well—we seem to have in *Khovanshchina* an opera that succeeds because it is *not* drama. Individuals and events respond less to one another than to some higher type of time that renders them all powerless. And yet this operatic time and space is not mythic. The "collapse into historicity" that Wagner so lamented in German drama is thoroughly in force in Musorgsky's music-drama, which scrupulously recalls (and often reproduces) the documented historical event. This historical vision is sheathed in musical themes that recur with an almost obsessive regularity—suggesting, perhaps, that Musorgsky sought within the supremely temporal art of music some form to confirm the schismatics' faith that the passage of time no longer mattered. If his earlier operas explore the possibilities of interaction and dialogue, then *Khovanshchina*, it seems, explores the ways in which music can keep people apart. In the extremity of its final scene, it suggests how historical opera can stop history altogether.

[65] These final speculations owe much to David Geppert and Gary Saul Morson. Robert William Oldani and Richard Taruskin were kind enough to scrutinize the essay and make numerous suggestions and inquiries that greatly contributed to the final shape of the text.

Khovanshchina: Sequence of Episodes

MUSORGSKY'S OWN MANUSCRIPTS (piano-vocal 1872–80; Lamm reconstruction)	"BLUE NOTEBOOK" LIBRETTO (in Musorgsky's hand, 1879–80?)	RIMSKY-KORSAKOV VERSION (Bessell, 1883)
Act I	[1] [in six *kartiny*/scenes; no Acts]	*Act I*
1. Streltsy watch at dawn; Kuzka awakes	1. Streltsy watch; Kuzka	1. Streltsy watch; Kuzka
2. Clerk arrives; Shaklovity's denunciation	2. Clerk, Shaklovity [two sentences of dictation and one exchange omitted]	2. Clerk, Shaklovity [identical omissions of text (at Lamm 35, 49) as in libretto]
3. Clerk & Moscow folk. Clerk forced to read posted list of boyars condemned by streltsy; Clerk's booth smashed; Clerk's lament	3. Clerk & Moscow folk [complete]	3. ———
4. Ivan Khovansky enters; address to streltsy	4. Khovansky entry & address	4. Khovansky entry & address
5. Emma, Andrei & Marfa love/hate triangle	5. Emma/Andrei/Marfa [shortened]	5. Emma/Andrei/Marfa [shortened, but *not* as per libretto]
6. Ivan Khovansky appears, demands Emma; father-son quarrel dissolved by Dosifei	6. Khovansky father-son quarrel; Dosifei	6. Khovansky father-son quarrel; Dosifei
7. Dosifei's Lament over Russia	7. Dosifei's Lament	7. Dosifei's Lament
Act II [left incomplete]	[2]	*Act II*
1. Golitsyn reads letter from Tsarevna Sophia	1. Golitsyn reads letter from Sophia	1. Golitsyn reads letter from Sophia
2. Golitsyn reads letter from his mother	2. Golitsyn reads letter from his mother	2. ———
3. Lutheran Pastor arrives; pleads on behalf of Emma and for a Lutheran Church in Moscow	3. ———	3. ———
4. Marfa's fortune-telling	4. Marfa's fortune-telling	4. Marfa's fortune-telling
5. Ivan Khovansky arrives; quarrel with Golitsyn over abolition of princely rights	5. Khovansky arrives; quarrel	5. Khovansky arrives; quarrel [shortened with some paraphrase of text]
6. Dosifei arrives; teases about past identity	6. Dosifei arrives [teasing shortened]	6. Dosifei arrives [teasing *omitted*]
7. Marfa returns; Shaklovity announces arrest of Khovanskys	7. Marfa returns; Shaklovity	7. Marfa returns; Shaklovity [R-K ends with "Dawn" theme, Shostakovich with trumpets]
Act III	[3]	*Act III*
1. Old Believers' Chorus and Marfa's Song	1. Old Believers' Chorus, Marfa's Song	1. Old Believers' Chorus, Marfa's Song
2. Confrontation between Marfa & Susanna	2. Marfa/Susanna [shortened]	2. Marfa/Susanna [shortened as per libretto]
3. Dosifei drives Susanna away; Marfa's confession	3. Dosifei/Susanna/Dosifei [shortened]	3. Dosifei/Susanna/Dosifei [shortened as per libretto (12 bars at Lamm 30–31, 1 at 39)]

4. Shaklovity's Aria/lament
5. Streltsy drunken waking-up song
6. Streltsy wives: nagging countersong against drink
7. Kuzka's "Rumor Song" + chorus
8. Clerk arrives and tells of mercenaries moving against the streltsy camp
9. Appeal to Khovansky, who declines to lead streltsy into battle against Peter

Act IV

1. Khovansky and his serfgirl chorus
2. Dance of the Persian Slave Girls
3. Shaklovity's arrival and murder of Khovansky

4. Golitsyn sent into exile, mourned by Moscow folk
5. Dosifei's Aria; decision with Marfa to burn
6. Andrei confronts Marfa again over Emma
7. Andrei calls streltsy; they enter with gallows
8. Streltsy wives plead *not* to pardon drunken husbands
9. Streshnev delivers pardon from Tsar Peter

Act V [sketched; left incomplete]

1. Dosifei's Lament in pine forest near hermitage (generalized sacrificial language)

2. Dosifei appeals to faithful: burn for salvation
3. Marfa lovingly leads Andrei into fire

4. Dosifei leads faithful into hermitage

---

4. Shaklovity's Aria
5. Streltsy song
6. Streltsy wives' song
7. Kuzka's "Rumor Song" + chorus
8. Clerk arrives
9. Appeal to Khovansky

[4]

1. Khovansky and serfgirls
2. Dance of Persian Slaves
3. Shaklovity's arrival and murder of Khovansky

[5]

4. Golitsyn into exile
5. Dosifei's Aria, Marfa
6. Andrei/Marfa
7. Andrei with streltsy
8. Streltsy wives
9. Pardon of streltsy

[6]

1. Dosifei's lament

2. Dosifei appeals to faithful
——
——

---

4. Shaklovity's Aria
5. Streltsy song
6. Streltsy wives' song [cut by ¼]
7. ——
8. Clerk arrives
9. Appeal to Khovansky

Act IV

1. Khovansky and serfgirls
2. Dance of Persian Slaves
3. Shaklovity's arrival and murder of Khovansky

4. Golitsyn into exile
5. Dosifei's Aria, Marfa
6. Andrei/Marfa
7. Andrei with streltsy
8. Streltsy wives
9. Pardon of streltsy

Act V

1. Dosifei's lament [R-K *adds* 30 measures of his own text (political summary + lines "We shall burn, but we shall not surrender")]
2. Dosifei appeals to faithful
3. Marfa/Andrei [R-K *adds* 33 bars of dialogue]
4. [R-K *adds* final chorus: Marfa/Andrei farewell duet and Peter's trumpets on stage]

Boito and the 1868 *Mefistofele* Libretto as a Reform Text

Even with the hindsight of 120 years, it is difficult to conceive that the publication and circulation of an opera libretto could be the focus of a notable controversy that would have a whole city talking and taking sides. To understand the impact of Boito's original libretto for *Mefistofele*, with all its implications for reform, we need to have some picture of the circumstances that halted its composition for five years, to see how Boito's position as a critic indicated his innovative intentions while antagonizing part of his public, and to have some idea of the unusual circumstances that saw the libretto appear a full five weeks before the *prima* of the opera.

To begin with, reform was very apparent in the Milan of the 1860s. The Kingdom of Italy had come into being with the proclamation of 17 March 1861, and with it, at least to those parts of the peninsula included within its boundaries, came a marked easing of censorship. The proliferation of new journalistic projects in that decade is a clear consequence of this easing. Urban reform in Milan caused the demolition of a whole quarter of decaying tenements to make way for the Piazza del Duomo. The Duomo itself, after some centuries of neglect, was a-building once more and would achieve a Manzonian apotheosis as a shrine to contain the tomb of San Carlo Borromeo, a central figure in *I promessi sposi*. In mid-September 1867, just at the time Boito was working feverishly to complete *Mefistofele*, the Milanese Galleria was inaugurated: it made a fitting symbol, with its base at the Duomo, its right arm stretching toward Casa Ricordi in the via Berchet, the top giving on to the square in front of La Scala, and its left arm pointing northeast toward the fashionable quarter where dwelt influential segments of that theater's audience.

If reform was in the air, it had to compete, nonetheless, with a scarcely concealed sense of disillusion. The fervent afflatus aroused by the *Risorgimento* had been dispersed by factionalism, by the conflict of political and religious issues, by the inconclusiveness of the campaigns of 1859 and 1866, and by the consequence that unification still seemed a frustratingly elusive goal. Much of the disillusion stemmed from the sense of disparity between the two Italys, north and south, the former already participating in the nineteenth century, the latter seemingly immured in medieval immobility. Economically, the new country was in parlous condition, beset by financial problems that eluded solution, problems heightened by increasing migration from farm to city and by the pangs of incipient industrialization.

PERHAPS the earliest surviving reference to what was to become *Mefistofele* appears in a letter that Boito's brother Camillo addressed to him in February 1862, the month of Arrigo's twentieth birthday. Writing to Paris, where Boito and Franco Faccio had gone the previous November with prize money awarded them upon their graduation from the Conservatorio di Milano, Camillo inquires: "Have you made any further progress with the scoring of *Faust?*"[1] From this we can see that Boito had composed at least some parts of an opera that he was then calling *Faust* and had made some progress in orchestrating it. The following month Camillo addresses him again about the opera:

> If your *Faust* were complete and if Mazzucato should support you actively, Mefistofele would be able to shatter the globe on the stage of La Scala.[2]

Camillo refers to that moment in the Witches' Sabbath (Act II, scene 2) where, at the conclusion of his aria "Ecco il mondo," Mefistofele "forcibly hurls the globe of glass so that it shatters."[3] Alberto Mazzucato (1813–77), whose active support Camillo was hoping for, was then chief conductor at La Scala, a post he had held since 1859; and he had also been Arrigo's professor of composition at the Milan Conservatory. According to Alberto's son, Gianandrea Mazzucato, who contributed the article on Arrigo Boito to the 1904 edition of *Grove*, by the time Boito left the conservatory in 1861 he "had already written and composed several numbers of his *Faust*—the garden scene, just as it now stands in *Mefistofele.*"[4] Among the "several numbers" Boito is supposed to have composed as a student it seems plausible that one was the opening choral section of the Prologue in Heaven. This passage (with its striking enharmonic modulations and postponed resolutions, unusual practices in Italian music of the 1860s), played by Boito in various Milanese salons he

---

[1] Piero Nardi, *Vita di Arrigo Boito* (Milano, 1944), 92 (henceforth cited as *VAB*).

[2] *VAB*, 94.

[3] Arrigo Boito, *Tutti gli scritti*, ed. Piero Nardi (Milan, 1942), 142 (henceforth cited as *TGS*): "Getta con impeto il globo di vetro che si frange." Nardi reprints the original 1868 text of *Mefistofele* on 95–179.

[4] *Grove's Dictionary of Music and Musicians*, 2nd ed. (1900), I, 354. The younger Mazzucato exaggerates a little when he says Boito's Garden Scene remained unchanged from his student days; in 1875 he altered the title role from baritone to tenor range and revised the concluding quartet.

frequented, could well account for his being taken seriously by the more progressive faction of the public while he was still a relatively untried composer.[5]

That Boito in February 1862 was at work in Paris on an operatic *Faust* naturally raises the question of its relationship to Gounod's opera of that name. By 1862 Boito had probably not heard Gounod's *Faust* in the theater, although he could scarcely have been unaware of its existence. Gounod's score, in its original *opéra-comique* form with spoken dialogue, had received its premiere on 19 March 1859 at the Théâtre Lyrique, where it achieved a total of fifty-seven performances before the year was out; it was then dropped from the repertory and did not return to the Parisian stage until 18 December 1862, when it was revived by Carvalho's company, now in its new quarters at the Châtelet. Although the score had been fitted out with musical passages to replace the earlier spoken ones, these were not sung in Paris until September 1866. The first performance of Gounod's score with these replacements had taken place, apparently, at Bordeaux on 2 April 1860. I know of no evidence that Boito traveled to the provinces in 1862 to see Gounod's opera.

Certainly Boito must have been aware of a notice that appeared in *Le Ménestrel* (23 February 1862) that Marie-Caroline Miolan-Carvalho, the original Marguerite and the wife of the director of the Lyrique, was scheduled to appear in a benefit concert later that month and that her program would include the Garden Scene from Gounod's *Faust*.[6] It is highly likely that he had provided himself with copies of Barbier and Carré's libretto and either the first or second edition of the score published by Choudens. (The second edition contained the music substituted for the spoken dialogue.)

As it took shape through 1867, Boito's libretto would roughly parallel five episodes used by Gounod: Faust's study, the Kermesse, the Garden Scene, the Witches' Sabbath, and the Prison. Boito, however, presents his version of the Kermesse as the opening scene of Act I, following the Prologue in Heaven, causing it to precede the episode "Il patto" (The Contract) in the laboratory. In Boito's version, Margherita is not accosted by Faust in the scene at the fair, nor is she evoked by Mephisto as an inducement for Faust to sign away his soul (as she is in the Barbier-Carré *livret*); she does not enter the action until the scene in the garden. Boito elimi-

---

[5] Two of Boito's compositions, the cantatas *Il quattro giugno* and *Le sorelle d'Italia*, for which he supplied the text and part of the music (the rest being by Faccio), had been performed at the Milan Conservatory in 1860 and 1861 respectively.

[6] T. J. Walsh, *Second Empire Opera: The Théâtre Lyrique Paris: 1851–1870* (London and New York, 1981), 143, mentions this notice but adds: "It is not certain that it ever took place."

nated Gretchen's brother Valentine (who is given some prominence by Barbier and Carré), as he did the Church scene. Since Gounod's setting was restricted to Goethe's Part I, his work contains no equivalent to Boito's Acts IV and V and Epilogue, which derive from Part II.

At some point in the spring of 1862, Boito put his uncompleted *Faust* to one side. The most probable reason was his awareness of the first stages of the great vogue for Gounod's opera, whose tone Boito would later describe as "blandly voluptuous."[7] *Faust* was introduced to Italy at La Scala on 11 November 1862 in an Italian translation by Achille de Lauzières, with such success that it was revived in March 1863 and again in January 1865; it must have seemed to Boito an unpropitious moment for finishing and producing his own treatment of the subject. That he had hopes for the future is shown by a letter dated 19 March 1863, just ten days after the first revival of Gounod's *Faust* at La Scala. The letter is written on the letterhead of the Prefettura of Milan and addressed to the Directorship of the Royal Theaters in Milan:

> Messrs. Arrigo Boito and Francesco [*sic*] Faccio, graduates of the Royal Conservatory of Music, to whom the Minister of Public Instruction granted the means to travel for a year in France and Germany for the purpose of advancing their musical studies, would now like to have presented in the Theater [La Scala] the operas that each has composed [. . .][8]

The secretary of the Directorship appended a brief undated note: "[This letter] retained as a memorandum in case an opportunity presents itself; approved."

The first results of that letter favored Faccio, whose *I profughi fiamminghi*, to a libretto by Emilio Praga (1839–75), one of the Milanese *Scapigliati* and a close friend of both Faccio and Boito, had its premiere at La Scala on 11 November 1863 and ran for five performances. Boito's turn would not come for another five years.[9] Instead, he entered on a career of intense literary and critical activity.

His earliest journalistic efforts were occasional letters on the Parisian scene, written during his first visit there in the spring of 1862 and published in *La Perseveranza*. The chief music critic of *La Perseveranza* was Filippo Filippi, an authoritative figure and enthusiastic supporter of Boito. Also from 1862 comes Boito's libretto of *Amleto*, destined for Fac-

---

[7] *TGS*, 1124.

[8] Museo Teatrale alla Scala: CA 755.

[9] Boito's first appearance on the *cartelloni* of La Scala, however, was in his capacity as the librettist of Verdi's *Inno delle nazioni*, which was performed in the theater by the students of the Milan Conservatory on 24 June 1864.

cio. This text he completed by 2 June 1862, dispatching it from Poland where he was visiting his mother's relatives. The libretto is significant not only because it is Boito's first adaptation of Shakespeare, but also because it was his earliest to confront the opera-going public with a "reform" text. The work had its premiere at Genoa's Carlo Felice on 30 May 1865. Boito's *Amleto* has been discussed as a "reform" text by Guido Salvetti, who points to such unfamiliar devices as the use of Dante's *terza rima* for the Ghost and the "abolition of closed musical forms." He sums it up in this way:

> The working relationship between Boito and Faccio seems, therefore, to be unusually complex: the literary audacity of the libretto appears to be undoubtedly propitious for a radical renewal of the musical language, for new perspectives of musical drama, free of the recurrence of traditional episodes [*situazioni "canoniche"*]. Yet Faccio's setting demonstrates the inherent limitations of [Boito's] new ideas when seen in operatic terms, with due account taken of the special requirements of stage production.[10]

Much of Boito's effort in these years centered on trying to reform the musical and cultural climate of his country, Milan in particular. Along with Mazzucato and the Ricordis he was a founder of the *Giornale della Società del Quartetto*, which appeared between July 1864 and November 1865. For Boito, however, the cultivation of German symphonic and chamber music—a repertory not exactly disregarded in the conservatories, but one studiously ignored by the vast majority of the general public in Italy[11]—turned out to be a means to an end. It was ultimately intended to enrich the musical and dramatic resources of opera, opera being the noblest Italian contribution to music. In the issue of 14 May 1865 Boito says explicitly: "Esercitiamoci alla Sinfonia ed al Quartetto per poter affrontare il Melodramma" (Let us train ourselves on the Symphony and the Quartet in order to confront the [challenge of] Opera.)[12]

The *Giornale della Società del Quartetto* was, of course, not the only participant in the ensuing controversy, but it provides a useful focus for examining one of the chief shibboleths: *sinfonismo*. Twenty years later, Verdi would still feel strongly enough about this issue to write to Count Opprandino Arrivabene, "L'opera è l'opera; la sinfonia è la sinfonia."[13]

---

[10] "La Scapigliatura milanese e il teatro d'opera," in *Il melodramma italiano dell'ottocento* (Turin, 1977), 567–604, here 595.

[11] A Società del Quartetto had been formed in Florence some two years before its Milanese counterpart was launched.

[12] *TGS*, 1177.

[13] Letter to Arrivabene, 10 June 1884, in *I copialettere di Giuseppe Verdi*, ed. G. Cesari and A. Luzio (Milan, 1913), 630.

And the issue is pertinent to the topic at hand, for Boito's 1868 version of *Mefistofele* contains an *Intermezzo sinfonico* ("La battaglia"), a protracted series of fanfares spiced from time to time by something described as "detonazioni," by occasional rallying cries, and finally by Mefistofele's cry "Viva la chiesa!"

Boito's stance as a reformer had been definitively assumed some months before in the pages of the Milanese *Figaro* when he reviewed Giuseppe Rota's *Ginevra di Scozia*,[14] an operatic subject that had been treated by Mayr in 1801 and that goes back past Handel's *Ariodante* to the middle of the seventeenth century, deriving from Ariosto's *Orlando Furioso*. The antiquarianism of the subject and the vacuity of Rota's score provided Boito with just the sort of occasion he most enjoyed. Placing "of the present" in quotation marks, both to twit Rota for his old-fashionedness and to remind his readers of that other shibboleth of the times, Wagner's "music of the future," he states:

> An opera "of the present," in order to have vitality and glory and in order to attain the high goals that set it apart, must in our opinion arrive at:
>
> I. The complete obliteration of *formula*.
> II. The creation of *form*.
> III. The realization of the most immense tonal and rhythmic development possible today.
> IV. The supreme incarnation of the drama.

Near the end of the review, he fits Rota into a scene which he claims is inspired by Rabelais's Pantagruel, but which is really a parody of *I promessi sposi*:

> At least if there had been something in Rota's music that, however ugly, had been individual; however deformed, had been new; however wearisome, had been bizarre. But no, he follows the litany of the deacons, subdeacons, clerics, sacristans who tag along behind the High Priest;[15] he follows the procession very slowly [*lemme, lemme*] with his candle in his hand and with his thurible swaying, saying "Amen" at every step and genuflecting at every altar, with the outward devotion of a friar, with the pusillanimous humility of a nun.[16]

[14] Rota's work was mounted at La Scala on 19 January 1864; it had received its first performance at the Regio of Parma, 22 January 1862.

[15] There are those who have suggested that by his mention of the "gran Prete" Boito intended an allusion to Verdi; but it seems more likely, considering the age of the *Ginevra* subject, that he meant Rossini. After all, Boito had called on Rossini in Paris two years earlier, and on that occasion Rossini had allegedly returned Boito's calling card to him, assuring him that it was still clean and could be used again.

[16] *TGS*, 1107–1108.

This quotation not only indicates Boito's attitude toward outmoded operas, but also serves as a sample of his personal *scapigliato* style: humorous, anticlerical, pointedly *anti-manzoniano*, absorbed with words for their own sake, and delighting in a stance of shocking the establishment. He was, after all, not quite twenty-two when he wrote this review.

Writing in *La Perseveranza* the previous year (13 September 1863), Boito identifies the problem of Antonio Cagnoni's opera *Il vecchio della montagna* (libretto by Francesco Guidi) as one that "begins as usual with the libretto." The trouble with these manufacturers (*facitori*) of libretti is that they do not understand their responsibility. They "do not think for one moment that music in chains waits for them to deliver the blow that will liberate it." They are "happy [. . .] with their easy métier [. . .] completely uncaring about art."

And then he goes on to explain his distinction between *form* and *formula*:

> The Romans [. . .] made the second of these words the diminutive of the first; but then the Romans also knew how to speak and how to think more clearly than we do. *Form*, the extrinsic manifestation, the beautiful raw material of art, has as much in common with *formula* as an Horatian ode has with a jingle by Ruscelli, as much as the rays of Moses have with asses' ears. And what needs to be said is that from the time *melodramma* existed in Italy until today, we have never had the true form of *melodramma*, but instead always the diminutive, the *formula*. Born with Monteverdi, the formula for *melodramma* passed to Peri, to Cesti, to Sacchini, to Paisiello, to Rossini, to Bellini, to Verdi, acquiring gradually as it was handed on (especially at the hands of these last great masters) power, development, variety, yet remaining always *formula*, as *formula* it had been born. The terms aria, rondò, cabaletta, stretta, ritornello, *pezzo concertato* are all there, drawn up in orderly array to affirm this statement. The hour of changing style should have dawned; the form largely achieved in the other arts should also develop in our area; its time of maturity should be fully present; let us forgo the pretext and put on the toga, let us change name and method, and instead of saying *libretto*, that little conventional word, let us say and write *tragedia*, as the Greeks were wont to do.[17]

The brash idealism of the young Boito is here writ large. It should be remembered, furthermore, that it was against pronunciamentos such as these that *Mefistofele* would be assessed.

[17] *TGS*, 1078–81.

In the middle of 1866, Boito served three months with the Italian army in the campaigns against the Austrians. He returned to Milan during August, and not long after this again took up *Faust*, soon to be retitled *Mefistofele*. Boito was still composing in the spring of 1867, when he was again visiting his Polish relatives at Mystki. In a letter from Camillo, undated but stemming from this time, we read:

> You have had an excellent idea: that of expanding the concept of your *Mefistofele*; now you have the means, the time, the ease to flesh it out well. I am tearing out of my old booklet of memorabilia the verses by Tommaseo that you asked me for.[18]

The verses of Tommaseo, a speech for Helen of Troy that Camillo obligingly scanned for his brother, were written in classic hexameters, exactly resembling those of the soliloquy of Elena in the Classical Sabbath of *Mefistofele* that begins, "Notte cupa, truce, senza fine funèbre." Camillo's reference to "expanding the concept of your *Mefistofele*" suggests that the idea of combining material from both parts of Goethe's *Faust* into a single stage work dates from early 1867, about a year before the work was first performed.

In another letter of that spring, dated 23 April 1867, Camillo informed Arrigo:

> If your score can be ready before Carnival, I do not doubt that you can get it staged at La Scala, all the more so since the management has left with its heels in the air. Mazzucato's influence will increase, I believe, and you would do well to write to him [. . .] Come back soon with your score.[19]

The pages of the Milanese weekly *La Fama*, then under the editorial supervision of Pietro Cominazzi, give some clue to the problems facing La Scala. The Carnival-Lenten season of 1866–67 had proved tempestuous: the public was disillusioned by politics and by the country's financial woes, and ill disposed because of the incompetence of the management, which announced productions and then postponed or abandoned them. The operas that were given were inadequately cast. The final performance of that season was greeted by cries of "Abbasso la Direzione! Abbasso la Direzione!" and it was observed that "within human memory such a night of disorder had never occurred at La Scala."[20]

In late June 1867 it was reported that on the 18th of that month Parliament had voted to suspend its subsidies to the royal theaters; one orator

18 *VAB*, 236.
19 *VAB*, 237.
20 *La Fama*, XXV, no. 16 (16 April 1867), 64.

proclaimed that "Art had been cast in the mud!"[21] Shortly afterwards, a commission was appointed in Milan to solicit a public subscription to help keep the theaters open; by August it had managed to raise 54,000 lire. In its issue of 3 September 1867, La Fama[22] announced that a well-known theatrical agent named Giuseppe Bonola would become impresario of La Scala and would assume the obligation "to have performed an opera new to Milan by a composer of established reputation, as well as a completely new opera written by an Italian composer."[23]

The singers and repertory for the new season were announced in early October 1867. La Fama of 8 October 1867, after mentioning the forthcoming Italian premiere of Gounod's Roméo et Juliette (as Romeo e Giulietta) and a revival of Rossini's Guglielmo Tell, went on to report:

> We shall also have, for the new opera that has not been presented elsewhere, Mefistofele by Boito, former pupil of the Milan conservatory, a writer making his first appearance as an opera composer: we do not know, however, if this will suffice to fulfill the management's obligation to put on a new opera written by an established composer.[24]

Although the official announcement by the management of La Scala had spoken merely of "a completely new opera written by an Italian composer," the opponents of Boito were unwilling to admit that he was in any way qualified to be considered "an Italian composer" on the basis of what he had submitted to the public at large. The position of La Fama in the coming controversy is not hard to fathom, particularly as it returned to the same objections to Mefistofele two weeks later, expanding the discussion by charging the management with bad faith in entertaining such a work: "it should be excluded [from the repertory] because, as we have maintained, it is the work of an untried composer, and La Scala ought never to be the arena for beginners, even for those who have given the most worthy demonstrations [of their talent]."[25] A month later the journal was still harping on the same theme.[26]

The La Scala season of 1867–68 opened on 30 November with Gu-

[21] La Fama, XXV, no. 26 (25 June 1867), 103.

[22] Beginning in early 1865 La Fama had been publishing, in installments of fifty lines or so at irregular intervals, a translation of Faust Part II by one G. Rota. This continuing project had not been completed at the time of the prima of Mefistofele. (I have not been able to identify this G. Rota but would be surprised if he turned out to be the Giuseppe Rota whose Ginevra di Scozia had been pilloried by Boito.)

[23] La Fama, XXV, no. 36 (3 September 1867), 143.

[24] La Fama, XXV, no. 41 (8 October 1867), 163.

[25] La Fama, XXV, no. 43 (22 October 1867), 171.

[26] La Fama, XXV, no. 47 (19 November 1867), 187.

glielmo Tell. On 26 December Boito addressed a letter to the Directors of the theater asking that the chorus be given over exclusively to rehearsing *Mefistofele* if his opera was to be ready "by the end of January. [. . .] My opera, relying almost entirely on the performance of the chorus, will have to be rehearsed at length, very seriously, and more than any other to be performed at La Scala this season."[27] He was, furthermore, eager to have the scenery available for stage rehearsals a full week before the premiere.[28]

The rehearsals, however, did not begin much before the third week of January. On the 28th of that month *La Fama* reported:

At La Scala the rehearsals of *Mefistofele* have begun. Taking part in the new opera will be Signora [Melania] Reboux (Margherita and Elena), [Marcello] Junca (Mefistofele), the baritone [Gerolamo] Spallazzi (Faust), and Signora [Giuseppina] Flory (Marta). Strangely enough, the opera is written without a tenor, an innovation that will prove convenient to the management for economic reasons, but not for artistic ones, as it will be deprived of a vocal type of such importance.[29]

On 24 February 1868 Mazzucato, who had been in charge of the musical direction of *Mefistofele*, wrote to his colleague Angelo Mariani:

Boito's *Mefistofele* was proceeding well at the first rehearsals, but one of the usual random inspirations of [Filippo] Filippi suggested placing the composer himself as director of the orchestra, under the pretext of forming a complete trinity: poet, composer, and conductor; this has produced nothing but a complete demoralization of the executant forces, because of which everything is now going to the dogs.[30]

It seems likely that Mazzucato's description to Mariani tells only part of what happened, since Faccio (who was in Scandinavia conducting a touring company) had heard rumors of "dissension" [*dissapori*][31] between Mazzucato and Boito; and Faccio, who knew the strengths and limitations of Boito's musical talents as well as anyone, feared for the fate of *Mefistofele* with his friend wielding the baton. It seems likely that at some

[27] *VAB*, 249.
[28] A note in the original edition of the libretto informs us that "the costumes for the work are in imitation of engravings by Dürer, from Kaulbach's illustrations for Goethe, from old prints by Van Siehem, and from descriptions of the legends of Widman, Pfitzer, etc."
[29] *La Fama*, XXVI, no. 4 (28 January 1868), 16.
[30] *VAB*, 250.
[31] *VAB*, 251.

point in the rehearsals Mazzucato, acting in his capacities as conductor and as Boito's former professor of composition, may have suggested some modifications in the long score; at this point Boito balked and turned to Filippi for advice; Filippi in turn suggested that if Mazzucato would not conduct the opera as written, why then did not the composer, in spite of his inexperience, assume that function as well?

The delays in the preparation of *Mefistofele* had already started to cause scheduling problems at La Scala, as *La Fama* in its issue of 18 February was only too pleased to point out:

> What will be the remedies of the management to fill the void we do not know for certain [. . .] and we doubt that the *poema-leggenda Mefistofele*, whose performance is announced for this coming Saturday (22 February) will suffice, especially since it is said to contain almost insuperable problems of execution. Therefore, three times this past week *Guglielmo Tell* was put on.[32]

The following week *La Fama* intensified its attack:

> Still another *mystification* at La Scala. After the anticipatory announcements of sets hurriedly prepared by the full crew, after the printed promises, *Mefistofele* did not go on last Saturday, nor will it appear during the coming week, it being asserted by the management that a work of this scope required time and tranquil people, not the noise and jollification of Carnival. In fact Lent is a more appropriate time to go into the clouds, as the libretto directs, and the good public, if the truth be told, which was within a trace of being deprived of the new work that is judged by its own fabricators as close to unperformable, must resign itself to waiting and having the theater often closed at the height of Carnival.[33]

As one can infer from this sneering reference, Boito's libretto, contrary to the usual practice of the time, had been in circulation in advance of the premiere—in fact, since the latter half of January. Boito's supporters tried to explain this novelty. On 22 January, which must have been just about the time the libretto appeared, Filippi wrote in *La Perseveranza* that he refused to discuss it until he had heard how it went with the music, as if to forestall premature debate.[34] Antonio Ghislanzoni, in *La Gazzetta Musicale* two weeks later, praised Boito's skill in making a single coherent

[32] *La Fama*, XXVI, no. 7 (18 February 1868), 27–28.
[33] *La Fama*, XXVI, no. 8 (25 February 1868), 31.
[34] VAB, 251–52.

work out of the two parts of Goethe's drama.[35] Michele Uda, in an appendix of 15 February to *Il Pungolo*, raised the temperature of discussion: "If you wish to have an idea of the great good that I judge *Mefistofele* to be, as a poem, imagine the great number of bad things that the admirers of the *grand'aria di sortita*, the apostles of the *cavatina*, the fanatics of the *cabaletta*, will have to say about it."[36] *Il Politecnico* attacked the work, observing that even Verdi's *Il trovatore* had managed to survive an inept libretto.[37] Then, in its issue of 3 March, *La Fama* joined the controversy.

In a long article signed "P.A.," the critic, who claims to have been in possession of the text for one week, justifies dealing with it at length because it has already been prejudged an "extraordinary musico-literary masterpiece." After a show of erudition designed to match that of Boito's *Prologo in teatro* prefixed to the libretto, the critic takes exception to the "reform" aspects of Boito's text, beginning with its choice of subject:

> We remain deeply convinced that it is not possible to translate the second part of Goethe's poem to the stage, still less that it could serve as the plot of a musical score. Dramatic music wants emotions and passions; without them an author can never find the divine afflatus of inspiration that will communicate itself to his listeners to warm and exalt them.[38]

Before coming to specific instances, P.A. makes this transition:

> We state openly that in reducing Goethe's poem to a *melodramma* Signor Boito has created a work more improbable than praiseworthy. If he has displayed an uncommon power of ingenuity, we do not understand its purpose, and the result, considered just from a literary point of view, is certainly not such as to merit our approval.

To summarize P.A.'s particular objections: he censures rhymes too closely placed, images that do not make sense (he cites from the opening hymn of the Prologue the lines "E s'erge a Te per l'aure azzurre e cave / In suon soave" [and rises to Thee through the blue and empty breezes in sweet sound]). He objects to bizarre words, such as "allelujate," pointing out that although it appears as a verb in Dante's *Purgatorio* 30, recent authoritative editions substitute "alleviare" for it. His sense of propriety is offended by other lines and by the moment when Faust gives Margherita

---

[35] Issue of 9 February 1868. Ghislanzoni had been editor of *La Gazzetta Musicale* since 1866.
[36] *VAB*, 253.
[37] *VAB*, 252.
[38] *La Fama*, XXVI, no. 9 (3 March 1868), 33.

the narcotic for her mother; P.A. is concerned for mothers attending the performance "seated beside their comely young daughters."

It may be a coincidence, but three passages in the Witches' Sabbath ridiculed by P.A. were eliminated in Boito's revision of 1875. In dealing with one of these, P.A. turns to sarcasm without indicating that the words are for the Witches:

And oh what of these other lines, masterpieces of harmony, of elegance, and of common sense:

> Re! Re! Re! Tu despota
> Sei del nostro fato.
> Noi c'incurviam docili
> Al rege implacato.
> Re! Re! Re! Benevolo
> Mira l'alto fè
> Del tuo popol supplice,
> O Re! Re! Re! Re! Re!
> *Miserere*! Re! Re!
> *Miserere*! Di me!

(King! King! King! You are the despot / ruling our fate. / We bend docilely / to the implacable ruler. / King! King! King! Benevolently / notice the high faith / Of your supplicant people / O King! King! King! King! King! / *Have mercy*! King! King! / *Have mercy*! On me!)

Or the critic tries to score on Boito for using an inadmissible verb form ("Where has Signor Boito found that one can truncate the third person [singular] present indicative of the verb *bollire*?"), citing these lines from the scene in the Imperial Palace (former Act IV, scene 1):

> Non senti, più lesto,
> Più caldo, più presto,
> Il polso che palpita
> Il cuore che bol.

(Do you not feel, nimbler, / warmer, faster, / the pulse that throbs / the heart that boils.)

The article then turns to metrics. P.A. first takes up *il metro nonasillabo*, saying that although it has been used it is not sanctioned by accredited treatises on versification (he does not, however, indicate that he is quoting one of Boito's own footnotes to the libretto). The critic also fails to include Boito's point that he uses *nonasillabi* because he finds "they provide a very melodious cadence." What P.A. does say is that this meter, with its stresses on the second, fifth, and eighth syllables, is fre-

280

quently adopted in French opera librettos, and he conjectures: "perhaps this reveals likewise the probable tendency of the music." He is scornful of Boito's employment of hexameters; first because he cites a French model, Jodelle, when P.A. can name seven more plausible Italian antecedents; and secondly because not all the lines of Elena's soliloquy about Troy can be scanned as hexameters, even though Boito modifies the accentuation of a number of words in the hope of making them fit. He regards the use of this classical meter as an aberration, without acknowledging that Boito was following Goethe's example. In fact, P.A. remains stubbornly insensitive to the unusual closeness with which Boito followed his source: the self-protective irony behind Boito's scholarly citations in the *Prologo in teatro* and the learned footnotes that adorn his text incite the critic to ludicrous lengths of pedantry.

This review of the libretto is typical of the negative attitudes that raged around *Mefistofele* in the months before its disastrous premiere (5 March 1868) and even more ignominious second performance, spread over two evenings, when the ballet *Brahma* was performed as a sop between Acts IV and V of Boito's score. But P.A.'s review, however prejudiced and nit-picking it may seem, does have the merit of being circumstantial, and it confronts some experimental aspects of Boito's reforms.

A much more recent critic has less difficulty in identifying what he calls "the bold originality of [Boito's] conception":

> This originality seems all the greater when we consider that many of its most important features were present in 1868, about the time of *Don Carlos*. In a period when Verdi was patiently tinkering with the traditional structures of Italian romantic opera, Boito simply discarded them. Not a single scene of *Mefistofele* follows the old four-movement format [as described by Basevi], and some scenes—most notably the Prologue and the Romantic Sabbath—have no precedent whatsoever within the Italian tradition. No Italian had yet provided such weighty structural pillars as the prologue material to lend support and shape to his drama. No Italian had depended as little as Boito did in 1868 on the aria and duet . . .[39]

Considering this judgment, it is worthwhile remembering that Boito uses only one of Goethe's songs—assigning the Tomcat's song in the Witch's Kitchen, "Das ist die Welt," to Mefistofele in the Witches' Sabbath, as "Ecco il mondo." By omitting the rest of Goethe's interpolated songs, Boito avoids obvious opportunities for arias in his score.

[39] Jay Nicolaisen, *Italian Opera in Transition, 1871–1893* (Ann Arbor, 1980), 149.

TO LOOK at the 1868 libretto of *Mefistofele* as a reform libretto, we must first acknowledge the distortion that results from considering the text apart from the music, something especially important when the librettist and composer are the same person. The problem is heightened, in this case, because a fair amount of the music is no longer retrievable. I propose, however, that something useful, if necessarily incomplete, can be gained from looking at two aspects of the text: first its diction and rhetoric, and second its relation to its source.

Boito's vocabulary is notoriously large and exotic. Its exoticism, however, is not that of coining new words so much as disinterring uncommon words or employing unusual secondary meanings from the past. In fact, P.A.'s diatribe focuses on precisely these two points. Although he objects to unearthing the verb "allelujate," the usage is self-explanatory and appropriate in its context. P.A. found fault with the juxtaposition of "aure" and "cave," the latter having a primary meaning of "empty":

> Emana un verso—di supremo amor
> E s'erge a Te per l'aure azzurre e cave
> In suon soave.

(There emerges a verse of supreme love / and [it] rises to Thee / through the blue and empty breezes / in sweet sound.)

What P.A. fails to mention is that these lines are immediately followed by "Echoes" singing "Ave," the word with which this hymn begins—"Ave Signor"—or that the two succeeding strophes end with the same rhyme sound, similarly echoed by "Ave," and then immediately followed, with tremendous irony, by Mefistofele's address to the Lord, which also begins "Ave Signor." What is impressive here is the large-scale organization cued by verbal repetition and rhyme; no effect of comparable virtuosity occurs in any earlier Italian libretto that I know, nor is it carried over from Goethe's Prologue in Heaven.

One result of Boito's choice and combination of words in the 1868 *Mefistofele* is that his characters are, verbally at least, more sharply individual than was customary in librettos of this time; the individualization is, of course, most marked in Goethe's text as well. I should like to make a distinction here between individualization and characterization. By individualization I mean that Boito's characters express themselves in terms that are distinctive and unique, while characterization would mean that the terms in which they express themselves reveal something of the complexity and richness of a particular personality. Boito has to some extent both characterized and individualized Margherita, for example, while he has been less vivid, but just as individual, with Faust.

In the Prison Scene (Act III), the insane Margherita explains to Faust the order of the graves for her mother, herself, and her child. In the libretto, the passage appears as follows:

> Vien ... vo' narrarti il tetro ordin di tombe
> Che doman scaverai ... là... fra le zolle
> Più verdeggianti ... stenderai mia madre
> Dov'è più vago il cimiter ... discosto ...
> Ma pur vicino ... scaverai la mia ...
> La mia povera fossa ... e il mio bambino
> Poserà sul mio sen.

(Come ... I will tell you the gloomy order of tombs / that you must dig tomorrow ... there... under the / greenest turf ... you will lay my mother / where the cemetery is most pleasing ... a little apart / but yet close ... you will dig mine ... / my poor grave ... and my baby / you will place on my breast.)

While Boito follows Goethe fairly faithfully, he is at the same time creating a quite different effect with unrhymed *endecasillabi*, artful use of caesura, and irregular phrase lengths. Goethe, on the other hand, uses couplets of varying lengths:

> Ich will dir die Gräber beschreiben.
> Für die mußt du sorgen
> Gleich morgen;
> Der Mutter den besten Platz geben,
> Meinen Bruder sogleich darneben,
> Mich ein wenig beiseit',
> Nur nicht gar zu weit!
> Und das Kleine mir an die rechte Brust.

And there is a singular shift of emphasis: whereas Gretchen bids Faust provide for the graves ("Für die mußt du sorgen"); Margherita leaves no doubt (with her repeated use of *scaverai*) that she wants Faust himself to dig them. And there is a more overt effect of pathos in the repetition of "la mia / La mia povera fossa." In Goethe's text, Gretchen does not characterize her own resting place. Margherita is both more self-consciously pathetic than Gretchen and more exigent, but Boito has succeeded in both individualizing and characterizing her.

Another passage closely linking the libretto and its source is Faust's speech at the beginning of Boito's Act I, scene 2 (Goethe's two scenes in the Study combined and much condensed):

> Dai campi, dai prati, che innonda
> La notte d'un nuvolo nero,
> Ritorno e di quete profonda

Son pieno di sacro mistero.
Le torve passioni del core
Si assonano in placido obblio,
Mi ferve soltanto l'amore
Dell'uomo, l'amore di Dio.

(From the fields, from the meadows, that are engulfed / by night in a black cloud / I return, and I am filled / with profound calm and sacred mystery. / The grim passions of my heart / sleep in peaceful oblivion, / I am moved only by the love / of man, the love of God.)

(Verlassen hab' ich Feld und Auen,
Die eine tiefe Nacht bedeckt,
Mit ahnungsvollem, heil'gem Grauen
In uns die beßre Seele weckt.
Entschlafen sind nun wilde Triebe
Mit jedem ungestümen Tun;
Es reget sich die Menschenliebe,
Die Liebe Gottes regt sich nun.)

Although Boito follows the general sense of Goethe's eight-line verse, he conceives this moment as an aria opportunity, and he is as much concerned with achieving an Italianate lyrical euphony as with reproducing the externals of Goethe's text. Boito preserves Goethe's alternate rhyme, but instead of the German poet's alternate nine- and eight-syllable meter he maintains a regular *metro nonasillabo* (accentuating the second, fifth, and eighth syllables), as well as the main syntactical division into two four-line sentences. The Italian is less complex in its images (dropping *ahnungsvollem* and *ungestümen Tun*, for instance) but has the merit of being syntactically straightforward, uncommonly so for libretti of this period. Boito's use of caesura in the opening and closing lines allows for parallel phrasing that has obvious musical implications.[40]

That Boito's aged Faust does not make a more clearly characterized impression up to this point in the current (post–1875) performing version of the opera results from the suppression of a long exchange between Faust and Wagner in Act I, scene 1:

... Due anime discerno
Che dimorano in me con fato opposto.
L'una s'abbranca al mondo,
Alla carne vieta;

[40] In comparing Boito's versions with Goethe's in various passages, we see that he employed a French intermediary in working with Goethe's German; his annotated French translation is today in the Museo Teatrale alla Scala.

E l'altra nel profondo
Etere vola,
E squassando la creta,
Serenamente all'Ideal s'impola.
Oh! se vaga in quest'aure il molle coro
De' spiriti leggeri,
Deh! ch'io salga ai lor diafani sentieri,
Alle nuvole d'oro,
Alle plaghe di rosa,
Verso una vita nuova e luminosa!

(I see two souls / with opposing destinies that dwell within me./ One clings to the world, / to forbidden lust; / and the other flies / in deep space / and, shrugging off mortal clay, / serenely orbits the Ideal. / Oh! if there wanders in these spaces the delicate chorus of ethereal spirits, / ah! let me rise to their diaphanous paths, / to the golden clouds, / to the roseate expanses, / toward a new, luminous life!)

This passage links Faust's aspirations to the Prologue in Heaven; it anticipates the close of Act I, scene 2, when Faust and Mefistofele ride off through the air; and it prepares for the soliloquy of the dying Faust, "Giunto sul passo estremo." The metrical freedom is noteworthy, but even more so is the coherence that it gives to Faust, who becomes a cryptically symbolic figure in the 1875 revision of the libretto.

The major part of Boito's "reform" libretto, then, is more faithful to its source than was then the general practice. While Boito is necessarily selective in the material he includes, he normally follows the sequence of his source. One notable exception, however, is the last half of the Prologo, in which texts for the Seraphim and Penitents are only loosely adapted from the final scene of *Faust II*. There are other places, such as Mefistofele's "Son lo Spirito che nega" (Goethe's "Ich bin der Geist, der stets verneint!"), where Boito's text for his strophic aria freely adapts certain allusions from the German text and incorporates others not there, each verse ending with a resounding *fischio* (whistle), which has no counterpart in Goethe:

Son lo Spirito che nega
Sempre, tutto; l'astro, il fior.
Il mio ghigno e la mia bega
Turbi gli ozi al Creator.
Voglio il Nulla e del Creato
La ruina universal.
È atmosfera mia vital

Ciò che chiamasi peccato,
Morte e Mal.
Rido e avvento—questa sillaba:
⟨No.⟩
Struggo, tento,
Ruggo, sibilo,
⟨No.⟩
Mordo, invischio,
Fischio! fischio! fischio![41]

(I am the Spirit who denies / always, everything; the stars, the flowers. / My sneers and my dissent / disturb the leisure of the Creator. /
I want Nothingness and the / universal ruin of Creation. / And my
vital atmosphere / is that which is called sin, / Death and Evil. / I
laugh and spit—this syllable: / ⟨No.⟩ / I lay waste, I tempt, / I ruin, I
hiss, / ⟨No.⟩ / I bite, I entice, / I whistle! whistle! whistle!)

Here one observes Boito at his ingeniously adaptive best, versifying with
skill and sophistication; it was a proclivity that, when not constrained by
a practical sense of theater, contributed in large part to the fiasco of 5
March 1868. If the virtuosity of verbal tone-color is without precedent in
earlier Italian libretti, the emphasis on "reform" is strangely undercut by
Boito's adoption of traditional French *couplet* structure for this aria: two
verses, rounded off by the same refrain.

We have seen that the passages Boito cut when revising the libretto
robbed it of coherence and, in some places, of striking originality. Besides
episodes like the Emperor's Court, which was omitted entirely, those that
received the most cuts were: the opening scene of Act I, where two characters ("Un borghese" and "Un mendicante cieco," both paraphrased
from Goethe) were eliminated, as well as forty-seven lines of dialogue for
Faust and Wagner; and the Witches' Sabbath, which was pruned of almost ninety lines of text. Significantly, a large part of this material relates
closely to Goethe. Viewed in the main, Boito's 1868 text is more stimu-
lating to read than the revision of 1875 or the final version of 1881, but
that in no sense means that the original is a more effective libretto. Its
intention as a "reform" document is more patent, however, than the revisions, where conventional structures such as a second strophe to
Margherita's "L'altra notte in fondo al mare" or the duet "Lontano, lontano, lontano," both in the Prison Scene, provide the additions; and what
was excised were often the discursive, experimental passages that had no
prototypes in earlier Italian libretti. Examples of these excisions are the
Zig-Zag jingle for the Hobgoblin in the Witches' Sabbath, or the virtuoso

[41] *TGS*, 98.

286

metrics of the *buffo* duet text about the properties of gold in the scene at the Imperial Court. As nearly as one can tell, judging from the reviews of the first performance of 1868, the passages that Boito decided to cut were ones in which the audience seemed to object more to the ineffectiveness of the music than to the text. In 1875 Boito's chief concern, to judge by the conventional additions he made to his score, as well as by such adjustments as the changing of Faust into a tenor role, was to convert *Mefistofele* into a viable opera that audiences could appreciate without undue strain—just the sort of concern that had been uppermost for those composers he had listed as perpetrators of *formula*.

At the first performance of *Mefistofele*, the contestation of opposing factions in the audience—the later parts of the performance were, apparently, only fitfully audible—delayed the final curtain until 1:30 a.m., after five and a half noisy hours. In retrospect, that outcome seems inevitable. Boito at age twenty-six lacked a sense of proportion. In the mid-1860s his enthusiasm for the mastodonic works of Meyerbeer, then comparative novelties in Italy, encouraged self-indulgent dilation.[42] Nor can we ignore the special circumstances of the La Scala season of 1867–68, which afforded him both the unexpected chance to have his work performed and—in view of his inexperience—inadequate time to convert it into a work in which his notions of reform had a real chance to convince a singularly exigent public. He was genuinely heroic, if ill advised, to resist Mazzucato's demands for changes in the work during rehearsal, even though it meant he had to assume the conducting himself. It is fortunate that the libretto, if not the complete score, of the 1868 *Mefistofele* survives, because it shows that Boito's advocacy of *form* over *formula* was not mere journalistic glibness; it demonstrates a serious concern to capture something of the spirit of its source, rather than reshape selected events to conform to the clichés of mid-nineteenth-century librettistic practice. Of the thirteen libretti that Boito wrote, the 1868 *Mefistofele*, among the serious ones, shows least resemblance to the traditions of Italian *melodramma*. Very much a derivative work in its relationship to Goethe, it is at the same time a most original Italian libretto in its diction and versification; although undeniably compromised by events, its idealism as a reform document can still command our respect.

---

[42] The 7 March 1868 issue of *Il Pungolo* included an article by Leone Fortis, an intimate friend of both Boito brothers. Fortis maintains that Boito had originally intended not one opera but two, corresponding to the two parts of Goethe's work, the first to be called *Mefistofele*, the second *Elena*; this plan had been put in abeyance by the success of Gounod's *Faust* in Italy. The resulting conflation of the passages that appealed both to the *scapigliato* and to the classicist in Boito contained more material than he could take full advantage of (see *VAB*, 236).

On Reading Nineteenth-Century Opera: Verdi through the Looking-Glass*

I

Early in the nineteenth century, Jérôme-Joseph de Momigny, a Belgian musical theorist and composer little known today except to historians of musical analysis, published a *Cours complet d'harmonie et de composition*.[1] Toward the end of his first volume, Momigny offers a lengthy discussion of Mozart's String Quartet in D minor, K.421. His remarks have been noted more than once in recent years, and particular attention has been given to the manner in which Momigny's musical taxonomy seems to anticipate modern methods of musical analysis.[2] However, in the final section, "Du style musical de ce Morceau," Momigny offers a method of approaching the piece that bears little relation to modern-day practice. Indeed, so distant is it from what we regard today as the legitimate concerns of an analyst or critic, it may well seem bizarre, even risible:

> The style of this *Allegro Moderato* is noble and moving. I thought that the best way in which to make clear to my readers its true expression was to attach some words to it. But these verses, if one can give them that name, having been as it were improvised, must not be judged on any criterion but their agreement with the sense of the music.
>
> I have tried to make it clear that the feelings expressed by the composer were those of a woman in love who is about to be abandoned by the hero she adores: Dido, who had a similar misfortune to la-

---

* The present essay grows in part from ideas developed in collaboration with Carolyn Abbate (see in particular our "On Analyzing Opera," in Carolyn Abbate and Roger Parker, ed., *Analyzing Opera: Verdi and Wagner* [University of California Press, in press]). I should like to thank Professor Abbate for her critical reading of earlier versions of the essay, and for many important suggestions.

[1] 3 vols. (Paris, 1803–1806).

[2] The discussion is on 307–82; the accompanying musical diagram (which includes a score of the entire first movement) occurs in vol. 3 ("Volume des planches"), 109–56. For commentaries, see Albert Palm, "Ästhetische Prinzipien in der französischen Musiktheorie des frühen 19. Jahrhunderts," *Archiv für Musikwissenschaft*, 22.2 (1965), 126–39; and Ian D. Bent, article "Analysis" in *The New Grove Dictionary of Music and Musicians* (London, 1980), I, 348–49.

ment, came immediately to mind. The elevation of her station, the ardor of her love, the celebrity of her misfortune—all of these made me decide to make her the heroine of the plot.[3]

True to his word, in the accompanying musical example he attaches a kind of Gallic Dido's Lament to Mozart's first-violin part. Virtually every musical phrase of the first movement is underpinned with a phrase of dramatic text. Momigny has in effect attempted to explain the piece through an act of translation, by converting a string quartet's sonata form into a *scène lyrique*. With a fascinating mixture of the ingenious and the ingenuous, he then proceeds to offer a detailed commentary and justification for his choice of particular words. In the opening two lines, for example:

This [musical] verse contains two poetic verses.
> Ah! quand tu fais mon *déplaisir*,
> Ingrat, je veux me plaindre et non pas t'attendrir.

The word "déplaisir" is weak, and is there only because I did not find *under my hand* a rhyme for *ir* that could conveniently replace it. The true sense of this verse would, rather, be *Ah! quand tu t'apprêtes à désoler, à déchirer mon coeur.*[4]

The final sentence, with its reference to "the true sense," is most important, emphasizing the intimacy of the proposed relationship between music and words. Momigny clearly "read" his "text," crossed barriers of medium, genre, and language, understood music with a directness and lack of self-consciousness thoroughly alien to us today. His reading unquestioningly accepts the possibility of translation from one medium to another, and sees the aesthetic difficulties of such translation primarily in

[3] Momigny, I, 371: "Le style de cet *Allegro Moderato* est noble et pathétique. J'ai cru que la meilleure manière d'en faire connaître la véritable expression, à mes lecteurs, était d'y joindre des paroles. Mais ces vers, si l'on peut leur donner ce nom, ayant été pour ainsi dire improvisés, ne doivent être jugés sous aucun autre rapport que sous celui de leur concordance avec le sens de la musique.

"J'ai cru démêler que les sentimens exprimés par le compositeur étaient ceux d'une amante qui est sur le point d'être abandonnée par le héros qu'elle adore: *Didon*, qui a eu à se plaindre d'un semblable malheur, est venue aussitôt à ma pensée. L'élévation de son rang, l'ardeur de son amour, la célébrité de son infortune, tout m'a décidé à en faire l'héroïne de ce sujet."

[4] Momigny, I, 372: "Ce vers [musical] en contient deux de poésie.
> Ah! quand tu fais mon *déplaisir*,
> Ingrat, je veux me plaindre et non pas t'attendrir.

Le mot déplaisir est faible, et n'est là que parce que je n'ai pas trouvé, *sous ma main*, une rime en *ir* qui pût convenablement le remplacer. Le vrai sens de ce vers serait plutôt: *Ah! quand tu t'apprêtes à désoler, à déchirer mon coeur.*"

289

mechanical terms (finding appropriate rhymes, etc.). The arts of music and poetry—though clearly carrying their own systems of articulation— are at base directed by the same rules, governed by the same checks. As he says a little later, "Many people think that the language of Orpheus is a vague idiom and that in music, as in the clouds, one sees everything that one wants to see. If it were thus, would one note make us shed tears while another makes us shudder?"[5]

Such directness presents us with two options. We may simply dismiss Momigny's explanatory scenario as quaint, irrelevant, merely silly. But we can also use the strangeness as a point of entry, a chance to measure the distance between others' aesthetic attitudes and our own. As Robert Darnton puts it, "When we cannot get a proverb, or a joke, or a ritual, or a poem, we know we are on to something. By picking at the document where it is most opaque, we may be able to unravel an alien system of meaning."[6] We can, in this case, pose Momigny as an extreme point of reference from which to test our own unspoken assumptions about the vexed question of how words and music work together in a dramatic context.

For it is clear that modern-day incomprehension of Momigny's approach tells us something of the various ways in which we will choose to "read" a musical-dramatic text, something of what can be expressed of one medium in another's language. As stated above, what strikes us as centrally odd about Momigny is his certainty, his assumption that the connection between words and music is so inevitable and unchallengeable that the two matrices, the two systems, may enfold one another even when given no overt encouragement from the creative exterior. No matter that we have a string quartet, or that Mozart was German-speaking, or even that the first violin has music unsuited to the human voice (whether Dido's or anyone else's). Wherever there is music, Momigny seems to assume, words will lurk beneath the surface, ready to voice specific dramas when invoked for the purpose of critical understanding.[7]

Certainly the historical road toward our incomprehension has been long and rich: so much so that it would be presumptuous to attempt anything like a comprehensive summary. Nor would it be entirely fair to

[5] Momigny, I, 380: "Beaucoup de gens pensent que la langue d'Orphée est un idiôme vague, et que, dans la Musique, comme dans les nuages, on voit tout ce qu'on croit y voir. S'il en était ainsi, telle Note nous ferait-elle verser des pleurs, telle autre frissonner?"

[6] Robert Darnton, *The Great Cat Massacre and Other Episodes in French Cultural History* (New York, 1984), 5.

[7] I should, though, make clear that nowhere does Momigny claim that his *scène* is the only possible text that might clarify the music. Mozart's quartet does not carry a specific text—merely a specific expressive sentiment that can be made clear through words.

paint the issue in black-and-white terms. The history of operatic criticism has been punctuated by admissions of the rough edges that inevitably occur where words and music meet, this even during periods in which one might assume a strong resistance to such imperfections. To take an instance virtually at random: in the late seventeenth century, Dryden's collaboration with Purcell occasioned the poet's (perhaps grudging) admission that "the Numbers of Poetry and Vocal Musick, are sometimes so contrary, that in many places I have been oblig'd to cramp my Verses, and make them rugged to the Reader, that they may be harmonious to the Hearer."[8] A century later, Momigny himself was aware that the "perfect marriage" metaphor (still maintaining a robust usage today) was ideal rather than realistic: "Can Poetry agree in every detail with Music? No: in this amiable alliance, as in marriage, the contracted parties must make mutual sacrifices."[9]

In spite of these admissions, our incomprehension of Momigny, the sense of an unknown country of cultural attitudes, remains. There are doubtless numerous ways in which we might trace our path toward this feeling of unease and alienation; but there is one obligatory nineteenth-century port of call in any attempt to clarify our present-day position, our unspoken assumptions when we set out to "read" an opera. Whomever else we omit, however partial our gesture toward historical process, we cannot discuss the matter without some reference to the contribution of Richard Wagner.

II

Wagner is obligatory for the simple reason that in many senses we remain under the influence of Wagnerian ideals about how one might "read" an opera. This is less often recognized and stated than it should be. Musical historians will talk of certain places at certain periods undergoing "Wagnerian domination"—late nineteenth-century France is an obvious example—and of a subsequent emergence into bracing modernity. However, while this "emergence" may indeed have taken place so far as strictly musical influence is concerned, the manner in which we all evaluate opera still depends a good deal on Wagnerian criteria. *Pace* some modern directors, we have had no Artaud or Brecht of the operatic stage.

---

[8] John Dryden, Preface to Purcell's *King Arthur*, in *The Dramatic Works*, ed. Montague Summers, VI, 242; quoted from James Anderson Winn, *Unsuspected Eloquence: A History of the Relations between Poetry and Music* (New Haven and London, 1981), 242.

[9] Momigny, II, 622: "La Poésie peut-elle s'accorder en tout et partout avec la Musique? Non: dans cette aimable alliance, comme dans le mariage, les parties contractantes ont des sacrifices mutuels à se faire."

And in spite of a recent revival of interest in seventeenth- and eighteenth-century opera, our experience of the entire genre remains deeply rooted in the Wagnerian era.

Partly as a result of this unspoken acceptance (and partly, it must be admitted, owing to the opacity of his style), Wagner's theoretical and journalistic writings have become a kind of sacred text, a scripture within which one may find loose justification for a startling number of (often contradictory) theoretical formulations. As Carl Dahlhaus has pointed out, Wagner's mechanical and habitual Hegelian mode of argument often causes him to set up artificial—even arbitrary—opposites; forces that seem impressive when juxtaposed with each other, but that may crumble disconcertingly if considered individually. One sometimes has the impression that the entire construct holds true only by an effort of Wagner's (not inconsiderable) will. Details are there for the sake of the "synthesis" they "inevitably" lead to, and can be taken from their context only with caution. A typical example, one that Dahlhaus cites, is Wagner's contention that there was an historical *need* for musical drama, brought about directly by the decline of spoken drama on the one hand and of absolute music on the other.[10] When such techniques are in play, we do well to keep a wary eye out for the self-justifying subtext that runs just beneath the surface.

Certainly Wagner's views on the status of conventional operatic attempts to deal with words and music are not hard to find. He devoted many of his most influential essays to the topic. And whatever the confusions that arise from various changes in emphasis, one point is immediately obvious—has, in fact, become a commonplace. Rather than Momigny's *translation*, Wagner promulgated the Romantic notion of a *fusion* of words and music. What is more, the definition of this fusion required elaborate theoretical foundation; it was an aesthetic "ideal" and could not be attained without a struggle. Nor, of course, could its creative manifestations be achieved in the disarmingly prosaic manner of a Momigny. Sheer workmanlike application was not the Wagnerian Way. Indeed, Wagner's writings are littered with observations on the manner in which most operatic works fall depressingly short of expectations.

His arguments on the topic are presented most concisely in *"Zukunftsmusik"* (1860), an essay that sets out to restate some of the main issues raised in *Oper und Drama* (1851). There the grandiosity of past theories is set rudely against the contemporary, pragmatic context:

I found it highly illuminating that brilliant minds should so often have entertained these hopes [for a fusion of the arts in opera] with-

[10] See John Deathridge and Carl Dahlhaus, *The New Grove Wagner* (New York and London, 1984), esp. 68–88.

out their ever having been fulfilled. On the one hand it implied that the highest in drama might be attainable through a complete fusion of poetry and music. On the other hand it pointed to the fundamental defect of opera, a defect which in the nature of the case a musician would not be conscious of and which would also escape the attention of a poet. From the point of view of a poet who was not himself a musician, an opera was a firmly carpentered framework of musical forms that imposed specific rules for the invention and execution of the dramatic material he supplied. These forms only the musician could alter; and as to their content the poet commissioned to supply the libretto soon, without meaning to, exposed its worth in that he found himself obliged to degrade both his subject and his poetry to the level of triviality castigated in that pronouncement of Voltaire ["Ce qui est trop sot pour être dit, on le chante"]. In point of fact it is not necessary to lay bare the awkwardness, superficiality, not to say absurdity, of an operatic libretto; even in France the best efforts have been designed rather to conceal the evil than to remedy it. And so poets have always regarded the operatic form as a strange untouchable object to which they must perforce submit—which is why, apart from a few unfortunate exceptions, truly great poets have always steered clear of it.[11]

A crucial step in realizing Wagner's thesis comes with his account of the operatic achievement of Mozart, the only representative of the Teutonic pantheon who produced a body of stage works that could not be dismissed. This he did most completely in an extended late essay on words and music: "Über das Opern-Dichten und Komponieren im Besonderen" (On Opera Poetry and Composition), published in the *Bayreuther Blätter* in September 1879.[12] The most important passage is preceded by the usual series of brisk salvos aimed at early nineteenth-century operatic practice in Italy, France, and Germany:

The meagre doggerel verse, often built of mere empty phrases, the verse whose sole affinity to music, its rhyme, destroyed the words' last shred of meaning, and thereby made the best images quite valueless to the musician—this verse compelled the composer to take the formation and working-out of characteristic melodic motifs from a province of music which had previously been developed in the orchestral accompaniment as a kind of free language for instruments.

[11] Reprinted in vol. 7 of the *Gesammelte Schriften und Dichtungen*; English translation from Robert L. Jacobs, ed., *Three Wagner Essays* (London, 1979), 22–23.

[12] Reprinted in vol. 10 of the *Gesammelte Schriften und Dichtungen*; English translation (slightly modified) from Charles Osborne, ed., *Richard Wagner. Stories and Essays* (New York, 1973), 113–35.

Mozart had raised this symphonic accompaniment to such expressiveness that, wherever it was consistent with dramatic naturalness, he could let the singers merely speak to it in musical accents, without disturbing the rich melodic texture of themes or breaking up the musical flow. Thus violence towards the verbal text disappeared also; anything in it that did not call for vocal melody was clearly intoned. (p. 122)

Not all of this is clear. Its description of Mozartian opera—in which singers speak to the "symphonic accompaniment" without disturbing "the rich melodic texture of themes"—seems at worst opaque, at best rather partial. It seems to us much more like an account of Wagner's own musical style; and the resemblance is, of course, anything but fortuitous. Significantly (in view of the late nineteenth- and twentieth-century critical reception of Mozart), the passage makes most sense if applied to Mozart's central and closing finales, and seems least appropriate to the arias. But what is unmistakable is the tortuous path Wagner felt he had to follow to arrive at a conclusion: his perception that words and music created drama not through their natural affinity, through some automatic alchemy, but rather through a special effort of will, and by a very special sort of insight. The goal was not chimerical, but its attainment required a Mozart or—better still—a Richard Wagner. Though Wagner sometimes assumes an appalling modesty of diction, it is clear that he imagines his own music-dramas as the logical outcome of this line of argument: as the demonstration of words and music fused in the service of drama. And it is no accident that the terms of approbation he uses in discussing Mozart, "symphonic accompaniment," "dramatic naturalism," "musical flow," were all appropriated by disciples and became key critical expressions in their writings, both on Wagner's music and on that of other operatic composers.

We might at this stage measure our distance once again. The gap, seemingly so unbridgeable with Momigny, has narrowed considerably. In fact, most critical writing on Wagner's music (and on that of most other operatic composers) during our own century has taken as its starting point an implicit acceptance of Wagner's main argument: "serious" opera should aspire toward the condition of the symphonic, toward "naturalism," and it should do so in the larger aim of effecting drama through a fusion of words and music. We can take as an example the most obvious and most frequently discussed level: that of the leitmotif. Early generations of Wagnerian scholars were obsessed by leitmotifs, and they spent much energy and ingenuity in sorting and labeling them. Musical ideas that could be associated with dramatic issues seemed to offer reassuring evidence of Wagner's higher purpose. And scholars such as Wolzogen pursued the matter so thoroughly that they eventually found themselves in possession of a dictionary, an orderly presentation of how music could be expressed in words, and words in music. There seemed no better demonstration of the new level of fusion Wagner had achieved. The persuasiveness and longevity of this model should not be underestimated. Later generations of scholars found the inconsistencies and ambiguities in the dictionary increasingly confusing; but, rather than question the premises, they continued in dogged attempts to rewrite Wolzogen's semantic tags. As in much other writing on nineteenth-century opera, a reliance on escape clauses such as "dramatic irony" (by which the composer was licensed to state musically the opposite of his true dramatic intention) became ever more essential. The pattern was repeated, with varying degrees of success or distortion, in writings on other composers. To take an obvious extension, the use of recurring themes became one of the most common areas of interest in operatic studies; extensive use of such themes was nearly always regarded as an enrichment and development of a composer's technical apparatus; in some cases leitmotivic ingenuity (Richard Strauss) or casualness (Puccini) even became a standard of measurement and evaluation.

It is true that some of the most recent critical thought on Wagner's music has taken a rather different direction. If we again consider the example of the leitmotif, we find that some scholars have now renounced "brawling upon the labels"[13] in favor of more broadly-based pursuits. For them the dictionary has lost its potency and has become instead an historical document; the chimera of easy equivalence has lost its fascination.[14] Of course, much of the standard nomenclature still remains, but this itself can serve as a *point d'appui*, as an opportunity to rejoice in the ambiguities created when such a direct, perhaps even naïve, system of identifying words with music as the leitmotif is applied to a verbal, musical, and dramatic surface as complex and multi-layered as Wagner's.[15]

[13] In the *Oxford English Dictionary*, one of the illustrative phrases under "label" (one dated, curiously enough, 1850) reads: "It is but a very fond dalliance to brawl upon the labels before you agree upon the original verity."

[14] There is evidence that this revaluation is not restricted to operatic or even to musical studies. For a fascinating discussion of how a reliance on semantic labels may restrict our appreciation of a visual artist, see Charles Rosen and Henri Zerner, "Caspar David Friedrich and the Language of Landscape," *Romanticism and Realism: The Mythology of Nineteenth-Century Art* (New York, 1984), 51–70.

[15] Dahlhaus has again been a leading figure in this movement. See in particular the volume cited in n. 10 above, 111–14, and *Richard Wagner's Music Dramas* (Cambridge, 1979). The essays of Christopher Wintle and Carolyn Abbate in the present collection offer varying viewpoints on the topic.

Release from such long-standing strictures is often heady. Some are now content for leitmotifs to accrue meaning endlessly, for signifiers to release their signifieds. But, persuasive and influential as some of these writings have been, it is still an open case as to whether they have yet changed profoundly the general practice of operatic criticism. To explore the matter further we need a test case. What better than to examine the reception of the composer who, while an exact contemporary, is more than any other classed as the historical and cultural antithesis of Wagner? Is there a sense in which, despite our understanding of the differences between them, we "read" Verdi through Wagner?

III

But first some background. As is well known, in Wagnerian terms the Italian operatic school came at the bottom of the heap: Wagner habitually reserved his most withering tones for the egregiously successful Rossini (whom he characterized as a dispenser of eternally repeated cadential *felicitàs*). One can immediately see reasons for his lack of sympathy, and for the fact that Italian musical drama assumed a very different stance on the topic of words and music. For one thing, there was (Goldoni, Gozzi, and Alfieri notwithstanding) no comparable tradition of spoken theater with which to belittle the libretto: in most of nineteenth-century Italy, opera *was* drama. However, generations of Italian critics of the nineteenth century found themselves able to castigate their own literary operatic tradition in a manner reminiscent of Wagner, though admittedly from an entirely different viewpoint.

These men of letters, increasing numbers of whom made a living by writing feuilletons for the burgeoning daily and weekly press, often measured new works against the Metastasian, arcadian ideal, against a period in the mid-eighteenth century when words intended for opera had attained a self-sufficiency and elevated reputation they have never since equaled. There was a widespread assumption that the librettist (always called "il poeta"), as well as serving the composer, had somehow to fashion an artifact in words that could be read on its own terms. The fact that printed libretti were prepared for each revival of an opera, and were sold at the theater in remarkably large numbers until well into the nineteenth century, of course fostered this state of affairs—in a sense made it possible.[16] The reviewer would have only a memory of the music (and would often be technically unqualified to make detailed remarks); but the li-

[16] For detailed information about Milanese libretto production and sales from the period 1814–1848, see Marino Berengo, *Intellettuali e librai nella Milano della Restaurazione* (Turin, 1980), 198–201.

bretto was by his side; he found himself in an ideal (i.e. music-less) position from which to make extensive reference to the words, and especially to their shortcomings as poetic drama.

However, rather early in the century some composers seemed to realize that words for music were somehow a special case, could not be judged by the same standards as purely literary endeavors. Vincenzo Bellini, whose reputation, both today and among his contemporaries, rests heavily on his "gusto romantico"—an unsurpassed ability to respond musically to verbal nuance—showed in at least one of his letters a matter-of-fact recognition of this point:

> If my music turns out to be beautiful and the opera pleases, you can write a million letters against composers' abuse of poetry, etc., that will prove nothing. [. . .] Carve in your head in adamantine letters: "The opera must draw tears, terrify people, make them die through singing." [. . .] And you know why I told you that a good *dramma per musica* is the one that does not make good sense [*il buon dramma per musica è quello che non ha buon senso*]? Because I know what a ferocious and intractable beast the man of letters is, and how absurd he is, with his general rules of good sense.[17]

Much could be made of Bellini's "adamantine" dictum, with its uncanny resemblance to certain famous sayings of Artaud, but his central point is elsewhere: that *il poeta* must be prepared to sacrifice conventional literary and (at least, in this context) dramatic plausibility in the service of his art. However, statements such as Bellini's are rare, and certainly no Italian creative artist explored the theoretical issue in anything like a systematic manner. It is certainly no accident that Bellini wrote the above lines *in extremis*: to a librettist (Count Carlo Pepoli) who had very little experience of writing for the musical theater. When Bellini worked with Felice Romani (his long-standing and most adroit librettist) no such admonitions were necessary. One imagines that collaboration moved ahead all the more smoothly when such formulations remained understood but unspoken.

It is with this essentially pragmatic context in view that we should turn finally to Verdi. The obvious point of entry would seem to be the early 1850s, the period in which Wagner constructed many of his most influential theories and Verdi wrote, in quick succession, *Rigoletto* and *Il trovatore*. Wagner was establishing an elaborate theoretical rationalization against which he would write his mature music-dramas, laying out a pa-

---

[17] Undated letter (c. late spring 1834) to Count Carlo Peopli, quoted in Herbert Weinstock, *Vincenzo Bellini. His Life and Operas* (New York, 1971), 170–71.

tient argument for continuity of approach, for a framework within which words might definitively merge with music in the service of drama. At the same time Verdi, seemingly by accident, wrote in swift succession two operas which differ fundamentally from Wagnerian standards in their treatment of that same issue. Both *Rigoletto* and *Il trovatore* emphatically reveal that, at the period of his most productive maturity, Verdi moved freely between what are sometimes considered antithetical positions about the very basis of musical drama.

It is worth pausing to describe more precisely the variation in relationship between words and music in these two middle-period masterpieces. On the whole, *Rigoletto* invites description in terms that might loosely be called Wagnerian. At its dramatic center is a character (Rigoletto) who typically expresses himself in a musical style (free, orchestrally accompanied arioso) that delivers the words with a minimum of repetition or distortion, a style that minimizes the formal constraints music may place upon words. The moments of greatest dramatic articulation involve the active participation of semantic/verbal, musical, and scenic devices. Side by side with these moments come traditional, "Rossinian" fixed forms: areas in which words frequently lose their semantic freshness (through distortion, selective repetition, or rearrangement) in the service of strictly musical closure. But, so firm is Verdi's control over the dramatic pacing, this alternative strategy does not compromise the central, "naturalistic" flow of dramatic time identified with the protagonist. Indeed, it could be argued that the more conventional formal means of other characters (the Duke, Gilda) serve as indications of their distance from the work's emotional core. The Duke is musically immobile, and his opening *ballata* and final *canzone* are the most stylized numbers in the opera. On the other hand, as Gilda matures during the opera, grows in Rigoletto-like density of feeling, she casts aside the ornamental vocal effects and traditional forms that characterize her first appearance, and increasingly adapts her musical language to that of her father.

Conversely, *Il trovatore* seems a perfect example of the dramatic type Wagner most despised: the "firmly carpentered framework of musical forms that imposed specific rules for the invention and execution of the dramatic material." To talk of characterization through form is (with the partial exception of Azucena) impossible, as each character's most prominent moments are set in identical, conventional structures. There are comparatively few moments of Rigoletto-like arioso, the division between "recitative" and "aria" being unusually rigid. Similarly, the progression of events seems to avoid naturalism: physical actions are narrated rather than seen; the ordered pattern of confrontations discourages focus on the individual. And, as a direct result of this strict adherence to formalism, the words of *Il trovatore* constantly aspire toward the condition of music: their sounds and rhythms often overwhelm their sense. It seems that literary values have been completely subsumed by the musical imperative. Again there are important variations in the nature of the relationship between words and music, most noticeably in the sequence of narratives that punctuate the opening two acts. The narrative voice (of Ferrando, Leonora, and then Azucena) injects an important and dramatically defining new level of relationship between words and music. But this time there is no sense of tension between the two modes. The *Il trovatore* narratives are—typically for Italian opera—cast in a formal mold even more rigid than that of the "normal" discourse: they thus produce a kind of frame inside which the action will unfold and, in doing so, serve to reinforce the overall formalism of dramatic expression.

This is not the place to expatiate on the relative musical and dramatic merits of these two operas. But the progress of their critical fortunes is significant. *Rigoletto* has, until recently, fared consistently better; and some of the qualities for which it is praised will have a familiar ring. Apart from the "naturalism" of its protagonist's musical language (mentioned above), its finest moments are said to involve the use of a recurring theme, a theme that functions as a powerful musical symbol of the opera's essential dramatic meaning. What is more, it develops this theme in a restricted tonal context, and so has encouraged some to argue that the opera projects a "symphonic" structure, develops a single key that is itself neatly attached to this meaning. *Il trovatore*, on the other hand, was commonly regarded as a throwback, a "lapse" into formalism, an interruption in Verdi's pursuit of the True Nature of Musical Drama. Its sequence of cabalettas, its extravagant vocal display, its tableau-like dramatic effects, its refusal even to tell a story in orderly fashion—all this seemed of a piece, and all seemed cheerfully irresponsible. The essential terms according to which these comparative judgments were made, the sense of what made an opera serious, were usually implicit but lost none of their potency for being so.

It is in this sense a measure of our gradual emergence from the implicit acceptance of Wagnerian theories that critical revaluation of *Il trovatore* has been a recurring feature of Verdian critical writing in recent years. Although the most important stages in this revaluation, the writings of Gabriele Baldini and Pierluigi Petrobelli, do not specifically address this issue, both authors are rooted in traditions that ensure their distance from Wagnerian theories.[18] But again, as with the new Wagner scholarship to

---

[18] For Baldini, see the chapter on *Il trovatore* in his *The Story of Giuseppe Verdi* (Cambridge, 1980), 209–30; Petrobelli's essay "Towards an Explanation of the Dramatic Struc-

which it might usefully be compared, this "new wave" runs against a mass of what Baldini termed "Rigolettan" attitudes and has not as yet significantly altered the general view of Verdi's progress as a musical dramatist.

Two examples, from superficially similar dramatic moments, may clarify the situation. Near the end of Act II of *Rigoletto*, as Gilda appears on the scene, Rigoletto tells the assembled company, in breathless, broken phrases, the exact nature of his feelings for her: "Signori ... in essa ... è tutta la mia famiglia ..." (Gentlemen ... in her ... is my entire family ...) The verbal declamation could be transferred to a spoken drama virtually intact. At the end of Part II of *Il trovatore*, as Manrico appears, Leonora asks, in an impressively contoured musical line, a question whose literal meaning is completely submerged by the intense musical closure: "Sei tu dal ciel disceso, o in ciel son io con te?" (Have you descended from Heaven, or am I in Heaven with you?). No one even thinks to offer a reply. One wonders how many operatic critics would accept both moments as equally convincing in their dramatic seriousness of purpose.

IV

If we turn to Verdi's development after the early 1850s, one point becomes immediately clear: of the two musico-dramatic types he had juxtaposed so effortlessly and with such telling effect in mid-career, it was the first (the type associated with *Rigoletto*) that gained ascendency. As if to confirm the Wagnerian teleology, fixed musical and poetic forms became ever more fleeting, and in some cases took on a referential rather than a form-building function. Words became increasingly significant for their semantic value, and some words even took on an iconic function within the drama. By the 1870s, the time of *Aida*, Verdi was talking to his librettist of the *parola scenica*, "the word that sculpts [*scolpice*] the dramatic situation and makes it clear and evident." He continues with an even more radical manifesto:

And the verse, the line, the stanza? I don't know what to say; but when the action demands it, I would immediately abandon rhythm, rhyme, stanza; I would make *versi sciolti* [unrhymed lines of variable length] in order to say neatly and clearly everything the action de-

---

ture of *Il trovatore*" appears as part of a symposium on the opera published in *Music Analysis*, I, 2 (1982), 125–69. Both these essays originally appeared in Italian: Baldini's in his *Abitare la battaglia* (Milan, 1970), 234–59; Petrobelli's as "Per un'esegesi della struttura drammatica del 'Trovatore'" in *Atti del Terzo Congresso Internazionale di Studi Verdiani* (Parma, 1974), 387–400.

mands. Unfortunately, in the theater poets and composers must sometimes have the talent not to write either poetry or music.[19]

It is of course usual to see these developments as both "logical" (i.e. strengthening our implicit assumptions about the genre) and artistically successful. And there is also the comforting sense of historical inevitability: *all* opera was becoming more continuous, more naturalistic during this period. Verdi, in common with his major European contemporaries, began to take musical drama more "seriously" in the second half of his career, created fewer and more elaborate operas and, as a just reward, wrote better music. But there is an alternative viewpoint. According to this, the gradual release from tradition—however consciously it may have been sought by Verdi, and however inevitable it may have been historically—brought with it a gradual loss of creative energy. After the great period of the early 1850s, Verdi's rate of operatic production gradually but inexorably wound down. And eventually, after *Aida* in 1871, the flow of new works ceased altogether.

Although there are certainly a number of what we might term "external" reasons for this loss of creative energy (his dissatisfaction with the turns that Italian culture was taking, his gathering financial security), a glance at his correspondence shows a more basic cause. This is most succinctly and clearly stated in a letter of 1869 that Verdi wrote to his sometime French librettist and producer Camille Du Locle:

In your opera houses (I'm not trying to be epigrammatic) there are too many wise men! Everyone wants to judge according to his own ideas, his own tastes and, what is worse, according to a *system*, without taking account of the character and the individuality of the composer. Everyone wants to give an opinion, wants to voice doubts, and the composer living for a long time in this atmosphere of doubt eventually cannot help being a little shaken in his convictions and ends up revising, adjusting or, to put it better, ruining his work: in this way one finds in the end not an opera written in a single burst of creative activity [*un opera di getto*], but a *mosaic*: as beautiful as you want, but still a *mosaic*.[20]

Although the context of this letter restricts the composer's nervousness to the Parisian stage, it is tempting to extend its meaning, particularly as Verdi had devoted so much of his creative energy of the past two decades to Paris. The *opera di getto*, the unity of dramatic conception that had

[19] Letter to Antonio Ghislanzoni (the librettist of *Aida*) dated 17 August 1870, in G. Cesari and A. Luzio, ed., *I copialettere di Giuseppe Verdi* (Milan, 1913), 641.
[20] Letter dated 7 December 1869, in *I copialettere*, 220.

seemed to arrive almost automatically in earlier years, became harder and harder to achieve. And the symptom of his discontent was a dissatisfaction with *words*. As he came increasingly to demand liberation from the fixed forms of the early nineteenth century, libretti that stimulated his creative imagination became impossible to find. At the period in which Wagner was bringing to fruition his life's work, was offering seemingly undeniable creative justification for the ideals he had set forth in the early 1850s, Verdi, at what should have been the height of his powers, was becalmed. He could no longer find words sufficiently attuned to his new musical demands. He was poised, it seemed, on the edge of an abyss of freedom. The fact that it was an abyss his own earlier, revolutionary works had done so much to create can have made his position no less easy to bear.

The manner of Verdi's return to composition at the end of the 1870s may have a wider application to the world of late nineteenth-century opera. First and foremost, he found in Arrigo Boito an ideal collaborator, not only because Boito was an accomplished man of letters, but—most important—because he was also a composer of operas who knew from bitter personal experience the difficulties and obstacles that could arise in the making of a modern musical drama. Without Boito's selfless encouragement and devotion, and without his instinctive grasp of the restrictions imposed by a decaying tradition, it is almost certain that the last works, *Otello* and *Falstaff*, would have remained unwritten.

The nature of the subjects Boito and Verdi chose is also significant. It is a critical commonplace that Shakespeare's *Othello* is the most single-minded of his great tragedies, indeed of all his plays. There is no sub-plot, nor even a great deal of variation in tone: simply the inexorable progress of the tragic hero. In other words, the unity of conception Verdi had struggled so hard for in the past two decades was built into the subject.[21] It is an immediate indication of Boito's acumen that, from the very first, he eliminated the one potentially fragmenting aspect of Shakespeare's plot by cutting the Venetian first act. By doing so he presented Verdi with just the singleness of purpose he required: a libretto that cast aside equivocation by the sheer concentration of its dramatic impetus.

Falstaff is a different case, though the manner in which it is exceptional in Verdi's output is analogous, and ultimately allowed the same release. Here the question of genre is all-important. *Falstaff* (like no other mature

---

[21] George Bernard Shaw summed this up in an epigram that, typically for him, sacrificed sense in the first part to rhythmic dash in the second: "instead of *Otello* being an Italian opera written in the style of Shakespeare, *Othello* is a play written by Shakespeare in the style of Italian opera." Quoted in Julian Budden, *The Operas of Verdi*, III (London, 1981), 302.

Verdi opera) is a comedy, and the comic genre released Verdi from the artistic crisis of late nineteenth-century opera by allowing him to rejoice in diversity. All the new aspects of the opera—the increased level of musical variety achieved through minute attention to word–painting; the ironic references to various musical forms and compositions; the relative independence of individual scenes; the proliferation of identifying colors—all of these are possible only through the medium of comedy, and all of them served to stimulate Verdi's creative imagination to new levels of fecundity, to fill the abyss of freedom with a stunning variety of techniques and ideas. The example of *Falstaff* makes it all the more regrettable that *fin-de-siècle* opera composers so rarely found the comic genre suitable to their expressive intentions.

V

So, through a collaborative effort of will, Verdi and his selfless librettist managed to go on composing operas nearly into the twentieth century. But the example of the second half of his career encourages us to confront a striking paradox—one that will bear on the phenomenon of "reading" opera with ever-greater insistence as the nineteenth century comes to a close. The words of an opera from Verdi's later years seem (at least from a Wagnerian point of view) to be treated musically with a respect far greater than they had been accorded earlier in the century; but music's apparent accommodations, its detailed attentions, were as ever ministered at a price. As has been hinted at earlier, freely-structured arioso (increasingly prevalent after the 1850s) essentially approaches the words as semantic rather than phonetic/metrical units. True, it tends carefully to preserve accentuation, but at the same time it interprets and articulates, giving key words and phrases their own particular musical weight. For this reason, the natural counterpart to arioso is unstressed, unrhymed verse: poetry that has little tendency toward periodicity and pattern. And it was this prose-like verse that began to dominate the genre as the century progressed. In other words, the old, reassuring links between the poetic and the musical period that had allowed Momigny to "explain" his music through words, that Wagner had theorized about and elevated so persistently, and that Verdi in his middle-period works had used with such startling variety and to such persuasive dramatic effect was finally breaking up. Hence the paradox. Words may seem to be granted more importance on the surface of the music but, as they are, they relinquish their effect on other, deeper aspects of the musical and dramatic structure.

One could of course argue (indeed, it is a frequent critical assumption) that the essential relationship between words and music had not changed, that words began to free themselves from their fixed rhythmic bonds precisely as music was becoming less periodic, more prose-like. But this is to fall into the common trap of assuming that, merely because we habitually describe music in terms of language, the relationship between them is anything other than at base metaphorical. The link between the periodicity of certain poetry and certain music (and hence the musical "form-building" properties of certain libretto traditions) provides one area in which the metaphor is vivid and helpful. But to relate verbal prose to musical prose is on quite another level. Music of the later nineteenth century, however "prosaic," could not respond to the semantic directness of prose in the same way as early nineteenth-century music had been nourished by the periodicity of poetry. Its response, its echo of the word, was to be sure often intense and immediate; but—notwithstanding the much-vaunted "form-building" effect of recurring motives—the sum total of such effects was no substitute for structure. Other methods of formal articulation (some of them more purely musical) and other means of ensuring a degree of stylistic continuity played an increasing part.

THE picture of this incomplete, broken analogy between music and language is a fitting point at which to end—just as it is fitting to leave the progress of opera in the free-for-all of the *fin de siècle*, where each work was forced to create its own aesthetic world out of whatever materials were available: local color, orchestral complexities, philosophical ideas. We seem to have come a long way since Momigny. His was a casual certainty about the way in which words might co-exist with and eventually even "explain" music; and his simple, un-selfconscious creation of a Mozartian *scène lyrique* was unnerving precisely because of its unprepossessing context, its obvious lack of a high artistic purpose. The *fin de siècle*, the age of *Literaturoper*, seems in this sense a comforting point of repose—a fact that in part explains the great attention the period now seems to attract. There, attempts to bring together the verbal and musical systems were typically undertaken with the loftiest of aesthetic intentions and with a minimum of aesthetic compromise. Each blending of words and music was unique: no simple equations between the two could pretend to encompass the mystical creative purpose in hand. Our Wagnerian assumptions about an ideal fusion of the arts can remain unchallenged, no matter what our views of individual successes and failures.

But, as I suggested at the beginning of this essay, the search for and acceptance of distance between two attitudes may not in the end simply lead to confusion and fragmentation. It may lend perspective, causing us to ponder why we find one of them so comparatively strange and the other so "natural." And, at least on the basis of the Verdian examples offered above, one conclusion seems to become insistent. It is that, whatever Momigny's *Cours complet* or Wagner's theories or Verdi's operas may suggest to us (and whether the example we draw is one we choose to nurture or reject), an acceptance of the seriousness of all three means that we can espouse no "ideal" way in which words and music will make drama together, and that we should be careful not to approach the issue with unconscious *a priori* assumptions, to see things in terms of "improvement" from one composer, period, or national school to another. Out of a desire to congratulate our favored opera composers or to find rational explanations of the pleasure they afford us, we may be tempted to repeat the old cliché about a "perfect marriage" of words and music. But, alas (to echo Momigny in an uncharacteristic moment of skepticism), perfect marriages are not of this earth. What is more, even their idealization may prove dispiritingly dull, encouraging us again and again to search across repertories, revealing the same generic jewels, the same types of skillful adaptation between words and music, music and words. The best operas have, for the most part, been read as model unions, as works in which the words and the music function together with the minimum of stress, with the maximum cooperation and good will. But the terms of these value judgments are themselves historical and need not be immutable. It may well be that, as Wagner and the nineteenth century become ever more distant, we will increasingly wish to question the uncertain response that Jérôme-Joseph de Momigny now awakens and, as a result, to approach the works of composers such as Verdi with a greater aesthetic flexibility.

SANDER L. GILMAN

Strauss and the Pervert

The following essay poses a series of questions about the social context of an opera libretto, a composer's intention in selecting a theme, and the cultural significance of setting a text to music. Its object will be one of the most popular operas of the *fin de siècle*, Richard Strauss's *Salome*, first performed at the Dresden Opera on 9 December 1905. My contention is that composers take into consideration much more than aesthetic appropriateness when selecting an operatic subject. They are aware of the cultural implications of that choice, and of the force that cultural presuppositions have in shaping the audience and drawing it into the work or—perhaps even more important—into the theater.

The problem of Strauss's *Salome* seems trivial at first glance, since the composer, according to his own testimony, simply "purge[d] the piece [i.e. Oscar Wilde's French drama of 1892] of purple passages to such an extent that it became quite a good libretto."[1] Would it not therefore suffice to read the play in order to understand the genesis and content of Strauss's libretto? I hope to demonstrate that more is involved; that the culturally determined reading of any text in its historical (and, indeed, national) context determines its particular meaning. There is a text in this opera, to paraphrase Stanley Fish,[2] but it is a text constructed through the demands of the interpretative community in which it functions.

Some background information is necessary in order to understand the detailed analysis of this context that will follow. Oscar Wilde (1854–1900) had been dead only three years when the Viennese poet Anton Lindner approached Richard Strauss about a libretto based on *Salome*, a project that Strauss merely toyed with, as a potential pendant to his *Feuersnot* (1902).[3] As the break between the "folkloric" *Till Eulenspie-*

[1] "Reminiscences of the First Performance of My Operas" (1942), in *Richard Strauss, Recollections and Reflections*, ed. Willi Schuh, trans. L. J. Lawrence (London, 1953), 150. On the differences between Wilde's text and the libretto, see Ernst Krause, *Richard Strauss: The Man and His Work*, trans. John Coombs (London, 1964), 296–98.

[2] Cf. *Is There a Text in This Class? The Authority of Interpretive Communities* (Cambridge, Mass., 1980), 303ff.

[3] Strauss praises Lindner for having recognized *Salome* as a "covert opera text" in "The History of *Die schweigsame Frau*," printed as an appendix to *A Confidential Matter: The Letters of Richard Strauss and Stefan Zweig, 1931–1935*, ed. Edward E. Lowinsky, trans. Max Knight (Berkeley, 1977), 107. On the general background, see Ludwig Kusche, *Rich-*

gel's Merry Pranks (1895) and the "Nietzschean" *Thus Spake Zarathustra* (1896) suggests, Strauss had already begun to identify with the "moderns" in the programs for his symphonic tone poems. But the break with his attempts to write mock-Wagnerian operas, or at least operas to mock-Wagnerian texts, did not come until after he saw Max Reinhardt's production of Wilde's play in the Kleines Theater in Berlin. A friend (the cellist Heinrich Grünfeld) suggested that the composer use the play for an opera; Strauss answered that he was already at work.[4] It was a decisive moment. In setting Wilde's *Salome* rather than Lindner's adaptation, Strauss discovered the avant-garde and was in turn discovered by them.[5]

According to the composer's recollections in 1942, the idea of setting Wilde's play directly sprang from the belief that "Oriental and Jewish operas lacked true Oriental color and scorching sun."[6] It is important to note the hyphenated phrase "Orient- und Judenoper." Other works in this genre, Biblical operas such as Verdi's *Nabucco* (1842) and Saint-Saëns' *Samson et Dalila* (1877), or post-Biblical works such as Halévy's *La Juive* (1835), lacked the "orientalism" Strauss thought necessary for a "Jewish" topic. His words reflect a concept of the Jew held by two disparate groups in the German-speaking world: anti-Semites who charged that Jews were merely Orientals and would always be outsiders in the West; and early Zionist writers such as Theodor Herzl and Martin Buber. Strauss's acceptance of this form of projection and his association of the Jew with the cultural avant-garde influenced his selection of the *Salome* libretto in a complicated manner. Even the impetus to set Wilde's play derived from a production by a Jewish leader of the dramatic avant-garde, Max Reinhardt, and a suggestion from another Jew, Heinrich Grünfeld, that Wilde's play could provide material for an opera.[7] And

---

ard Strauss im Kulturkarussell der Zeit 1864–1964 (Munich, 1964), 129–50 (with illustrations), and Roland Tenschert, *7 × 7 Variationen über das Thema Richard Strauss* (Vienna, 1944), 91–101.

[4] *Recollections*, 150. The German text is in Richard Strauss, *Betrachtungen und Erinnerungen*, ed. Willi Schuh (Zürich, 1949), 224–29. See Norman Del Mar, *Richard Strauss: A Critical Commentary on His Life and Works* (1962; rpt. Ithaca, N.Y., 1986), I, 243.

[5] On the popularity of Salome at the turn of the century, see E. W. Bredt, "Die Bilder der Salome," *Die Kunst*, 7 (1903–1904), 249–54; Hugo Daffner, *Salome: Ihre Gestalt in Geschichte und Kunst* (Munich, 1912); Reimarus Secundus, *Geschichte der Salome von Cato bis Oscar Wilde*, 3 vols. (Leipzig, [1907–1909]). More recent overviews: Helen Grace Zagona, *The Legend of Salome and the Principle of Art for Art's Sake* (Geneva, 1960), and Mechthilde Hatz, "Frauengestalten des Alten Testaments in der bildenden Kunst von 1850 bis 1918: Eva, Dalila, Judith, Salome" (diss., Heidelberg, 1972).

[6] References to Lindner and Grünfeld (but not to Reinhardt, a non-person in 1942) are in Strauss's *Recollections* (see n. 1 above), 150–54.

[7] I apply the term "Jew" to an individual only within the strict limits set by anti-Semites

finally there is the link between Wilde, the homosexual poet, and the Jews, representatives of the avant-garde.

The following discussion examines three major contexts for the interpretation of Strauss's libretto: (I) the contemporary image of Oscar Wilde in German-speaking countries as the homosexual writer *par excellence*; (II) the reflection of this image in Strauss's presentation of the opera's characters as stage Jews, with their connotation of disease; (III) Strauss's creation of his audience in light of these two factors. I cannot, of course, present an exhaustive reading of the libretto, but I shall attempt to reconstruct a set of cultural presuppositions about disease and difference that existed in Germany and Austria at the turn of the century, and inquire how these presuppositions shaped the choice of the libretto and its contemporary interpretation.[8]

I. THE PERVERT: WILDE IN GERMANY

Wilde's *Salome*, written in French for Sarah Bernhardt in 1891 and 1892, had been performed in Paris only in 1896 (and without the Divine Sarah). But Wilde's *oeuvre* had an extraordinary success in Germany during the early twentieth century. Between 1900 and 1934 there were more than 250 publications of Wilde's work (more than any other British author except Shakespeare); and during the 1903–1904 season alone 248 performances of his dramas were seen on the German stage, including 111 performances of *Salome*.[9] While Reinhardt's production was not the German premiere (that took place in 1901 at the Freie Literarische Vereinigung in Breslau), it was by far the most famous of the period.[10]

Wilde's popularity grew in Germany almost in inverse proportion to its decline in Britain following his trials and conviction on charges of homosexuality. The trials, held in London during 1895–96, were reported in detail. A long, factual report ran in the liberal newspaper *Die Zeit*, and two extraordinary essays were published in the socialist magazine *Die Neue Zeit* by the exiled politician Eduard Bernstein.[11] The first of these

of the period. Cf. the standard anti-Semitic reference work, Theodor Fritsch, *Handbuch der Judenfrage*, 38th ed. (Leipzig, 1935).

[8] This essay is indebted to Norbert Kohl, *Oscar Wilde: Das literarische Werk zwischen Provokation und Anpassung* (Heidelberg, 1982), and J. E. Chamberlin, *Ripe Was the Drowsy Hour: The Age of Oscar Wilde* (New York, 1977).

[9] Peter Funke, *Oscar Wilde in Selbstzeugnissen und Bilddokumenten* (Reinbek, 1969), 7.

[10] More than a hundred reviews of and articles on this production are preserved in the Max Reinhardt Archive of the State University of New York at Binghamton.

[11] *Die Zeit* (15 June 1895), signed by "Dr. Handl"; and Eduard Bernstein, "Aus Anlass eines Sensationsprozess" and "Die Beurteilung des widernormalen Geschlechtsverkehrs," *Die Neue Zeit*, 2 (1894–95), 171–76, 228–33. On the image of Wilde before the trials, see

stresses the popular British image of Wilde as the effete aesthete; the second presents Bernstein's thesis concerning the nature of homosexuality, arguing that only complex societies view homosexuality as deviant. It was a "commonplace" in the British attack on Wilde "that with increased wealth and luxury sexual excesses increase" (230). This popular equation, which Bernstein opposes, formed the basis for the German conservative attack on Wilde as a product of British capitalism. The Socialists, in contrast, generally supported the cause of homosexual emancipation in Germany.[12] Wilde thus became part of the litmus test between the right, which condemned him as the representative of British decay, and the left, which saw the persecution of homosexuality as a sign of the inherent hypocrisy of German society.

Bernstein was arguing against writers such as the conservative commentator Moeller van den Bruck, who used Wilde's homosexuality to condemn British imperialism.[13] Wilde is van den Bruck's prime example of British degeneration, an unnatural reaction to the materialism that dominates the British soul. His "sexual insanity" (van den Bruck uses the English words to stress the nature of this disease) is quintessentially British, typical of the ideology of colonialism:

Morally this people does not know what else to do. It seeks a replacement for morals in eccentricity. The proverbial British brutalization of the masses is nothing more than misdirected sexuality in a society deeply embedded in the perversions of all quarters of the earth. (251)

Bernstein's response stresses the parallels between the persecution of Wilde and the potential for similar public persecution of homosexuals under German imperial law, not recognizing the racist subtext of the conservative's argument. This emerges in van den Bruck's image of the homosexual's discourse, the "dissipation of thoughts in sophistry," a term long used to represent the discourse of the Jews (250). The British, seen as the most degenerate nation in Europe, become by extension the new Jews of Europe.[14] Nietzsche's Antichrist[ian] had already denounced this view:

Max Nordau, *Degeneration* (New York, 1895), 318–22, which speaks of Wilde as an aesthete and mentions "his buffoon mummery," but does not use him as an exemplary figure for the author's conservative attack on "degeneration."

[12] For general background, see James D. Steakley, *The Homosexual Emancipation Movement in Germany* (New York, 1975).

[13] Rpt. in Moeller van den Bruck, *Die Zeitgenossen: Die Geister—Die Menschen* (Minden, 1906), 238–56.

[14] According to Barbara W. Tuchman, *Bible and Sword: England and Palestine from the*

The Jews are the antithesis of all decadents: they have had to *represent* decadents to the point of illusion; with a non plus ultra of histrionic genius they have known how to place themselves at the head of all movements of decadence (as the Christianity of Paul), in order to create something out of them that is stronger than any *Yes-saying* party of life.[15]

Nonetheless, the association remained in German conservative thought. The trials of Oscar Wilde also had a significant impact in making German homosexuals realize the importance of repealing the law against homosexual activity, which had been in force from 1872, continuing older laws in the Prussian Criminal Code. In 1896, Oscar Sero wrote a detailed account of Wilde's trial in a monograph published in Leipzig by Max Spohr, who served as the major outlet for popular as well as scholarly works on homosexuality.[16] Sero appends to his account of the trial a long "dialogue" on the treatment of and attitude toward homoerotic activity in Germany, repeating Bernstein's parallel between British and German society. The appearance in 1896 of Adolf Brand's homophile periodical *Der Eigene* was to no little degree stimulated by the trials of Wilde, as was the founding in 1897 (by Max Spohr, the sexologist Magnus Hirschfeld, and the civil servant Erich Oberg) of the first homosexual emancipation organization, the Wissenschaftlich–Humanitäres Kommittee. In spite of its initially broad political base, the homosexual emancipation movement quickly became identified with the avant-garde (and therefore Jewish) left. The image of the Wilde trials in Germany was shaped by individuals who were seen as liberals—but also very clearly understood as Jews (especially Eduard Bernstein and Magnus Hirschfeld). This link also remained in the popular mind.

Much as he had become the quintessential dandy of the 1880s, after the trials Wilde became the exemplar of the persecuted artist—persecuted by aesthetic conservatism in avant-garde Germany, represented by Victorian (read: Wilhelminian) prudery. In the obituary of Wilde published in Magnus Hirschfeld's *Jahrbuch für sexuelle Zwischenstufen*, for example, "Numa Prätorius" (the pseudonym of lawyer Eugen Wilhelm) centers his account on the trials and their impact in Germany. He represents

---

Bronze Age to Balfour (New York, 1984), this link was made overt in the conception that in the *Realpolitik* of the Middle East "Jews [were] a possible *avantgarde* of England's imperialism" (212).

[15] Friedrich Nietzsche, *Sämtliche Werke: Kritische Studienausgabe* (Berlin, 1980), VI, 192–93. Cited, in Walter Kaufmann's translation, from my essay "Nietzsche, Heine and the Otherness of the Jew," in *Studies in Nietzsche and the Judaeo-Christian Tradition*, ed. James C. O'Flaherty, Timothy F. Sellner, and Robert M. Helm (Chapel Hill, N.C., 1985), 206–25.

[16] *Der Fall Wilde und das Problem der Homosexualität: Ein Prozeß und ein Interview* (Leipzig, 1896).

Wilde as an artist persecuted by the state for his sexual orientation and his membership in the intellectual avant-garde.[17] By 1905 the merger of artist and works is complete. Hugo von Hofmannsthal sees Wilde as the symbolist poet whose life and art are inseparable.[18] Wilde takes on this role not merely because of the nature of his work but also because his life was created from a series of symbolic masks, including the final mask of degradation, Sebastian Melmoth (Wilde's pseudonym after his release from prison and escape to the Continent). Hofmannsthal, following Wilde's own suggestion in "The Truth of Masks," reads nature, even the nature of the poet, through the work of art. For Hofmannsthal, "Wilde's essence and his fate were one and the same. He approached a catastrophe with steps like Oedipus, the seeing-blind" (89). Significantly, the reference to Oedipus evokes the essential symbolic actor in the fantasy of the *fin de siècle*, representing sexual perversion, incest, and divine punishment.

This image of the persecuted artist doubtless received its most elaborate presentation by Karl Kraus in a series of essays in the influential periodical *Die Fackel*.[19] In December 1903 (about the time that Strauss became seriously interested in the Salome theme), Kraus opened his discussion of Wilde with a polemic against a German book on sex in Britain:

The uncomplicated German can only gaze upward jealously at the British nation, so far above the Continent in the culture of sexual perversion and the development of sexual hypocrisy, which, as well as murder, can bring forth the genius of Oscar Wilde, and which has flagellation-bordellos and laws that can threaten the nuances of sexual activity with a ten-year jail sentence.[20]

In addition to revealing parallels between British sexual attitudes and those in contemporary Viennese society, Kraus—like Bernstein before him—also introduces a term central to understanding the complex links between Wilde, Strauss, the Jews, and the avant-garde: *Perversität*. Kraus's indirect citation reveals that he is using a term from contemporary discourse on difference. The category of the "perverted," not merely the unnatural but the anti-natural, provides another link in our understanding of Wilde's reception in the opening decade of the twentieth century. At the close of that issue of *Die Fackel*, Kraus reports two items of

---

[17] 3 (1901), 265–74.

[18] See *Die prosaischen Schriften Gesammelt* (Berlin, 1917), II, 85–94. On the general context, see Thomas A. Kovach, *Hofmannsthal and Symbolism: Art and Life in the Work of a Modern Poet* (New York, 1985).

[19] The only essay on this topic is narrowly focused: Hugh Salvesen, "Zu den Wilde-Übersetzungen in der 'Fackel,' " *Kraus Hefte*, 24 (1982), 5–11.

[20] *Die Fackel*, 148 (2 December 1903), 19–20.

Viennese gossip: anti-Semitic attempts, abetted by the city government (with its publicly anti-Semitic mayor, Karl Lueger), to limit the promotion of Jewish civil servants; and the granting of permission to perform Wilde's *Salome* only "if the head of John the Baptist, which Salome brings in, is covered with a cloth" ("Too dumb!" Kraus retorts).[21] This apparently random juxtaposition illustrates how closely Kraus—Jew, cripple, aesthete—relates such varied categories of difference as anti-Semitism and homophobia, the Jews and Oscar Wilde.

Kraus devoted the first fourteen pages of the 1903 Christmas issue of *Die Fackel* to a detailed review (and review of the reviews) of *Salome* at the Deutsches Volkstheater, which had circumvented Austrian censorship by inviting Adele Hartwig's production from the Neues Theater in Berlin.[22] The guest appearance, which opened on 12 December 1903, was a *succès de scandale*. Kraus begins his review in typical fashion with an attack on Friedrich Schütz's review of the play in the *Neue Freie Presse*, a paper edited by Kraus's *bête noire*, Moritz Benedikt. It is important to read the opening of Kraus's review in light of the rhetoric to which he is responding and in which he clothes his understanding of the play:

"When critics disagree the artist is in accord with himself," wrote Wilde in his wonderful preface to *The Picture of Dorian Gray*. In the arena of his noble culture of the spirit, the argument of proletarian idea-mongers can only be heard as the Yiddish-accented German [*Gemauschel*] of the Pharisees, though in this case mitigated by the excellent direction of the play *Salome*. I do not have the pleasure of enjoying works of art as an observer. A fatal sharpness of hearing forces me to listen to the voices that come from the depths, and I cannot pray before I curse the sacrilege. Like the *Gemauschel* of the Pharisees in *Salome*, "One sees that he is not the Elias!," someone cries out who has forced himself, gesticulating, into the front row and whose name is Friedrich Schütz. (1)

Kraus's main concern is the role of the Jews, represented by their discourse, the language of the "Pharisees" in the debate before Herod. According to Schütz, Wilde was merely an anti-Semite, a "Briten-Goi" who attacks Jews in the basest manner. Kraus quotes Schütz's assertion that the Jews are reduced to "a quintet of tottering Jews represented with ugly gestures that fulfill the deepest sense of subjugation," adding that

The direction of the Volkstheater does even more and "lets these Hebrews *mauscheln*." And that has to be inflicted on Mr. Schütz, for

[21] Ibid., 31.
[22] *Die Fackel*, 150 (23 December 1903), 1–14.

whom every work of art must have but one law: "There is no Jewish ill-breeding." (9)

Even Kraus admits that the use of *Gemauschel* on the Viennese stage was tasteless: "Indeed, the jargon of the group of Pharisees should have been moderated—at least with an eye toward the audience at the premiere" (9). The emphasis on *Gemauschel* illustrates, as I have suggested elsewhere, the double-bind of a Jew writing in German.[23] The *Gemauschel* of Wilde's Jews points to the incompetence of a specific group of Jews, the Eastern Yiddish-speakers from the provinces of the Austro-Hungarian Empire, parvenus onto whom Viennese Jews projected their anxieties. These anxieties arose from the charge—popularized by Wagner's "Judaism [*Judentum*] in Music" and repeated by anti-Semites of various persuasions[24]—that all Jews (not merely the newly arrived) did not, and could not, command German, the discourse of high culture. Kraus separates himself from those designated by this charge with his own "translation" of Wilde's characterization of these argumentative figures. According to Kraus, Wilde's stage Jews are not merely "Juden" (that designation, read as a racial category by a German reader, would also include Karl Kraus); they are "Pharisees," with all of that term's negative connotations in Christian-German rhetoric.

Although Kraus's review condemns the German (i.e. Berlin) version for unnecessarily altering Wilde's intent, it condemns even more the thin-skinned critic for the *Neue Freie Presse* (a journal that both anti-Semites and Jews regarded as "Jewish") for seeing an attack in every representation of the Jews. Kraus mockingly asks Schütz to allow some "perverted" views, so that the theater can serve up peacock's tongues as well as peasant dumplings [*Bauernknödel*] (12). The word "perverted" in this context ironically links the defender of the Jews (Schütz/Benedikt) with the "perversion" of homosexuality that he defends. "Perversion" becomes a positive label of libertarian aesthetics, with which Kraus identifies himself. He therefore closes his review with the acerbic observation that the clerical newspaper *Vaterland* has followed Benedikt's *Neue Freie Presse* in condemning the play. Both Catholics and Jews conspire to damn true art; Kraus defends the "perverted."

KRAUS's view is no more an unambiguous affirmation of the "perverted" label for the cultural avant-garde than Nietzsche's aphorism glorifying the "degenerate" as the sole image of the true artist. On 4 January 1904

---

[23] See my *Jewish Self-Hatred: Anti-Semitism and the Hidden Language of the Jews* (Baltimore, 1986), esp. 209–60.

[24] See Jacob Katz, *Richard Wagner: Vorbote des Antisemitismus* (Königstein/Taunus, 1985), as well as *Jewish Self-Hatred*, 209–11.

Kraus followed his review with a further attack on Schütz entitled "The Picture of Dorian Gray (Toward a Picture of Friedrich Schütz)," which again begins with a paraphrase of the homophobic rhetoric of the period:

In that rag, the advertising pages of which are open to the offering of every perversion and whose owners in a notorious manner financially benefit from the procuring of pederastic contacts, a certain F. Sch. has fumed about Oscar Wilde in a moral wrath.[25]

Kraus begins by condemning the homophobic Schütz for writing for a mere homosexual rag. The Jew who condemns the homosexual is not above pandering to (and for) him. The importance of Kraus's statement lies in his ambiguous use of the term "perversion," applying it not only to the homosexual but also to the Jewish press. Jews such as Moritz Benedikt are no better than their own image of the homosexual.

The image of Oscar Wilde and *Salome* in the *fin-de-siècle* press thus ties together a string of apparently unrelated qualities: an anti-British attitude, a sense of sexual pathology, the image of an author as identical with his work, popular images of the language of deviance. All are linked through the association of accepted stereotypes of the Jews with qualities of difference ascribed to the homosexual. This occurred, moreover, during a period of growing concern over homosexual scandals among the nobility and the upper class in Germany and Austria, such as the Krupp scandal of 1902.[26] The awareness of difference—sexual, cultural, racial—set the stage for the most notable of these scandals, involving Wilhelm II and his friend Philipp Eulenburg, which broke in 1906, shortly after the premiere of Strauss's *Salome*.

II. *Salome* AND THE PERVERT

The reception of Wilde and his play in Germany enables us to understand the extent to which contemporary reception of the opera was shaped by that representation of difference labeled "perversion." The term had been used ubiquitously to designate Wilde as well as his drama, and it soon became associated with the opera. Strauss was perfectly aware of the implications of selecting a text by Wilde,[27] and it is not surprising that dur-

---

[25] "Das Bildnis Dorian Gray's (Zum Bildnis des Friedrich Schütz)," *Die Fackel*, 151 (4 January 1904), 18–23.

[26] On the political background to the homosexual scandals and their close association with images of Jewish discourse (especially the idea of journalism as a form of Jewish discourse), see Isabel V. Hull, *The Entourage of Kaiser Wilhelm II, 1888–1918* (Cambridge, 1982), 57–145, and James D. Steakley, "Iconography of a Scandal: Political Cartoons and the Eulenberg Affair," *Studies in Visual Communication*, 9 (1983), 20–51.

[27] In 1948 he remarked on the publication of Hesketh Pearson's biography of Wilde,

ing rehearsals for the first performance in Dresden the producer required the singer cast as Salome to play the role full of "perversion and outrage," a demand that she, "the wife of a Saxon Burgomaster," refused to obey.[28] A review of the dress rehearsal in the *Dresdner Nachrichten* (10 December 1905) begins with a reading of Wilde's play as "raw actions, the exaggeration of everything that Wilde's text demands of normal feelings by its perverted actions," but adds that "the disgusting nature of the material is transfigured through the music."[29] The idea that Strauss's music redeems the perversion of Wilde's text occurs again and again, but the charge of perversion remained. When Gustav Mahler, head of the Viennese Court Opera, submitted Strauss's opera to the court censor for approval, the rejection notice not only objected to the representation of Biblical characters on stage but also rejected the drama—in light of the opposition and critical reaction to the 1903 production of Wilde's play—as a work of sexual pathology:

> Aside from the fact that the representation of actions from the New Testament raises difficulties for the Court Theater, the presentation of perverted sensuality, as incorporated in the figure of Salome, is morally repugnant.[30]

The first scholarly reactions to the opera, such as Eugen Schmitz's monograph of 1907 on Strauss, defend it against the accusation that "Wilde's *Salome* is an artistic representation of perversion."[31] Oscar Bie's monograph of 1906 asks whether it is "possible to represent perversion," answering: "Childish catchwords—perversion and decadence."[32] But Strauss's French correspondent, the novelist Romain Rolland (whom he had asked to check the French version of the libretto), launched a series of attacks on Wilde and his "literary jargon."[33] In 1907, after the initial performance of *Salome* in Paris, Rolland wrote Strauss a long and detailed condemnation of the text as

> not worthy of you [. . .] it has a nauseous and sickly atmosphere about it: it exudes vice and literature [. . .] Wilde's Salome and all

---

"How times have changed!" *Richard Strauss—Willi Schuch: Briefwechsel* (Zürich, 1969), 153.

[28] *Recollections* (see n. 1 above), 151.

[29] The review is reprinted in Friedrich von Schuch, *Richard Strauss / Ernst von Schuch und Dresdens Oper* (Leipzig, n.d.), 72–73.

[30] From Clemens Höslinger, " 'Salome' und Ihr Österreichisches Schicksal 1905 bis 1918," *Österreichische Musikzeitschrift*, 32 (1977), 301.

[31] *Richard Strauss als Musikdramatiker* (Munich, 1907), 45.

[32] *Die moderne Musik und Richard Strauss* (Berlin, 1906), 69.

[33] Trans. Rollo Myers, *Richard Strauss and Romain Rolland: Correspondence* (Berkeley, 1968), 37.

those who surround her are unwholesome, unclean, hysterical or al-
coholic beings, stinking of sophisticated and perfumed corruption. I
fear [. . .] that you have been caught by the mirage of German decadent literature. However talented these poets may be [. . .] the difference between them and you is the difference between an artist who
is great (or famous) at one time (a fashion)—and one who is, who
should be, great for all time. [. . .] You are worthy of better things
than *Salome*.   (83)

The resemblance to Bernstein's remark about the stereotypical association of sexual perversion and increased sophistication and luxury is unmistakable.

Rolland echoes contemporary views of the homosexual found in the
popular press during the so-called Eulenburg scandal, but he also reflects
the popular (and literary) perception of Jewish sexual pathology. The
connection is made in one of the pamphlets that circulated in 1906 as a
result of the premiere of Strauss's opera,[34] labeling the Wilde play an example of a "medical" [gynecological?] theme in Biblical clothing (16); a
play that reveals the inner workings of the author's mind: "The play
should be called *Oscar Wilde* rather than *Salome*" (17). While condemning Wilde's "bigoted fellow countrymen" (16) for their persecution of the
poet, it still damns Wilde's immorality and his creation of this "song of
perverted love" (23). Turning to the opera, it claims that "if you tell me
what you set to music, I'll tell you what you are" (24), and proceeds to
link Strauss with another figure to illustrate the relationship between the
theme of a work of art and its true essence—Max Liebermann (24–26),
the dean of German Impressionism and the most visible "Jewish" artist
of the avant-garde, who had suggested that art is form and is not dependent on subject matter. The linking of Strauss with the "Jewish" avant-
garde further labels both as diseased: only "sick artists produce sick art"
(27), and their disease is Jewish modernism.

If homosexuals and their advocates, the Jews, are perverted, then so are
their fictional characters; perversion becomes the label that joins all forms
of sexual deviance, linking heterosexuality and homosexuality. Salome's
"perversion" has nothing to do with homosexuality but, rather, with the
representation of a sexual hysteric and the source of her neurosis: she
would have represented, in a German reading of 1905, a study in hysteria.
The symptom, sadism (represented by her desire to possess a fetish, the
severed head of a man who has rejected her), has its origin in the trauma
of her attempted seduction by her stepfather, Herod. Just as Salome desires to possess the eyes, hair, and lips of Jochanaan from the beginning
of the opera, Herod exhibits a fetishistic wish to possess the cup from

---

[34] H. Ernstmann, *Salomé an den deutschen Hofbühnen* (Berlin, 1906).

316

which Salome drinks or the fruit she eats. A simple case for the master solver of cases of hysteria, Sigmund Freud:[35] Salome suffers from memories, memories acted out for the audience in Herod's attempts to seduce her. Is Salome then perverted because she is a victim who in turn victimizes, or because she is a mentally ill hysteric whose signs, symptoms, and etiology are clearly present? This would, of course, be no more than a superficial reading of the libretto.

Actually, Salome is perverted because she serves as the audience's focus for a set of representations of difference, all of which are understood as perverted. These include the signs and symptoms as well as the resultant psychosexual pathology, which further reflect Strauss's sophisticated understanding of his ideal audience and their self-representation. There is one social group Strauss would have desired for his ideal audience, a group with roots in seduction and incest, and one understood by *fin-de-siècle* medicine as especially at risk for hysteria: the Jews.[36] Contemporary clinical psychiatry assumed that Jews were prone to mental illnesses such as neurasthenia and hysteria. The latter had its source in Jewish sexual selectivity, which European medicine understood in eugenic terms as "inbreeding." Jews, both male and female, are hysterics because they indulge in perverted sexuality; the signs and symptoms are clearly marked on their physiognomy. But incest was not only a source of disease—it was also a crime. There is a complex literature that attempts to document or refute the special nature of Jewish criminal sexuality, the higher incidence of "moral crimes" among Jews.[37] The sexual "perversions" of the Jews have both a medical and a legal dimension and are understood as parallel to the "perversions" of homosexuals.

As the contemporary reception suggests, Strauss clearly provided his audience with a set of signs and symptoms that enabled them to understand his work as a "Jew-opera" (*Judenoper*) about Jewish sexuality and criminal incest, a reading carefully prepared by his adaptation and setting of the play. As is the case with almost any transposition of a drama into a libretto, Strauss pared down Wilde's text, cutting it almost in half and removing peripheral characters such as Tigellius and Salome's slaves. Al-

[35] The reference is to Freud's and Breuer's *Studies in Hysteria* (1895).

[36] See my "The Madness of the Jews," *Difference and Pathology: Stereotypes of Sexuality, Race and Madness*, 2nd ed. (Ithaca, N.Y., 1986), 150–162, and Jan Goldstein, "The Wandering Jew and the Problem of Psychiatric Anti-Semitism in Fin-de-Siècle France," *Journal of Contemporary History*, 20 (1985), 521–52.

[37] See the anonymous *Der Juden Antheil am Vebrechen: Auf Grund der amtlichen Statistik über die Thätigkeit der Schwurgerichte, in vergleichender Darstellung mit den christlichen Confessionen* (Berlin, 1881); Ludwig Fuld, *Das jüdische Verbrecherthum: Eine Studie über den Zusammenhang zwischen Religion und Kriminalität* (Leipzig, 1885); and S. Löwenfeld, *Die Wahrheit über der Juden Antheil am Verbrechen: Auf Grund amtlicher Statistik* (Berlin, 1881).

though he reduced the appearance of the Jews to one major scene, they first appear in musical form with a leitmotif during the opening scene of the opera. Narraboth, Herod's guard, observes: "How beautiful is the Princess Salome tonight" (Wie schön ist die Prinzessin Salome heute Abend!). A din breaks out in the banquet hall: Strauss labels a subsidiary motif in the cacophony as "howling" (*heulend*). It appears as the first soldier turns to the second and asks: "What an uproar! Who are those wild beasts howling?" (Was für ein Aufruhr! Was sind das für wilde Tiere, die da heulen?). And the second soldier replies: "The Jews. They're always like that. They're disputing about their religion" (Die Juden. Sie sind immer so. Sie streiten über ihre Religion).[38] The music later reappears as one of the themes characterizing Jewish discourse, depicting it as aggressively argumentative. Strauss is hardly subtle in his musical representation, associating the Jews' leitmotif with one particular instrumental sonority, the thin, whining sound of the oboe. He also brings the "howl-

EXAMPLE 1

[38] *The Complete Works of Oscar Wilde* (Garden City, N.J., 1923), IX, 106.

ing" cacophony of the orchestra to its peak when the first and second soldiers use the words "howling" and "Jews": Ex. 1.

This theme reappears later to herald the entry of a quintet of Jews who protest at Herod's refusal to turn Jochanaan over to them. The quintet consists, for comic effect, of four high tenors and a low bass. Strauss, as he notes in a letter written in 1935 to Stefan Zweig, caricatures the five Jews as well as Herod, but within a German rather than a British mode of representation.[39] The overt topic of their debate is whether or not Jochanaan has seen (or perhaps even is) the Messiah. A quintet of contradictory themes is presented that borders on unintelligibility, a cacophony that is musically "avant-garde" and also characterizes the Jews' discourse. This cacophony clearly contrasts with the opera's two other principal modes of musical discourse, the shimmering, chromatic world of Salome and the firm diatonicism of Jochanaan. Unlike them, Jews argue

EXAMPLE 2

[39] *A Confidential Matter* (see n. 3 above), 90.

and do not make sense, hence their music is "out of key." This point is made particularly clear when their musical language is set against that of Jochanaan and his followers. Both in the opening scene of the opera and in the quintet, Strauss follows shrill Jewish cacophony with deep-voiced Christian repose and diatonicism. The most extreme juxtaposition comes in the argument over the appearance of the Messiah, in which one Jew (described as "screaming") shows complete disregard for the prevailing "Christian" tonality: Ex. 2.

Herod, to whom the Jews are appealing, becomes part of this debate; it is significant that, like four of the Jews in the quintet, he has a high tenor voice. In fact, throughout the scene, Strauss makes every effort to forge a sense of musical identity between Herod and the Jews. Even after the cacophonous quintet has finished, Herod continues the Jews' musical role, responding with jarring dissonance to the comforting diatonicism that announces Jesus's power to raise the dead: Ex. 3. The message is clear: Herod is (musically) another Jew.

The discourse of the Jews would have been marked for Strauss's audience not only by their "howling" and "screaming" argumentation, but also by the sexualized nature of their voices. Indeed, Strauss introduces a musical joke on their discourse and sexual identity halfway through the quintet, by placing the highest note in the piece on the word "beschnitten" (circumcised): Ex. 4. The late nineteenth century associated religious circumcision with castration, the unmanning of the Jew by making him a Jew.[40] The high-pitched note points toward this association, as well as that between the Jews' discourse and that of the homosexual, the feminized male.

This theme haunts the pseudoscientific literature written against the Jews during the nineteenth and early twentieth centuries, and its most representative work became a topic of discussion just as Strauss was setting Wilde's text. Otto Weininger's *Sex and Character*, published posthumously after the author's suicide in 1903, was seen as a major scientific contribution to the discussion of human psychology. It sought to create parallel categories of difference, showing that all Jews are merely women. Discourse for Weininger is an important marker of difference, and the male Jew's song and speech reveal his nature:

> Just as the acuteness of Jews has nothing to do with true power of differentiating, so his shyness about singing or even about speaking in clear positive tones has nothing to do with real reserve. It is a kind of inverted pride; having no true sense of his own worth, he fears being made ridiculous by his singing or his speech.[41]

[40] See *Difference and Pathology* (n. 36 above), 33–35.
[41] Cited from the English translation (London, 1906), 324.

EXAMPLE 3

EXAMPLE 4

This view finds its clearest representation in the unclear language—
Mauscheln—spoken by comic Jews on the *fin-de-siècle* stage. By the
twentieth century, this becomes one of the stereotypical signs of the Jews'

321

language: "one says that he *mauschelt*. His voice often breaks."[42] In Strauss's opera the break is signified by the nature of the musical voices. Herod is thus as much of a Jew as is the disputatious quintet, his discourse signifying his incestuous sexuality. Strauss's audience would have heard in the high-pitched, breaking voice an audible sign of the Jews' difference, a sign that would have been understandable given the "perverted" nature of the sexuality represented on stage.

Strauss's setting of the discourse of the Jew is central to any reading of the opera, the key to the incestuous father and child, the seducer and object of seduction, the hysteric and her father-surrogate. In fact, Thomas Mann had just made such a link overt in his tale of mock-Wagnerian passion, "Wälsungenblut" (1905), in which the use of Yiddish by the incestuous twins marks them as Jews of the cultural elite.[43] Although Mann subsequently suppressed the "Yiddish" characterization because of the objections of his father-in-law, the Jewish educator Alfred Pringsheim, it was a basic cultural assumption that the upper class, especially Jews, were perverts, and that perversion took the form of incest. Incest was the ultimate form of sexual selectivity, of "inbreeding." Popular medical knowledge of the period believed that "inbreeding" led to a weakening of the stock and to illnesses such as hysteria. This is the subtext of Freud and Breuer's *Studies in Hysteria* (1895), a fact that accounts for the Jewish authors' suppression of the religious identity of their patients even though it looms relatively large in their case notes.[44]

Here the link with the idea of "perversion" incorporated in the figure of Oscar Wilde finally becomes overt. According to late nineteenth-century medicine and popular culture, the feminizing "break of the voice" is one of the standard stigmata of degeneration borne by the homosexual.[45]

---

[42] Although this citation is from the Nazi child's introduction to Jew hatred, *Die Giftpilz* (The Poison Mushroom), published by Julius Streicher in 1938, it represents a tradition that reaches back to the representation of the stage Jew in the late nineteenth century. See *Jewish Self-Hatred* (n. 23 above), 312.

[43] See *Jewish Self-Hatred*, 292. "Perversion" is also associated with the cultural elite and Wagner. Romain Rolland pointed out to Strauss that "the incest in the *Walküre* is a thousand times more healthy than the conjugal and legitimate love in such and such a dirty Parisian comedy, which I don't want to name" (83). Oskar Panizza also noted ironically the homoeroticism of Wagner and its relationship to actual homosexual practices: "Bayreuth und die Homosexualität," *Die Gesellschaft*, 11 (1895), 88–92.

[44] See Breuer's notes to the case of "Anna O." in Albrecht Hirschmüller, *Physiologie und Psychoanalyse im Leben und Werk Josef Breuers* (Bern, 1978).

[45] See, for example, Richard Krafft-Ebing, *Psychopathia Sexualis mit besonderer Berücksichtigung der conträren Sexualempfindung: Eine klinisch-forensische Studie* (Stuttgart, 1893), which regularly records the nature of the patient's voice. On the popular signs of degeneration, see Nordau, *Degeneration* (n. 11 above), 17–18. For an overview, see *Degeneration: The Dark Side of Progress*, ed. J. E. Chamberlin and Sander L. Gilman (New York, 1985).

In the work of Krafft-Ebing, Tarnowski, Moll, and others, homosexuality was generally understood as an innate biological error manifested not only in "perverted" acts but also in visible signs. One of the most evident degenerative stigmata, cited in almost all case reports, is the quality of the voice. The change of voice signaled the masculinization of the male; continued breaking of the voice indicated a male's inability to assume any but a "perverted" sexual identity.

But *fin-de-siècle* nosological systems also accepted the theory that those who become homosexuals, usually through seduction, have some inborn predisposition to homosexuality that may announce itself through the stigmata of degeneration. The tension between two models of homosexuality, based on "nature" and "nurture," also had a parallel in attitudes toward race. It was assumed that the stigmata were "real" signs of perversion, whether present or future, endogenous or exogenous; and this assumption was internalized, often in the most complex manner, by those who were stereotyped. Highly acculturated German and Austrian Jews would have projected the stigmata of difference onto a subgroup of Eastern Jews, understood as quarrelsome, materialistic, and speaking with a different intonation—speaking *Mauschel*. Their degeneration is further manifested in perverted sexuality. Thus Herod is understood to be an Eastern Jew because he is rich and materialistic and his voice breaks; he tries to seduce his stepdaughter because he is an Oriental Jew in this "Orient- und Judenoper." Salome is an hysteric, not merely because her stepfather wishes to seduce her but because Eastern Jews are particularly at risk for such forms of mental illness. Two models of the East are combined in the perspective of the German-Jewish observer.

Wilde had indicated that Jews are at special risk for the madness that results from incest, for they permit a form of marriage—parodied in his play—that fascinated Christians by its perversion. An unmarried Jewish man was required to marry his brother's widow, a practice that as early as the seventeenth century was one of the major focuses of Christian accusations of Jewish incest.[46] This type of marriage appears in Jochanaan's opening solo with its charge of incest against the house of Herod, a charge substantiated more in the relationship between father and stepdaughter than between Herod and Herodias. The parodic element comes with the reason for Herod's "incest," his Claudius-like murder of Salome's father and marriage to her mother. All Jews in the court are, from a Christian point of view, marked by the stain of incest and thus of madness. They are as clearly marked by the signs of innate, biological degeneracy as are

---

[46] See Hjalmar J. Nordin, "Die eheliche Ethik der Juden zur Zeit Jesu," trans. W. A. Kastner and Gustave Lewi, *Beiwerke zum Studium der Anthropophyteia*, 4 (1911), 99–104, for a rebuttal of the general discussions of the Levirate marriage circulating at the turn of the century. See also *Jewish Self-Hatred* (n. 23 above), 74.

the homosexuals, whatever the cause of their deviance. And both groups reveal their criminal perversion not only through their sexual activities, but also through their high or breaking voices.

III. STRAUSS CREATES HIS AUDIENCE

Strauss seems to have read Wilde against the German grain, subversively contravening one of the basic tenets of German anti-Semitism, which saw the Jews of the Bible, especially of the New Testament, as different from contemporary Jewry. As early as the German Enlightenment, there had been complicated attempts to separate the discourse of the New Testament from the language of the Jews heard in the streets of Frankfurt and Berlin.[47] The British, however, accepted the continuity of contemporary Jewry from the Bible, including the New Testament.[48] This was often understood positively, as when Christian Hebraists persuaded Oliver Cromwell to readmit the Jews to England as part of a Puritan theology of Biblical continuity, or negatively, as in the anti-Semitic doggerel written by one of the founders of the Fabian movement, G.D.H. Cole.[49] On the other hand, Houston Stewart Chamberlain, Wagner's son-in-law, argued in one of the most influential presentations of the science of race during the nineteenth century that the modern Jews had little or nothing to do with the pure race inhabiting the Near East during the time of Jesus.[50]

What sort of audience would Strauss have had in mind when he selected Oscar Wilde's play, with its references to disease and difference coming together under the term "perversion"? Why should Strauss signal to his audience that this is an opera about rich, decadent Jews, their crimes, and their perversions? And why should he accept a model of the Jews that provided a sense of continuity between the Jews of the past and the Jews of the present? How did Strauss construct his audience when he undertook *Salome*?[51]

---

[47] See K.W.F. Grattenauer, *Über die physische und moralische Verfassung der heutigen Juden* (Leipzig, 1791). On the general background see Jacob Katz, *From Prejudice to Destruction: Anti-Semitism, 1700–1933* (Cambridge, Mass., 1980), 51–62.

[48] Barbara W. Tuchman's *Bible and Sword* (see n. 14 above) can be read as the British parallel to Katz's history of anti-Semitism.

[49] See Anne Fremantle, *This Little Band of Prophets: The British Fabians* (New York, 1959), 204.

[50] Houston Stewart Chamberlain, *Foundations of the Nineteenth Century*, trans. John Lees, 2 vols. (London, 1910), I, 388–89.

[51] I am playing with Strauss's own repudiation of the Nazi concept of "Volk" in the famous letter of 17 June 1935 to the "Jewish" poet Stefan Zweig, which was seized and delivered to the Gestapo. Strauss ironically attacks the solidarity Zweig shows with other victims of anti-Semitism as "Jewish obstinacy" and "pride of race," while condemning the Nazi view that true art must be "Aryan": "the people [*Volk*] exist for me only at the moment they become audience." *A Confidential Matter* (see n. 3 above), 99.

The answer is not as one might imagine. In choosing to set Oscar Wilde's play, Strauss draws on a fundamental ambiguity in German-Jewish self-understanding during the *fin de siècle*. He clearly plays on the increased popularity of Wilde's work, a popularity fostered by Wilde's iconic role among the German avant-garde. But he also echoes the association between the Jews, as defenders of homosexual emancipation, and the "perverted" text of *Salome*. The association of degeneration in Jews and homosexuals creates a category that Strauss's idealized "liberal" (read: Jewish) audience would have understood as the biological result of social prejudice. But they would also have distanced anti-Semitic charges concerning their own perverted nature by projecting these charges onto a subgroup, the Eastern Jews, just as Kraus read Wilde's representation of the "Jews" as a discussion of the "Pharisees." The need for a continuity of images from the New Testament to the present day underlines the Jewish understanding of degeneration as the result of centuries of anti-Jewish attitudes and actions upon Eastern Jews. The conflation of "Oriental" and "Eastern" was one that acculturated Western Jews of the *fin de siècle* made easily. Liberal Jews were not portrayed onstage; it was rather the ancestors of those loud, aggressive, materialistic, incestuous, mad Jews whom the Viennese and Berlin Jews saw every day on streets and in shops; it was the Jews from the East, the embodiment of the anti-Semitic caricatures that haunted the dreams of the assimilated Jews. It was the "Pharisees," already condemned as the "bad" Jews of the New Testament, who now walked the streets of Vienna dressed in their long, black caftans, gesticulating and arguing.

Strauss believed himself to be appealing to such a German-Jewish audience of the avant-garde. He takes a "perverted" text that can also be read as an attack on the nouveau riche, conservative, materialistic, and disputatious (read: Eastern) Jews of his time, accepts the self-hating model of Jewish identity with its pathological image of the Eastern Jew, and presents a text that fulfills all the necessary categories for acceptance by this idealized, self-hating audience. He knew he could not be the new Wagner; this was evident from the reception of both his *Parsifal* (*Guntram*) and his *Meistersinger* (*Feuersnot*).[52] But he could become the creator of new opera for the avant-garde. The Wagnerians by 1905 had clearly allied themselves with the political and cultural anti-Semites, following Wagner's own views. The uneasy alliance between Jewish advocates of Wagner (such as the conductor Hermann Levi) and the non-Jewish Wagnerians had collapsed by the turn of the century, and the house

---

[52] See the early letter to Cosima Wagner, printed under the title "Erlebnis und Bekenntnis des jungen Richard Strauss," *Internationale Mitteilungen: Richard-Strauss-Gesellschaft*, 30 (1961), 1; and A. A. Abert, "Richard Strauss und das Erbe Wagners," *Die Musikforschung*, 27 (1974), 165–71.

organ of the Wagner Society, the *Bayreuther Blätter*, had become a mouthpiece of cultural anti-Semitism.[53] This is not to say that Jews as part of the general public, desiring to share in the German cultural patrimony that defined membership in the middle class for all Germans, did not remain in the Wagner camp. But it was the musical avant-garde, rather than the world of conservative music, that was perceived as Jewish, and to them Strauss directed his appeal.

Strauss read his audience extraordinarily well; with *Salome* he became nothing less than the opera composer of the avant-garde. How he appealed to the ambiguity of the acculturated Jews whom he saw as the source of his potential popularity can be seen in his relationship with Gustav Mahler. For German anti-Semites, Mahler was an essentially "Jewish" composer, even though he was baptized in 1897.[54] As head of the Vienna Court Opera, Mahler was one of Strauss's (and *Salome*'s) strongest supporters in his (unsuccessful) efforts to have the opera produced. The correspondence between the two composers reveals Mahler's unalloyed enthusiasm for the opera and Strauss's energetic desire to see it produced in Vienna. If we look at Mahler's personal correspondence, however, other concerns appear. Prior to his baptism in 1894, Mahler wrote to his sister Justine mocking Strauss as the new cultural "pope," the new Wagner, and suggesting that "[Mahler's] being Jewish is closing all the doors" to advancement.[55] The suspicion that he was less successful than Strauss because of prejudice against him as a Jew echoes in Mahler's behavior after his baptism. He would often ask his wife to "stop him when he emphasized his speech with too much gesticulation."[56] This was clearly a response to having been labeled the arch-Jewish composer, a composer of "Oriental" music.[57]

But there is an even more telling moment in Mahler's internalization of this image. Mahler later characterized a journalist in Paris as being so "perverted" that "Strauss might one day set him to music."[58] Mahler had internalized the negative associations between Jews and homosexuals in *Salome*, a work that overshadowed the first performance of his own Sixth

---

[53] See Peter Gay's essay on Levi in his *Freud, Jews, and Other Germans* (New York, 1978), 189–231.

[54] Strauss, recording Mahler's death in a diary entry for 18 May 1911, refers to him as "der Jude Mahler." Herta Blaukopf, ed., *Gustav Mahler—Richard Strauss: Briefwechsel 1888–1911* (Munich, 1980), 211.

[55] *Briefwechsel*, 152.

[56] Egon Gartenberg, *Mahler: The Man and His Music* (New York, 1978), 47.

[57] See the entries under "Mahler" in Nicolas Slonimsky, ed., *Lexicon of Musical Invective* (New York, 1965).

[58] Alma Mahler Werfel, *Gustav Mahler: Erinnerungen und Briefe* (Amsterdam, 1940), 360.

Symphony. He understood that he remained a Jew, with his own "perverted" discourse, while Strauss could appropriate the essence of this discourse and thus the leadership of the cultural avant-garde. This was not merely a reading of the difference between the "insider" and the "outsider" by one acculturated (indeed, assimilated) Jew. At least one "Jewish" observer also saw in the two composers the "eternal conflict between the successful-blond [Strauss] and the fateful-dark [Mahler]."[59] This dichotomy, expressed by a coach at the Viennese Court Opera, Thomas Mann's Jewish brother-in-law, Klaus Pringsheim, points to the internalization (and projection) of Mahler's sense of difference, a sense of difference that heightened his need to see Strauss's *Salome* performed in his house, to show that he was not one of those loud, gesticulating Eastern Jews but part of the avant-garde, distanced from the world of those characters, their perversion, their contaminated discourse. In Mahler's case, Strauss's opera magnificently served its function as a litmus test for assimilated Jewish identity.

Strauss succeeded beyond his wildest expectations. *Salome* became the touchstone of German avant-garde opera. According to his own contemporary testimony, he became the "leader of the Moderns," the "head of the avant-garde." At the same time, however, he felt the need to retrench, to declare that he was in truth opposed to modernity, was a "reactionary"; he even denied that the avant-garde existed. True, in this rejection of the avant-garde (read: of his presumed Jewish audience) he still criticized those who would limit opera to Wagner's "Teutonic legends" and demanded that "Biblical topics be taboo."[60] But his retrenchment and the basic reason for it are clear. Strauss, the arch-manipulator of audiences, had been overtaken by events: he had become, against his will, a "Jewish" composer, a "pervert."[61] The financial and artistic breakthrough of *Salome* was achieved with a double-edged sword. He had conquered the avant-garde; but in doing so he had engendered a "perverted" creation from which—protest as he might—he could not distance himself.

[59] Klaus Pringsheim, "Zur Uraufführung von Mahlers Sechster Symphonie," *Musikblätter des Anbruch*, 2 (1920), 497.

[60] "Is There an Avant-Garde in Music?" (1907), in *Recollections* (see n. 1 above), 12.

[61] See Fritsch (n. 7 above), 325: "man erinnere sich, daß der größte Vertreter der Vorkriegsmusik, Richard Strauß, 'an den Geist der Zersetzung verlorengegangen ist' (Eichenauer), daß er nicht nur von der jüdischen Presse gelobhudelt wurde, sondern daß seine Textdichter (Hofmannsthal, Stefan Zweig), sein Verleger (Fürstner) und sein Biograph (Specht) sämtlich Juden sind."

A Deconstructive Postscript:
Reading Libretti and
Misreading Opera

My observations here are intended as a polemical dissent from certain assumptions informing the essays in this collection and, indeed, informing most operatic criticism that I have read. I take it as axiomatic that polemics should overstate the case, seeking to disturb or provoke, where a more balanced expression of opinion might pass relatively unnoticed. As the reader will ultimately learn, my own convictions are less unorthodox than I like to let on. But throughout the essay I have self-consciously adopted a contrary—not to say contentious—point of view, since the assumptions I examine are, I believe, misguided and largely regrettable.

My theme, which I will risk repeating to the point of canonic monotony, is that an opera cannot be read from its libretto. Put another way, a libretto is not a text as we ordinarily understand that term. Because the meaning of opera is at bottom musical—because its essential argument is posed in musical language—any interpretation of opera derived exclusively, or even primarily, from the libretto is likely to result in a misreading.

I have put my proposition in categorical form. Naturally, its truth varies considerably from one operatic tradition to another, from one composer to another, from one work to another, even from one passage to another in the same opera. It is, for example, more true of the operas of the nineteenth century than of those of the seventeenth and eighteenth centuries; more true of Verdi than of Rossini; more true of *Il trovatore* than of *Otello*; more true of concerted passages than of recitative. One of my purposes will be to specify what factors—historical, compositional, and vocal—influence the balance (or, more precisely, the imbalance) between musical and textual elements in the logic of opera.

I intend to pursue this theme largely through what Thomas Aquinas called the *via negativa*, discussing four distinctive aspects of opera that serve to undermine a purely textual approach to it. These are, you might say, the four great operatic enemies of intelligibility, four characteristics of the genre that interfere with our ability to decipher the words and thus limit the interpretive usefulness of any analysis centered on the libretto.

My purpose, however, is not to lament these antitextual forces in opera. Far from it. I am delighted with opera in all its radical musicality. If anything, my object is to liberate opera from the textual fetters that literary interpreters seem determined to impose on it.

The intelligibility of an operatic libretto is inhibited, in varying degrees, by the following considerations: (1) opera is in a foreign language; (2) opera is sung, and much that is sung by an operatic voice cannot be understood; (3) opera contains a good deal of ensemble singing—passages where two or more voices sing at the same time, sometimes to identical words, sometimes to different words—and if one operatic voice is often unintelligible, two or more are almost always so; (4) operatic singers must compete with a full symphony orchestra—at least from the nineteenth century onward—and, as every opera-goer knows, the sheer volume of that orchestral sound further limits our ability to make out the words.

Before I examine these factors in detail (and qualify my assertions in certain ways), let me note that I am going to pay no attention to what composers themselves have written about the relative importance of words and music in opera. Scholars and critics love to quote the dicta of Wagner or Verdi or Strauss on this subject. Thus we often read, for example, of Strauss's "Golden Rule" for conductors: "It is not enough," he wrote, "that you yourself should hear every word the soloist sings. You should know it by heart anyway. The audience must be able to follow without effort. If they do not understand the words they will go to sleep." The pronouncement might make sense had it been issued by Monteverdi; but coming from Strauss it is merely laughable. Think, for example, of the final trio from *Rosenkavalier* and try, if you can, to square it with Strauss's statement here. By and large such statements are best understood in strategic terms: they represent an effort to persuade singers to be more attentive to the text and conductors to be more considerate of singers. Or perhaps they might be said to reveal the contradictory aspirations of the operatic composer: the impossible wish to be fully loyal to the traditions of both drama and music. But however one interprets them, they are an unreliable guide to what actually happens when language is set to music in opera. Only one source is authoritative in this regard: the operas themselves.

In arguing against the overvaluation of a textual approach to opera—against the usefulness of "reading opera," as the title of this collection would have it—I am of course doing battle with the imperialistic textualism of today's literary culture. "Text" has in fact become one of the great buzzwords of our time, its only competitor being the equally literary (and equally imperialistic) "discourse." I will readily confess that I find the pro-

329

miscuous use of these terms annoying even when applied to artifacts that are a good deal more literary than is opera. Indeed, on the grounds that one ought to cherish precision and avoid the clichés of the hour, I make a point of saying "book" or "essay" or "poem" or whatever else might be appropriate, reserving "text" for its legitimate function as a covering term. Students of opera, however, should resist the urge to "textual talk" not just for the sake of intellectual cleanliness but, more crucially, because such talk disfigures the object of their love. In this regard, they might attend to the example of the art historian Michael Baxandall, whose new book, *Patterns of Intention*, makes exactly the same point with regard to painting: painting, Baxandall suggests, remains at bottom a matter not of words but of images, and historians of painting who reduce those images to language (who interpret them according to a textual model) distort the aesthetic object. Opera, by analogy, is in its essence not a textual but a musical phenomenon, and interpreters of opera, accordingly, should proceed with great delicacy when they come to discuss its textual component.

Let me turn now to my four operatic adversaries of intelligibility in order to specify my claim and examine its implications.

I

That opera is sung in a foreign language is the least significant of the four, but I place it first because in the minds of many, I suspect, it ranks as the most significant. Certainly it is the main inspiration behind the practice of performing operas with supertitles—a subject about which I will have more to say later on. And I have no doubt that many opera-goers, especially Americans, believe that the main thing standing between them and the singers' words is the quaint but annoying fact that those words are uttered in a foreign tongue. Yet, important as the foreign-language issue may be, it does not go to the structural heart of the matter.

For one thing, opera is performed in a foreign language only under particular historical and geographical circumstances. The practice, in other words, is specific to certain times and places. In the three countries that have produced the majority of the works heard in the opera house today—that is, in Italy, France, and Germany—the repertory has always been dominated by native composers, although the domination is more recent in the case of France and Germany. Moreover, since the nineteenth century, in virtually all European countries, works by foreign composers have generally been performed in translation. Needless to say, there have been significant deviations from this norm: in Mozart's Vienna, even operas by indigenous composers were often composed and sung in Italian, as were Handel's operas (though written by a German) in London; and, as every reader of Balzac and Flaubert knows, Italian operas were sung in Italian in mid-nineteenth-century Paris, at least if they were performed at the Théâtre Italien. Nonetheless, for most Continental Europeans going to the opera has not meant, as it did for Dr. Johnson, attending "an exotick and irrational entertainment."

One must also note that until fairly recently opera singers sang in only one language, namely their own. Anybody who, like myself, collects historical recordings of opera will be familiar with this phenomenon. And, if the truth must be known, one can become positively addicted to operas sung in the "wrong" language. Likewise, persons who began attending opera as little as two decades ago will be able to recall some odd residue of this long-standing nativist tradition. As a student in Berlin in the early 1960s, I saw a performance of *Otello* with Renata Tebaldi in which the soprano sang in Italian while the rest of the cast and the chorus sang in German. As a variation on the same theme, there is a notorious pirate recording of Mario Del Monaco singing Don José with the Bolshoi Opera: everybody sings in Russian except the tenor, who alternates between Italian and French.

The proposition that opera is in a foreign language, then, holds true mainly for recent generations in English-speaking countries. And even there opera in translation has sometimes flourished, as at the New York City Opera in the 1950s and 1960s, or the English National Opera in the 1970s and 1980s.

Up to now I have considered the foreign-language issue—and its relation to intelligibility—strictly from the standpoint of composers and performers. But it must also be considered from the perspective of listeners, whether live in the theater or at home with their recordings. The important point here is that the foreignness of a foreign language is always a matter of degree. Listeners boast varying levels of competence in a given language, and while the number who enjoy true fluency is probably small, even a rudimentary knowledge will increase a work's intelligibility and therewith the aesthetic weight of its textual component.

In spite of these mitigating factors—the dominance of indigenous operatic works in most European countries, the prevalence of translation, and the linguistic skills of the audience—I would insist that the foreign-language issue is still an important one, especially in America. When, for example, I attend performances of the operas of Musorgsky or Janáček—operas that I am extraordinarily fond of—I can understand virtually nothing of what is said. And I know that the majority of American operagoers find Italian, French, and German just as mysterious as I do Russian and Czech. Even in Europe, operas are now performed in the original language much more often than they were as little as two decades ago.

When I returned to Berlin in the late 1970s virtually every opera, including the Mozart operas, was being sung in the original. Naturally, the proliferation of operatic recordings and the increasingly international careers of major singers have played crucial roles in revitalizing original-language performances. And since this development corresponds, unhappily, with a decline in the study of foreign languages, the result is a situation where the foreignness of opera now constitutes probably a greater barrier to comprehension than it has any time in the past.

Still, no one who has spent much time listening to opera will delude himself into thinking that opera's being in a foreign language is the fundamental source of its unintelligibility. For one thing, such a listener will have attended too many English-language operas in which passage after passage has defied all efforts at comprehension. In its 1985–86 season, for example, the Metropolitan Opera broadcast performances of *Porgy and Bess* and *Samson* (the latter admittedly not an opera but an oratorio), and, except for the singing of Jon Vickers as Samson, the text of both works was largely incomprehensible. Or, to cite a more absurd example, anyone who was rash enough to buy a ticket to the San Francisco Opera's 1986 production of Gian Carlo Menotti's *The Medium* would have made the surprising discovery that the opera, although of course sung in English, had been supplied with supertitles—and from the point of view of intelligibility they were anything but gratuitous. So having opera performed in one's own language—although there is much to be said for it—in no sense comes to terms with the issue of intelligibility. The matter goes much deeper.

I hope it will be noted that I have not taken sides in the argument over translation in opera. This is not merely because I am of two minds on the issue, but, more important, because the really interesting question is why there should be a controversy at all. Such a controversy is, for example, inconceivable with regard to drama, which virtually without exception is performed in translation—even though, as the cliché reminds us, much is lost in the process. So why do we continue to argue about translating opera?

Obviously, we do so for musical reasons. The argument, one might say, pays ongoing tribute to opera's fundamentally musical nature. In the narrower sense, this takes the form of insisting that there is a crucial link between the notes a composer writes and the particular vowels he intends to be sung on those notes. When you change the vowels—as inevitably happens in translation—you change the musical fabric and thus alter the essential character of the work. But there is, I think, a simpler reason why translation has not carried the day (and, indeed, seems to be losing ground): and that is because translation often makes so little difference in the way we experience opera—in the way opera works its effects on us. By far the larger burden of operatic argument is carried by the music, and the music matters most when the burden becomes heaviest. That is why people will sit for hours listening to singing they do not understand, although they would not be caught dead under the same circumstances at a stage play.

II

Operatic singing itself, I wish to suggest, represents the most intractable enemy of intelligibility. It is above all because opera is sung—and sung, of course, in a particular way—that it can at best approximate the level of verbal communication regularly achieved in spoken drama. Furthermore, opera singers are not incomprehensible because their diction is slovenly (although sometimes it is) but because composers write music for them that can be produced only through certain specialized physical procedures one of whose effects is that intelligibility must, in varying degrees, be sacrificed. In the final analysis, opera is unintelligible for musical reasons.

This is not the place for a lecture on vocal technique, and I am not qualified to deliver one. But let me consider briefly, and necessarily in layman's terms, what operatic singing involves in order to suggest how it serves to undermine comprehension. The most basic demand made on an operatic voice is that it produce an enormous volume of sound. Indeed, a modern operatic voice is distinguished from an ordinary voice not so much by its beauty, flexibility, or even range as by its sheer loudness. This demand increases, moreover, as one moves forward through the repertory of the nineteenth century and the orchestral forces with which singers must compete grow larger. The first premise of an operatic career, one might say, is the ability to produce a certain amount of noise.

Operatic volume is achieved essentially by putting pressure on the voice and thereby fundamentally altering the nature of the sound it produces. One can hear this difference quite vividly by contrasting two recordings of Eileen Farrell, one operatic and the other popular. When Farrell sings in a light pop voice (a voice that, in performance, would be amplified by microphone, as it never is in opera), every word is as clear as if she were speaking. But when she employs her operatic voice, the large, penetrating sound she emits often overwhelms the words she is seeking to reproduce, and the same singer who was so splendidly lucid in Rodgers and Hart's "He was too good to me" becomes very difficult to understand, despite her excellent diction, in Verdi's "Tacea la notte placida." This drowning of the words in vocal sound can be explained, technically, in terms of increased overtones, the distortion of vowels, and several other particulars that high-pressure operatic vocal production inexorably brings in its wake. For our purposes it is sufficient to note that words sung in an operatic voice are significantly less understandable than in the spoken voice or the light singing voice. Indeed, this is a home truth that all of us know and accept—including Richard Strauss with his Golden Rule for conductors.

The sheer volume of the operatic voice, then, stands as a mighty bulwark against intelligibility. It is complemented, so to speak, by the requirement that an operatic voice be able to encompass two full octaves—a substantially wider range than the normal singing voice encompasses. Operatic voices, in other words, must be able to sing both lower and, more important, higher than ordinary untrained voices. (As a point of reference, "The Star-Spangled Banner," which is notoriously difficult to sing, encompasses only an octave and a fifth.) The demand for altitude might be thought of as a variation on the demand for volume, since from the point of view of the words it has the effect of exaggerating the distortions created by putting operatic pressure on the voice. When a singer moves to the top of his range (that is, when sopranos, mezzos, and tenors reach the area around top C, or when baritones and basses reach upward toward top G), words must be sacrificed even more ruthlessly than they are lower down in the register. Thus many a singer who is perfectly lucid in the middle of the range becomes incomprehensible at the top. One might say that the amount of non-verbal interference emitted by a voice increases as it approaches the upper register. Moreover, not only singers but conductors and composers as well are absolutely delighted to hear any sound at all when the voice moves into this territory; nobody is much inclined to quibble about diction on high C.

The crucial thing about high notes in opera is that these altitudinous, incomprehensible tones occur precisely at the moments of greatest dramatic significance, when the text, in theory, ought to matter most. In effect, the musical logic of opera exploits vocal altitude to express particularly intense or significant responses, but that very logic also conspires to undermine the intelligibility of those responses. Opera, in other words, grows inarticulate just when it seeks to say the most important things. Again, it is governed by a musical rather than a textual rationale.

Besides volume and altitude, operatic singing boasts—or ought to—one further characteristic that interferes with intelligibility: what aficionados refer to as "legato." Legato is essentially the singer's ability to sustain the tone inviolate as the voice moves from one pitch to another, or from one syllable to another on the same pitch. In its ideal form, operatic singing consists of an even, uninterrupted column of vocal sound, which undergoes no fundamental alteration in character as it abandons one note to embrace another or as it seeks to articulate different words. In reality, of course, singers achieve greater or lesser degrees of perfection of legato, and a bad singer will chop up the vocal line with aspirates marking each change of pitch or syllable (the tone will stop and start—even if ever so slightly—as the singer attempts to move the voice). But the goal of operatic singing is to achieve the most flawless legato possible.

That legato—that seamless, sustained vocal tone—stands in the service of opera's musical logic. In particular, it abets the composer's object of creating sonic shapes—that is to say, phrases—whose contours will emerge with the same lucidity as they might from a violin or a clarinet. Musical language traffics precisely in such sonic commodities: phrases, one might say, are the fundamental units of musical expression, whose cumulative weight and configuration constitute the essence of musical argument. And singing, in its effort to contribute to that argument, aims to produce musical shapes that approximate the aural qualities more readily produced by an instrument. Opera singers themselves will often refer to their voice simply as "the instrument," as if it were some alienated, mechanical appendage to the body—a kind of clarinet in the throat.

The significance of this ideal for the intelligibility of opera is vast. Spoken language becomes intelligible only through articulation: that is, through the interruption of sound. Or, put another way, speaking consists of both sound and silence. Singing, by way of contrast, allows no place for silence; it seeks to eliminate precisely those essential articulations that make language possible in the first place. Singing moves away from words toward vocalise. Indeed, a good deal of operatic singing, especially in bel canto opera, is nothing but vocalise, where the singer sustains the same vowel through a large number of notes. Even when singers try to articulate words, they remain under the more insistent (and opposite) imperative to make their voices into instruments, to bind the notes together, in spite of the words, so that we may hear the real language of opera, the language of musical phrases.

As if this were not enough, we must also reckon with the simple yet awesome fact that the only "singable" sounds are vowel sounds. One cannot produce an operatic noise on a consonant, not even on such accommodating consonants as *l*, *m*, or *n*. In other words, just as the fundamental articulations of language are consistently undermined by the ideal of legato singing, so also the shape or rhythm of language is radically distorted in opera because all the notes in a vocal part are written to be sustained on vowels. In order to be sung—to be rendered musical—words are pummeled and bent so that their vowels are dramatically extended, while their consonants are reduced to mere shadows of their spoken selves. Thus

335

when Radamès sings his final line in Act III of *Aida*—"Io resto a te"— what we actually hear is a sequence of elongated vowels trumpeted on the tenor's high A. If in speaking we were to redistribute vowels and consonants in the manner in which they are regularly redistributed in opera, our talk would be no less incomprehensible than is much operatic singing. The sovereignty of vowels in singing partly explains why a language like Italian, in which virtually all words end in vowels, is more gratefully operatic than is, say, English, where most words end in consonants.

It will doubtless have occurred to some readers that the generalizations I have just advanced invite all sorts of qualifications. The demands for volume, altitude, and legato do not affect the intelligibility of opera in a uniform manner. Rather, their effect is now more or less drastic, now more or less innocuous. Moreover, certain broad qualifications in this area are worth contemplating for a moment, because they help explain why some operas and some operatic roles are more intelligible than others. In particular I wish to call attention to a historical and a sexual variable in this domain.

The first qualification I have already alluded to: operas of the seventeenth and eighteenth centuries are generally more comprehensible than those of the nineteenth century. This is so because, for the most part, seventeenth- and eighteenth-century opera does not demand singing that is either loud or (in the case of male singers) as high as nineteenthcentury opera. As a result, some of the pressure comes off the voice, with the effect that the words are more apt to be understood. Recitative— which disappears from opera in the early nineteenth century—provides the most striking illustration of this process. One might fairly describe recitative as "talk music," since it tends to be set in the middle of the voice and at a reasonable volume (the competition coming not from an orchestra but from a harpsichord), and it also involves very little distortion of the natural ratio between consonants and vowels. Hence recitative—assuming one knows the language—is often as intelligible as spoken dialogue. The operas of the early Baroque, of course, were constructed virtually in their entirety from recitative. In his new book, *Osmin's Rage*, Peter Kivy even argues that Monteverdi's *Orfeo* is not properly an opera at all, since it is governed by literary rather than musical imperatives. Appropriately, the Monteverdi operas are perhaps the most intelligible in the entire repertory. In the next generation, the high Baroque operas of Handel, consisting as they do of a string of arias separated by recitative, actually gain in intelligibility from what is generally regarded as their undramatic (and unliterary) addiction to repetition. A Handel aria involves as much textual distortion as a representative vocal passage from Verdi or Puccini, but because each phrase is reiterated many times (particularly if the full *da capo* is respected), the listener gets several shots at deciphering the text. I am surely not the only person who has managed to piece together the words of a Handel aria simply by listening very hard to the repetitions.

Intelligibility, then, varies according to a broad historical pattern reflecting changes in the demands made on operatic voices, with the early nineteenth century marking a watershed. A second, and no less important, variable is sex. In general, male voices are more intelligible than female voices. Whatever the reason, all opera-goers know that the sound emitted by a female singer is more apt to overwhelm the words than is the sound emitted by a male singer. Listen, for example, to the splendid 1940 Met recording of *Otello* with Giovanni Martinelli, Lawrence Tibbett, and Elisabeth Rethberg. All three of the principals sing magnificently. The difference is that Martinelli and Tibbett make a good part of the text comprehensible, whereas we can catch only an occasional phrase from Rethberg. That difference, moreover, has nothing to do with the singers' intentions, and everything to do with the fact that the first two are men and the last a woman. Even female singers known for their attentiveness to the words (singers like Maria Callas or Elisabeth Schwarzkopf) are extraordinarily difficult to understand—much more so than an indifferent tenor or baritone—while female singers mainly concerned with producing a smooth and beautiful sound (singers like Joan Sutherland or Gundula Janowitz) are usually unintelligible from start to finish: the words are simply liquefied in a sea of operatic tone.

This almost categorical difference between male and female voices goes a long way toward explaining why certain composers, certain operas, and certain roles are more readily understood than others. Not surprisingly, operas dominated by male voices reveal more of the text than operas dominated by female voices. This is a principal source of the relative intelligibility of the Musorgsky operas (*Boris* and *Khovanshchina* each contain only one important female role), of the later Wagner operas, of Debussy's *Pelléas*, and also of Gilbert and Sullivan (where virtually everyone but the soprano heroine can be understood). Conversely, the same principle explains why we often hear very little of the text in the operas of Puccini and Strauss: both composers have a special proclivity for the high female voice. Indeed, Richard Strauss, with his notorious addiction to this voice (which he exploits to glorious effect in the climactic moments of *Salome, Elektra, Rosenkavalier, Arabella,* and *Capriccio*), was probably the composer least entitled to promulgate the so-called Golden Rule for conductors.

The overall effect of both the historical and sexual distinctions I have drawn is that intelligibility in opera is an uneven phenomenon. In a given opera, it will vary from passage to passage, indeed from phrase to phrase, depending on whether we are listening to recitative or an aria, whether the singer is a baritone or a soprano, and whether the passage lies low or high. When, at that splendid moment at the end of *The Marriage of Figaro*, the Count begs for forgiveness and the Countess grants it, the Count's words, set in the middle of the baritone voice, can be understood by everybody, whereas the Countess's, set in the upper-middle part of the soprano register, are intelligible only to someone who has seen the libretto. This may appear an embarrassingly mundane consideration, unworthy of mention in so lofty an aesthetic context as Mozart's great finale. But in fact we ignore such humble matters only at the risk of misrepresenting Mozart's actual achievement: for the Countess's forgiveness is realized not verbally but musically. Indeed, even if her words *could* be apprehended, they would not begin to convey the intensity and exaltation of Mozart's musical gesture. The passage illustrates why students of opera who construct their analyses from the text—from "reading the libretto"—will as often as not "misread the opera"—or, perhaps accurately in this instance, "underread" it.

III

My last two "enemies of intelligibility" will not require such extensive exposition, as they are at once less pervasive and more obvious than the matter of operatic voices. Each represents a further instance of the tension between verbal and musical logic in opera, a tension that is occasionally a source of aesthetic delight but more often simply results in decreased comprehension. Both, furthermore, are exacerbated in the operas of the nineteenth century.

Ensemble singing—my third adversary—is of course crucial to the musical logic of opera from Mozart to Strauss, although as the century comes to a close there are important defections from the tradition, notably Musorgsky, Debussy, the mature Wagner, and, to a lesser extent, the Verdi of *Otello* and *Falstaff*. Ensembles generally occur at moments of heightened dramatic interest, and they function as musical centerpieces. Moreover, as everybody knows, when two or more people sing at the same time the words generally suffer. So once again we are confronted with an illustration of what is perhaps opera's central paradox: the most important words are the least likely to be understood.

To be sure, the range of intelligibility in operatic ensembles is fairly broad. At one extreme is the duet for two male voices singing the same text in thirds and sixths (such as one often hears in bel canto opera), where the words can remain exceptionally clear. At the other extreme is the quartet, quintet, or even larger grouping (often supported by a chorus), where the characters sing different words set to extremely intricate music, and hardly anything can be deciphered. The singers, in effect, cancel out one another's lines. There are, of course, degrees of intelligibility even within the latter pattern. For example, the ensemble writing of Rossini skilfully uses repetitions and the strategic liberation of individual voices from the ensemble block to achieve a surprising level of verbal clarity. Rossini is a particularly interesting witness, moreover, because in the Act I finale of *L'italiana in Algeri* he satirizes the entire tradition of operatic ensembles by having his characters sing onomatopoeic noises, as if they were instruments rather than voices:

> Din din din,
> Cra cra cra,
> Bum bum bum,
> Tac tac tac.

Rossini's point is splendidly trenchant: what one normally hears in an operatic ensemble verges on the instrumental—a confection of homogenized, interwoven musical lines, whose inarticulateness grows more pronounced as the music moves toward its climax. "The crowning glory of opera," writes Auden, "is the big ensemble," to which one must add that the coronation is generally mute.

The operatic analyst, then, must approach ensembles with caution. Before assigning particular significance to this or that utterance, he must ask whether the words stand any chance of being heard. More often than not, the answer is No. Even more than is the case for opera as whole, the logic of ensembles is musical rather than verbal. Admittedly, unintelligibility is sometimes exactly their point. Such is true, for example, of the ensemble in which Act II of *Die Meistersinger* culminates. The piece, of course, represents a civic riot, and the hundred odd lines of poetry Wagner squanders on it are intentionally transformed into verbal chaos by the music. But Wagner's creative exploitation of incoherence is the exception rather than the rule. More representative is the sextet from *Lucia di Lammermoor*, where, once past the solo tenor introduction, very little can be understood, although incomprehensibility is hardly its dramatic point. This wonderful piece works its effect on us in spite of our not understanding what is being said, and it does so almost entirely through musical means.

IV

Finally, we come to the operatic orchestra. Its significance for my topic can be stated very easily: from the point of view of intelligibility the orchestra is simply a source of interfering noise. It stands between us and

339

the words. I can think of not a single instance where the orchestra increases rather than decreases our ability to make out the text. The only conceivable exception would be the verbal associations suggested by certain orchestral effects, such as the ringing of the triangle that Verdi uses to underline Falstaff's allusions to money. But even in such instances the connection between orchestral sound and intelligibility is indirect and, at best, approximate; when judged in strictly aural terms, even these orchestral allusions actually interfere with our ability to hear the words.

Naturally, the great opera composers know how to minimize that interference—how to make the orchestra as considerate of the text as possible. Indeed, intelligibility in opera is often a function of a composer's skill in restraining his orchestra. Or, put more drastically, it is a function of a composer's willingness to sacrifice the surefire effects that can be achieved through orchestral volume. Here one could cite Debussy's *Pelléas et Mélisande* as an especially noteworthy example—it being surely among the most orchestrally recessive of all great operas and, accordingly, also one of the most intelligible.

Perhaps we ought to ask why operas are orchestrated at all. Why not just a piano or harpsichord? or, even better, why isn't the whole thing sung *a cappella*? The answer has little to do with keeping singers on pitch. Rather, it is because opera would lose its fundamental character without the orchestra. It would become something that it is not. Orchestral sounds give an opera its basic contour—its overarching shape—just as they also carry the burden of establishing the distinct mood or flavor of an opera. They do many other things as well—all of them, needless to say, musical. In fact, the question is worth asking only because it reminds us of just how profoundly unliterary opera actually is.

Viewed structurally, orchestral noise bears the same relation to intelligibility as do high notes and ensembles: it asserts itself just when the words are most important. Moreover, in the nineteenth century this essential supporting and shaping sound grew several times more powerful—or, if you prefer, several times more noisy—than it had been in the seventeenth and eighteenth centuries. Not only is the nineteenth-century orchestra much larger than its predecessors, but its modernized instruments also produce louder and more incisive sounds. The change is reflected in the increased size of nineteenth-century opera houses, as Michael Forsyth has shown in his study of opera houses and concert halls from the seventeenth century to the present, *Buildings for Music*.

The larger orchestras and larger houses had two effects on operatic singing, both of them detrimental to intelligibility. Especially in the United States, where "barn" theaters have proliferated, singers have had to produce ever greater quantities of sound in order to fill the void, and their efforts in this direction have often resulted in yet further sacrifices in articulation and thus intelligibility. Many opera-goers find performances in medium or small European theaters relatively comprehensible, while the very same singers in a 4000-seat auditorium like the Metropolitan sound altogether wordless. This contrast between the lucidity of the small theater and the opacity of the large is sometimes overrated by devotees of the former (the evidence of recordings shows that theater size is a mitigating, not a determining, factor), but it is nonetheless an authentic distinction. I need hardly point out that it has manifestly elitist implications: opera, it suggests, is for the few; it can maintain its verbal integrity only within the small, aristocratic venues for which it was originally created. It was never meant to be a democratic entertainment.

A second effect of the larger orchestra is that operatic singing itself actually grew louder in the nineteenth century, especially in its closing years. This phenomenon is well known to students of the history of singing. It is associated above all with the emergence of artists like Enrico Caruso and Titta Ruffo, who made decidedly more noise than their counterparts in the previous generation and who were forced by their method of production to let many of the words go by the boards. Still, even the new singers could hardly keep pace with what was happening to the orchestra. If I might paraphrase Malthus, orchestral volume grew geometrically, while singing at best grew arithmetically. When the full Wagnerian or Verdian orchestra is unleashed, it expunges not merely the singers' words, but their voices as well. Indeed, at the climactic moments of nineteenth-century opera, whole choruses can be drowned out by the deafening orchestral racket. I hardly need add that no one would wish it otherwise. What is merely interference from a textual standpoint is of the essence of the thing when we view opera in the whole.

V

This concludes my survey of the enemies list. In each instance, as I have tried to suggest, intelligibility is sacrificed to music. Moroever, these sacrifices are not marginal to the logic of opera but central to it. From a consideration of them follows at least one important practical implication for the operatic analyst. The master question for any interpreter of opera must be not What does the text say, but How is the text realized, or at least addressed, in the music? How does it embed itself in the opera's musical fabric? That embedding may not always result in consonance—in an "isomorphism" of text and music—since there are situations in which the music responds to the text by antithesis. The important point, however, is that an operatic text really has no meaning worth talking

341

about except as it is transformed into music. The failure to come to terms with this hard reality explains why many literary studies of opera hold so little interest for musicologists. Such studies too often treat the language of opera as if it were as transparent as the language of stage drama. They may tell us a great deal about literature or about cultural history broadly conceived (and I have benefited from reading many of them), but so long as they do not speak about music, and about the way words become musical, they are condemned to remain on the periphery of opera—on the outskirts, so to speak, of the operatic village.

Some readers will have noted that these strictures view the question of "reading opera" from a very particular perspective. Everything I have said—about foreign language, operatic singing, ensembles, and the orchestra—presumes that we should settle the question of operatic intelligibility in terms of what can be discerned of the words while seated in an opera house during an actual performance. Or, to use the jargon of contemporary criticism, I have "privileged" a "house reading" of opera. This is indeed the case. But let me demonstrate my intellectual flexibility—such as it is—by suggesting that I am prepared to consider this reading simply one of a number of possible readings each of which, if it is not equally valid or useful, can at least claim our attention.

I am not sure exactly how many such possibilities exist, but five that I know actually play a role in any opera-lover's experience. The first, of course, is the "house reading" taken for granted up to this point: hearing the work in the the theater and doing one's best to make out the words in spite of the hindrances posed by my four "enemies." A second reading would be opera as heard on record. In terms of intelligibility, opera on record differs from opera in the house in only one respect: the solo singers generally have spot microphones on them, thus lending them unnatural prominence and giving the words a better chance of being understood because the relative volume of the orchestra is reduced. A third approach might be termed the "libretto-in-hand" reading. This, I suspect, is the way that we listen to opera most often—at least, it is the way we get to know most operas: while listening to a performance on record, we follow the text, both in the original language and in the line-by-line translation just to the right, with the effect that many of the words that could not be deciphered by the unaided ear become intelligible. What is going on here, I believe, is in fact a dual process: on the one hand listening, on the other reading, which through years of practice become fused in our minds into a more or less unitary experience. In fact, we become convinced that we actually hear words that are in reality being fed to us by our eyes.

Now, before Wagner the distinction between my first and third readings—between a "house reading" and a "libretto-in-hand" reading—may not have been so sharp as it is today. Most important in this regard, before Wagner the house was not darkened during performance, with the result that members of the audience could follow their librettos. Moreover, we know that librettos (often with a translation on the facing page) were on sale at the entrance to the theater, and that they were often printed afresh for each new production of an opera. Hence the option of following the text during a live performance was very real, and that option was abetted, so to speak, by stagings that were a good deal more static than those one normally sees at present—and thus a good less compelling to the eye. It may well be, therefore, that what I have called the "libretto-in-hand" reading is a distinctly post-Wagnerian phenomenon.

A variation on the "libretto-in-hand reading" is the "supertitle reading": we hear the work performed live while a version of the text (in translation) is flashed above the stage. Again, what actually happens with supertitles is that two processes are carried out more or less simultaneously: reading and hearing. Many people seem to be under the illusion that supertitles serve merely to translate opera out of a foreign language. But that is surely erroneous. As with the "libretto-in-hand reading," supertitles introduced a textual explicitness quite foreign to what one actually experiences in the theater. Perhaps the practice can be refined, but right now it often invites us, for example, to read the text of the *Lucia* sextet as if it were just as intelligible as the recitative in *The Marriage of Figaro*. Still, providing we are disabused about its actual function, the "supertitle reading" can be defended as a usefully different way to experience opera, or perhaps as a heuristic device. (I will not pretend to have exhausted the pros and cons of supertitles here, only to have related them to the issue of intelligibility.)

Finally, at the opposite end of the spectrum from what I have called the "house reading" stands reading the libretto without listening to anything. This is at once a drastically impoverished and an unrealistically intelligible reading, but it is nonetheless a reading, and one of particular importance to scholars and critics. It shades off, moreover, into all sorts of other textual approaches, which might be usefully lumped together as "approximate or ancillary readings." These would include synopses, record-album notes, scholarly books and articles, the literary source, even anecdotes recounted on the Metropolitan Opera Quiz.

All five of the readings I have mentioned feed into and inform one another. In other words, we seldom "read" opera one of these ways without being influenced by having read it another way before. Thus, a "house reading" of opera seldom occurs in its purest form. By the time most of us see an opera in the theater, we have listened to it on record with libretto in hand. In some instances we may actually have memorized the text—or

large portions of it. At the other extreme, even the most cursory examination of the plot synopsis in the program notes already means that a
seemingly virgin house experience has been "textually anticipated."

Because of this complex and, so to speak, layered set of experiences,
my earlier pronouncements about operatic meaning must be modified to
suit a variety of ways in which opera is actually appropriated. But I would
like to return, here at the end, to the archetypal primacy of the "house
reading." In spite of the significant role played by readings that draw us
away from its purity, I am convinced that it remains at the center of the
operatic experience and, indeed, that we move back toward it again and
again, even after it has been supplemented by more explicitly textual approaches. In fact, those textual readings have a way of receding from consciousness, as we gradually forget the language of operatic texts we once
knew—something that never quite happens with the music.

I was reminded of this primitive truth recently when I heard Gounod's
Romeo and Juliet for the first time in my life. I somehow expected that I
would not like the opera, but then a friend happened to give me a tape of
the 1947 Metropolitan Opera Broadcast with Jussi Bjoerling. Conrad Osborne calls it "the finest singing of a complete romantic tenor role, beginning to end, I've ever heard," and the singing is indeed so wonderful that
I found myself listening to the performance over and over. I listened without a libretto; nor did I consult a synopsis of the opera. I simply indulged
myself in the thing itself. I know French well enough, but I found I could
make out only a few of the words in the performance. Bjoerling was a
scrupulous linguist, but the special plangency of his voice (just the quality
that makes it for some the most beautiful voice ever recorded) renders his
diction less easily understood than that of some lesser tenors.

Of course, my listening benefited from an important extra-operatic
source, namely, Shakespeare's play (and its derivatives), which I have
read and seen many times. This, along with the odd phrase that I managed to understand, provided me with enough information to follow the
general contours of the plot, identify most of the characters, and get the
general sense of what was being said. Still, the opera compelled my attention, indeed my fascination, above all because of its music. Put simply, I
found it extraordinarily beautiful and moving. Later, when I heard a live
radio broadcast of the work from the Metropolitan Opera, some of the
charm was lost because the singers, at least by comparison, were so inadequate. But the opera itself still worked its magic. Its music—and,
above all, its singing—powerfully conveys the essential ingredients of
Shakespeare's play: the unconstrained rapture of young love, the violence
of adult hatreds, the sense of doom, the sweet pain of the lover's simultaneous fulfillment and separation, the agony yet transcendence of their

final meeting. Shakespeare's dramatic arc achieves an immediacy in Gounod's music (and in Bjoerling's singing) greater than anything I have witnessed in a performance of the play. As in all good operas, the loss of narrative explicitness is handsomely repaid in emotional resonance. Listening to the piece, I was convinced all over again of how little the words count for in opera. Or perhaps I should say, I was convinced all over again of how much their meaning is a function of their musical embodiment.

But I prefer to end on a more ambiguous—and a more prudent—note. While the words in opera sometimes count for little, they never count for nothing. Even when unintelligible, their existence—or the effort of singers to bring them into existence—is an important component of operatic reality. Above all, they are important as symbols of the human subjectivity that lies at the heart of opera: whether actual or potential, they identify operatic singing as an expression of will. Their willfulness, moreover, is aptly reflected in the extraordinary athleticism of operatic singing: the bulging eyes, throbbing arteries, thickening necks, and reddening faces caused by the effort to produce sounds of impossible volume and extension.

Conrad Osborne makes this connection between the operatic word and human action in his discussion of Bjoerling's singing in *Romeo and Juliet*:

[Bjoerling's tone] has emotive properties, the power to sadden or to thrill. It has this power in and of itself, independent of the meanings of words (though not of their sounds) . . . The tone, independent of the word in all these ways, nevertheless bears the word's encoding, which rides within it like a written scroll embedded in richest amber, and sends its messages therefrom with an aesthetic life and finish it could not otherwise know. As we hear the tone sail and arc, swell and fall, we know that all these properties are not simply those of some phenomenon with whose symmetry and gleam Nature has, as they used to say, chosen to astonish us. Instead, they are the deliberate creations of human behavior.

One might argue that this is an artful if eloquent dodge. But it nicely suggests that, while we cannot always understand the words, they remain a significant constituent of our experience: even when they are unintelligible, their presence identifies the singer as a human actor with specific feelings, giving voice to specific thoughts. This explains, at least in part, why we will not tolerate pure vocalise even in place of words we cannot hear. Indeed, the passion and heartbreak of Bjoerling's singing in *Romeo and Juliet* would largely evaporate if the sound of his voice were disso-

345

ciated from this particular character, in this particular situation, and, above all, saying—or attempting to say—these particular things. I am inclined to suggest, therefore, that words in opera are emblems of human volition. As such, they are part of our experience of opera even, as it were, when they are not.

INDEX

Annunzio, Gabriele d': as opera source, 108–11; plays by, 108; *Fedra*, 126; *La figlia di Iorio*, 108, 110, 111; *Francesca da Rimini*, 109–10, 112, 122–25; *Parisina*, 111–22
Asafiev, Boris, 245–46, 258n, 262
Auden, W. H., 222, 339

Bakaeva, Galina, 246–47, 255n
Baldini, Gabriele, 299, 300
Barthes, Roland, 179, 183, 184, 186
Baxandall, Michael, 330
Bellini, Vincenzo, 6, 297
Benedikt, Moritz, 312, 313, 314
Benveniste, Emile, 192n
Bernstein, Eduard, 308–309, 315
Bertin, Louise-Angélique, *La Esmeralda*, 92–93
Bie, Oscar, 315
Bizet, Georges: composition of Habañera, 176–77n; political views, 169. See also *Carmen*; Carmen, story of
Bjoerling, Jussi, 344–46
Boieldieu, François Adrien, *La Dame blanche*, 130
Boito, Arrigo: ideal collaborator for Verdi, 302–303; as journalist and reformer, 271–74; libretti by, 93, 96; libretto of *Amleto*, 271–72; selection as librettist for *Otello*, 41–47; Shakespeare as source, 34–38, 40, 272, 302; style, 185; use of translations, 35, 38. See also *Mefistofele; Otello*, libretto
Boito, Camillo, 269, 275
Boris Godunov (Musorgsky), 337
    libretto: dealing with sources, 239; and *Khovanshchina*, 247–48; Kromy Forest scene in, 238, 240, 245, 246; language in, 252, 253; two versions of, 237–38
    reviews of, 240
Budden, Julian, 55, 185–86

Cagnoni, Antonio, 109; *Il vecchio della montagna*, 274
Cardoze, Michel, 180

Carmen (Bizet): characters, 173, 175–80, 181–83; fate in, 170; Habañera, 176–77, 178–79, 182; libretto, 169, 173, 174; theme of love, 169–70, 174–75, 176–81, 182; war between the sexes, 173, 174. *See also* Carmen, story of
Carmen, story of, 169; different revivals of, 168, 169; interpretations, 171–73; plot summary, 170–71; status of myth, 168. *See also* Mérimée, Prosper
Cixous, Hélène, 174; *The Newly Born Woman*, 178
Clément, Catherine, 172
Coleridge, Samuel Taylor, 51, 56
Cossa, Pietro, *Nerone* (play), 93
Corsaro, Frank, 173

Dahlhaus, Carl, 178, 292
Dante Alighieri, *Divina Commedia*, 109–10
Darnton, Robert, 290
Debussy, Claude: Maeterlinck's need for, 61–62, 90; and Wagner, 62, 76, 167. *See also Pelléas et Mélisande*
Delius, Nicolaus, edition of Shakespeare, 35–36
Donizetti, Gaetano, 6; *Lucia di Lammermoor*, 339

Eisenberg, Evan, 260n

Faccio, Franco, 269, 277–78; *Amleto*, 271–72
Fama, La, 275, 276, 277; article by P.A. in, 279–81, 282
Farrell, Eileen, 333
Filippi, Filippo, 271, 277, 278
fin-de-siècle: composers, 303; libretti, criticism of, 97; operatic culture, 93; press, *Salome* in, 314; progress of opera in, 304; views of language, 62, 63. *See also Literaturoper*
fliegende Holländer, Der (Wagner): conventional score of, 135, 138; Erik's Dream, 129, 130, 139–47; love in, 169–70; Senta's Ballad, 130, 134, 135, 138–39, 145, 147

DATE DUE